A LEADERSHIP
ODYSSEY

*Muslim Separatism and the Achievement
of the Separate State of Pakistan*

A LEADERSHIP
ODYSSEY

Muslim Separatism and the Achievement
of the Separate State of Pakistan

SIKANDAR HAYAT

OXFORD
UNIVERSITY PRESS

OXFORD
UNIVERSITY PRESS

Oxford University Press is a department of the University of Oxford.
It furthers the University's objective of excellence in research, scholarship,
and education by publishing worldwide. Oxford is a registered trade mark of
Oxford University Press in the UK and in certain other countries

Published in Pakistan by
Oxford University Press
No. 38, Sector 15, Korangi Industrial Area,
PO Box 8214, Karachi-74900, Pakistan

ISBN 978-969-734013-2

Typeset in Minion Pro
Printed on 68gsm Offset Paper

Printed by The Times Press (Pvt.) Ltd., Karachi

Acknowledgements
Cover illustrations: Pioneers of Freedom Series (1990) Sketches by Saeed Akhtar
© Saeed Akhtar/Pakistan Post Foundation Press

For

Samina

Contents

Preface

My interest in Muslim separatism in British India, which eventually developed into the Pakistan movement and led to the creation of Pakistan in 1947, and its charismatic leader Quaid-i-Azam Mohammad Ali Jinnah, the founder of Pakistan, dates back to the late 1970s—more than four decades.

In 1979, for my doctoral dissertation, I decided to focus on Jinnah. Ever since, I have not only sustained interest in the subject but found myself deeply interested in its many aspects, especially leadership as a political phenomenon. In fact, leadership has fascinated, intrigued, and inspired me since my days at Columbia University (1974–7), where I was encouraged by my academic advisor (late) Professor W. Howard Wriggins who himself wrote a very interesting book on leadership titled, *The Ruler's Imperative: Strategies for Political Survival in Asia and Africa* (1969).

In the course of my studies and research, I realised that the achievement of Pakistan was not a given—it was not inevitable. It was a result of the conscious, deliberate, and dedicated efforts of several prominent Muslim leaders led, of course, by Jinnah. Other prominent leaders were Syed Ahmad Khan, Aga Khan, Syed Ameer Ali, Maulana Mohamed Ali, and Allama Muhammad Iqbal. All of them contributed in their own way, successively, reinforcing one another through what I term the Muslim separatist political movement. Founded by Syed Ahmad Khan, the main basis and rationale of this movement was that the Muslims were a separate political community and had separate interests and demands. The British system of representative government—newly introduced in India—was based on numbers. It made Muslims a 'minority' community in India, and a permanent one at that, which necessitated the need for separate political life and processes for them. The growth and development of a separatist movement at the hands of these aforementioned leaders

was in response to British rule, the attitude and working of the
Indian National Congress leadership, and, of course, emerging
'Indian nationalism' that catered only to Hindu majority interests.
There was little prospect of Muslims sharing power with Hindus,
especially after the British departure (as was apparent during
and after World War II). For most of his political career, Jinnah
laboured relentlessly for Hindu–Muslim unity and for a joint
struggle for self-government and freedom. But the Congress (and
the Hindu Mahasabha) leadership—who felt secure with their
numbers and with a system inherently biased in their favour—
were not interested in any deal. They did not care much about
Muslims and did not want to share power with them. Thus, all
options exhausted, Jinnah joined the mainstream separatist
political movement, and through his Pakistan Movement,
achieved the goal of a separate state, that is, Pakistan.

Muslim separatism, that separatist sentiment, indeed a tradition
and norm, prevailed in India before the advent of the British, in
spite of all the efforts of varying degrees on part of the Muslim
rulers, especially the Mughals. There was clear, discernible
separatism on the part of both Muslims and Hindus. What
made this separatism so different, intense, and irreconcilable in
British India was the introduction of a representative system of
government that bifurcated Muslims and Hindus permanently as
minority and majority communities respectively, and which was
further reinforced by the Congress' reluctance and eventual refusal
to share power with Muslims. The Muslim leaders, particularly
Jinnah, tried in vain to persuade Congress to accommodate
Muslim rights and interests for the common cause of India and
its freedom. Consequentially, the separatist legacy evolved and
developed into a concrete, tangible separatist political movement,
culminating in the Pakistan Movement, and the eventual struggle
for the achievement of the separate state of Pakistan.

This book is about the role and relevance of these Muslim
leaders—Syed Ahmad Khan, Aga Khan, Ameer Ali, Mohamed
Ali, Iqbal, and Jinnah, the ultimate achiever, in making this
achievement possible. It was an integrated, consistent, and,
indeed, persistent effort on their part, and essentially a long-drawn

struggle. The demand for a separate state on 23 March 1940 was the historic moment. It will also help explain, much to the chagrin of 'conspiracy' theorists, as to why it became possible to achieve Pakistan in a short span of seven years, 1940 to 1947; it was a long time coming.

I am grateful to my friends and colleagues at the Forman Christian College, particularly Dr Saeed Shafqat, Professor and Director, Centre for Public Policy and Governance, for going through the first draft of the manuscript and providing useful feedback and suggestions. I am also grateful to other colleagues both at the Centre for Public Policy and Governance and the Department of History for hearing me out and sharing their thoughts, particularly Dr Arfa Sayeda Zehra, Dr Farzand Masih, Dr Umber Bin Ibad, Dr Saadia Sumbal, Khizar Jawad, Raheem-ul-Haque, Dr Raja M. Ali Saleem, Dr Imdad Hussain, and Saba Shahid. I am, of course, thankful to Dr James A. Tebbe, my Rector, for encouraging all of us at the university to pursue research along with our teaching and administrative responsibilities. None of my colleagues, however, are responsible for the views expressed in the book. I myself am responsible for all the facts presented here and their interpretation to develop and advance an argument.

In completing the manuscript of this book, I was helped, as always, by Muhammad Irfan who typed numerous drafts before I could come up with the final draft. I am thankful. I also wish to thank my staff in the Dean's office—Tania Hamid, Shazia Sharif, and Fayyaz Raza—for all administrative and clerical tasks they performed.

I would also like to thank Oxford University Press, my old publisher, for the publication of this book. I am particularly grateful to Ghousia Gofran Ali, Managing Editor for academic and higher education books, and Raheela Fahim Baqai, Marketing Director, at the Press. They have always been so forthcoming and helpful. It has been a pleasure working with them. I am much obliged to my editor, Sunara Nizami, for her personal interest, dedication, and diligence in converting the raw manuscript into its present, refined form of a book. It could not have been done better.

Finally, I am indebted to my family: my wife Samina; our children Tehnia (Tina), Umar, and Ali; son-in-law Nauman; and grandchildren Ayaan and Emaad, for all their love and care. I am particularly indebted to my wife for her patience, understanding, and encouragement as I worked on this book for long hours during the last two years. The book is lovingly dedicated to her.

Introduction

Muslim separatism in India, especially in British India, has been a subject of considerable interest among scholars working on modern South Asia, and is reflected in books, articles, theses, and dissertations published over the years.[1] Two eminent scholars— American political scientist Paul Brass and British historian Francis Robinson (publishing, interestingly, at the same time)—have not only contributed the most but have also offered different and divergent explanations of Muslim Separatism: 'instrumentalist' versus 'primordial'. There are other explanations as well but these two are the most cited, debated, and discussed ones, and the following discussion too, essentially, revolves around them.

Francis Robinson in his seminal work, *Separatism among Indian Muslims: The Politics of the United Provinces' Muslims, 1860–1923* (1974),[2] highlighted four explanations of Muslim separatism. The first explanation came from W. W. Hunter, a British historian, statistician, and civil servant in post-1857 India, who, in 1870, presented a theory of separatism based on 'Muslim backwardness' which was promoted by the Muslim leadership in their political discourse henceforth.[3] The second explanation suggested '*Divide et impera*' on the part of British rulers in India 'for their own imperial purpose', thus breaking 'an evolving synthesis of Hindu-Muslim culture'—a favourite theme of most Indian historians today.[4] The third explanation, an 'important' one and directly opposed to the second, argued that 'Indian nationalists would do well to look at their own record ....'[5] Muslim 'communalism', it stressed, 'was due to the failure of [Indian] nationalism to develop a truly non-communal ethos. Nationalism was associated with a frequently aggressive Hindu revivalism, and its symbols, its idiom and its inspiration were all Hindu.'[6] The fourth explanation, offered by most Pakistani historians, takes cue from the third explanation and emphasised that 'Muslim separatism was no Pavlovian reaction to

1

Hindu organisation, but the natural expression of the realisation that Indian Muslims were a separate community.'[7]

Paul Brass, in his *Language, Religion, and Politics in North India* (1974),[8] however, put much of these explanations differently and in two broad sets of arguments pressed by two parties. In his opinion, one party argued that 'the development of separate Hindu and Muslim nations on the subcontinent was pre-ordained from pre-modern times [i.e. before the advent of the British] because of the fundamental differences between Islamic religion and civilization and Hindu religion and civilization.'[9] The other party, 'including both scholars and Indian nationalists', disagreed with that and:

> pointed to the objective similarities of race, language, and culture—even religion—among the common mass of Muslims and Hindus, to the development in India of a composite culture and nationality embracing both Hindus and Muslims from medieval times, and to the very late and seemingly fortuitous acceptance by the Muslims of the idea that they formed a separate nation in India.[10]

Brass himself did not support 'either of these polar views'.[11] He contended that:

> There have been, in fact, both objective similarities and dissimilarities in language, religion, culture, diet, and dress between Hindus and Muslims in India, upon which either two separate nations or a single composite nation might have been built.[12]

He held that 'even accepting the predominant historical view that religious and cultural separatism had become the standard at the elite level in pre-modern times, the translation of this separatism into politics was not pre-ordained'.[13] In fact, he maintained that:

> 'Muslim separatness did not flow necessarily and inexorably out of the objective differences between Hindus and Muslims, but uses which were made of those differences through the manipulation of symbols of Muslim unity and Hindu-Muslim separateness by an elite concerned to preserve its political privileges.'[14]

Brass developed this 'instrumentalist' position through his study of Muslim politics in the United Provinces (UP) of North India in particular. He pointed out that both the Aligarh Movement—'the ideology of Muslim separatism'—and the Muslim League—'the political organization of the Muslim community'—began their journey from north India, especially the UP, where 'far from being a backward people, the Muslim elite constituted a dominant elite bent upon preserving its dominance ....'[15] The 'ideology' of this dominant elite, he claimed, went on to 'ultimately spread throughout eastern and western India'.[16] Thus, he insisted, 'what stands out in the history of Muslim separatism is not the ineluctable movement of events on an historically predetermined course, but the process of conscious choice by which men decide, because it suits their interests to do so ....'[17] The Muslim elite consciously manipulated 'selected symbols of Muslim identity' to help them 'in economic and political competition with each other and with elite groups among Hindus.'[18] The competition, he further explained, was for 'administrative and political power and for employment, and for whom the symbols of religion [Islam and Hinduism] and language [Urdu and Hindi] were both subjectively meaningful and politically useful.'[19] Religion and language were the instruments. In his own words, 'Religion and language were the symbolic instruments in this essentially political conflict.'[20]

Thus, as opposed to the ulema for whom religion and language defined the Muslim community, for these 'modernizing Muslim elites', from Syed Ahmad Khan to Mohammad Ali Jinnah, the community was essentially a 'political one'.[21] In the case of Jinnah, in particular, Brass emphasised that it was not only 'entirely different from the definition used by the ulema', it 'also moved away from the historical-political definition of the early leaders of the Aligarh movement.'[22] It was no longer 'an abstract historical-political entity' of 'historical importance' but 'a contemporary political force', indeed a 'minority' comprising 'a separate people with distinct interests'.[23] More importantly, this was not a 'shifting' minority 'in a representative system [of government] who could be voted down on one issue, but would have a chance to prevail on other issues.'[24] The Muslim minority 'represented a permanent and persistent political interest and could not be treated only as a minority.'[25] In the 1930s and 1940s, it all came down to 'political power' for a 'self-determining nation, distinctive in religion, history, philosophy of life, literature, and language from the Hindus....'[26] The 'primordial' sentiment came to the fore only to help and sustain the struggle for power.

This brings us to Robinson, the main architect of the primordial theory of Muslim separatism in India. Like Brass, Robinson too, in his detailed work on the UP Muslims,[27] traced the history of Muslim separatism till the early 1920s and claimed that the Muslims of UP 'were at the heart of Muslim separatism'.[28] Led by Syed Ahmad Khan, they established the Muhammadan Anglo-Oriental (M.A.O) College at Aligarh, 'which directed much early Muslim political activity and nurtured many Muslim League politicians.'[29] The 'most powerful position' in the Muslim League, that of the Secretary, 'between 1906 and 1910 ... was held by UP Muslims in Aligarh, and between 1910 and 1926 by UP Muslims in Lucknow.'[30] The League persuaded the government 'to give Muslims representation which in most councils took into account not only their proportion of the population but also their alleged political importance.'[31] This was done through 'separate electorates' granted in the Indian Councils Act of 1909. The result, according to Robinson, was that, 'By 1909, a Muslim identity was firmly established in Indian politics.'[32] The British, on their part, had accepted the Muslims as a 'separate, distinct, and monolithic' group.[33]

But did 'this mean that the British divided and ruled?'[34] Robinson's answer, in 'the crude sense', was, of course, 'no'.[35] While he argued that the 'British policy in the second half of the nineteenth century made a great contribution to the development of Muslim separatism', he insisted that the 'division was not intended'.[36] There was 'no deliberate attempt' by the British government 'to foster communal hostility; indeed the aim was to avoid it.'[37] But, 'they had to isolate areas of opposition and discover areas of support. Then, with these divisions in mind, they had to formulate policies and hand out patronage. Inevitably, the effect of imperial rule was to exacerbate some divisions and to break down others.'[38]

Robinson believed that 'being Muslims under British imperial rule did give them some common experience',[39] especially 'common religious experience', which helped them organise for 'politics on a communal basis'.[40] However, he emphasised that, 'It would be wrong ... to see government's marked responsibility to Muslim pleas as a constant factor in the growth of Muslim separatism .... Instead, Muslims themselves became increasingly effective in sustaining their separate identity in politics.'[41]

Robinson observed that 'the formation of separatist movements on the basis of religious confession' and, hence, 'the assertion of a political identity on the basis of religion' was a 'special characteristic of Muslims'.[42] He maintained that 'Islamic ideals had a moulding and on occasion a motivating role to play amongst the elites of the UP,' and, therefore, 'the continuing power of these ideas suggest that the balance of the argument should shift more towards the position of primordialists.'[43] He was convinced that 'objective differences between Hindus and Muslims were not great enough of themselves to fuel a separatist movement', until we 'add the religio-political ideas of Islam, in particular those that stress the existence of a Muslim community.'[44] Thus, in his opinion, 'the example of Muslim separatism' in the UP, and indeed in India, clearly demonstrated that 'politics as an autonomous must be cut down' more than Brass had been 'prepared to admit'.[45] His instrumentalist approach was not of much help.

A number of writers have taken either the instrumentalist or the primordial approach to explain Muslim separatism in India as they saw it. A few are discussed here to illustrate the phenomenon further before I delineate my own position in this respect and present the scheme of the book accordingly.

Farzana Shaikh, in her important work, *Community and Concensus in Islam: Muslim Representation in Colonial India, 1860–1947* (2012), followed Robinson and his primordial theory. She held that 'Indian Muslims conceived of the purpose of politics as the expression of their religious ideals rather than as search for consensus with other communities ....'[46] This 'perceived "primordial" basis of my analysis,' she explained, 'aimed simply to correct dominant interpretation of Indo-Muslim politics that roundly dismissed the power of ideology, except as an "instrument" for manipulation of competing elites to mobilize popular support.'[47] The idea, she insisted, was not 'to say that Indian Muslims were in any sense determined in their pursuit of separatist politics by the normative concerns of their religion.'[48] It was to argue 'that their motivations are best understood and appreciated in the light of these religious traditions, whose complex relationship to power acted as a significant constraint against the accommodations judged necessary to strengthen liberal-democratic arrangements in late colonial India.'[49]

In the end, after analysing the whole Muslim separatist case at length, Farzana Shaikh concluded that: 'there was more at stake here than power for power's sake. The dictates of their faith have led Muslims, more often than not, to presuppose the division of society into Muslims and non-Muslims.'[50] That, in the case of Indian Muslims, explained 'what the League and its Muslim followers sought to establish, therefore, was not only that Congress did not represent the vast majority of Muslims in India, but that as a non-Muslim body, it *could not* represent a Muslim consensus [ijma].'[51] This 'denial of Congress' representative mandate' indeed formed 'the cornerstone of Muslim separatism'.[52]

Venkat Dhulipala too, in his study of the Muslims of UP— like Brass, Robinson, and Farzana Shaikh before him—took the primordial, 'religio-political' route to explain Muslim separatism in India. In his book, *Creating a New Medina: State Power, Islam, and the Quest for Pakistan in Late Colonial North India* (2015),[53] Dhulipala tried to show how the 'men of religion', the ulema, 'utilized a common political vocabulary that intertwined concepts of modern politics and Islamic political theology in order to make the most compelling arguments in favour of Pakistan.'[54] Islam, he claimed, 'became the language of politics in Pakistan precisely as a result of the trajectory of the Pakistan movement in the last decade of the [British] Raj.'[55] Indeed, he contended, 'my argument is that the origins of the "ideological" state in Pakistan lie not just in its post-independence insecurities, but at the very core of its nationalist ideology that developed in the run up to 1947.'[56] In this sense, he disagreed with 'Studies of Pakistan that emphasize its "insufficient imagination",' for, in his opinion, 'Pakistan was not insufficiently imagined, but plentifully and with ambition.'[57] Pakistan was 'imagined and contested in a Muslim minority province like UP', but the ultimate goal was 'a new Medina, which accounts for the crises that confront Pakistan today.'[58]

As opposed to Dhulipala's emphasis on Islam as the basis for Muslim separatism, Ram Gopal, in his major work, *Indian Muslims* (1976),[59] argued that 'Islam was not the cause but was employed as an excuse'[60] by the Muslim leadership. In his opinion, 'Government jobs during the post-Revolt [1857] period' provided the 'starting-point of a separatist movement which grew in the last quarter of the 19th century in the north-west of India under patronage of Sir Syed Ahmad Khan's Aligarh school ...'.[61] Eventually, 'starting from a humble beginning', this movement went on to 'develop into a turbulent stream'.[62] The result was that, in the end, Indian nationalism 'stood defeated' for 'exhortation made in the name of Islam reduced nationalism virtually to mean Hinduism.'[63] The Congress, a 'national' organisation, 'was reduced, by the elections of 1936 and 1946, to a Hindu organization', making the League 'even more popular among Muslims',[64] and thus the creation of Pakistan. Clearly, Gopal adopted the instrumentalist position to explain the rise and growth of Muslim separatism in India.

In a similar vein, S. R. Mehrotra, in *Towards India's Freedom and Partition* (2007),[65] pursued an instrumentalist approach to Muslim separatism. 'It was the determination of the All-India Muslim League—the carrier of Muslim separatism in India—to dominate the Muslim-majority provinces,' he argued, 'which led directly and inevitably to the partition of India and the creation of Pakistan.'[66] Jinnah's leadership, he continued, had 'relevance' only because 'he became both the architect and the symbol of alliance between Muslim separatism and Muslim will to rule the Muslim-majority provinces.'[67] He credited Jinnah for making 'a tremendous appeal to the hopes and fears of the Muslims' which 'made a steadily growing number of thinking Muslims favour the idea of a separation of "Muslim India" from "Hindu India"... an easy and perhaps the only practicable solution to the chronic and extremely intractable Hindu-Muslim Problem.'[68] By Muslim India, Mehrotra obviously meant 'Muslim-majority regions in India which could be easily separated from the rest of India.'[69] In fact, he emphasised that the 'Muslim desire for a separate homeland of their own could not, even if it had arisen, have found fulfilment in the manner in which it ultimately did unless there were clearly demarcable regions in which the Muslims were in a majority and which they could turn into their own separate homeland.'[70] Still, he insisted, it was 'the Muslim will to power which proved decisive.'[71]

Walter Bennett Evans, in his study of the origins of Pakistan, *The Genesis of the Pakistan Idea: A Study of Hindu-Muslim Relations* (2013),[72] projected a primordial view of Muslim separatism by plainly stating that 'Nationalism in India was tied up with religion.'[73] But, more significantly, he stressed, this nationalism was 'plural. The Hindu renaissance caused a Muslim renaissance. The two revivals could not be alike.'[74] Interestingly, he went on to suggest that: 'Had there been no nationalist movement[,] the points of agreement would have been emphasized. Nationalism emphasized the points of difference.'[75] While the Hindus and the Muslims had 'lived side by side in the subcontinent of India', he believed,

> two diametrically opposed forces have been at play. The one force has moved in the direction of unity and cooperation, while the other force has moved in the direction of particularism and diversity. The Lahore Resolution marked the triumph of the latter and the acceptance of the Pakistan idea.[76]

Curiously enough, Evans was also of the view that,

> Had the Round Table Conference [1930–2] granted Dominion Status or had the Congress and the League been willing to cooperate with the Liberals in the working of the federal scheme in the Act of 1935 India might have solved the communal problem and remained a united country ....[77]

It is an unusual claim, but still clearly an instrumentalist position.

Hafeez Malik too, in his book, *Moslem Nationalism in India and Pakistan* (1963),[78] presented an instrumentalist view of Muslim separatism. Islam in India, he observed, 'not only referred to a system of belief' but also 'stood as a symbolic expression of the total cultural, religious and historical experience of the Moslems of India.'[79] In this sense, he maintained, 'Islam was also used as a label to describe the Moslem's aspirations and to indicate their separate future destiny.'[80] He thus disagreed with those writers who claimed that 'Pakistan as a state' was founded on religion, simple and pure, for, in spite of the fact that 'Islam as a religion' had played a significant role in 'the creation of Pakistani nationalism', the Muslim leaders' 'eyes were fixed on the secular affairs of the Muslims.'[81] Malik, indeed, felt that 'Moslem nationalism in India had been obscured by religious terminology.'[82] He, thus, insisted that 'when the name Pakistan was coined the secular national ambitions of the Moslems were clearly set forth and it became evident that the actual aim of the Moslems in India was a political state of their own.'[83]

Ayesha Jalal also pursued an instrumentalist approach to Muslim separatism. In her study, *The Sole Spokesman: Jinnah, the Muslim League and the Demand for Pakistan* (1985),[84] she emphasised 'the uses made by Jinnah and the League of religion or the importance of communal consciousness at the social base.' However, she claimed that 'Jinnah's appeal to religion was always ambiguous' and, more importantly, 'his use of the communal factor was a political tactic, not an ideological commitment.'[85] In deploying 'the communal card', it was a different matter how 'far it constrained or helped him in achieving his political aims.'[86] For one thing, 'the "two-nation" theory with which Jinnah had hoped to get the League a share of power at the centre was the sword which was now cutting his Pakistan down to size.'[87] Jinnah had to concede the division of Punjab and Bengal on communal lines. Earlier, she rejected 'the most common argument … that the Indian Muslims were always a separate and identifiable community.'[88] She also dismissed the theory that 'emphasized the role of imperialism in dividing two communities which history and tradition had joined.'[89] However, she did not deny that 'British policies and initiatives were a vital factor in Indian political calculations and responses ....'[90] In the end, she went on to assert that, 'It was Congress that insisted on partition. It was Jinnah who was against partition.'[91] This, of course, seemed more like a case for Hindu separatism, not Muslim separatism, and that Jinnah did not want the separate state of Pakistan.

Ishtiaq Hussain Qureshi, the earliest and most influential historian of Pakistan, explained Muslim separatism in India, like Robinson suggested in case of most Pakistani historians referred to earlier, in terms of Indian Muslims being a separate community from the Hindus. In his classic study, *The Struggle for Pakistan* (1969),[92] he challenged the 'fallacious assumption that the Muslims of the subcontinent had everything in common with the Hindus except their religion.'[93] He argued that 'Islam and Hinduism build two entirely different kinds of society', but it went beyond 'social structure' into 'variance through all details.'[94] He, therefore, considered it a misnomer to call the Muslims a 'religious minority.'[95] In fact, they were 'a distinct' nation 'without a name', although they themselves were quite conscious of it from the early days of the British rule as they, while demanding separate electorates, plainly told 'the Viceroy [Lord Minto] "that the Muslims of India should not be regarded as a mere minority, but [sic] as a nation within a nation whose rights and obligations should be guaranteed by Statute."'[96] Their 'status of minority' worried them till they, in the wake of World War II and the imminent departure of the British from India, realised that they 'would have nothing to do with one India if that one India was to be ruled by the Hindus.'[97] It was 'fortunate', Qureshi observed, that the Muslims at this juncture, after the passage of the 1940 Lahore Resolution, 'possessed a leader of Jinnah's caliber during the struggle for Pakistan.'[98] But he maintained most emphatically that 'Even without Jinnah[,] Pakistan would have come, but it would have been delayed for decades and would have entailed much greater conflict and travail.'[99]

Abdul Hamid, another eminent Pakistani historian, in his pioneering study on Muslim separatism, took a position different from that of Qureshi. In his book, *Muslim Separatism in India:*

A Brief Survey, 1858–1947 (1967),[100] he took an instrumentalist position. Beginning his study with the 1857–8 Revolt 'which marked the failure of a mass uprising against the British', Hamid highlighted the role of Syed Ahmad Khan 'who awakened the communal consciousness of the Indian Muslims and propagated the impulses that ultimately broadened into the demand for a separate homeland in the subcontinent.'[101] This was not an easy undertaking for, on the one hand, he 'had to fight the religious conservatism and intellectual stagnation of Muslim society' and on the other, the 'frigid hauteur of Britons towards Indians.'[102] But Syed Ahmad Khan dedicated himself wholeheartedly to 'political rehabilitation and social regeneration of his people.'[103] His Aligarh College and the associated Aligarh Movement soon 'became the visible emblem of Muslim hopes and desires.'[104] Indeed, Syed Ahmad Khan's 'period was the seed-time of vast changes' when pertinent 'issues were framed, propositions laid down, attitudes defined and the persistent pattern of Hindu-Muslim relations cast.'[105] Hamid did not agree that Syed Ahmad Khan was 'consciously creating the separatist movement.'[106] But then, he acknowledged that 'The contributory causes of all movements in history are found in the environment itself. Leaders are seldom aware of the full implications and possibilities of the attitudes they strike and tendencies they initiate.'[107] Syed Ahmad Khan did '"drive a stream of tendency" through the Muslim affairs in this sub-continent',[108] strengthening 'separatist tendencies',[109] which culminated in the separate state of Pakistan.

Khalid bin Sayeed, in his influential book, *Pakistan: The Formative Phase, 1857–1948* (1994),[110] promoted the primordial aspect of Muslim separatism in India, and lamented that this aspect 'has not been fully understood in the West.'[111] As he put it: 'To the West, nationality based on religion is an alien and often incomprehensible phenomenon. This is because religion in the West has come to play such a restricted role.'[112] Western scholars fail to appreciate that 'Hindus and Muslims in India' represented 'two separate cultural entities ...'.[113] Indeed, Sayeed claimed,

... there has never taken place a confluence of the two civilizations in India—the Hindu and the Muslim. They may have meandered towards each other here and there, but on the whole the two have flowed their separate courses—sometimes parallel and sometimes contrary to one another.[114]

Thus, he insisted that 'the roots of Pakistan can be found in the pre-British period, but its [sic] full germination took place on the eve of the British departure from India.'[115] In the meantime, he credited both Iqbal for his 'comprehensive' conception of a 'separate state' for the Muslims 'based on both geographical and ideological factors'[116] and Jinnah, 'the Quaid-i-Azam—the Great Leader of a national movement' for the achievement of the separate state of Pakistan.[117] Jinnah 'achieved something which no other Muslim leader had even dreamt of. Muslims, especially in Northern India, regarded him as a successor of great Moghul Emperors, Emperors like Babur and Aurangzeb.'[118] Sayeed rejected the thesis that 'Muslim separatism really started with separate electorates to Muslims in 1909'[119] or, for that matter, 'Hindu short-sightedness or exclusiveness was the sole factor which created Pakistan.'[120] In fact, after the passage of the Lahore Resolution in 1940, 'the dominant theme in Muslim politics was not complaint against Hindu injustice but a demand for a separate political existence.'[121] Thus, Sayeed forcefully 'argued that ... separatism rather than Hindu exclusiveness was the principle cause behind the creation of Pakistan.'[122]

In my opinion, Muslim separatism in India, as it grew and developed, leading up to the achievement of Pakistan, can best be explained through the instrumentalist approach, through the conscious, careful, and deliberate role played by the Muslim political leadership in promoting and securing Muslim interests in an inherently biased system of representative government introduced in the country. This role was political and for political ends. However, it essentially had a religious basis; the struggle was for the Muslims, the Muslim community who, obviously, professed and, indeed, pursued Islam as a 'religio-cultural force' in their lives.[123]

Both Islam and Hinduism affected Hindu–Muslim relations and contributed to the ultimate split and separation between the two communities. Hindu separatism was as pronounced as Muslim separatism. As early as the eleventh century, Al-Beruni, a Muslim traveller to India, pointed out that 'Hindus totally differ from us in religion as we believe in nothing which they believe, and vice versa ....'[124] Nirad C. Chaudhri, writing several centuries later, in the twentieth century, was 'shocked' to 'read Al-Beruni's account of Hindu xenophobia for the first time', but agreed that 'Al-Beruni was substantially right' and that 'hatred of the Hindu is directed against all men who are not fellow Hindus or, theoretically, blood-kins ....'[125]

However, there was no denying that, depending upon the circumstances in the political arena and the will of political actors involved, this Hindu–Muslim relationship kept changing for better or for worse. During Muslim rule in India, especially under the Mughals, the relationship kept moving up and down depending on a particular ruler and his dispensation, whether it was Emperor Akbar or Emperor Aurangzeb, for example, and then within their reigns, in different periods. The 'difficulties', as Tara Chand pointed out, 'arose out of the practical exigencies of government over a vast population different in religion, customs, language and culture .... Some levied the Jaziya, others refrained from doing so; some differentiated between Hindus and Muslims, others did not.'[126] Hence, it was all about politics, and what goes with it, including power, influence, and conduct.

The situation was more 'political' during British rule, as the British were quite mindful of the fact that the difference between Islam and Hinduism was 'not a mere difference of articles of religious faith. It is a difference in life, in tradition, in history, in all the social things as well as articles of belief that constitute a community.'[127] Thus, the British came to see and accept the Muslims as a separate community as the Muslims were insistent in the first place, through the exhortation of Syed Ahmad Khan in the immediate post-1857 Revolt period, followed by the Aga Khan and Syed Ameer Ali soon after. Given the constitutional framework of representative electoral system of government being introduced in India then, Syed Ahmad Khan's common refrain was, 'The larger community [i.e. Hindus] would totally override the interests of the smaller community'.[128] The majority–minority syndrome took roots. The Muslims, given their numbers, became a 'minority' community and a permanent one. There was no way they could turn the system around in their favour. It was inherently and indeed permanently biased against them. Separate electorates, granted under the Indian Councils Act 1909, and its continuation was meant to help lessen the burden of a majority rule under the system. Interestingly, at this point in time, the British were not so sure of the kind of system suitable for India, 'akin to the instinct of the many races composing the population of the Indian Empire.'[129] No wonder, Lord Morley, the Secretary of State for India, and the architect of the Act which is also popularly known as the Morley–Minto Reforms, went on record to say that: 'I am no advocate of "representative government for India" in the Western sense of the term.'[130] Eventually, of course, by the early 1940s, the British were wondering if 'the Swiss constitutional system might have a better chance of succeeding in an Indian province than the British.'[131] But then, it was too late. The British went on with their representative system of government, essentially based on numbers.

With devolution of authority to the Indians under the Government of India Act 1919 (also known as the Montagu–Chelmsford Reforms), particularly with the so-called provincial autonomy under the system of 'dyarchy', the relations between the Hindus and the Muslims became severely strained with the passage of time. There was the 'issue of ministries, distribution of seats in the legislative councils and municipal bodies, and the proportion of representation in the government jobs.'[132] The 'Hindu-Muslim unity' spirit of the Lucknow Pact of 1916 between the Muslims and the Hindus, and the Muslim League and the Congress, was no more. As H. M. Seervai aptly stated, 'Perhaps the explanation lies in the fact that the "war of succession" to the British Raj had not begun in 1916, but had begun in 1928, because full provincial autonomy was the obvious line of political advance in India'.[133] The Nehru Report of 1928 reflected this 'war'. It was time for 'the struggle for political power and for the opportunity

which political power confers.'[134] The Government of India
Act 1935, with the prospects of power in the hands of Hindus at
the centre, raised this struggle to another, more ominous level—
the threat of Hindu rule in India—and a permanent, enduring
one given the inexorable logic of majority rule. The haughty,
disdainful, and indeed distressful Congress rule of the provinces
in 1937–9[135] made it all the more real and revolting for the Muslims
in particular. They clearly saw that:

> [The Congress rule] foreshadowed a permanent Hindu government
> ruling over the minorities and demonstrated the unworkability of
> parliamentary rule, the constitutional safeguards for minorities
> proving fragile. The Muslims felt that the remedy of minority
> troubles did not lie within a federal framework, because the
> advantages offered by provincial autonomy would be negatived
> if the central government was placed, as it was bound to be under
> Hindu domination.[136]

This was the making of an existential crisis in which the Muslims,
having lost power to the British earlier in 1857–8 (after the Revolt of
1857), were now confronted with the possibility of losing it forever—
this time, to the Hindus. World War II and the imminent departure
of the British from India made it critical for the Muslims to find
a way out of their present predicament and, more importantly, to
seek a safe and secure future. The Muslim leadership responded
in the form of the Lahore Resolution of 1940, indeed demanding
partition of India and the separate state of Pakistan, not only to
save them from the Hindu majority rule but also to provide power
and security in a separate homeland to live their lives in their own
way, following their own faith, values, traditions, and norms.

In shaping, formulating, and eventually realising this separatist
goal, the Muslims, of course, passed through a number of phases,
led by different leaders pursuing a steady, evolving, and maturing
separatist political movement, founded by Syed Ahmad Khan. The
central plank of this separatist movement was separate Muslim
political identity, with its own separate interests, rights, and
demands. Separate electorates, a separate political organisation,
the All-India Muslim League, and Urdu were some of the early

components. It was essentially a political movement. The main
leaders of the movement, after Syed Ahmad Khan, were the
Aga Khan, Syed Ameer Ali, Maulana Mohamed Ali, Allama
Muhammad Iqbal, and indeed Quaid-i-Azam Mohammad Ali
Jinnah. While his predecessors, the Aga Khan and Ameer Ali,
faithfully followed the movement, Mohamed Ali deviated for a
while because of his intense involvement with the Khilafat–non-
cooperation movement before returning to the fold and reviving
and putting the separatist political movement back on track
and, indeed, onwards. Allama Iqbal furnished the intellectual,
philosophical, and 'national' basis for the demand for a separate
state and directed the separatist movement towards a tangible
national goal. Jinnah, though an 'Ambassador of Hindu-Muslim
Unity' for most part of his political career, especially his early
career, finally embraced separatism and assumed leadership of
the movement, transforming and developing it into a nationalist
movement—the Pakistan Movement—and eventually bringing
the struggle for a separate, sovereign state of Pakistan to a historic
end. India was partitioned to accommodate the new nation-
state of Pakistan, home of the Muslim nation. Thus, 'while Islam
inspired and moved the Muslims in the struggle for Pakistan and
was indeed the basis', the Muslim separatist political movement,
and, eventually, the Pakistan Movement, was primarily 'a political
project', with distinct 'political character and functions', and
operated 'in a political way and for political ends, that is, the
creation of Pakistan.'[137]

In order to pursue this argument in some detail and depth, this
book is divided into seven convenient chapters.

- Chapter 1, 'Origins and Development of Hindu-Muslim
  Separatism in India: A Survey of Muslim Rule', explores
  'separatism' between the two communities during the
  Muslim rule of India, in spite of all the efforts on the part of
  some rulers to unite them, before the arrival of the British.
- Chapter 2, 'Syed Ahmad Khan and the Foundation of the
  Muslim Separatist Political Movement in British India',
  highlights Syed Ahmad Khan's efforts to respond to and deal

with British rule and, in the process, promote and pursue
Muslim separatism in politics and thus lay the foundation of
a Muslim separatist political movement.

- Chapter 3, 'Aga Khan and the Growth of the Muslim
  Separatist Political Movement in British India', follows the
  role of Aga Khan in the growth of the separatist political
  movement through the establishment of the All-India Muslim
  League and the granting of separate electorates.

- Chapter 4, 'Syed Ameer Ali and the Consolidation of the
  Muslim Separatist Political Movement in British India',
  emphasises the critical role played by Syed Ameer Ali in
  promoting the separatist movement in Bengal, independent
  of Syed Ahmad Khan's efforts in UP, and forcing the British
  to concede separate electorates through his London Muslim
  League and thus further institutionalising separatism and
  consolidating the movement.

- Chapter 5, 'Maulana Mohamed Ali and the Revival of the
  Muslim Separatist Political Movement in British India', traces
  Maulana Mohamed Ali's split from the separatist political
  movement for the sake of Khilafat and the resultant Khilafat-
  non-cooperation movement, and then his eventual return
  to it with greater clarity and for the pursuit of its enhanced
  goals and objectives, indeed preparing the movement for its
  ultimate realisation.

- Chapter 6, 'Allama Muhammad Iqbal and the Formulation
  of the Idea of a Separate State in India', examines Allama
  Iqbal's role in formulating the idea of a separate state for
  the Muslims of India, based on the concept of nationalism,
  'Muslim nationalism'. This formulation not only helped the
  Muslims in demanding the separate state of Pakistan but
  it also encouraged Jinnah to accept and promote Muslim
  separatism and lead the Pakistan Movement for the resolution
  of the perennial Hindu–Muslim problem in India.

- Chapter 7, 'Quaid-i-Azam Mohammad Ali Jinnah, the
  Pakistan Movement and the Achievement of the Separate
  State of Pakistan', evaluates Jinnah's political life and career
  in British India, concentrating upon his transformation

from being the proponent of Hindu–Muslim unity to the fiercest champion of Muslim separatism and nationhood, indeed helping the Muslim separatist political movement develop into a more focused, deliberate, and practical Pakistan Movement, achieving its ultimate goal of Pakistan. This, being the most eventful and crucial phase of Muslim separatism, is the longest chapter of the book.

There were, of course, some more leaders who contributed to the development of Muslim separatism in India, both at the national and provincial levels, and are duly recognised for that, but these six leaders—Syed Ahmad Khan, Aga Khan, Syed Ameer Ali, Maulana Mohamed Ali, Allama Muhammad Iqbal, and Quaid-i-Azam Mohammad Ali Jinnah—were the most prominent, influential, and decisive in their contributions. Hence, the present emphasis on their leadership.

Four chapters, 1, 2, 5, and 6, are revised, expanded, and updated versions of the articles published long ago in the *Pakistan Journal of History and Culture*, Vol. V, No. 2, July–December 1984; *Pakistan Journal of Social Sciences*, Vol. VIII, No. 1 and 2 (January–July–December 1982); *Pakistan Journal of History and Culture*, Vol. VI, No.1 (January–June 1985); and *Pakistan Journal of Social Sciences*, Vol. IX, No. 1 and 2 (January–July–December 1983), respectively. I am grateful to the publishers. The other three chapters, on the Aga Khan, Ameer Ali, and Jinnah, are fresh and original, especially written for this volume. The idea is to explain Muslim separatism in India through the struggle of these prominent Muslim leaders who led and pursued the separatist political movement and through their consistent, cumulative efforts—indeed an 'odyssey', to borrow the title of an ancient Greek epic poem, for want of a better expression—made the achievement of a separate state of Pakistan possible.

While accounts of some individual leaders pursuing Muslim separatist agenda and goals are available, including my own work on Jinnah, to the best of my knowledge, no study so far has examined the growing, systematic effect of such a common pursuit in the hands of so many leaders, one after the other. In this sense, it will be a distinct study on the subject of Muslim separatism in India, with leaders, a succession of leaders, as explanatory variables. Hopefully, this will help explain the phenomenon better than any other explanation offered so far, especially to Indian historians and some others who hold Jinnah alone responsible for Pakistan. It was Muslim leadership, one and all.

Notes

1. This is not to suggest that less attention has been paid to Hindu separatism in British India, especially with reference to the All-India Hindu Mahasabha, Rashtriya Swayamsevak Sangh (RSS), Jana Sangh, Bharatiya Jana Singh, and the present-day Bharatiya Janata Party (BJP) and indeed the rise and role of their leaders in the process. Mahasabha leader, Bhai Parmanand, in 1933, had no qualms in declaring that: 'Hindustan is the land of the Hindus alone, and Musalmans and Christians and other nations living in India are [sic] only our guests.' RSS leader, Madhavrao Sadashiv Golwalker, a few years later, in 1939, asked the Muslims in particular that they 'must either adopt the Hindu culture and language, must learn to respect and hold in reverence Hindu religion, must entertain no idea but those of glorification of the Hindu race and culture … or must stay in this country, wholly and subordinated to the Hindu nation, claiming nothing, deserving no privileges …—not even citizen's rights.' This was a few months before the passage of the 1940 Lahore Resolution, demanding a separate homeland for the Muslims. Jana Sangh, under the leadership, first of Keval Malkani, and then of Syama Prasad Mookherjee, went on to adopt 'Hindutva' for India, an ideology and agenda pursued later by the Bharatiya Jana Sangh and the BJP. The Hindu Mahasabha, the oldest separatist political party, heavily influenced the Indian National Congress, especially in the 1920s and 1930s, till they were convinced in the late 1930s that the Congress had, based both on the will of its leadership and the sheer numbers at its command in a representative system of government, had transformed 'Indian nationalism' into 'Hindu nationalism', and had finally and fully refused to share power with the Muslims. They did not even agree to a genuine federal system of government for India where the Muslims could have had some relief in the Muslim–majority provinces. However, in closing, it needs to be stressed that this Hindu separatism had a unique characteristic which set it apart from Muslim separatism as such. It did not simply say that Hindus were separate from the Muslims and thus had separate interests and demands. It denied Muslims their place in the society and politics of India as will be evident from the above two quotes from their most representative leaders. Additionally, they did not need to act separatists, demanding a separate state, because the

numbers were on their side, under all circumstances. They represented the Hindu majority community. India belonged to them. The system helped them, facilitated them in their pursuit of power, absolute power. For some details on these separatist parties and their leaders, see Craig Baxter, *Jana Sangh: A Biography of an Indian Political Party* (Philadelphia: University of Pennsylvania Press, 1959), 19, 13, and especially chapters II, III, and IV. Also see Muhammad Mujeeb Afzal, *Bharatiya Janata Party and the Indian Muslims* (Karachi: Oxford University Press, 2014).

2. Francis Robinson, *Separatism Among Indian Muslims: The Politics of the United Provinces' Muslims, 1860–1923* (Cambridge: Cambridge University Press, 1974).
3. Ibid., 1.
4. Ibid., 2.
5. Ibid.
6. Ibid.
7. Ibid.
8. Paul Brass, *Language, Religion, and Politics in North India* (Cambridge: Cambridge University Press, 1974).
9. Ibid., 119.
10. Ibid.
11. Ibid.
12. Ibid.
13. Ibid., 119–20.
14. Ibid., 120.
15. Ibid., 121.
16. Ibid.
17. Ibid., 179.
18. Paul Brass, 'Elite Groups, Symbol Manipulation and Ethnic Identity among the Muslims of South Asia', in *Political Identity in South Asia*, eds. David Taylor and Malcolm Yapp (London: Curzon Press, 1979), 41.
19. Brass, *Language, Religion, and Politics in North India*, 137.
20. Ibid., 138.
21. Ibid., 56.
22. Ibid., 60.
23. Ibid.
24. Ibid.
25. Ibid., 61.
26. Ibid., 66.
27. Robinson, *Separatism among Indian Muslims*.
28. Ibid., 4.
29. Ibid.
30. Ibid.
31. Ibid., 173.
32. Ibid.
33. Ibid.

34. Ibid., 348.
35. Ibid.
36. Ibid., 131.
37. Ibid., 348.
38. Ibid., 349.
39. Ibid., 345.
40. Ibid., 348.
41. Ibid., 349.
42. Robinson, 'Islam and Muslim Separatism', in *Political Identity in South Asia*, eds. David Taylor and Malcolm Yapp (London: Curzon Press, 1979), 78.
43. Ibid., 107.
44. Ibid., 106–7.
45. Ibid., 107.
46. Farzana Shaikh, 'Introduction', in *Community and Consensus in Islam: Muslim Representation in Colonial India, 1860–1947*, 2nd ed. (Delhi: Imprint One, 2012), xvii.
47. Ibid., xxiv.
48. Ibid., xxv.
49. Ibid.
50. Ibid., 236.
51. Ibid.
52. Ibid., 231.
53. Venkat Dhulipala, *Creating a New Medina: State Power, Islam, and the Quest for Pakistan in Late Colonial North India* (Cambridge: Cambridge University Press, 2015).
54. Ibid., 499–500.
55. Ibid., 498.
56. Ibid., 501.
57. Ibid.
58. Ibid., 500–1.
59. Ram Gopal, *Indian Muslims: A Political History (1858–1947)* (Lahore: Book Traders, 1976).
60. Ibid., Preface, vii.
61. Ibid.
62. Ibid., viii.
63. Ibid., ix.
64. Ibid., 330.
65. S. R. Mehrotra, *Towards India's Freedom and Partition* (New Delhi: Rupa & Co., 2007).
66. Ibid., 252.
67. Ibid.
68. Ibid., 255–6.
69. Ibid., 251.
70. Ibid.

71. Ibid., 252.
72. Walter Bennet Evans, *The Genesis of the Pakistan Idea: A Study of Hindu-Muslim Relations* (Karachi: Oxford University Press, 2013).
73. Ibid., 43.
74. Ibid., 289.
75. Ibid., 290.
76. Ibid., 284.
77. Ibid., 287–8.
78. Hafeez Malik, *Moslem Nationalism in India and Pakistan* (Washington DC: Public Affairs Press, 1963).
79. Ibid., 298.
80. Ibid.
81. Ibid.
82. Ibid.
83. Ibid., 298–9.
84. Ayesha Jalal, *The Sole Spokesman: Jinnah, the Muslim League and the Demand for Pakistan* (Cambridge: Cambridge University Press, 1985).
85. Ibid., 5.
86. Ibid.
87. Ibid., 255.
88. Ibid., 1.
89. Ibid.
90. Ibid., 5.
91. Ibid., 262.
92. Ishtiaq Hussain Qureshi, *The Struggle for Pakistan* (Karachi: University of Karachi, 1974).
93. Ibid., 10.
94. Ibid.
95. Ibid., 15.
96. Ibid., 10,15.
97. Ibid., 15, 127.
98. Ibid., 302.
99. Ibid.
100. Abdul Hamid, *Muslim Separatism in India: A Brief Survey, 1858–1947* (Lahore: Oxford University Press, 1967).
101. Ibid., xv.
102. Ibid.
103. Ibid.
104. Ibid., 42.
105. Ibid.
106. Ibid.
107. Ibid.
108. Ibid.
109. Ibid., 225.

110. Khalid bin Sayeed, *Pakistan: The Formative Phase, 1857–1948*, 2nd ed. (Karachi: Oxford University Press, 1994).
111. Ibid., 12.
112. Ibid.
113. Ibid.
114. Ibid.
115. Ibid., 13.
116. Ibid., 103.
117. Ibid., 227.
118. Ibid.
119. Ibid., 4.
120. Ibid., 9.
121. Ibid.
122. Ibid.
123. Aziz Ahmad, *Studies in Islamic Culture in the Indian Environment* (Oxford: Clarendon Press, 1964), 73.
124. Edward C. Sachau, ed., 'Preface', in *Alberuni's India*, Vol. I (Lahore: Sh. Mubarak Ali, 1962, rep.), xxix.
125. Nirad C. Chaudhri, *The Autobiography of an Unknown Indian* (London: Macmillan, 1951), 410.
126. Tara Chand, *Society and State in the Mughal Period* (Lahore: Book Traders, 1979), 63.
127. Anil Chandra Banerjee, ed., *Indian Constitutional Documents: 1757–1945* (Calcutta: A. Mukherjee & Co., 1946), 158.
128. Gulam Allana, ed., *Pakistan Movement: Historic Documents*, 3rd ed. (Lahore: Islamic Book Service, 1977), 2.
129. Banerjee, *Indian Constitutional Documents*, 139.
130. Ibid.
131. N. Mansergh and Penderel Moon, eds., *Constitutional Relations between Britain and India: The Transfer of Power*, Vol. VI (London: Her Majesty's Stationery Office, 1976), 402.
132. Sikandar Hayat, *Aspects of the Pakistan Movement*, 3rd rev. ed. (Islamabad: National Institute of Historical & Cultural Research, 2016), 100.
133. H. M. Seervai, *Partition of India: Legend and Reality* (Rawalpindi: National Services Club Book, 1991), 12.
134. Government of India. Statutory Commission. *Report of the Indian Statutory Commission*, Vol. I (London: Her Majesty's Stationery Office, 1930), 30.
135. K. K. Aziz, indeed, went on to claim that 'the Musims owed the creation of Pakistan to the Congress, in the sense that had the Congress treated the Muslims differently there would have been no Muslim separatism and therefore no Pakistan.' K. K. Aziz, *The Making of Pakistan* (London: Chatto & Windus, 1970), 184.
136. Hamid, *Muslim Separatism in India*, 23.
137. Hayat, *Aspects of the Pakistan Movement*, 197.

1

Origins and Development of Hindu–Muslim Separatism in India: A Survey of Muslim Rule

The history of Muslim rule in India, Aziz Ahmad writes, is 'a history of Hindu–Muslim religio-cultural tensions, interspersed with movements or individual efforts at understanding, harmony and even composite development'. These efforts, however, he felt, touched 'the fringe' and 'the external element of their coexistence'. The Hindus and Muslims failed to imbibe the 'cohesive' features and this soon gave way to 'divisive forces'.[1] Even Tara Chand, an ardent advocate of composite development of Hindu–Muslim culture, admitted that, 'the content of the two did not quite coincide and fuse'.[2] This failure, indeed, had the effect of pushing the two communities into 'separate traditions' to await the outcome of the British Raj in the nineteenth century.[3]

This chapter highlights the origins of these 'separate traditions', delineating the role of both 'cohesive' and 'divisive' forces in the evolution of Hindu–Muslim separatism in India. The appraisal comprises political, social, economic, and religious factors that had a direct bearing on Hindu–Muslim relations. The upshot is that the balance of these relations always weighed on the side of separateness and both communities, notwithstanding some conscious and careful efforts of the Muslim rulers and centuries of contact and living together, moved in separate directions.

Muslim rule in India began with the Arab invasion and conquest of Sind (Sindh) in 711 A.D. Led by Muhammad bin Qasim, the Arab rule opened the Muslim chapter in Indian history, but the rule itself did not last long. Later, in the eleventh century, Mahmud of Ghazni (d.1030), after having consolidated his rule, turned his attention to India, but even after breaking the back of Hindu resistance in his seventeen invasions (1000–26), did not settle in India. He always returned to Ghazni, leaving his possessions to his governors. In this sense, one may argue that Muhammad bin Sam Ghori (d. 1206) truly laid the foundation of Muslim rule in India which continued to thrive at the hands of his slave governor, Qutab al-Din Aibak, the architect of both the 'Delhi Sultanate' and the so-called 'Slave Dynasty' (1206–90). This dynasty, in turn, prompted the rise of successive Turco-Afghan dynasties for more than three centuries, Khaljis (1290–1320), Tughlaqs (1320–1414), Sayyids (1414–50), and Lodhis (1450–1526). In 1526, the Mughals, led by Zahiruddin Muhammad Babur and followed by a host of other rulers, consolidated and expanded Muslim rule for the next three centuries till they were exhausted and the British, inside India by then, through the East India Company, took over India in the wake of the failed 'Revolt of 1857', in 1858. It needs to be stressed here that, while the Mughals, in the end, succeeded in establishing a monolithic Muslim empire, the Sultanate rulers, more often than not, coexisted with the Hindu rulers in the same region. For instance, Ranthambhor and Chittor remained Hindu states during the Khalji and Lodhi periods, in spite of Sikandar Lodhi's conquest of Rajputana. Thus, Muslim rule was far from a settled fact of life in India.

Initially, the Mughal rulers' attempts to rule over the local Hindu rulers and people of India met with strong opposition. Hindus in general and the Rajputs in particular put up a very stiff resistance. It was not until the Second Battle of Panipat (1556) that Muslim powers, under Jalaluddin Muhammad Akbar, emerged victorious over the contending Hindu forces, thereby establishing the supremacy of Muslim rule in India.[4] A century and a half of Muslim rule under successive Mughal emperors—Akbar (1556–1605), Jahangir (1605–27), Shah Jahan (1627–58), and Aurangzeb (1658–1707)—was indeed the high point of Muslim power and glory in India. While the Mughal dynasty remained in power until the last emperor, Bahadur Shah Zafar, was deposed in 1857, paramount Muslim power in India barely lasted beyond the middle of the eighteenth century.[5]

Muslim rule in India began with an effort at Hindu–Muslim understanding and accommodation. The Muslims considered India their home as much as the Dravidians and the Aryans of the old,[6] and tried to make their rule in India acceptable to their subjects in as many ways as possible. Right from the days of Muhammad bin Qasim and Mahmud of Ghazni, Muslim rulers such as Muhammad bin Tughlaq, Alauddin Khalji, Sher Shah Suri, Islam Shah Suri and others sought Hindu–Muslim 'amity and equality of rights', and even entrusted important civil and military responsibilities to the Hindu officers. In fact, Tughlaqs and Khaljis could be described as forerunners of the Mughal ruler Akbar in the way they treated Hindus. Tughlaqs too appointed Jains to senior ranks of their administration. Muhammad bin Tughlaq, in particular,

> showed a greater regard for the religious susceptibilities of the Hindus than his predecessors had ever done .... His culture had widened his outlook, and his converse with philosophers and rationalists had developed in him a spirit of tolerance for which Akbar is so highly praised. He employed some of them in high positions in the state, and like the great Akbar, he tried to stop the horrible practice of *sati*. The independent Rajput states were left unmolested ....'[7]

During the reign of Islam Shah, the Hindus rose to the most important positions in the government.[8] The result was that not only did the Hindus come to share with the Muslims the responsibilities of power and office but great strides were made in the progress of common cultural institutions. Hindi, Bengali, Marathi, Punjabi, and other northern Indian languages absorbed elements from Persian and Arabic and paved the way for a renaissance of literary activity.[9] Still, the fact remained that there was 'no bond of sympathy between the Hindus and Muslims and they often fought among themselves.'[10] This, ironically, was in spite of the common threat to both communities at the hands of the invading Mongols from time to time.

However, the efforts to promote Hindu–Muslim harmony reached their full potential under Akbar's concept of an Indian 'synthesis'.[11] This synthesis had three aspects: political, economic and religious. Politically, Akbar realised that the Hindus would not support Muslim rule unless they were allowed to join in 'a partnership in the empire',[12] and so incorporated them, particularly the Rajputs, into 'the top officialdom as a matter of policy'.[13] Raja Todar Mal became Akbar's finance minister and, for some time, even his prime minister. Man Singh, Bhagwan Das, Rai Singh, and Todar Mal served at various times as governors of provinces. Out of his 137 *mansabdars* (a ranking service, based upon a command of a number of horsemen) of 1,000 and above, 14 were Hindus, while out of 415 *mansabdars* of 200 or above, 51 were Hindus.[14] Akbar, indeed, encouraged the formation of the Mughal army in India into a 'true example of the synthesis of Hindu and Muslim ways'. Though the cavalry, so important in the Turco-Afghan rule of India, remained an elite corps and a Muslim monopoly, an elephant branch, which was to be massed behind the infantry, was filled with Hindus.[15] The result was a 'politico-military service' that brought 'the motive of honour to the service of the crown and united the communities in a joint membership.'[16]

By abolishing *jizya* (poll tax) in 1564,[17] Akbar not only removed a 'major source' of Hindu 'economic discontent' with Muslim rule but also created 'a common citizenship' for all his subjects, Hindus and Muslims alike.[18] In addition, Akbar encouraged tax remission in times of famine or other natural calamities, expressing 'greater understanding and sympathy' with the predominantly Hindu peasant population.[19]

In order to establish 'a permanent harmony' between the Hindus and the Muslims,[20] Akbar even pushed the 'synthetic' effort on to the religious plane. He secured a 'document',[21] signed by the principle ulema and jurists of the day,[22] stating:

> … that the king of Islam, Amir of the Faithful, shadow of God in the world … whose kingdom God perpetuate, is a most just, a most wise, and a most God-fearing king. Should therefore, in future, a religious question come up, regarding which the opinions of

the Mujtahids are at variance and His Majesty, in his penetrating understanding and clear wisdom, be inclined to adopt, for the benefit of the nation and as a political expedient, any of the conflicting opinion which exist on that point, and issue a decree to that effect, we do hereby agree that such a decree shall be binding on us and on the whole nation ...This document has been written with honest intentions, for the glory of God, and the propagation of the Islam ...[23]

No sooner had he obtained this document, assuming a higher authority than the traditional religious scholars, that Akbar propounded his 'divine faith'—*Din-i-Elahi*. But apparently, it was not meant to propagate Islam.[24] He prohibited the slaughter of cows and the eating of their flesh,[25] initiated Hindu ceremonies in the court, and began to wear the Hindu mark on his forehead.[26] In addition, he started worshipping the sun. He kept a perpetual fire burning as he sat in the *Jharoka Darshan* (the Salutation Balcony) muttering spells which the Hindus strung together in Sanskrit for his benefit. He not only brought Zoroastrian priests to the court to explain the mysteries of their religion but also had the solar year reckoned in all official records (in place of the Arab/Muslim lunar year). He even initiated the festival of the solar New Year as an official reckoning.[27] This Parsi-Hinduism, in all probability, remained with Akbar till his death,[28] causing some alarm and indeed anguish among orthodox Muslims.[29] As Ishtiaq Hussain Qureshi expressed it:

Akbar had changed the nature of the polity profoundly. The Muslims were still the dominant group in the state, but it had ceased to be a Muslim Empire .... Tolerance and abdication of power are not the same; tolerance and conciliation of the Hindus had been the policy of the previous dynasties as well, but they had accorded greater importance to the interests of Islam than to the endeavour to identify the state with the entire population. Akbar had strengthened his dynasty but made it subservient to interests other than those of Islam to a remarkable degree, so that it took three generations to restore the laws of Islam to their previous position.[30]

However, in the opinion of Sri Ram Sharma, a leading Hindu writer, the net result of the religious policy of the Mughals was:

.... fraternization of the learned in the two communities, as they were drawn together, their angularities were rubbed off, their hatred of each other decreased. The Hindus came to consider the Muslims less of a defiling influence, when they met them on terms of equality in the private audience chamber, on the battlefield, and in the administrative secretariat. The Muslims ceased to think of the Hindus as an offence against their religion when they stood shoulder to shoulder with them in the greater enterprise of governing India.[31]

Akbar not only encouraged religious 'toleration' in official circles but also promoted a 'tolerant attitude' at the public level.[32] It was only because of Akbar's keen reception of the influence of the Bhakti movement[33] that Hindu artisans, traders, weavers, cultivators, and shopkeepers could pursue their professions without having to suffer any loss at the hands of Muslim officers of the State.[34] Akbar, in fact, created a climate of opinion in which the Bhakti movement could even succeed in winning the allegiance of some of the Muslim people. In the 1580s, Akbar ordered the Sanskrit Mahabharata translated into Persian 'Razmuamah (Book of War)' which 'would prove a seminal work in imperial circles for decades ... even incorporated into the education of royal princes.'[35]

But, apparently, all of this was in vain. This 'path of sincere syncretism' did not work. 'The way for Hindu-Muslim harmony,' S. M. Ikram suggested, 'was not through integration but through peaceful coexistence ... [recognising] the separateness of the two cultures', as Mujaddid Alif Thani 'advocated'.[36] In fact, in Ikram's view, Akbar's 'efforts at religious syncretism were doomed to failure' for the roots of his failure,

went even deeper—to the fundamental differences between Islam and Hinduism and the basic reluctance of the two communities to merge. By now Hindus and Muslims had co-existed for centuries— occasionally in conflict, generally in peace—but they had never coalesced. The over-ambitious attempt at merger went against the genius of the two people, and could find acceptance only in the circle of court sycophants. It failed, as it was bound to, but the aggressive attitude of the Hindu revivalists, and the offence which some of Akbar's ill-advised measures gave to the Muslims, compounded the failure.[37]

However, Akbar's policy of 'religious toleration' was followed by his successors—Jahangir, Shah Jahan, and Aurangzeb. Jahangir did not differentiate between Muslims and non-Muslims in public employment. Under Shah Jahan, a Hindu was considered 'the mightiest subject and the highest public servant'. The imperial finance minister and several provincial ministers of finance, besides several military commanders of great fame, continued in the Mughal service. Maharaja Jaswant Singh rose to the rank of a *mansabdar* of 6,000. Aurangzeb, like Akbar, continued with the policy of incorporating Hindus into his administration. During his reign, no less than 148 *mansabdars* above the rank of 1,000 were Hindus. Among them were the only three *mansabdars* of 7,000— Raja Jai Singh, Maharaja Jaswant Singh, and Raja Sahu, Shivaji's grandson.[38] Aurangzeb insisted that 'public services must accrue only on the basis of ability and merit'.[39] In fact, as one particular estimate showed:

> ... Aurangzeb's ascension [to the throne] initially changed little about the Hindu share in Mughal administration. Under Akbar, for example, Hindus were 22.5 per cent of all Mughal nobles. That percentage hardly budged in either direction under Shah Jahan, and, in the first twenty-one years of Aurangzeb's reign (1658–79), it stayed level at 21.6 per cent. But between 1679 and 1707, Aurangzeb increased Hindu population at the elite levels of the Mughal state by nearly 50 per cent. Hindus rose to 31.6 per cent of the Mughal nobility. This dramatic rise featured a substantial influx of Marathas as a strategic aspect of expanding Mughal sovereignty across the Deccan.[40]

Although Aurangzeb revived the collection of *jizya* in 1679, it was 'not necessarily the outcome of any feeling of dislike that Aurangzeb entertained towards the Hindus or their faith'. His own religious disposition made it necessary for him to order the levy of *jizya* on non-Muslims as a substitute for military service which was obligatory on all Muslims.[41] J. N. Sarkar was not right in suggesting that 'the "true objective" of Aurangzeb was to establish such an Islamic state in India', for such views 'have been questioned, and are no longer subscribed to in scholarly circles.'[42] Aurangzeb's religious policy 'went through a number of phases' and indeed became 'more pragmatic' during the later part of his reign after he was in the Deccan region (1689).[43] Thus Aurangzeb exempted minors, women, slaves, the blind, the mentally deficient, the unemployed, the handicapped, and the impoverished from the payment of *jizya*. Of course, Hindus who were willing to serve the state were exempt from its payment.[44]

Interestingly, Aurangzeb 'suspended *jizya* in the Deccan in 1704 "for the duration of the war" in view of the distress caused by famine and the Maratha war.'[45] Indeed, as Satish Chandra noted, 'Sufficient importance has not been given by historians to this suspension of the *Jizyah* in the Deccan.'[46] In his opinion, this 'suspension of *Jizyah* was tantamount to its abandonment and a virtual admission on Aurangzeb's part of the failure of the religious policy proclaimed by him in such fanfare in 1679.'[47] But then, the question arises: apart from his religious fervour, were there any worldly considerations in imposing *jizya* after it had been abolished a century ago, since the days of Akbar? A number of explanations have been offered, the most important being the following three.

First, this was a tax, as Khaliq Ahmad Nizami observed, prevalent 'long before the advent of the Prophet of Islam [PBUH] .... Nausherwan had formulated rules about it ... in lieu of exemption from military service. When the Prophet of Islam [PBUH] imposed this tax, after giving it the Arabic form of *jiziyah*, he followed a tradition long before him.[48] In fact, Nizami maintained, 'such taxes were not unknown to other countries in the middle ages. The nature of *Turushkidanda* in India, *Host Tax* in France, *Common Penny* in Germany, and *Scutage* in England, despite all the differences, was almost identical.'[49] Secondly, this re-imposition of *jizya* helped address 'the acute unemployment among the theological classes', especially the *qazis*.[50] It was 'an additional avenue for employment' for them.[51] Thirdly, and most importantly, it was reflective of Aurangzeb's own view of kingship, of 'combining religion and worldly affairs' for 'restoring peace and the rule of Islam in the realm so as to be able to answer on the Day of Reckoning.'[52]

One thing should be clear here. The imposition of *jizya* had nothing to do with Hindu conversions in spite of the fact that 'conversion meant freedom from the tax'. This freedom 'could also be gained by joining government service of any kind because *jizya* was not levied on government servants.'[53] Indeed, as Satish Chandra explained it at some length:

> If Aurangzeb had been keen to effect the forcible conversion of the Hindus, as [J. N.] Sarkar believed, he might have attempted it in the Deccan. But there is no evidence of any such attempt on his part. Conversions in West Punjab, Kashmir and East Bengal had been effected much earlier, and are in no way related to Aurangzeb or his religious policies. Occasional cases of conversion during Aurangzeb's reign did take place, some of them being highlighted by contemporary historians. What is noteworthy, however, is that in the bulk of the recorded cases, the converts were either small zamindars or petty state employees or their wards. Such converts either expected confirmation or grant of zamindari or preferential treatment after their conversion, competing with the Muslims for official posts which were in short supply.[54]

Thus, it can be safely argued that when Aurangzeb 'imposed *jizyah* after a lapse of 115 years, no sudden spurt in the number of conversions is recorded.'[55] While assessment of the revenues collected and its importance varied among the historians, with Ishtiaq Qureshi claiming that 'at no time did *jizyah* form an important source of revenue'[56] to Ishwari Prasad insisting that the 'revenue yielded was considerable and in Gujarat alone it amounted to five lakhs of rupees a year',[57] the fact was that because of *jizya* and related measures, 'it does not appear that a single Hindu suffered death, imprisonment, or loss of property for his religion, or indeed, that any individual was ever questioned for his open exercise of the worship of his fathers.'[58]

Aurangzeb granted land and money to Hindu temples and Hindu priests.[59] Much to the chagrin of his critics, there were 'numerous gaping holes in the proposition that Aurangzeb razed temples because he hated Hindus.'[60] In fact, there was much evidence to the effect that he 'counted thousands of Hindu temples within his domain and yet destroyed, at most, a few dozen.'[61] The large number of documents found all over India vouchsafe for Aurangzeb's religious tolerance.[62] Aurangzeb neither interfered with the religious worship of his Hindu subjects nor forbade the Hindu priests from teaching the Hindus.[63] The trouble, as Audrey Truschke, in her recent study, observed, was that:

> Many modern assessments of Aurangzeb's reign have been marred by unhelpful value judgments that frame Aurangzeb as a religious conservative at best and a bigoted fanatic at worst. These analyses are generally based on some truth in that, so far as we can tell, Aurangzeb personally subscribed to a more conservative interpretation of Islam than his ancestors. For example, he prayed with great regularity and abstained from wine. However, until recently, few scholars have investigated why Aurangzeb's religious inclinations informed Mughal policy. Even today it is alarmingly common to see entirely unsubstantiated comments about Aurangzeb's purported religious influence and his alleged penchant for destroying temples, manuscripts, anything else of cultural value.[64]

Truschke, in fact, claimed that all 'Mughals cultivated a thoroughly multicultural and multilingual image' that, for instance, 'involved repeated attention to Sanskrit texts, intellectuals, and knowledge systems ....'[65] No wonder then that in the end, one of the leading figures of the Indian National Congress and eventually President of India, Rajendra Prasad (1950–62), did not hesitate to admit that:

> The attitude of the Muslim conquerors had, on the whole, been one of toleration, and in spite of the fanatical zeal manifested by some of them at times, it may be safely asserted that there had been a continuous attempt from the earliest days to deal with the Hindus fairly.[66]

There were certainly difficulties along the way. However, as Tara Chand, in his classic study of society and state under the Mughals, perceptively noted:

> [These] difficulties arose out of the practical exigencies of government over a vast population different in religion, customs, language and culture .... Some levied the Jaziya, others refrained from doing so; some differentiated between Hindus and Muslims, others did not.[67]

In the end, the Mughal rule was political, first and foremost, not religious.

In encouraging the spirit of Hindu–Muslim understanding and harmony, the Muslim rulers were not alone. An equally keen effort was made by some of the most prominent Sufis of the time who tried to build 'ideological bridges' between the two communities.[68] The contribution of Sufis such as Nizamuddin Auliya (1238–1328) is a case in point who, with his piety and exemplary conduct, inspired following not only from Muslims but also from the Hindus. The leaders of the Bhakti movement, Kabir (1440–1518) and Guru Nanak (1469–1538) in particular, were inspired by his preaching and practices.[69] Acknowledging this influence on the Bhakti message, Rabindranath Tagore, thus, noted: 'We should have no hesitation in admitting freely that this message was inspired by contact with Islam.'[70]

However, this powerful religious impulse, which drew its inspiration from Islamic sources, did not last long. As 'the line of these enlightened, large-hearted, generous humanists began to shrivel',[71] the Hindus reacted sharply. The followers of Guru Nanak indeed went on to create a new religion—the Sikh religion—under their sixth Guru, Govind. Kabir's verses became part of the Sikh scripture.[72] The Bhakti movement developed into some sort of 'neo-Hinduism'.[73] The 'bridges' devised or sought to be built to unite the Muslims and Hindus collapsed under the sheer weight of 'mutual fear and antipathy', leading to further estrangement.[74] The efforts of Akbar and his successors and all the contributions of Nizamuddin Auliya and his followers proved to be futile. Hindu resilience and separatism refused to yield to Muslim authority and rule. Hindus and Muslims remained separate entities even within the body politic of one set of powerful rulers, the Mughals.

Major trouble started in the later part of Aurangzeb's reign,[75] though it developed into a full-blown crisis only after his death in 1707. The immediate cause of the crisis[76] were Aurangzeb's military campaigns against the Marathas and other southern rulers. Aurangzeb's efforts to extend Mughal authority beyond the northern plains not only broke the so-called 'Indian synthesis' that emerged under Akbar[77] but also ensured that 'besides the Marathas, organized in a loose confederacy of chiefs', there were quite a few who opposed Muslim rule.[78] Shivaji (1627–80), the Maratha rebel,[79] raised the slogan of Hindu rule, *Hindu Pad Padshahi* (Hindu Empire), and fought numerous guerrilla battles against Aurangzeb. Although he himself could not succeed against Aurangzeb, he laid the foundation of a movement towards the political regeneration of the Hindus. Mahadev Govind Ranade, in his study of the Marathas, thus wrote:

> … the rise of the Maratha power was due to the first beginnings of what one may well call the process of nation-making. It was not the outcome of the successful enterprise of any individual adventurer. It was the upheaval of the whole population, strongly bound together by the common affinities of language, race, religion and literature, and seeking further solidarity by a common independent political existence …. It was a national movement or upheaval in which all classes cooperated.[80]

The Maratha rising was not isolated. In northern India, Jats, Rajputs, and Sikhs, taking advantage of the Mughal empire's weak, dwindling position, were also in revolt. The Jats went so far in their anger against the Muslims and Muslim rule that they desecrated Akbar's tomb 'as a [sic] vengeance for his having married Hindu women.'[81] The Rajputs were the 'last defenders of Hindu power' in India.[82] They had remained fiercely independent till they eventually saw it to their advantage to join hands with the Mughal rulers, particularly Akbar, and help him complete the conquest of India.[83]

Now, as before, they began to assert their independence.[84] In Central India, the grip of the Mughals was broken by the Sikhs, who took control of Punjab. These forces, strong and ambitious, demanded Hindustan for the Hindus. It was, according to Stanley Lane-Poole, 'a religious war, centered round the phantom of the Mughal empire.'[85]

This was not surprising. India was held by the Muslims mainly by the strength of their arms at the centre. The weak centre revived the age-old 'persistent principle of regional autonomy'[86] once again. The 'communal units' became isolated, indeed divisive. Political unity, 'centralized, imposed, or constructed' from outside, by some external force or authority, as witnessed in the earlier cases of Rome or Persia, was not feasible in India. The 'magnitude' and the 'peculiarity' of the Indian situation, wrote Mackenzie Brown, a keen writer on India, was such that,

> the easy method of a centralized empire could not truly succeed in India … yet … seemed the only device possible and was attempted again and again with a partial success that seemed for the time and a long time to justify it, but always with an eventual failure.[87]

Besides 'the practical exigencies'[88] of government over a vast population and a large area, a major cause of the failure was the absence of cultural unity in India.[89] Indeed the 'inherent weakness' of Muslim rule[90] in India was that the Hindus regarded the Muslims as 'Outsiders',[91] quite 'different in religion, customs, language and culture'.[92] The Muslim rulers, thus, could do no more than try and win the political support of 'the higher castes', brought out in the organisation of the *mansabdari* system, and that too, at times, 'forcibly'.[93] The Hindu masses, by and large, remained indifferent and distant.

But then it could not be helped either. Hinduism, as Wilfred Cantwell Smith stated, could never 'outgrow its tribalism', could never aspire or claim to be 'anything higher than the religion of a group', or rather 'a series of sub-groups' embodied in the 'caste system'.[94] To the Hindu, a Muslim was 'an outcast out-caste, an Untouchable with whom dealings must not be so intimate as to transgress formal rules'. This exclusion was 'religious', but with Hinduism, religion means 'social' in a highly evolved traditional way. The result was that Hindu attitude presented India with 'a communal situation' throughout the centuries, sometimes less, sometimes more, of a problem.[95] Indeed, according to Qureshi, Hindu communalism was 'never entirely dormant', though it made its 'peace' with the Muslim conquerors and a substantial number of Hindus were even 'reconciled' to Muslim rule but, deep down, 'hostility' always 'persisted among conscious sections'.[96] The efforts of Marathas, Jats, Rajputs, and Sikhs constituted in reality 'a continuation and externalisation' of Hindu communalism.[97]

There was no way the Muslims could contain or control Hindu communalism. This is how the Hindu social order was created and, indeed, operated. Hinduism, with its distinctive customs and practices, traditions and norms, and ways of life and social behaviour, revealed how rigid and, in some respects, hostile the communal sentiment could be. Hindu laws prohibited marriages and even socialising with the Muslims. The interaction between the two communities thus could not help but foster 'a greater degree of mutual withdrawal, antipathy, and orthodox insularity.'[98]

This naturally led to the rise of Muslim 'separatism' in the eighteenth century. Shah Waliullah (1703–62), a religious scholar of Delhi, who saw the sad plight of the Muslims in India, not only propounded a philosophy of the 'ideal state' which sought the establishment of 'an independent Muslim state', where 'true Islam, freed from semi-pagan practices could be practiced', but also invited Ahmed Shah Abdali (1722–73), the ruler of Afghanistan, to India to defend Islam 'in a situation where Muslims were losing the physical power to do so.'[99] Abdali came to India and defeated the Maratha-Jat forces at Panipat in 1761. But the Muslims had, by then, lost so much in strength and spirit that they could not hold India back. Their plight was indeed too severe to be arrested at this point in time.[100] The coming of the British on the scene further aggravated the elemental clash between the Muslims and the Hindus.

The advent of the British stirred the Hindus. They lost no time in demonstrating awareness of the need 'to protect and promote' their special interests, particularly 'religious' ones.[101] 'When the British took over the rulership of North India', thus wrote K. M. Panikkar, 'Hinduism for the first time in 700 years stood on a plane of equality with Islam'.[102] There developed 'a new self-conscious awareness' of differences and distinctions,[103] promoting 'religious revivalism' based on different 'sources of inspiration',[104] the Hindus falling back on the Vedas, Brahamas, and the Mahabharata and the Muslims on the Holy Quran, Hadith, and the early community of Islam.

Muslim revivalism sprang from the reforms movements of Sayyid Ahmad Barailvi (1786–1831) and of the Fara'izis[105] aimed at the transformation of the Muslim community from 'an aggregate of believers' into 'a political association with a will for joint action'.[106] Sayyid Ahmad strove to free Punjab from the stranglehold of the Sikhs in the hope that it would one day inspire Muslims to hold India for Islam of the early days.[107] He, however, did not succeed in his fight against them and died in the battle of Balakot in 1831.[108] The movement failed not only because it was confronted by powerful foes and difficult circumstances but also because the fighters, who were also reformers, in their zeal to create 'a facsimile' of the Muslim community in the areas they liberated, did not wait to postpone the establishment of their concept of the Islamic Sharia till the gains could be consolidated, leading to internal dissensions, divisions, and ultimate loss.[109]

The movement nevertheless did succeed in some important respects. It succeeded in keeping alive the prospects of 'political resistance' against the encroachment of the non-Muslim powers together with a conscious effort to 'reforms and rejuvenate' Muslim society in ridding the religion of its accretions and corruptions. It also succeeded in creating 'a passionate urge' for the establishment of *Dar-al-Islam* in the Indian subcontinent, encouraging the succeeding generations of Muslims to advance towards the idea of a separate homeland.[110]

Hindu revivalism, directed against the Muslims, emerged from the Hindu movements of reforms and re-interpretation of religion, symbolised, in particular, by the Arya Samaj, founded in 1875. The Arya Samaj attacked the Muslims with increasing ferocity, demanding that the Muslims should either leave India or convert to Aryanism.[111] Arya Samaj wanted a return to the Vedas, simple and pure. They held the Vedic period as the ideal and endeavoured to persuade its followers 'to re-establish and revive its pristine unity and the ancient civilisation'. Founded by Dayananda Saraswati (1824–83), this 'militant puritanical sect of Hinduism' continued with the leadership of Swami Shraddhanand, Lala Lajpat Rai, Lala Hans Raj, Pandit Lekh Ram, and Bal Gangadhar Tilak well into the twentieth country. Hindus, according to Duni Chand, were convinced that Arya Samaj was 'the deliverer of the Hindus'.[112]

The two revivalisms clashed with each other in their 'emotional responses' to the history of Muslim India.[113] The Muslims remembered that they once were the conquerors and ruling people of India and the Hindus were their subjects. The splendour of their rule seemed 'all the more brighter [sic]' in contrast with the long period of decline and decay that followed it.[114] The Hindus revered the memory of Shivaji and others who had fought against the Muslims.[115] Thus, the two revivalisms, as Beni Prasad put it, not only clashed against each other but also:

> stimulated each other, competed with each other and became more and more different in outlook …. Hindus and Muslims alike began to give up many practices which they had imbibed from one another and which had served to bridge the chasm between the two communities.[116]

The Hindus and Muslims, however, had to deal with a third party in India—the British. History possibly provided the two communities an opportunity to make amends. But the religio-cultural differences—together with communal instinct on the one hand, contending with an instinct for communal separateness on the other—that were nurtured by centuries of contact and conflict, drove deeper the wedge of differences dividing them in their response to the British challenge at the doorstep. Their different responses to the British, politically, socially, and economically, went on to radically affect the final outcome of events in India's modern history. While the majority of the Hindus, mainly due to the efforts

of Brahmo Samaj—founded in 1828 under the inspiration of a
Bengali reformer, Raja Ram Mohan Roy (1774–1833), who sought
to meet the challenge through the promotion of Western education
and social reforms—reconciled with the British presence without
any serious fear of losing their religious bearings,[117] the Muslims
proclaimed a sort of war against the British.[118] In their aversion to
the new situation and its demands, they fell back on old traditions,
set by Shah Waliullah and Sayyid Ahmad Barailvi, of resistance to
the concentration of power in non-Muslim hands,[119] resulting in
the Revolt of 1857.[120]

Although no definite assessment of the contribution of Muslims
in the Revolt has been made, the British took no time in regarding
the Muslims as the arch rebels. This was in spite of the fact that
both Hindus and Muslims were involved. The Rani of Jhansi and
Nana Fadnavis along with the Mujahids of Baraeli and Prince Birjis
Qadr of Oudh 'led the rebellion against the British in the name
of the Mughal emperor Bahadur Shah.'[121] To the British, it was 'a
Muslim intrigue and Muslim leadership' that converted a 'sepoy
mutiny' into a 'political conspiracy aimed at the extinction of the
British Raj'.[122] But then, there was no denying that,

> Even if the Muslims had been differently inclined and had found
> it opportune to seek conciliation with the British, they would not
> have found it easy. The very fact that they had been the rulers and
> still had a political consciousness would have militated against their
> assurances being taken at face value ....[123]

Thus, the Muslims were dispossessed of all positions of power and
authority that remained with them even during the final collapse
of the Mughal Empire. The doors of civil and military services
as well as professions were closed on them. In Bengal alone, for
instance, in 1871, of the 773 Indians holding responsible positions,
the Muslims, though almost equal to Hindus in the province in
numbers, occupied only 92 positions. The British indeed put a seal
on the decline of Muslims in all walks of life.[124]

This new and unprecedented situation reinforced the realities
of separatism in India. These realities were bound to develop into

Hindu–Muslim separatism and separate group life for the Muslims in the days ahead, when the British system of representative government, based on numbers and creating conditions in which 'religious grievances' could be satisfied politically, was to make the Muslims realise 'the full weight of the Hindu majority'.[125] They had become a 'minority' community for all times to come. Indeed, this predicament left them no choice but to think, act, and plan as a separate community. While some historians blamed the separate electorates granted to the Muslims in 1909 for separating 'the Moslems from the mainstream' of Indian nationalism 'as represented by the [Indian] National Congress', there was an argument to the effect that these 'separate electorates were the legal acknowledgment of the prior existence of a Moslem nationality.'[126] It was only a matter of time, and a couple of instrumental political choices on part of the Hindu and Muslim leaders, that the Hindus and Muslims would indeed come to grow and develop into two separate 'nations'.

Notes

1. Aziz Ahmad, *Studies in Islamic Culture in the Indian Environment* (Oxford: Clarendon Press, 1964), 73–6, 89–90. In this estimate, Ahmad is joined by a host of important writers. See, for instance, Stanley Wolpert, *India* (Englewood Cliffs, New Jersey: Prentice Hall, 1965), 56–60; Wilfred Cantwell Smith, *Islam in Modern History* (Princeton: Princeton University Press, 1957), 268; M. Mujeeb, *The Indian Muslims* (London: George Allen & Unwin, 1967), 396; B. R. Ambedkar, *Pakistan, or the Partition of India* (Bombay: Thacker & Co., 1945), 18, 48; Hugh Tinker, *India and Pakistan: A Political Analysis* (New York: Frederick A. Praeger, 1967), 13; D. Mackenzie Brown, *The White Umbrella: Indian Political Thought from Manu to Gandhi* (Berkeley: University of California Press, 1964), 133; Ishtiaq Husain Qureshi, *The Administration of the Sultanate of Delhi* (Karachi: Pakistan Historical Society, 1958), 186; and Bernard S. Cohn, *India: The Social Anthropology of a Civilization* (Englewood Cliffs, New Jersey: Prentice-Hall, 1971), 66.
2. Tara Chand, cited in Ahmad, *Studies in Islamic Culture*, 73.
3. Hugh Tinker, *South Asia: A Short History* (New York: Frederick A. Praeger, 1966), 92.
4. Tinker wrote that the second battle of Panipat was 'probably the most decisive encounter in Indian history. Akbar raised the Mughal position

from that of the most important of many Muslim States in India to that of the paramount power over all India'. Tinker, *South Asia*, 30.

5. While Wolpert claimed that the British were a 'paramount power' in the eighteenth century, many are convinced that it was only in the nineteenth century (in 1818, after the British had finally overcome the Maratha forces) that they managed to lay claim to a 'paramount' position in India, holding as its direct territory the Gangetic Valley up to Delhi, the Maratha homelands in the Deccan, the littoral of the Arabia Sea, and the coastal strips extending from Bengal to the south. See K. M. Panikkar, *Asia and Western Dominance* (New York: Collier, 1969), 81; and Wolpert, *India*, 17.

6. H. K. Sherwani, *Cultural Trends in Medieval India* (Bombay: Asia Publishing House, 1968), 4. 'Differently to the English,' wrote Sherwani, 'who never tried to make India their home, the Perso-Turks, the Mughals and others professing Islam, who became the founders of dynasties in different parts of India, lost sight of where they came from and made the country their own.' Ibid., 3–4.

7. Ishwari Prasad, *A Short History of Muslim Rule in India: From the Advent of Islam to the Death of Aurangzeb* (Allahabad: The Indian Press, 1956), 111–12.

8. See Fathullah Mujtabai, *Aspects of Hindu-Muslim Cultural Relations* (New Delhi: National Book Bureau, 1978), 139–40; Iqtidar Husain Siddiqui, *Some Aspects of Afghan Despotism in India* (Aligarh: Three Men Publication, 1969), 83; Muhammad Abdur Rahim, *History of the Afghans in India, A.D. 1545–1631, with especial reference to their relations with the Mughals* (Karachi: Pakistan Publishing House, 1961); and Tara Chand, *Society and State in the Mughal Period*, 60.

9. Qureshi, *The Administration of the Sultanate*, 186; Chand, *Society and State*, 99–107; Mujtabai, *Aspects of Hindu-Muslim Cultural Relations*, 135; and Rahim, *History of Afghans*, 50. Bahmani rule in the south was even more accommodative. See Mahomed Kasim Ferishta, *History of the Rise of the Muhammadan Power in India, till the year A.D. 1612*, trans. John Briggs (Calcutta: Editions Indian, 1966).

10. Prasad, *A Short History of Muslim Rule in India*, 168.

11. Percival Spear, *India, Pakistan and the West* (London: Oxford University Press, 1958), 66. Akbar and his Mughals, wrote Spear, 'had something of the same vivifying effect upon Muslim Indian Policy as William the Conqueror and his Normans had on Saxon England. There was a new vigour, a new unity, a new constructive purpose leading on to a synthesis'. Ibid., 66–7. On Akbar's synthetic efforts also see, Ramkrishna Mukherjee, *The Rise and Fall of the East India Company: A Sociological Appraisal* (Bombay: Poplar Prakashan, 1958), 198; Wolpert, *India*, 57–9; Sri Ram Sharma, *The Religious Policy of the Mughal Emperors*, (Bombay: Asia Publishing House, 1962), 15–19; Cohn, *India*, 73, and Tinker, *South Asia*, 66.

12. Spear, *India, Pakistan and the West*, 66.

13. Cohn, *India*, 73.
14. Sharma, *The Religious Policy*, 22.
15. Wolpert, *India*, 55.
16. Spear, *India, Pakistan and the West*, 66.
17. Abu'l-Fazl Allami, *The Akbar Nama*, trans. H. Beveridge (Lahore: Sang-e-Meel Publications, 1975), 31.
18. Sharma, *The Religious Policy*, 19.
19. Wolpert, *India*, 58–9.
20. Mukherjee, *The Rise and Fall of the East India Company*, 205.
21. Also referred to as the 'Infallibility Decree'. Sharma, however, took an exception to this terminology. He argued that the nature of the document was 'a little misunderstood in the heat of arguments raised over it. It gave Akbar no power until and unless the divines failed to agree. Even then he had the power to interpret the Muslim law and not to make it', (Sharma, *The Religious Policy*, 31–3). Malleson, however, suggested that, 'The signature of this document was a turning-point in the life and reign of Akbar. For the first time he was free. He could give currency and force to his ideas of toleration and of respect for conscience. He could now bring the Hindu, the Parsi, the Christian, into his councils...The document is, in fact, the Magna Charta of his reign.' G. B. Malleson, *Rulers of India: Akbar and the Rise of the Mughal Empire* (Lahore: Islamic Book Service, 1979), 158–9.
22. Abu'l-Fazl Allami, *The Ain-i-Akbari*, trans. H. Blochmann (Lahore: Sang-e-Meel Publications, 2003), 195.
23. Ibid., 196.
24. For different viewpoints on the subject see, in particular, Abu'l-Fazl, *The Ain-i-Akbari*, 203–16, 221; Abdul Qadir Badaoni, *Muntakhab-ut-Tawarikh*, Vol. II, trans. W. H. Lowe (Karachi: Karimsons, 1976), 339. Henry Miers Elliot and John Dowson, eds., *The History of India, as Told by its Own Historians*, Vol. V (Lahore: Islamic Book Service, 1976), 526–33; George Dunbar, *A History of India: From Earliest Times to 1939*, Vol. I (London: Nicholson & Watson, 1943), 208; Malleson, *Rulers of India*, 160, 168–9; Michael Prawdin, *The Builders of the Mogul Empire* (London: Allen & Unwin, 1963), 153; Ishtiaq Husain Qureshi, *The Muslim Community of the Indo-Pakistan Subcontinent (610–1947): A Brief Historical Analysis* (The Hague: Mouton & Co., 1962), 167–8; Sharma, *The Religious Policy*, 39–45; and Shaikh Muhammad Ikram, *Raud-i-Kausar* (Lahore: Institute of Islamic Culture, 1958), 130–2.
25. The Hindus devoutly worship cows, and some even esteem their dung. This remained the abiding source of Hindu–Muslim tension, indeed communal riots, throughout the history of Modern India, during the British period, and happens to be so even today, especially now under the Prime Minister of India, Narendra Modi, and his BJP government (since 2014). In fact, killing cows and the consumption of beef is banned in most states of India.

26. He even married a Hindu Rajput princess (Hira Kunwari) who gave birth to the next Mughal Emperor, Jahangir. There was lot of controversy about Jodha Bai as Akbar's wife. See Malleson, *Rulers of India*, 130, 184–5. In fact, he claimed that, being 'mother of the heir apparent, she held the first place in the Harem.' Ibid., 185. But there was no mention of Jodha Bai by name, in Akbar's biography, Akbarnama.

27. Khafi Khan, *Muntakhab al-Lubab*, in Elliot and Dowson, *The History of India*, Vol. VII, 241; Sharma, *The Religious Policy*, 41–2; and Abu'l-Fazl, *Ain-i-Akbari*, 221.

28. While Jahangir's memoirs indicated that Akbar 'repented' on his deathbed of his efforts to combine the opposing elements of Hinduism, Zoroastrianism and Islam, Blochmann strongly felt that 'Akbar, in all probability, continued worshipping the sun, and retained all other peculiarities of his monotheistic Parsi-Hinduism, dying as he had lived'. Blochmann, Abu'l-Fazl, *Ain-i-Akbari*, 221.

29. Wolpert, *India*, 59.

30. Qureshi, *The Muslim Community*, 167–8.

31. Sharma, *The Religious Policy*, 60–1.

32. Sharma in fact claimed that Akbar's 'toleration was more comprehensive than that of his contemporary, the English Queen, Elizabeth. Indeed it was not till the latter half of the nineteenth century that England was able to adopt religious toleration and freedom from civic disabilities to the extent to which Akbar had done in India in the sixteenth century'. Ibid., 49.

33. Akbar, besides the desire to create harmony among his Hindu and Muslim subjects, might also have been influenced by 'the trend of society to promote production and commerce'. Mukherjee, *The Rise and Fall of the East India Company*, 205.

34. Sharma, however, suggested that Akbar's policy, 'had not been willingly accepted by many of his officers and they had no enthusiasm for it'. Sharma, *The Religious Policy*, 152–3.

35. Audrey Truschke, *Culture of Encounters: Sanskrit at the Mughal Court* (New Delhi: Penguin Random House India, 2017), 101.

36. S. M. Ikram, *History of Muslim Civilization in India and Pakistan: A Political and Cultural History* (Lahore: Institute of Islamic Culture, 2013), 278.

37. Ibid., 356.

38. For a detailed account of Hindu–Muslim relations, particularly the role played by Hindus in public services under emperors Jahangir, Shah Jahan, and Aurangzeb see, Sharma, *The Religious Policy*, 71, 76, 85, 119, 124.

39. C. P. Roy, a noted literary figure of Bengal. Cited in Syed Tufail Ahmad Manglori, *Musalmanon Ka Roshan Mustaqbil* (Delhi: Ilmi Delhi 1945), 27–8.

40. Audrey Truschke, *Aurangzeb: The Man and the Myth* (Karachi: Oxford University Press, 2017), 57.

41. Sharma, *The Religious Policy*, 157–8.

42. Satish Chandra, 'Religious Policy of Aurangzeb during the Later Part of his Reign—Some Considerations', *Indian Historical Review*, Vol. XIII, nos. 1–2 (1987): 88–101.
43. Ibid., 100.
44. Zahiruddin Faruki, *Aurangzeb: His Life and Times* (Lahore: Al-Biruni, 1977, rep.), 155.
45. Chandra, 'Religious Policy of Aurangzeb', 95.
46. Ibid.
47. Ibid.
48. Khaliq Ahmad Nizami, *Some Aspects of Religion and Politics in India during the Thirteenth Century* (Bombay: Asia Publishing House, 1961), 310.
49. Ibid.
50. Chandra, 'Religious Policy of Aurangzeb', 94.
51. Ibid.
52. Ibid., 96.
53. Qureshi, *The Muslim Community*, 76.
54. Chandra, 'Religious Policy of Aurangzeb', 93.
55. Qureshi, *The Muslim Community*, 77.
56. Ibid.
57. Prasad, *A Short History of Muslim Rule in India*, 486.
58. Mountstuart Elphinstone, *Aurangzeb*, ed. Sri Ram Sharma, with introduction by Robert Nichols (Karachi: Oxford University Press, 2008), 131.
59. Manglori, *Musalmanon Ka Roshan Mustaqbil*, 24.
60. Truschke, *Aurangzeb*, 77–8.
61. Ibid., 78.
62. Ishtiaq Husain Qureshi, *The Administration of the Mughal Empire* (Karachi: Karachi University, 1966), 215.
63. Sharma, *The Religious Policy*, 176
64. Truschke, *Culture of Encounters*, 235.
65. Ibid., 5. This, of course, may not necessarily have been 'for the benefit of their population but rather mainly for themselves'. Ibid.
66. Rajendra Prasad, *India Divided* (Bombay: Hind Kitab, 1947), 85.
67. Chand, *Society and State*, 63.
68. Wolpert, *India*, 51.
69. See, in particular, Wolpert, Ibid., 50; Chand, *Society and State*, 96; and Tinker, *South Asia*, 90.
70. Rabindranath Tagore, *A Tagore Reader*, ed. Amiya Chakravarty (Boston: Macmillan Co., 1966), 271.
71. Chand, *Society and State*, 112.
72. Kabir's followers, *Kabirpanthis*, still sing his songs and follow the religion of Bhakti. But they are now merely sub-castes of the different castes to which their members originally belonged. Tinker, *South Asia*, 89; Ikram,

Raud-i-Kausar, 465; and Tara Chand, *Influence of Islam on Indian Culture* (Lahore: Book Traders, 1979), 145–65, 166–77.

73. Pakistan History Board, *A Short History of Hind-Pakistan* (Karachi: Pakistan Historical Society, 1955), 184.

74. Sharif al Mujahid, *Quaid-i-Azam Jinnah: Studies in Interpretation* (Karachi: Quaid-i-Azam Academy, 1981), 321. Also see, William Theodore de Bary, ed., *Sources of Indian Tradition* (New York: Columbia University Press, 1958), 370.

75. Wolpert was of the opinion that 'the primary cause' was 'economic'. 'The inevitable increase in revenue demands,' he thought, 'drove more and more zamindars as well as peasants to risk death from rebellion rather than accept inevitable starvation.' Stanley Wolpert, *A New History of India* (New York: Oxford University Press, 1977), 159.

76. For different opinions on the subject, see Tinker, *South Asia*, 35; Sharma, *The Religious Policy*, 175–7; Elphinstone, *Aurangzeb*, 160–2; Spear, *India, Pakistan and the West*, 20; Qureshi, *The Muslim Community*, 168; and Ishtiaq Husain Qureshi, 'Chapter 11', in *Akbar: The Architect of the Mughal Empire* (Karachi: Ma'aref, 1978).

77. Cohn, *India*, 58.

78. Tinker, *South Asia*, 31.

79. Shivaji, according to Khafi Khan, 'assembled a large force of Maratha robbers and plunderers and set about reducing fortresses.' Elliot and Dowson, 'From 1662 to 1681', in *The History of India*, Vol. VII, 257. Also see, Elphinstone, *Aurangzeb*, 54–87.

80. Mahadeo Govin Ranade, *Rise of the Maratha Power*, cited in *Modern India: An Interpretative Anthology*, ed. Thomas R. Metcalf (London: Macmillan, 1971), 51. Also see Mountstuart Elphinstone, *The History of India* (London: John Murray, 1889), 658.

81. Ahmad, *Studies in Islamic Culture*, 95.

82. Tinker, *South Asia*, 19.

83. Brown, *The White Umbrella*, 136.

84. Tinker, *South Asia*, 31–2.

85. Stanley Lane-Poole, *Mediaeval India under Mohammedan Rule, 712–1764* (Lahore: Sang-e-Meel Publications, 1979), 419.

86. Barring short phases under the Maurya and Guptas, India, was never united. Even this rare unity was short-lived and very fragile. As soon as the imperial hold weakened, India was torn into pieces. The only unity India had was in term of 'geography'. But there too, in the words of Spear, 'geography has promoted partial and hindered complete unity. It has encouraged aspirations to empire and hindered its maintenance.' Spear, *India, Pakistan and the West*, 19.

87. Brown, *The White Umbrella*, 128–33.

88. Chand, *Society and State*, 63.

89. Brown, *The White Umbrella*, 132.

90. Ahmad, *Studies in Islamic Culture*, 94.

91. Smith, *Islam in Modern History*, 159.
92. Chand, *Society and State*, 63.
93. Ibid., 68.
94. On the exclusive nature of social relations in the caste system, also see, Tinker, *South Asia*, 13; George Rosen, *Democracy and Economic Change in India* (Berkeley: University of California Press, 1966), 79; Smith, *Islam in Modern History*, 268; M. N. Srinivas, *Social Change in Modern India* (Berkeley: University of California Press, 1973), 1–45; W. H. Morris-Jones, *The Government and Politics of India* (London: Hutchinson & Co., 1971) 64–5; and W. Norman Brown, *The United States and India, Pakistan, Bangladesh* (Cambridge, Massachusetts: Harvard University Press 1972), 32–5.
95. Smith, *Islam in Modern History*, 159.
96. Ishtiaq Husain Qureshi, 'Hindu Communal Movements', in *A History of the Freedom Movement*, Vol. III, Part I, Karachi, Pakistan Historical Society, (1961), 240.
97. Ahmad, *Studies in Islamic Culture*, 95.
98. Wolpert, *India*, 56.
99. Ahmad, *Studies in Islamic Culture*, 213–14; Peter Hardy, *The Muslims of British India* (Cambridge: Cambridge University Press, 1972), 30. The full text of Shah Waliullah's letter to Ahmad Shah Abdali is available in Khaliq Ahmad Nizami's *Shah Waliullah Kay Siyasi Maktubat* (Aligarh: Aligarh Muslim University Press, 1950), 97–114.
100. Qureshi, *The Muslim Community*, 198.
101. Francis Robinson, *Separatism Among Indian Muslims, 1860–1923* (Cambridge: Cambridge University Press, 1974), 77.
102. Panikkar, *Asia and Western Dominance*, 240.
103. Ainslie T. Embree, *India's Search for National Identity* (New York: Alfred A. Knopf, 1972), 18.
104. Beni Prasad, *India's Hindu-Muslim Questions* (London: George Allen & Unwin, 1946) 31.
105. The religious and social movement of Dudu Miyan and Titu Mir in Bengal. In the conditions of Bengal under the Permanent Settlement of Lord Cornwallis, where majority of *zamindars* (landowners) were Hindus, the conflict between the exploited Muslim tenants and exploiting Hindu landlords was inevitable. What triggered the movement under Dudu Miyan was that the Hindu landlords levied illegal cess on Muslim peasants and then spent this levy on Hindu religious rites. The movement declined by the late nineteenth century. See Hardy, *The Muslims of British India*, 56–7; and Ahmad, *Studies in Islamic Culture*, 216.
106. Hardy, *The Muslims of British India*, 58. Generally, though erroneously, Sayyid Ahmad of Bareilly and his followers have been dubbed as 'Wahabis'. The political objectives of Sayyid Ahmad of Bareilly and his followers were derived from the teachings of Shah Waliullah and not from the doctrines of Abdul Wahab of Nejd (d. 1787). For some of the discussion

on the controversy, see, in particular, Qeyamuddin Ahmad, *The Wahabi Movement in India* (Calcutta: Firma K. L. Mukhopadhyay, 1966); K. M. Ashraf, 'Muslim Revivalists and the Revolt of 1857', in *Rebellion 1857*, ed. P. C. Joshi (Delhi: People's Publishing House 1957); and W.W. Hunter, *The Indian Musalmans* (Calcutta: Comrade Publishers, 1945).

107. Hardy, *The Muslims of British India*, 58.

108. A certain element of mystery surrounded the death of Sayyid Ahmad of Bareilly and in fact for nearly half a century after the battle of Balakot, the belief was common among many of his followers that he had not been killed but had simply disappeared and was still alive. For a scholarly analysis of this uncertainty about the Sayyid's death, see Mahmud Husain, 'The Mystery of Sayyid Ahmad Shahid's Death', *Journal of the Pakistan Historical Society*, Vol. III (July 1955): 167–71.

109. Qureshi, *The Muslims Community*, 231.

110. See Ziya ul-Hasan Farooqi, *The Deoband School and the Demand for Pakistan* (Bombay: Asia Publishing House, 1963), 9; Qureshi, *The Muslim Community*, 231; Mujahid, *Studies in Interpretation*, 336; Ahmad, *Studies in Islamic Culture*, 217; and Smith, *Islam in Modern History*, 210–11. A noted historian, Hameed-ud-Din, in an article referred to the battle of Balakot as 'the first battle for Pakistan'. Cited in S. M. Burke, *Mainsprings of Indian and Pakistani Foreign Policies* (Minneapolis: University of Minnesota Press, 1974), 257.

111. The Hindu leadership was still obsessed with Aryanism as late as 1936. In his presidential address to the eighteenth session of the All India Hindu Mahasabha, Shri Sankaracharya stated: 'it must be remembered that minorities can't claim to have any superior political rights and powers which prove detrimental to the interests of Hindus and subversion of the Aryan culture.' N. N. Mitra, ed., *The Indian Annual Register, 1936*, Vol. II (Calcutta: Annual Register Office, 1936), 255–6.

112. See Duni Chand, *The Ulster of India* (Lahore: Navajivan Press, 1936), 18–31; Panikkar, *Asia and Western Dominance*, 295; and Nancy Wilson Ross, *Three Ways of Asian Wisdom: Hinduism, Buddhism, Zen, and their Significance for the West* (New York: Simon & Schuster, 1966), 67–73; and Spear, *India, Pakistan and the West*, 118–19.

113. Ahmad, *Studies in Islamic Culture*, 264.

114. Reginald Coupland, *The Indian Problem, 1833–1935* (London: Oxford University Press, 1968), 31–2.

115. Ambedkar, *Pakistan or the Partition of India*, 18.

116. Prasad, *India's Hindu-Muslim Questions*, 31.

117. Spear, *India, Pakistan and the West*, 120–1; and Panikkar, *Asia and Western Dominance*, 241–3.

118. Shah Waliullah's son and successor, Shah Abdul Aziz, declared that India had become '*dar-al-harb* because the infields' had taken control of it. Shah Abdul Aziz, *Malfuzaat-e-Shah Abdul Aziz* (Karachi: Pakistan Educational Publishers, 1960), 25. Also see Hunter, *The Indian Musalmans*, 105.

119. Ahmad, *Studies in Islamic Culture*, 208.

120. According to Sir Reginald Coupland, a noted authority on British Indian history, 'It was a mutiny but more than a mutiny … [it] was the natural reaction of one civilization under pressure from another of an old order threatened by a new of Asia invaded by Europe.' But, he maintained, 'if the outbreak was more than a mutiny, it was not a national rebellion against foreign rule. Some sepoy regiments fought bravely besides the British. The Sikhs made no attempt to recover their independence … Southern India, on the whole stayed quiet. None of the rulers of the leading States, who held the strategic keys of Central India, joined in the revolt.' *India: A Re-Statement* (London: Oxford University Press, 1945), 38–9.

121. Ikram, *History of Muslim Civilization*, 683.

122. Thomas Metcalf, *The Aftermath of Revolt* (Princeton: Princeton University Press, 1964), 298. Also see Sir Syed Ahmad Khan, *The Causes of the Indian Revolt*, with an Introduction by Francis Robinson (Karachi: Oxford University Press, 2000); and Mohammed Ahsen Chaudhry, 'The Impact of the Revolt of 1857 on British Colonial Policy', *Journal of the Pakistan Historical Society* (July 1963): 208–19. 'Had the spirit of Indian Nationalism inspired the struggle,' wrote Wolpert, 'all those revolting would have joined force. But Marathas and Mughals, Hindus and Muslims were still jealous and suspicious of one another, despite many examples of Hindu-Muslim unity in this year of travail.' Wolpert, *India*, 98. In the words of Metcalf, the Revolt of 1857 was 'something more than a sepoy mutiny, but something less than a national revolt', Metcalf, *The Aftermath of Revolt*, 60.

123. Qureshi, *The Muslim Community*, 213.

124. Khalid bin Sayeed, *Pakistan: The Formative Phase, 1857–1948*, 2nd ed. (Karachi: Oxford University Press, 1994), 13–14: Metcalf, *The Aftermath of Revolt*, 298; Mujeeb, *The Indian Muslims*, 432; Hunter, *The Indian Musalmans*, 161; and Ishtiaq Husain Qureshi, *The Struggle for Pakistan* (Karachi: Karachi University, 1969), 18.

125. Robinson, *Separatism among Indian Muslims*, 85. Syed Ahmed Khan, leader of the Muslims in the latter half of the nineteenth century, thus described the majority–minority situation as 'a game of dice in which one man had four dice and the other only one.' It is certain, he said, that Hindus would obtain four times as many votes as Muslims because their population was four times as large. *Syed Ahmad Khan, The Present State of Indian Politics: Speeches and Letters*, ed. Farman Fatehpuri (Lahore: Sang-e-Meel Publications, 1982), 36.

126. Hafeez Malik, *Moslem Nationalism in India and Pakistan* (Washington DC: Public Affairs Press, 1963), 297.

2

Syed Ahmad Khan and the Foundation of the Muslim Separatist Political Movement in British India

Many writers have suggested that Hindu–Muslim separatism in British India and the 'two-nation theory' as such, is reflected in Syed Ahmad Khan's policies and pronouncements.[1] Some others claimed that Syed Ahmad Khan was not a 'separatist', much less a Muslim 'nationalist'. Admittedly, they say, he was disappointed with the Hindu leaders who sought to replace Urdu with Hindi; he was also unhappy with the Hindus advocating the Congress' demands but Syed Ahmad Khan never spoke in terms of Muslim nationalism.[2] There may be some truth in both these viewpoints but it would be worthwhile to remember that 'nationalism' as a consciously held political idea was a twentieth century phenomenon even in Europe from where it was transplanted into India.[3] The spirit of the late nineteenth century India was far from it. Of course, Syed Ahmad Khan talked of Indian Muslims as a 'qaum' (readily translated into 'nation' by indulgent translators and compilers) but it would not be correct to equate this expression with the concept of 'nation' or 'nationhood', not yet. Muslim nationhood had to wait till Quaid-i-Azam Mohammad Ali Jinnah came up with the 'two-nation theory' and the demand for a separate state in 1940, almost half a century later. Syed Ahmad Khan's usage of the term *qaum* is indicative more of 'group consciousness' than a case of Muslim nationhood. Muslims and Hindus lived side by side, equally subjected to the newly imposed British rule, devoid of any national feeling or national identity at that time. It was not that the Muslims were not a nation—the Hindus, too, presented no different a picture. Indeed, India, as a whole, lacked consciousness of national unity. In fact, as Anil Seal pointed out, 'there were not two nations, there was not one nation, there was no nation at all.'[4]

The purpose of this chapter is to argue that Syed Ahmad Khan was a 'Muslim separatist' who, in presenting Muslims as a separate political group in Indian politics, laid the foundation of a Muslim separatist political movement in India. His successors in Muslim politics, such as Aga Khan, Syed Ameer Ali, Maulana Mohamed Ali, Allama Muhammad Iqbal, and Jinnah, subsequently used this foundation to build the edifice of Muslim nationalism and eventually led the Muslims towards the goal of a separate sovereign state of Pakistan. Even prior to the foundation of this separatist political movement, in fact during Muslim rule in India, Muslims and Hindus had pursued their separate paths, following their separate values, norms, and traditions.[5] But what was implicit in Muslim separatism then became explicit and definite in Syed Ahmad Khan's efforts to mobilise Muslims to deal with the reality of British rule in India, with the Hindus becoming the 'majority' community and taking charge and the Muslims on the receiving end of the new dispensation. The Muslims indeed began to feel, more than ever, that they were separate from the Hindus, that their interests were separate from those of the Hindus, and that their interests could be secured and promoted only through a separate group life and activity.

In order to evaluate and assess Syed Ahmad Khan's role in bringing about this paradigm shift, his contribution to Muslim politics will be analysed here. Particular emphasis will be on his efforts to help the Muslims in meeting the challenges of British rule and the associated English/Western system of education, his consideration of the British system of representative government, his understanding of Hindu–Muslim relations, and most importantly, his position on the aims and objectives of the Indian National Congress, founded in 1885, and their impact on the Muslims as a newly formed 'minority' community in India.

Syed Ahmad Khan (1817–98) was born on 17 October 1817 to a traditional noble family of Delhi. His ancestors, who had been 'oppressed' during the Ummayad rule (because of being Fatimids), had fled from Arabia to Iran and had finally settled in Afghanistan (Herat) before moving to India in the reign of Emperor Shah Jahan (1627–58). They went on to secure important positions under the Mughals. However, Syed Ahmad Khan, after the death of his father, Mir Muttaqi, did not hesitate in joining the dominant East India Company. In 1857, he was serving as a 'sub-judge' in Bijnor (Meerut).[6]

Syed Ahmad Khan's move towards the English was understandable. The Mughal Empire had become 'nothing more than an apparition of its former self'.[7] In fact, Mughal sovereignty had been lost for more than a hundred years now. The administration of the empire, for all practical purposes, was in the hands of the East India Company. The last Mughal emperor, Bahadur Shah Zafar, was forced to live on a modest pension from the Company, biding his time. Soon, the final, dismal end of the Mughal rule in 1857–8 saw the British government assume direct control of India, replacing both the Mughals and the East India Company.

In the wake of the unsuccessful Revolt of 1857,[8] the Muslims were confronted with a new situation. They had lost their pre-eminent position in Indian body politic. The East India Company, which had displaced Muslim authority, had given way to the British government with full and paramount control of India. India now began to experience a strong British drive to change Indian social, economic, and political life and institutions, and to Westernise India.[9] The Muslims were not willing or able to adjust themselves to the new demands. The substitution of Persian with English and traditional education with Western education made them resentful, even hostile, to the new order.[10] They found it easier 'to look backward to their glorious past, and painful to consider the realities of the present and future.'[11] Hindus, on the other hand, under the influence of the early Brahmos,[12] rushed to government or missionary schools in large numbers and readily accepted Western education.[13] 'The truth is,' wrote W. W. Hunter in 1871, that:

our system of Public instructions, which had awakened the Hindus from the sleep of centuries, and quickened their inert masses with some of the noble impulses of a nation, is opposed to the traditions, unsuited to the requirements, and hateful to the religion of the Musalmans.[14]

The result, particularly in Bengal, as he reiterated in 1872, 'painted a grim picture of the pitiable plight of the Muslims' and indeed showed that 'there is no Government office in which a Muslim could hope for any post above the rank of porter, messenger, filler of inkpots and a mender of pens.'[15]

Syed Ahmad Khan clearly saw the danger to Muslims if they did not adjust and realign themselves to the realities of new life in India. He wanted to help. He was the man of the moment too: 'His aristocratic background, combined with his employment in a responsible office of the British government and his recently demonstrated loyalty, fitted [sic] him admirably for this role.'[16] He wanted the Muslims to find a *modus vivendi* with the British and to take advantage of Western education. Interestingly, at this point in time, he 'did not look to the arena of political activity as crucial for his community's future'.[17] In fact, as John Wilder aptly put it:

> He saw the decline of Indian Muslims as due to their own internal weaknesses, their backward-looking stagnation [sic], and not to any political reasons. He was convinced that the solution to Indian Islam's ailments lay in the areas of education and Westernisation. Instead of seeking to preserve the glorious past, and apply past remedies and philosophies to the radically changing present, Muslims should adjust to the present and adopt new remedies. Muslim youths should enter the new educational institutions which were rising on every side. They should learn English ....[18]

Syed Ahmad Khan was convinced that if the Muslims did not accept the new system of education introduced by the British, they would not only remain a backward community but would also suffer increasingly until no hope was left for their revival at all. Already, the community had 'found itself diminishing in influence. It was not securing its fair share in Government Offices;

it was being left behind in the race for wealth, it was having little influence on public opinion. In short, the community was a mass without weight'.[19] This distressful situation brought forth Syed Ahmad Khan as 'undoubtedly the most commanding Muslim figure during the period.'[20] As Abdul Hamid noted:

> It was he who awakened the communal consciousness of the Indian Muslims .... He was quick to perceive the British had come to stay in India and entreated his co-religionists to make the necessary adjustments to, and compromise with, the new order. He had to fight the religious conservatism and intellectual stagnation of Muslim society as well as the frigid hauteur of Britons towards Indians.[21]

In 1858, Syed Ahmad Khan wrote his famous pamphlet, *Risala Asbab-i-Baghawat-i-Hind*, 'privately printed' by him in 1859 'and sent to the Indian and Home governments' which, given the turbulent years of 1857–8, 'was an act of considerable risk and daring'.[22] It was translated into English much later (*The Causes of the Indian Revolt*),[23] spelling out in concrete terms for the English readers what he thought were the 'evils' of British policy in India which had been responsible for the Revolt of 1857, and indeed claimed that 'the revolt was an outcome of the frustrations and accumulated wrongs of decades'.[24] He identified a host of causes—political, social, cultural, economic, religious, and administrative. But the most important cause of them all, he pointed out, was the 'non-admission of natives' into the Imperial Legislative Council. The government, he argued,

> could never know the inadvisability of the laws and regulations which it passed. It could never hear as it ought to have heard the voice of the people on such a subject .... But the greatest mischief lay in that the people misunderstood the views and the intentions of Government. They misapprehended every act, and whatever law was passed was misconstrued by men who had no share in the framing of it, and hence no means of judging its spirit. At length the Hindustanees fell into the habit of thinking that all the laws were passed with a view to degrade and ruin them, and to deprive

them and their fellows of their religion. Such acts as were repugnant to native customs and character, whether in themselves good or bad, increased their suspicion .... There was no man to reason with them, no one to point out to them the absurdities of such ideas .... Because there was not one of their own number among the members of the Legislative Council. Had there been, these evils that have happened to us, would have been averted.[25]

The admission of Indians into the Legislative Council, Syed Ahmad Khan stressed, was all the more important because the British were in India as 'foreigners' and 'differed from the natives in religion, in customs, in habits of life and of thought'. As such, they not only failed to grasp the realities of the Indian situation but had unwittingly committed themselves to policies which were harmful to the people. 'The more one thinks the matter over,' he felt, 'the more one is convinced that there we have the one great cause which was the origin of all smaller causes of dissatisfaction.'[26] However, he was candid enough to admit that:

I do not wish to enter into the question as to how the ignorant and uneducated natives of Hindustan could be allowed a share in the deliberations of the Legislative Council; [sic] or as to how they should be selected to form an assembly like the English Parliament.[27]

Indeed, the Revolt revealed a complete lack of contact and understanding between the Indians and the British government in general, and Muslims and the British in particular. Here, it is worth noting that, interestingly, Syed Ahmad Khan also suggested in his pamphlet that the Muslim 'regiments' may not have joined the Hindus in 1857 'if their concerns had been isolated from their Hindu counterparts then they would have not followed suit', thus creating a sense of 'exceptionalism' for the Muslims.[28] Hafeez Malik highlighted this aspect in the following manner:

Although the Hindus and Moslems cooperated with each other, they fought on different fronts and independently of each other. Their aims too were different. The wars of 1857 were undoubtedly

fought for political liberation, but there were no common
nationalistic goals to forge a joint Hindu-Moslem nation in India.
Two distinct nationalisms fighting for their separate aims, were in
simultaneous conflict with the British.[29]

Syed Ahmad Khan, thus, promptly moved to bridge the gulf
between the Muslims and the British. He addressed himself wholeheartedly to this task in his *Loyal Mahomedans of India* (1860), a
series of pamphlets (only three appeared) narrating the eminent
services rendered by the Muslims during 1857–8, and even claimed
that Muslims were 'loyal' subjects of British India. He did not deny
that some Muslims had revolted. But, then, he observed, 'good and
bad are to be found in every class and creed ....' He, eventually,
went on to maintain that when all the 'truth' about the events of
1857–8 was revealed, it will show that,

> ... if in Hindustan there was one class of people above another who,
> from the principles of their religion, from habits and associations,
> and from kindred disposition, were fast bound with Christians, in
> their dreaded hour of trial and danger, in the bounds of amity and
> friendship[,] those people were the Mohammedans ....[30]

Syed Ahmad Khan pointed out that both Christians and Muslims
were the followers of revealed religions and, therefore, had much
in common. He challenged Hunter's thesis that Muslims were
bound by their religion to rebel against their Christian rulers.[31] In
a review of Hunter's book, originally published in the *Pioneer* (a
newspaper published from Allahabad), he charged that Hunter was
not only ignorant about the Indian Muslims but also had no idea of
Islam as such, representing 'Wahabiism and rebellion against the
British Government as synonymous'. 'His work', he insisted, 'was
politically a grave, and in a minor degree an historical mistake'.[32]
While he told 'the West that its version of Islam was a gross
distortion', he tried hard to impress upon the Muslims the fact
'that there was a strong affinity between Islam and Christianity',
and thus there was a need to establish 'a *rapprochement* between the
Christian government and its Muslim subjects.'[33] He explained to
them that 'as long as they could freely practice their religion under

the British, they had no reason to rebel' against the rulers.[34] In fact, in a letter to *Pioneer* on 14 April 1871, he declared: 'Mohammedans, be they dwellers in *Darul-Harb* or *Darul-Islam*, are prohibited from rebellion against a government which interferes in no way with the free worship of their religion.'[35] Earlier, in 1869–70, he had visited England to meet with his son, Syed Mahmud, later a judge of the High Court, who was studying law at Cambridge University. There, he had met and talked with 'prominent intellectuals and scholars', and addressed public meetings, which reinforced his belief that:

> the only hope for Indian Islam was to turn from the past and interact boldly with Western thought and customs. Islam must be rejuvenated with fresh thought, and be willing to rationalize and adapt its customs and laws wherever possible.[36]

Syed Ahmad Khan thus pleaded with the Muslims not to oppose the British. The lives and properties of the Muslims, he assured them, were safe under the British and no restrictions were placed on their religious practices. Jihad was incumbent on the Muslims only if they were denied peace and could not practise their religion without fear of persecution. Since none of these conditions prevailed in India, he stressed that they should be 'loyal' to their British rulers.[37] In addition, he warned them that, with the ultimate failure of the Revolt and the reprisals that followed, there was no other way to recover except by cooperating with the British and accepting their rule.[38] He was convinced that they would succeed only with the assistance of the government. Indeed, that is why Syed Ahmad Khan's entire political struggle was meant to seek, secure, and promote Muslim interests and demands through the British government.[39] Whether it was his insistence on loyalty to the British or an enthusiastic advocacy of Western education, his end goal, as he plainly stated, was to secure 'honour, prosperity and high rank' for the Muslims.[40]

Syed Ahmad Khan realised that European countries had developed economically and politically as a result of the acceptance of science and new skills and techniques of learning. In India, too, the Hindus had taken advantage of the new learning through

English schools. Therefore, Syed Ahmad Khan, who, ironically, was himself not educated in English,[41] insisted that Muslims must learn English and Western sciences. In emphasising this, he was by no means suggesting that the Muslims should ignore their traditional disciplines or languages such as Persian and Arabic. What he tried to emphasise was that the Muslims should acquire Western education too. They must acquire knowledge suited to 'the present age', otherwise they would be lost. As he explained it:

> The old Mohammadan books and the tone of their writings do not teach the followers of Islam independence of thought, perspicuity and simplicity, nor do they enable them to arrive at the truth of matters in general; on the contrary, they deceive and teach men to veil their meaning, to embellish their speech with fine words, to describe things wrongly and in irrelevant terms, to flatter with false praise, to live in a state of bondage, to puff themselves up with pride, haughtiness and self-conceit, to speak with exaggeration, to leave the history of the past uncertain, and to relate facts like tales and stories …. All these things are quite unsuited to the present age and to the spirit of the time, and thus, instead of doing any good, they do much harm to the Mohammadans.[42]

In addition, the connection between education and government was too obvious for Syed Ahmad Khan to ignore. 'When you should have fully acquired [English] education, and true education shall have made its home in your hearts,' he told the Muslims, 'then you will know what rights you can legitimately demand of the British Government. And the result of this will be that you will also obtain honourable positions in the Government, and will acquire wealth in the higher ranks of trade.'[43]

Defying opposition from the traditional theologians and the orthodox sections of the Muslim community who were opposed to his efforts to promote Western education and science and who saw them as 'sweet poison (*meetha zehr*) that is fatal'[44] and indeed a threat to their Islamic moorings,[45] Syed Ahmad Khan kept pressing that modern education was neither forbidden by Islam nor dangerous to the Muslims.[46] Modern science, he emphasised, did not, in any way, 'undermine true Islam; indeed there could be no contradiction "between the word of God and the work of God".[47] However, he advised the Muslims to 'adopt the world, not for its own sake, but for that of religion ....'[48] As he put it:

> If you get high education and shine like stars in heaven but leave the fold of Islam, then the relationship between you and me will be snapped asunder ... the tether that binds you to me and the rest of the Muslim community is that of God and his Prophet [PBUH] ... It is my earnest desire that you gain perfection in science and Western literature but I shall enjoin on you all not to forget the *Kalma*—that God is one and Muhammad [PBUH] is His Prophet.[49]

In pursuit of his educational goals, in 1874, Syed Ahmad Khan drew up the scheme of a college at Aligarh. While the location of Aligarh 'proved to be a felicitous choice',[50] it was 'almost by accident ... that he had pitched on Aligarh for his university town of the future.'[51] In 1875, he established the Muhammadan Anglo-Oriental School which, after two years of its inception and strenuous efforts at fund-raising and construction of buildings at the site, in 1877, ultimately evolved into the full-fledged Muhammadan Anglo-Oriental College (MAO, later Aligarh College), a centre for modern education for Muslims.[52] However, the College, modelled on Cambridge University which Syed Ahmad Khan had visited during his stay in England, soon assumed 'a form and personality of its own'.[53] Although there was not much difference in academic standards and achievements between the Aligarh College and other Indian colleges,[54] and the College also accommodated a fair percentage of Hindu students[55] who were exempt from Islamic instruction, it eventually developed into a centre of educational, cultural, and political aspirations of the Muslims. Its primary aims and objectives, highlighted at the official ceremony of its launching at the hands of Governor General Robert Bulwer-Lytton, were 'to reconcile Oriental learning with Western literature and science, to inspire in the dreamy minds of people of the East, the practical energy which belongs to those of [the] West'.[56] In the end, of course, not only did the College ensure a steady increase of educated Muslims in government services and professions but, inevitably and more importantly, it also produced 'the leadership for Muslim political separatism in India as a counter-balance to the growing influence of the Indian National Congress.'[57]

The bold and timely initiative of the College did not go down well with many, including some non-Muslims. They, in 'a section of Anglo-Indian newspapers' published 'virulent' articles against such a 'Muslim College for Western education', even insinuating that the 'College will disseminate the doctrine of *jihad*.'[58] The *Pioneer* blasted Syed Ahmad Khan and the College, in these harsh words:

> [with such plans in his head, Sayyid Ahmad] looks just like a huge dog facing a mirror, grimly watching its own reflection, attacking its imaginary rival in a fit of fury, smashing the mirror into pieces and hurting itself fatally. This is how the Sayyid is going to end himself.[59]

The College, of course, went on to develop into a principle seat of learning for the Muslims of India, attracting students from all over the country. In the process, it produced,

> a class of Muslim leaders with a footing in both Western and Islamic culture, at ease both in British and Muslim society and endowed with a consciousness of their claims to be the aristocracy of the country as much in British as in Mughal times.[60]

Indeed, as one writer summed up its most remarkable contribution to the Muslim community: 'The College, together with the All-India Muhammadan Educational Conference, founded by Sayyid Ahmad in 1886, provided the first All-India platform to the Muslims of the sub-continent and thus became the nursery of ideas that led to Pakistan.'[61] Syed Ahmad Khan served as Secretary of the Educational Conference for years, ensuring its regular meetings every year. Its proceedings were published and circulated among the Muslim intelligentsia in various provinces of India.

Syed Ahmad Khan was not only interested in spreading Western education among the Muslims, he was equally keen to inculcate confidence in the Muslim community and also to impart to them a kind of 'training in character'. He believed that things are, constantly changing, and the method suited to the past is not suited to the present. Hence, unless we give the children of our nation along with education a training in character adapted to the times, we cannot reap these advantages which we desire.[62]

Syed Ahmad Khan thus started publishing *Tahzib al-Akhlaq* (subtitled in English as *The Muhammadan Social Reformer*), a monthly periodical in Urdu, in 1871. As he explained its aim and objectives in its very first issue,

> The aim of publishing this periodical is to make the Muslims of India desirous of the best kind of civilization, so that it shall remove the contempt with which civilized people regard the Muslims, and the latter shall become reckoned among the respected and civilized people in the world.[63]

The periodical, modelled on the pattern of Sir Richard Steele's *Tatler* and Joseph Addison's *Spectator*, helped in lifting the Muslim spirit from sullenness and apathy.[64] As Aziz Ahmad noted, it covered articles from 'public hygiene to rationalist speculation on religious dogma', and indeed, in the process, went on to raise 'storms of bitter controversy'.[65] While most of the articles were written by Syed Ahmad Khan himself, other distinguished writers of the day, such as Moulvi Syed Mehdi Ali Khan, Moulvi Chiragh Ali, and Altaf Hussain Hali, too, contributed regularly.[66] In 'its brilliant pages,' of course, 'modernism emerged as a potent force and considerably changed the course and the direction of Islam in India.'[67] However, the fact remained that only 'moral and social ideas won general acceptance'.[68] The religious controversies never ended.

Still, it was a great achievement for Syed Ahmad Khan who was severely critical of contemporary Indian Muslim society and was in particular wary of what he called the 'old method' of social life. 'It is like a broom', he lamented, 'of which the string binding the twigs has been broken, so that they have all fallen apart, and cannot be re-united unless a fresh cord be provided.'[69] He believed that Islam, a dynamic social order, was compatible with progress and that it was not at all opposed to reason and science. He, therefore, insisted, that the Muslims must examine social ethics of the day critically and rationally and bring them into conformity with the true spirit of Islam.[70]

In order to pursue and promote their particular political interests too, Syed Ahmad Khan advised the Muslims to reflect upon their religion and its 'principles'. This would help them develop a 'national feeling'. As he explained in a public meeting:

> At this moment, when all of us Mahomedans have come together [,] the assembly itself has an effect on our hearts, and an involuntary emotion gives birth to the thought—'Our Nation!' 'Our Nation!'— but when we separate [,] the effect vanishes. This is not merely my assertion; I trust that all here will acknowledge its truth. If you will reflect in [sic] the principles of religion, you will see the reason why our Prophet [PBUH] ordered all the dwellers in one neighbourhood to meet five times a day for prayer in the mosque, and why the whole town had to meet together on Fridays in the city mosque, and in Eid [sic] all the people of the district had to assemble. The reason was that the effect of gathering should influence all, and create a national feeling among those present, and show them the glory of the nation.[71]

Syed Ahmad Khan, thus, made it abundantly clear to the Muslims that Islam was the basis of their nationhood and indeed 'national well-being'. Islam and Islam alone bestows upon them the membership of the Muslim 'nation'. In his own words:

> All individuals, joining the fold of Islam, together constitute a nation of the Muslims. As long as they follow and practice their beloved religion they are a nation. Remember, you have to live and die by Islam and it is by keeping up Islam that our nation is a nation ... if someone becomes a star of the heaven but ceases to be a Muslim, what is he to us? He is no longer a member of our nation. Thus, achieving progress by keeping up [sic] Islam means national well-being.[72]

In fact, one could clearly see the roots of 'Muslim nationalism' of Allama Muhammad Iqbal and Quaid-i-Azam Mohammad Ali Jinnah being planted here—nationalism on the basis of Islam. As he elaborated further, conceptually:

Some reflection is required to grasp the nature of Muslim nationality. From time immemorial, communities have been held together by ties of common descent or common homeland. The Prophet Muhammad [PBUH] obliterated all territorial and ancestral conventions and laid the foundations of a broad and enduring kinship which comprehends all those who subscribe to the formula of faith .... This tribe divine assimilates all human beings, regardless of colour or place of birth.[73]

Syed Ahmad Khan was, of course, conscious and considerate of the other larger community, the Hindu community, in India. Indeed, he recognised that the Hindus were the majority community of India and thus sought 'agreement and friendship' with them. He likened India to 'a bride whose two eyes are the Hindus and the Mahomedans.' He insisted that if the two eyes were to be 'beautiful', they must be 'of equal lustre'.[74] In fact, he repeated this 'eloquent illustration' of eyes off and on, in different ways, but to the same effect. For instance, he wrote thus:

If one community makes progress and the other does not, the condition of India can never be good, and India will be like a one-eyed man. But if both communities advance side by side, the name of India will be honored, and instead of being called a one-eyed, dishevelled, toothless old widow, she will become a very beautiful, attractive bride![75]

Syed Ahmad Khan never accepted Hindu–Muslim unity as a '*fait accompli*'.[76] It had to be secured. The Hindu majority community, he believed, had a special role and responsibility in this regard. They had to be responsive to Muslim interests and demands. They should not hurt the Muslims. Otherwise, there would be no unity or friendship and the Muslims will have no option but to defend themselves from their 'attacks'. In a speech addressed to the Bengalis (Hindus), in particular, he articulated these concerns at some length:

I always honour the Bengalis for the progress and the high position they have attained in learning. I have always said that in the

matter of learning the Bengalis are the crown of all the nations of
India, and I say it again now. Than myself there is also no person
more desirous that in religious matters, too, that agreement and
friendship should exist. I have often given my nation to understand
that slaughtering cows for the purpose of annoying Hindus is the
height of cantankerous folly. If friendship really exist between us
and them, that friendship is far to be preferred to the sacrifice of
cow. My advice about all the religious ceremonies of the Hindus
is that though they be forbidden by my religion, yet it is necessary
both for us to respect their ceremonies and for them to respect
ours. In those matters which my Hindu brothers are doing for
their prosperity, honour and glory, I am always ready to give my
best advice with the utmost sincerity of heart. These are all things
which one friend may do for another. But when my Hindu brothers
and Bengali friends devise such a course of action as will bring us
loss and heap disgrace on our nation, then indeed we can longer
remain friends. Without doubt it is our duty to protect our nation
from those attacks of the Hindus and Bengalis by which we believe
that she will be injured.[77]

However, the first of these attacks came in 1867, when the Hindus
in the United Provinces (UP), in order that the 'cultural aspirations
and employment opportunities' for their own community 'might
be better served',[78] demanded the replacement of Urdu (Persian
script) with Hindi (Devanagari script) as the official language of
the province. According to M. Hadi Hussain, a biographer of Syed
Ahmad Khan,

> the Hindu agitation against the continuance of Urdu ... shattered
> his [Syed Ahmad Khan's] dream of a single Indian nation
> combining the best features of its heritage with the best of what it
> could acquire from the West and evolving into a modern nation
> with a distinctive character of its own.[79]

This 'linguistic controversy', of course, continued 'unabated from
his day till half a century after his death'.[80] He himself 'broke
many a lance with Hindu publicists and it was during this debate
that he was driven to the belief that Hindu-Muslim unity was a
forlorn hope'.[81]

In disowning Urdu, the Hindus demonstrated not only their linguistic and cultural differences with the Muslims but also betrayed a clash of political interests. The Urdu language which was a factor of unity among Hindus and Muslims of the province—and indeed of India (developed during the Muslim rule)—came to symbolise the widening rift between the two communities. Syed Ahmad Khan was disillusioned with the prospects of Hindu–Muslim unity and friendship. The Urdu–Hindi controversy convinced him that the Hindus and Muslims would not be able to see eye to eye on the political future of India. In fact, he expected that the hostility between the two communities would increase with the passage of time. Indeed, he claimed that they will not be able to work and stay together in the future. Though he felt bad about it, he was absolutely sure of his 'prophecy' coming true eventually.[82] In a prophetic manner, as he told a British civil servant, Alexander Shakespeare, 'the current disputes had convinced me of the futility of expecting the two communities to join hands on any issue whatever. At present the danger is almost imperceptible. But disruptive elements are too strong to be held in check. They are bound to triumph in the long run. Those who live after me will bear me out.'[83]

This transformation in Syed Ahmad Khan's outlook was completed with the political activities of the Indian National Congress,[84] demanding not only expansion in the role of representative institutions in India[85] and a greatly enhanced presence in the administration of the country but also the right to speak on behalf of the 'Indian nation'. Syed Ahmad Khan did not agree. 'The aims and objects of the Indian National Congress,' he claimed,

> are based upon ignorance of history and present[-]day realities; they do not take into consideration that India is inhabited by different nationalities; they presuppose that the Muslims like the Marhattas, the Brahmins, the Kashtriyas, the Banias, the Sudras, the Sikhs, the Bengalis, the Madrasis, and the Peshawaris can all be treated alike, and all of them belong to the same nation. The Congress thinks that they profess the same religion, that they speak

the same language, that their way of life and customs are the same, that their attitude to history is similar and is based upon the same historical traditions.[86]

The proponents of the Congress themselves, he pointed out, readily admitted that some of the 'aims and objects' of the Muslims were different from those of Hindus. Should Muslims and Hindus, therefore, Syed Ahmad Khan asked,

... have their own Congress for their special objects in which they differ from one another? If so, as their aims are conflicting and contradicting, these two Congresses will go on fighting each other to death; but when they meet in that Congress which my friends call the National Congress, they will then say:- 'No doubt you are my nation: no doubt you are my brother; no doubt your aims and my aims are one. How do you do, my brother? Now we are united on one point.'[87]

But, obviously, what bothered Syed Ahmad Khan most was the fact that when compared with the Hindus, the Muslims were numerically fewer, educationally backward, and economically weak. Clearly, 'an educationally backward and impoverished minority like the Muslims would be permanently submerged under a democratic constitution. In the popularly elected legislatures, the incidence of authority would always be biased against them.'[88] He, therefore, did 'not wish to run a race with them'.[89] He was also convinced that the British mind was still fresh with the memories of 1857. He felt that the agitational activities of the Congress would surely lead to a confrontation between the government and the people.[90] He recalled the fateful events:

What took place in the Mutiny? The Hindus began it; the Mahomedans with their eager disposition rushed to it. The Hindus having bathed in the Ganges became as they were before. But the Mahomedans and their noble families were ruined. This is the result which will befall Mahomedans for taking part in political agitation.[91]

But most important of all, Syed Ahmad Khan was opposed to the demands put forward by the Congress. He was opposed both to the Congress' demand for holding competitive examinations for civil services and the extension of representative principle in India. Competitive examinations, Syed Ahmad Khan knew, would result in the rule of one community—the Bengalis (Hindus)—over others, in particular, 'shutting out from it the educationally backward Muslims'.[92] No wonder, then, that the 'essential aim' of his 'strategy of Muslim politics' was 'reconciliation with the British, and the delaying of political reforms in India until the Muslims were sufficiently educated to compete with the more advanced Hindus, especially the Bengali Hindus.'[93] It seemed like Syed Ahmad Khan had moved away from his *asbab* stance, but he had a good, justifiable reason for doing so:

> There would remain no part of the country in which we should see at the tables of justice and authority any face except those of Bengalis [Hindus] making progress, but the question is[—]what would be the result on the administration of the country? Do you think that the Rajput and the fiery Pathan … could remain in peace under the Bengalis? This would be the outcome of the proposal if accepted.[94]

Similarly, representative institutions in India, Syed Ahmad Khan realised, would result in the domination of Hindus over the Muslims.[95] Hindus would obtain four times as many votes as Muslims because their population was four times as large. How then would the Muslims guard their interests? In fact, how could they: 'It would be like a game of dice in which one man had four dice and the other only one.' Even if the electorate was limited through a method of qualification, like income,[96] he reckoned, Muslims had no chance:

> Suppose, for example, that an income of Rs. 5,000 a year be fixed on, how many Mahomedans will there be? Which party will have the larger number of votes? … In the normal case no single Mahomedan will secure a seat in the Viceroy's Council.[97]

Syed Ahmad Khan believed that the representative system of government was 'the best system' only when voters belonged to a homogenous population, 'of one race and one creed'. But,

> ... in a country like India where caste distinctions still flourish, where there is no fusion of the various races, where religious distinctions are still violent, where education in [the] modern sense has not made an equal or proportionate progress among all the sections of the population, I am convinced that the introduction of the principle of election, pure and simple, for representation of various interests ... would be attended with evils of greater significance than purely economic considerations ... The larger community would totally override the interests of the smaller community ....[98]

'The object of the promoters of the National Congress,' indeed, Syed Ahmad Khan charged,

> is that the Government of India should be English in name only, and that the internal rule of the country should be entirely in their own hand. They do not publicly avow that they wish it for themselves: they speak in the name of the whole of India; but they very well know that the Mahomedans will be unable to do anything, and so the rule of the country will be monopolized by them.[99]

Thus, being 'a realist in politics'[100] and mindful of the precarious position of the Muslims in the system of government, Syed Ahmad Khan opposed 'the yoking together of the strong and the weak'.[101] He even warned that if the demands of the Congress for competitive examinations and representative institutions were accepted, the result would be a 'civil war'. In fact, he warned:

> We also like a civil war but not a civil war without arms; we like it with arms. If [the] Government wants to give over the internal rule of the country from its own hands into those of the people of India, then we will present a petition that, before doing so, she pass a law of competitive examination, namely, that the nation which passed first in this competition be given the rule of the country; but that

in this competition we be allowed to use the pen of our ancestors, which is in truth the true pen for writing the decrees of sovereignty. Then he who passes first in this shall rule the country.[102]

Evidently, it was 'fear of the Hindu majority that caused Sir Saiyid to steer Muslims away from the Congress.'[103] But that also showed how much he cared for his own community, the Muslim community. Their interests were supreme for him. His opposition to the Congress at the time was no ordinary affair. It was like an official party. Both the British and Indian governments were fully behind it. The Congress enjoyed the support of Governor-General Lord Dufferin, Secretary of State for India and the British Parliament, indeed the whole British establishment.

Syed Ahmad Khan's opposition to the Congress reached its crescendo with the formation of the United Indian Patriotic Association, in 1888. The major aim of the Association was to persuade the British that the Congress' demands were not representative of India as a whole. The Association received the support not only of the majority of the Muslims but also of those Hindus who did not approve of the stance taken by the Congress on representative institutions and 'democracy'.[104] Such Hindus, under the leadership of Raja Uday Pratap Singh, joined hands with Syed Ahmad Khan. While Raja Pratap Singh failed to carry enough support of his community, and perhaps was not much motivated himself, Syed Ahmad Khan achieved great success in mobilising Muslim opposition all over India.[105] He was able to win the support of a number of Muslim associations from Bengal, Punjab, Madras (Chennai), and the Central Provinces (CP).[106] Of particular importance was the Central National Muhammadan Association (in Calcutta, Kolkata) of Syed Ameer Ali, who, like him, was helping the Muslims, particularly in Bengal, to revive their fortunes in the new dispensation. In spite of their differences with the Patriotic Association on the nature of the political role of the community, Syed Ameer Ali assured Syed Ahmad Khan of their support against the Congress.[107] This really strengthened his cause.

The result was that Badruddin Tyabji, the only Muslim leader of standing who joined the Congress and was elected its president in 1888, could not help but confide to Allan Octavian Hume, the British founder-secretary of the party, that:

> The fact exists and whether we like it or not, … an overwhelming majority of Mahomedans are against the movement … If then the Mussalman community as a whole is against the Congress—rightly or wrongly does not matter—it follows that the movement *ipso facto* ceases to be a general or National Congress.[108]

Within a few months of its formation, however, the Patriotic Association disintegrated. Hindu and Muslim supporters of the Association fell apart. Despite their opposition to the Congress, the Hindu supporters of the Association could not agree with their Muslim counterparts on the future course of political action in India. Syed Ahmad Khan was not surprised or dismayed. It merely went on to reinforce his conviction that Hindus and Muslims had separate interests and that their interests could only be pursued and secured separately.

In 1893, Syed Ahmad Khan founded the Muhammadan Anglo-Oriental Defence Association, an exclusively Muslim concern, to bolster his anti-Congress campaign.[109] The Defence Association, however, like its predecessor, was not only opposed to competitive examinations and representative institutions but also, given the experience of municipality elections of the West UP and the Doab municipalities, insisted on separate electorates (first time) for the Muslims. They demanded separate electorates with Muslims voting only for Muslims, in addition to equal representation for the Muslims on the UP Legislative Council on account of their historical importance, and weightage in representation on municipal and district boards. These new demands were circulated particularly through the *Aligarh Institute Gazette*.[110]

The 'explicit denial of the Congress' faith in one nation'[111] and Syed Ahmad Khan's emphasis on 'Muslim particularity',[112] carried with it all the elements of an evolving Muslim separatist political movement in India, though, as Hamid cautioned:

Let us not make the facile assumption that Sayyid Ahmad was consciously creating the separatist movement. The contributing causes of all movements in history are found in the environment itself. Leaders are seldom aware of the full implications and possibilities of the attitude they strike and the tendencies they initiate. Movements easily overflow their original banks, sluices widen into flood-gates. Sayyid Ahmad did no more than 'drive a stream of tendency' through Muslim affairs in this sub-continent and in doing so he was making the future.[113]

The main characteristic of this 'tendency', of course, remained an awareness that representative institutions in India, based on numbers, would cause the permanent subjugation of Muslim minority to Hindu majority. Elections were merely a way of securing the representation of the Hindu majority community. The political interests of the Muslims were not the same as those of the Hindus; the Muslims had particular interests. Muslims and Hindus were separate political groups. Islam was the basis of the Muslim concept of group. The Muslim political group was the group Muslims should advance in their political life and processes. Muslims could not expect the other group, Hindus, to join hands with them and make fair and equitable demands on the system. They had to fend for themselves. They had to promote and pursue their own separate interests. These thoughts, feelings, and aspirations became even more pronounced as, eventually, the end of the British rule in India came in sight, during World War II. It was then, more than ever,[114] that the Muslim leadership came to grasp the true significance of the now familiar assessment of the Indian situation as foretold by Syed Ahmad Khan:

Now, suppose that all the English and the whole English army were to leave India ... then who would be rulers of India? Is it possible that under these circumstances two nations—the Mahomedans and the Hindus—could sit on the same throne and remain equal in power? Most certainly not ... To hope that both could remain equal is to desire the impossible and the inconceivable.[115]

Jinnah, the ultimate leader of the Muslims in the late 1930s, realised the implications of this, and indeed went on to demand the partition of India and a separate state for the Muslims, Pakistan. But, of course, there were some prominent political leaders, contemporarily and after Syed Ahmad Khan, who played their part in setting the stage for such a demand by leading the separatist political movement along the way. The Aga Khan was one of the first and foremost among those leaders.

Notes

1. See, for instance, Aziz Ahmad, *Studies in Islamic Culture in the Indian Environment* (Oxford: Clarendon Press, 1964), 265; S. M. Ikram, *Modern Muslim India and the Birth of Pakistan* (Lahore: Sh. Muhammad Ashraf, 1970), 57; Mary Louise Becker, 'Some Formative Influences on the Career of Quaid-i-Azam M.A. Jinnah', in *World Scholars on Quaid-i-Azam Mohammad Ali Jinnah*, ed. Ahmad Hassan Dani (Islamabad: Quaid-i-Azam University, 1979), 83; Francis Robinson, 'Islam and Muslim Separatism', in *Political Identity in South Asia*, eds. David Taylor and Malcolm Yapp (London: Curzon Press, 1979), 91–2; Percival Spear, *India, Pakistan, and the West* (New York: Oxford University Press, 1967), 122; and Hafeez Malik, *Sir Sayyid Ahmad Khan and Muslim Modernization in India and Pakistan* (New York: Columbia University Press, 1980), 244. Hafeez Malik, however, likened Syed Ahmad Khan's 'nationalism' to Bolingbroke's concept of nationalism, which in a word, represented 'the most natural and reasonable means not only of safeguarding Muslim national interests but also of achieving amiable relations with the Hindus'. Ibid.

2. S. K. Bhatnagar, *History of the M.A.O. College Aligarh* (Lahore: n.p. n.d.), 21–5. Also see Marietta Stepaniants, 'Development of the Concept of Nationalism: The Case of Muslims in the Indian Sub-continent', *The Muslim World*, Vol. LXIX, No. 1 (January 1979): 34; Sachin Sen, *The Birth of Pakistan* (Calcutta: General Printers & Publishers, 1955; Lahore: Sh. Muhammad Ashraf, 1978), 42.

3. This is not to suggest that we do not find different concepts of the national ideal in the writings of Bolingbroke, Montesquieu, Rousseau and Sieyes, Jefferson, Herder, and Fichte, Alferi and Mazzini. For the development of this ideal in the twentieth century, see especially Anthony D. Smith, *Nationalism in the Twentieth Century* (Oxford: Oxford University Press, 1979).

4. Anil Seal, *the Emergence of Indian Nationalism: Competition and Collaboration in the Later Nineteenth Century* (Cambridge: Cambridge University Press, 1968), 339. For an opposite, rather polemical, view that

'Indian Nationality is not a plant of mushroom growth, but a giant of the forest, with Millenia behind it', see Annie Besant, *The Future of Indian Politics* (London: Theosophical Publishing House, 1922); and Ishwa Nath Topa, *Sidelights on the Problems of Indian Nationality* (Allahabad: Kitabistan, 1933).

5. See, for instance, Ahmad, *Studies in Islamic Culture,* 73–6, 89–90; Wilfred Cantwell Smith, *Islam in Modern History* (Princeton: Princeton University Press, 1957), 268; M. Mujeeb, *The Indian Muslims* (London: George Allen & Unwin, 1967), 396; Mackenzie Brown, *The White Umbrella* (Berkeley: University of California Press, 1964), 133; Stanley Wolpert, *India* (Englewood Cliffs: New Jersey: Prentice-Hall, 1965), 56–60; and Bernard S. Cohn, *India: The Social Anthropology of a Civilization* (Englewood Cliffs: New Jersey: Prentice-Hall, 1971), 66.

6. Hafeez Malik, *Moslem Nationalism in India and Pakistan* (Washington DC: Public Affairs Press, 1963), 208–9.

7. Bhatnagar, *History of the M.A.O. College*, 1–2.

8. Syed Ahmed Khan was a senior official at the court in Bijnor and remained loyal to the British throughout the Revolt. Syed Ahmad Khan retired from government service in 1876, and soon was knighted. He served the Viceroy's Legislative Council from 1878 to 1883. Walter Bennett Evans, *The Genesis of the Pakistan Idea: A Study of Hindu-Muslim Relations* (Karachi: Oxford University Press, 2013), 73.

9. See especially Valentine Chirol, *India: Old and New* (London: Macmillan, 1921); Reginald Coupland, *India: A Re-Statement* (London: Oxford University Press, 1945); Hugh Tinker, *India and Pakistan: A Political Analysis* (London: Frederick A. Praeger, 1967); Eric Stokes, *The English Utilitarians and India* (London: Oxford University Press, 1959); W. W. Hunter, *The Indian Musalmans* (Calcutta: Comrade Publishers, 1945); and P. Woodruff, *The Men Who Ruled India: The Founders, Vols. I and II* (London: Jonathan Cape, 1953 and 1954).

10. Alfred Lyall, *Asiatic Studies: Religious and Social* (London: John Murray, 1884), 246.

11. John W. Wilder, 'Introduction', in *Selected Essays by Sir Sayyid Ahmad Khan*, trans. John W. Wilder (Lahore: Sang-e-Meel, 2006), 13.

12. The Brahmo Samaj movement, founded in 1828 under the inspiration of a Bengali reformer, Raja Ram Mohin Roy (1774–1833), sought to reconcile Hindus with the Western education.

13. In 1860–2, there were ten Hindus to one Muslim in these schools. In 1870–1 there were still nine Hindus to one Muslim. As late as 1875, the number of Muslim graduates all over India was only 20—17 Bachelors of Arts (BA) and three Masters of Arts (MA). Hindu graduates were 846, 715 BAs, and 131 MAs. F. W. Thomas, *The History and Prospects of British Education in India* (Cambridge: Cambridge University Press, 1891), 94. For Syed Ahmad Khan's analysis of the pathetic state of Muslims in English education in India at the time, both before and after the establishment of the Aligarh

College, see, Maulana Altaf Hussain Hali, *Hayat-i-Javed* (Lahore: National Book House, 1986), 359–61.

14. Hunter, *The Indian Musalmans*, 168–9.

15. Abdul Hamid, *Muslim Separatism in India: A Brief Survey, 1858–1947* (Lahore: Oxford University Press, 1967), ix. While Hunter's argument 'applied only to Bengal' and 'not … all the Muhammadans of India', it did provide 'Muslim elites of northern India', led by Syed Ahmad Khan, 'a pretext to promote their own specific class and regional interests'. Ayesha Jalal, *Self and Sovereignty: Individual and Community in South Asian Islam since 1850* (Lahore: Sang-e-Meel Publications, 2007), 59.

16. Wilder, 'Introduction', in *Selected Essays*, 16. Syed Ahmad Khan 'risked his own life in saving the lives of a party of English men and women in the same city [Bijnor]'. Ibid., 15.

17. Ibid., 16.

18. Ibid.

19. Ramsay Macdonald, *The Awakening of India* (London: Hodder & Stoughton, 1910), 173.

20. Hamid, *Muslim Separatism*, xv.

21. Ibid.

22. Wilder, 'Introduction', in *Selected Essays*, 16.

23. Hali, *Hayat-i-Javed*, 803–46. For the English translation of the treatise, see *The Causes of the Indian Revolt*, translated by His Two European Friends (Lahore: reprint). The more recent one of course is the Oxford edition, with an 'Introduction' by Francis Robinson. This is the one used here. Syed Ahmad Khan, *The Causes of the Indian Revolt*, with an Introduction by Francis Robinson (Karachi: Oxford University Press, 2000).

24. Hamid, *Muslim Separatism*, 2. This publication, as one author argued, 'was not without its attendant dangers. Sir Sayyid's biographer, Altaf Hussain Hali cautioned us that post-rebellion India "was an exceedingly dangerous period. There was no freedom whatsoever to voice one's opinions" … conditions were exceedingly harsh for the Muslims.' '"To incriminate a Muslim," he warned, "there was no need for any proof."' Masood Ashraf Raja, *Constructing Pakistan: Foundational Texts and the Rise of Muslim National Identity, 1857–1947* (Karachi: Oxford University Press, 2010), 21.

25. Khan, *Causes of the Indian Revolt*, 13–14. 'The extent to which Sir Sayyid's memorandum,' wrote Hafeez Malik, 'influenced the formulation of British policy after 1857 is not precisely known, although it can be stated most confidently that his views were seriously considered by the India Office in London.' Malik, *Sir Sayyid Ahmad Khan and Muslim Modernization in India and Pakistan*, 123.

26. Khan, *Causes of the Indian Revolt*, 14.

27. Ibid., 15.

28. Raja, *Constructing Pakistan*, 33.

29. Malik, *Moslem Nationalism in India and Pakistan*, 207.

30. G. F. I. Graham, *The Life and Work of Sir Sayyid Ahmad Khan*, with a new introduction by Zatuna Y. Umer (Karachi: Oxford University Press, 1974), 41–2. Also see Hali, *Havat-i-Javed*, 102.
31. 'Probably,' Hafeez Malik opined, 'Hunter's interpretation corresponded to British imperial interests of the time' and, he wrote, 'evidently without consulting original sources which undoubtedly would have been available to him.' Malik, *Moslem Nationalism*, 191.
32. See the detailed discussion in Hali, *Hayat-i-Javed*, 174–83; Graham, *The Life and Work of Sir Syed Ahmad Khan*, 142–56; and Hunter, *The Indian Musalmans*, esp. Chps. II and III.
33. Hamid, *Muslim Separatism*, 20.
34. Raja, *Constructing Pakistan*, 49.
35. Ram Gopal, *Indian Muslims* (Lahore: Book Traders, 1976,), 25.
36. Wilder, 'Introduction', in *Selected Essays*, 17.
37. These efforts, in turn, caused certain ulema to take a more active role in political life, and thus found in 1867 a *Dar-al-Ulum* at Deoband, to help oppose the British and to secure the cultural and religious identity of the Muslims. For a detailed discussion of the founding principles of the *Dar-al-Ulum*, see Ziya al-Hasan Farooqi, *The Deoband School and the Demand for Pakistan* (Bombay: Asia Publishing House, 1963), 25–6. Also see Mushirul Hasan, *Nationalism and Communal Politics in India, 1916–1928* (Delhi: Manohar, 1979); Peter Hardy, *Partners in Freedom and True Muslims: The Political Thought of Some Muslim Scholars in British India, 1912–1947* (Lund: Student Literature Scandanavian Institute of Asiatic Studies, 1971); Mushir-ul-Haq, *Muslim Politics in Modern India, 1858–1947* (Meerut: Meenakshi Parakashan, 1970); and Ishtiaq Husain Qureshi, *Ulema in Politics: A Study Relating to the Political Activities of the Ulema in the South-Asian Subcontinent from 1556 to 1947* (Karachi: Ma'aref, 1977).
38. Syed Ahmad Khan, however, made it clear that the attitude of the Muslims towards the British would, in the long run, depend on the treatment meted out to them. He sought the stability and strength of the British rule for the sake of the Muslims. This, he was convinced, was the only way that they could get out of their present predicament. Hali, *Hayat-i-Javed*, 600. Also see, Ahmad, *Studies in Islamic Culture*, 59; Mujeeb, *The Indian Muslims*, 432; and Graham, *The Life and Work of Sir Syed Ahmad Khan*, 53. 'If, in 1856, the natives of India had known anything of the mighty power which England possesses, a power which would have impressed the misguided men of the Bengal army with the knowledge how futile their efforts to subvert the empire of Her Majesty in the East would be, there is little doubt but that the unhappy events of 1857 would never have occurred.' Ibid.
39. This explained why Syed Ahmad Khan was so keen to contain pro-Khilafat sentiment in the later years of his life. He feared it may upset his plans. For a critical discussion of this aspect of Syed Ahmad Khan's political role see, in particular, Sir Syed Ahmad Khan, *Akhri Mazameen* (Lahore:

Matba Rafai Aam Press, 1898); Ahmad, *Studies in Islamic Culture*, 64; Peter Hardy, *The Muslims of British India*, (Cambridge: Cambridge University Press, 1972), 178–9; Shan Muhammad, *Sir Syed Ahmad Khan: A Political Biography* (Lahore: Universal Books, 1976), 131; and M. Naeem Qureshi, *Pan-Islam in British India: The Politics of the Khilafat Movement, 1918–1924* (Karachi: Oxford University Press, 2009), 31. Syed Ahmad Khan, wrote Qureshi, 'deprecated the Indian Muslims' "extraterritorial romance" saying that the sultan of Turkey was not their ruler and could claim no temporal or spiritual allegiance from them.' Ibid.

40. Sir Syed Ahmad Khan, *The Present State of Indian Politics: Speeches and Letters*, ed. Farman Fatehpuri (Lahore: Sang-e-Meel Publications, 1982), 47.

41. This is not to deny his intellectual abilities and prowess as a man of letters. In 1847, he wrote *Asar al-Sanadid*, a considerably important work on the monuments of Delhi. In 1855, he edited Abul Fazl's *Ain-i-Akbari*, 'collating various manuscripts' related to Akbar. In 1862, he 'collated four manuscripts of another great historical work of medieval India, *Tarikh-i-Firuz Shahi*, to edit it for the Asiatic Society of Bengal.' In 1870, he published *Essays on the Life of Mohammad [PBUH]* in English and as *Khutbat-i-Ahmadiya* in Urdu to 'refute' William Muir's 'polemical' *Life of Mahomet* (1858). Aziz Ahmad, *Islamic Modernism in India and Pakistan* (London: Oxford University Press, 1967), 39–40.

42. Cited in Hamid, *Muslim Separatism*, 11.

43. Ahmad, *The Present State of Indian Politics*, 77.

44. Malik, *Moslem Nationalism in India*, 196.

45. Hamid, *Muslim Separatism*, 41. Also see Hasan, *Nationalism and Communal Politics in India*, 23–6; Farooqi, *The Deoband School and the Demand for Pakistan*, 24; and Ahmad, *Islamic Modernism in India and Pakistan*, 20. Being a 'progressive Muslim', Syed Ahmad Khan obviously was 'hated' by the orthodox Muslims. S. R. Mehrotra, *Towards India's Freedom and Partition* (New Delhi: Rupa & Co., 2007), 406.

46. See Muhammad Ismail Panipati, ed., *Maqalat-i-Sir Syed*, Vol. II (Lahore: Majlis-e-Tarraqi-e-Adab, 1962), 206. Also see Ahmad, *Islamic Modernism*, 32; and Ishtiaq Hussain Qureshi, *The Struggle for Pakistan* (Karachi: Karachi University, 1974), 19–20.

47. Ishtiaq Hussain Qureshi, *The Muslim Community of the Indo-Pakistan Subcontinent (610–1947)* (The Hague: Mouton & Co., 1962), 240.

48. Ahmad, *The Present State of Indian Politics,* 89.

49. *Lectures*, cited in Bhatnagar, *History of the M.A.O. College Aligarh*, 5. Also see, Hali, *Hayat-i-Javed*, 213.

50. Wilder, 'Introduction', in *Selected Essays*, 18.

51. Ibid. This was stated by Syed Ahmad Khan himself to a British civil servant, J. Kennedy, 'an acquaintance and admirer'. Ibid., 15.

52. For a useful and informative history of the development of the College (and eventually the Aligarh Muslim University), see Bhatnagar, *History of the M.A.O. College Aligarh*.

53. Ahmad, *Islamic Modernism*, 37. In Aligarh, 'the budding Moslem intelligentsia was inspired by ideals of Moslem nationalism; even their outward appearance underwent a radical change. They wore a special college uniform consisting of a black Turkish coat, white trousers and a *fez*.' Syed Ahmad Khan himself 'adopted Turkish dress and required it of the Moslem students in Aligarh College …. The nationalistic atmosphere at Aligarh College eliminated provincial differences.' Malik, *Moslem Nationalism in India and Pakistan*, 215.

54. Hali, *Hayat-i-Javed*, 367. Also see Ahmad, *Islamic Culture*, 65.

55. Hali, *Hayat-i-Javed*, 357–8; and Bhatnagar, *History of the M.A.O. College Aligarh*, 28. Incidentally the first BA graduate of the University was a Hindu, as was the first MA.

56. Cited in Hamid, *Muslim Separatism*, 13–14.

57. Ahmad, *Islamic Modernism*, 37. Hali, *Hayat-i-Javed*, 436; and Hardy, *The Muslims of British India*, 104; Mukhtar Zaman, *Students Role in the Pakistan Movement* (Karachi: Quaid-i-Azam Academy, 1979), 3; and M. S. Jain, 'Chapter 4', in *The Aligarh Movement: Its Origins and Development, 1858–1906* (Agra: Sri Ram Mehra, 1965).

58. Hamid, *Muslim Separatism*, 19.

59. Ibid. Syed Ahmad Khan, in fact, 'received numerous letters in which the writers said they had sworn on the [Holy] Koran to take his life. But threats did not change the course of his life.' Gopal, *Indian Muslims*, 47.

60. Hardy, *The Muslims of British India*, 103.

61. Hamid, *Muslim Separatism*, 19.

62. Ahmad, *The Present State of Indian Politics*, 93. Also see Ahmad, *Akhri Mazameen*, 28.

63. Wilder, 'Introduction', in *Selected Essays*, 20–1.

64. Hali, *Hayat-i-Javed*, 162–7. Also see R. H. Zobairi, 'Sir Syed Ahmad Khan's Interpretation of Muslim Society and his Reform Movement in the Indian Context', *Islamic Culture*, Vol. VII, No. 3 (July 1983), 173.

65. Ahmad, *Islamic Modernism*, 38.

66. Wilder, 'Introduction', in *Selected Essays*, 21.

67. Ahmad, *Islamic Modernism*, 38.

68. Wilder, 'Introduction', in *Selected Essays*, 25.

69. Ahmad, *The Present State of Indian Politics*, 93.

70. Bashir Ahmad Dar, ed., *Religious Thought of Sayyid Ahmad Khan* (Lahore: Institute of Islamic Culture, 1957), 148; S. M. Ikram, *Modern Muslim India*, 57; Qureshi, *The Muslim Community*, 240, 245; Ahmad, *Islamic Modernism*, 32. However, quite a few of his 'closest friends and supporters' did 'not accept his rationalistic ideas', including Deputy Nazir Ahmad, Maulana Shibli Nomani, Nawab Mohsen-ul-Mulk, and even Altaf Hussain Hali, 'his admiring biographer'. Wilder, 'Introduction', in *Selected Essays*,

26. For a 'modernist' interpretation of Syed Ahmad Khan's thought, also see Muhammad Aslam Syed, Chp. 3, 'The Modernists', in *Muslim Response to the West: Muslim Historiography in India, 1857–1914* (Islamabad: National Institute of Historical & Cultural Research, 1988), 34–70.

71. Ahmad, *The Present State of Indian Politics*, 94.

72. G. Allana, ed., *Pakistan Movement: Historic Documents* (Lahore: Islamic Book Service, 1977), 1.

73. Cited in Hamid, *Muslim Separatism*, 39.

74. Syed Ahmad Khan, thus I. H. Qureshi observed, 'almost invariably thought of the Hindus and Muslims as separate entities. Even when he preached the need of unity, he spoke of the two communities separately, without whose equal progress India as a whole could not prosper'. Qureshi, *The Muslim Community*, 249.

75. The essay in *Tahzib-al-Akhlaq*. Cited in John W. Wilder, 'Preface', in *Selected Essays by Sir Sayyid Ahmad Khan*, 10.

76. Hamid, *Muslim Separatism*, 36.

77. Ahmad, *The Present State of Indian Politics*, 49–50.

78. Paul R. Brass, *Language, Religion and Politics in North India* (Cambridge: Cambridge University Press, 1974), 134.

79. M. Hadi Hussain, *Syed Ahmad Khan: Pioneer of Muslim Resurgence* (Lahore: Institute of Islamic Culture, 1970), 241–2. Persian was the official language of the government in India till 1837.

80. Hamid, *Muslim Separatism*, 36.

81. Ibid., 37.

82. Hali, *Hayat-i-Javed*, 138–9.

83. Hamid, *Muslim Separatism*, 38.

84. According to Aziz Ahmad, his 'active opposition to the Indian National Congress did not begin until 1887 when a Muslim, Badr al-din Tayyabji, was elected its president. From Sayyid Ahmad's viewpoint this was the beginning of an erosion in Muslim political solidarity, disastrous for the future of Muslim community'. Ahmad, *Islamic Modernism*, 34.

85. Incidentally, the British never meant to introduce representative institutions into India like they had in England. The representative system in India was intended to be more in the form of traditional '*durbars*'. As late as 1909, Lord Morley, the architect of the 1909 Reforms, went on to declare in the House of Lords that, 'If it could be said that this chapter of reforms led directly or necessarily up to the establishment of a parliamentary system in India, I for one would have nothing at all to do with it.' The signs of ultimate representative government (based on the 1917 declaration), however, began to surface in the Government of India Act, 1919. Macdonald, *The Awakening of India*, 167; Reginald Coupland, *The Indian Problem: 1830–1935* (London: Oxford University Press, 1968), 50; and J. Coatman, *Years of Destiny, 1926–1932* (London: Jonathan Cape, 1932), 76.

86. Allana, *Historic Documents*, 3.

87. Ahmad, *The Present State of Indian Politics*, 83.
88. Hamid, *Muslim Separatism*, 31.
89. Ibid., 51.
90. The 'submissiveness' implied in Syed Ahmad Khan's political lead, wrote Abdul Hamid, 'prevented the growth of political maturity'. Hamid, *Muslim Separatism*, 31–2. Ayesha Jalal felt that: 'In urging Muslims to reject politics and make humble submissions to the colonial authorities, Sayyid Ahmad was angling for continued government support for the Muslim Anglo-Oriental College. This was the line of an educationist, not a wily political operator with a hidden agenda for a religiously informed cultural nationalism.' Jalal, *Self and Sovereignty*, 93. Maulana Mohamed Ali who led the Indian Muslims during the tempestuous years of the Khilafat movement, however, was of the view that it was 'a mistake to consider that Syed Ahmad Khan took little interest in political matters. Unlike other politicians of India, he was more anxious for construction than destruction'. Mushirul Hasan, ed., *Muhammad Ali in Indian Politics: Select Writings* (Delhi: Atlantic Publishers, 1982), 4.
91. Ahmad, *The Present State of Indian Politics*, 86.
92. Hamid, *Muslim Separatism*, 42.
93. Morris Dembo, 'Introduction', in *Political Profile of Sir Sayyid Ahmad Khan: A Documentary Record*, ed. Hafeez Malik (Islamabad: Institute of Islamic History, Culture and Civilization, Islamic University, 1982), xxii.
94. Ibid., 35. Here it needs to be noted that Syed Ahmad Khan was not opposed to the basic principle of representation emphasised in the *Asbab*. What he desired was that the system of representation in India must take into account the peculiar demographic situation of India, and must thus ensure justice and fair play for the minority communities, the Muslim community in particular.
95. Even Rejendra Prasad, a leading figure of the Indian National Congress in the twentieth century, could not help but admit 'that movement for self-government resting on the principle of majority suggested the possibility of a Hindu Raj'. See, *India Divided* (Bombay: Hind Kitab, 1977), 45.
96. Representative institutions in India, in fact, started off with educational and economic qualifications than adult suffrage. These qualifications included ownership of land, payment of income tax, and graduation from a university. For a detailed analysis of the subject see, in particular, Norris Steven Dodge, 'Political Behavior and Social change: Causes of the Growth of the Indian Electorate in the last half Century', Unpublished PhD Dissertation, Cornell University, 1971.
97. Ahmad, *The Present State of Indian Politics*, 36–7.
98. Allana, *Historic Documents*, 1–2.
99. Ahmad, *The Present State of Indian Politics*, 51–2.
100. Qureshi, *The Muslim Community*, 245.
101. This is how Maulana Mohamed Ali eventually defended Syed Ahmad Khan's political lead. See Afzal Iqbal, ed., *Selected Writings and Speeches*

of Maulana Mohamed Ali, Vol. II (Lahore: Sh. Muhammad Ashraf, 1969), 134.

102. Ahmad, *The Present State of Indian Politics,* 52.

103. Evans, *Genesis of Pakistan Idea,* 74.

104. 'Democracy,' said the Maharaja of Benares in a lecture on 20 July 1888, 'is an occidental idea. A Hindu cannot comprehend it as long as he is a Hindu. It is against his religious belief.' Ahmad, *The Present State of Indian Politics,* 149.

105. M. Yusuf Abbasi, 'Sir Syed Ahmad Khan and the Re-awakening of the Muslims', *Journal of Pakistan Studies,* Vol. II (1980): 31.

106. Hali, *Hayat-i-Javed,* 258–9; and Ahmad, *The Present State of Indian Politics,* Appendix, 'List of Affiliated Muhammadan Associations', 241–57.

107. The main difference between the two associations was that Syed Ameer Ali believed that the Muslims should not only concentrate on their educational and economic reconstruction but should also organise themselves in politics on lines parallel with that of the Congress. They must actively involve themselves in political activities. But then, according to Yusuf Abbasi, Syed Ahmad Khan and his supporters like Nawab Abdul Latif of Calcutta (Kolkata) also regarded the National Mahomedan Association 'as an intruder in their sphere of provincial influence'. M. Yusuf Abbasi, 'Syed Ameer Ali (Pioneer of Muslim Politics)', *Journal of Pakistan Studies,* Vol. II (1980), 58–9.

108. N. R. Phatak, ed., *Source Material For a History of the Freedom Movement in India, (1855–1920)* Vol. II (Bombay: Government Central Press, 1957). Cited in Matiur Rahman, *From Consultation to Confrontation: A Study of the Muslim League in British Indian Politics, 1906–1912* (London: Luzac & Co., 1970), 5.

109. Matiur Rahman, however, insisted that it was through two non-political institutions, the Aligarh College and the All-India Muhammadan Educational Conference, that Syed Ahmad Khan 'exercised his great influence over the Indian Muslims'. Ibid., 4.

110. Jain, *The Aligarh Movement,* 128–9.

111. Ainslie T. Embree, *India's Search for National Identity* (New York: Alfred A. Knopf, 1972), 38.

112. Raja, *Constructing Pakistan,* 34.

113. Hamid, *Muslim Separatism,* 42. In this sense, 'scholars inclined to take a longer view have attributed the emergence of a distinct Muslim identity and separatism to the work of Sir Syed Ahmad Khan and his clique at Aligarh in the late nineteenth century if not earlier'. Venkat Dhulipala, *Creating a New Medina: State Power, Islam, and the Quest for Pakistan in Late Colonial North India* (Cambridge: Cambridge University Press, 2015), 25. Similarly, Masood Ashraf Raja suggested that Syed Ahmad Khan's 'discursive treatment of Muslim particularity eventually becomes the basis for the idea of a separate Muslim nation'. Raja, *Constructing Pakistan,* 34. Hafeez Malik went one step further and asserted that, 'In judging his policies one

must constantly remind oneself that [he] was a Muslim nationalist first, and an Indian second, and he saw no contradiction between these two orientations.' Malik, *Sir Sayyid Ahmad Khan and Muslim Modernization in India and Pakistan*, 253.

114. 'The present artificial unity of India,' declared Jinnah in his presidential address at the League Lahore Session on 23 March 1940, 'dates back only to the British conquest and is maintained by the British bayonet, but termination of the British regime, which is implicit in the recent declaration of His Majesty's Government, will be the herald of the entire break-up with worse disaster [*sic*] than has even taken place during the last one thousand years under Muslims. Surely that is not the legacy which Britain would bequeath to India after 150 years of her rule, nor would Hindu and Muslim India risk such a catastrophe.' Jamil-ud-Din Ahmad, ed., *Speeches and Writings of Mr. Jinnah*, Vol. I (Lahore: Sh. Muhammad Ashraf, 1968), 170.

115. Ahmad, *The Present State of Indian Politics*, 61.

3

Aga Khan and the Growth of the Muslim Separatist Political Movement in British India

The Aga Khan was Syed Ahmad Khan's contemporary and a political successor to the leadership of Muslim India who readily agreed with him that Indian Muslims had to pursue their particular interests separately and for their own sake. The self-proclaimed 'national' party, the Indian National Congress or, for that matter, its brand of 'Indian nationalism' catering essentially to the Hindu majority community, could not secure or serve their interests which, more often than not, were different from and even opposed to Hindu interests. The Muslim leadership had to build on the separatist legacy, and more importantly, strengthen and develop the separatist political movement founded by Syed Ahmad Khan. There was no other way out. The Aga Khan realised it and, soon after Syed Ahmad Khan, stepped forward, and succeeded in ensuring the growth of the separatist political movement in a critical, formative phase of British rule in India.

Sir Sultan Muhammad Shah Aga Khan III (1877–1957) was born in Karachi on 2 November 1877, and grew up in Bombay (Mumbai) and Poona.[1] He was educated at Eton and Cambridge University. The British government helped 'in securing him a place at these prestigious institutions', thus 'smoothing his transition' to British life and 'environment'[2] at a young age.

The Aga Khan was a hereditary leader, or Imam, of the Ismaili sect, having inherited all 'the titles, wealth and responsibilities, spiritual and temporal.'[3] His grandfather, Mahomed Shah Aga Khan

I, was 'confirmed' as Imam through a judgement of the Bombay High Court in a suit, 'Aga Khan Case', in 1866.[4] Upon the death of his father, Aga Ali Shah, in 1885, the Aga Khan was installed as Imam (forty-eighth Imam) at the tender age of eight years 'through public support of and from the colonial state'[5] and the British rulers in London. As a 21-year-old, during his first European tour that started from Britain in 1898, he was 'received in audience' by the monarch, Queen Victoria, and was also knighted. During this visit, he also 'made acquaintance' with Prince of Wales, later King Edward VII, setting 'the foundation of a lasting friendship' with the British royalty and its officialdom.[6] Another title, Knight Grand Commander (GCIE), was bestowed upon him on the eve of King Edward's coronation in 1902.

In 1902, when he was just 25 years old, he was nominated a member of the Imperial Legislative Council of India. He gratefully acknowledged 'a letter from the Viceroy, Lord Curzon asking [him] to become a member of his Legislative Council', and indeed went on to exclaim that: 'This was a considerable honour to a young man still in his 20s (I was by far the youngest member), for the Viceroy's Legislative Council in those days was a small, select body of influential people, wielding real authority.'[7] The Aga Khan was offered nomination for the second time in 1904, after the expiry of his tenure, but he politely 'refused'. He did, however, admit that this unique experience of the Legislative Council had a 'profound and permanent effect' on his 'life and character, in their private and personal as well as their public aspect.'[8]

One of the most striking effects of his membership of the Council was his exposure to Indian politics in general, and that of the Indian National Congress in particular. He was able to see the working of the Congress at close quarters. It did not impress him, especially with regard to the Muslims and their interests. He found it deficient and disappointing. In fact, he felt bad that 'the Congress Party, the only active and responsible political organisation in the country, would prove itself incapable—was already proving itself incapable—of representing India's Muslims, or of dealing adequately or justly with the needs and aspirations of the Muslim community.'[9]

The Aga Khan found the Congress' attitude towards the Muslims disconcerting in spite of the presence of stalwarts, such as G. K. Gokhale who was 'a caste Hindu' but was beyond 'the barriers of creed and race',[10] and Pherozeshah Mehta, who was 'high in the counsels of the Congress Party' and was a family friend. Indeed, he 'begged' Mehta to 'use his influence and make Congress realise how important it was to win Muslim confidence, but all to no avail.'[11] The Congress 'persisted in ignoring the realities of [the] communal situation'.[12] The problem, of course, was the 'pressure of Hindu extremism' which was quite 'strong'.[13] To a large extent, this was reinforced by British constitutional reforms taking shape in India and their application based on numbers, that is, majority rule. 'Deep-seated and ineradicable differences' between the Muslims and Hindus, the minority and the majority community, respectively, 'expressed themselves once political activity and aspirations had advanced beyond the most elementary stage'.[14] This 'breach' between the two communities was self-evident in 'Hindu intransigence and lack of perception of basic Muslim ideals and hopes'.[15] Of course, the Aga Khan himself 'did' all he 'could to prevent the breach long widened'.[16]

In the end, disillusioned with the Congress and the Hindu leadership, the Aga Khan turned to his Muslim colleagues, particularly to Nawab Mohsen-ul-Mulk, who, he thought, 'had succeeded Sir Syed Ahmad as a Muslim leader.'[17] He trusted him. He believed that Mohsen-ul-Mulk 'was moderate and realistic, and was not at all antagonistic either to Congress or Hindus in general'. Indeed, he felt that,

> If there had been give-and-take in what were then quite minor matters [Mohsen-ul-Mulk] was willing to join forces with Congress. In such an atmosphere—assisted by the fact that there was a joint electorate and joint representation—a political alliance between the two communities was possible.[18]

But the Congress was not interested or ready for any such alliance. It remained indifferent to Muslims' 'legitimate claims and aspirations.'[19] The Aga Khan was truly frustrated. 'Our hope,' he deplored, 'was dashed again and again.'[20] Thus, as he put it:

> ... by 1906 Mohsen-ul-Mulk and I, in common with other Muslim leaders had come to the conclusion that our only hope lay along the lines of independent organization and action, and that we must secure independent political recognition from the British as *a nation within a nation*.[21]

This line of thinking clearly suggested that, as a 'representative' of the Muslims, the Aga Khan saw the Indian situation as Syed Ahmad Khan did before him, and 'prioritized the minority Muslim community over Indian national identity', indeed as a kind of 'response to the pressures exerted on minority groups by nationalism and its colonial legacy'.[22] He did not see the Muslims 'as merely a religious community' but, more importantly, as 'a national entity with the right to be represented by their own leaders.'[23] The experience of the working of 1892 reforms of the legislative council further showed him, clearly and convincingly, that 'there was no hope of a fair deal' for the Muslims 'within the fold of the Congress Party or in alliance with it'.[24] In this sense, the Aga Khan, given his first-hand, harsh exposure and experience of Indian politics, was left with no option but to follow 'in the footsteps' of Syed Ahmad Khan who 'campaigned for Muslim unity and progress' in its own right and for its own sake.[25]

Mindful of the inadequacy of the Indian Councils Act of 1892, however, John Morley, the Secretary of State for India, speaking in the British Parliament on 20 July 1906, announced that the government intended to advance constitutional reforms in India. It was prepared to increase the number of seats for the Legislative Council, with enhanced powers, and, above all, to extend 'the representative element' through elections. This reinforcement of the elective principle, indeed the setting up of an electoral system with its inherent bias in favour of the Hindu majority community, shook the Muslims like it had never before, not since the advent of British rule in India. Muslim leaders, particularly Nawab Mohsen-ul-Mulk and the Aga Khan, were greatly alarmed. They decided to act and act fast. A deputation led by the Aga Khan and comprising 35 nobles, ministers of various states, landowners, lawyers, and other influentials representing the Muslim elite of the time called upon the Viceroy, Lord Minto, in Simla on 1 October 1906, to apprise him of the Muslim position and perspective on these far-reaching changes. Most of the members of the deputation were closely associated with the Aligarh Movement through the All-India Muhammadan Educational Conference, founded by Syed Ahmad Khan. The Simla Deputation, as it came to be known later, submitted a memorial highlighting Muslim interests and demands, demanding not only 'the right of vote under [a] separate electoral system' but, more importantly, representation in the Legislative Council in excess of their population 'commensurate … [with] the position which they occupied in India a little more than a hundred years ago, and of which the traditions have naturally not faded from their minds.'[26] As the Aga Khan explained in his *Memoirs*:

> … we boldly asked the Viceroy to look facts in the face; we asked that the Muslims of India should not be regarded as a mere minority, but as *a nation within a nation* whose rights and obligations should be guaranteed by statute.
>
> … we asked for the establishment of a principle, a principle which would have to be embodied in any legislation as a consequence of these proposals for reform. We asked for adequate and separate representation for Muslims both on local bodies and on the legislative councils, we asked that this representation be secured by a separate communal franchise and electoral roll. In short, we Muslims should have the right of electing our own representatives on it.[27]

Although the Aga Khan was satisfied that 'our principle' of 'separate representation' was 'accepted' by the Viceroy,[28] its achievement went through many difficult stages. It was after a lot of concerted efforts by a host of Muslim leaders, especially Syed Ameer Ali in London and his London Muslim League, that the rules made under the Indian Councils Act of 1909 granted 'separate electorates' to the Muslims. However, it needs to be stressed here that this was not a special or unique concession to the Muslim minority. Its beneficiaries included other minority communities as well, such as Anglo-Indians, Indian Christians, Europeans, Sikhs, etc. Nonetheless, there was no denying that the Aga Khan and his deputation 'had established a major political principle' for the Muslims and 'its ... practice was to be a permanent feature of all constitutional developments in India henceforward.'[29] In the process, of course, 'Muslim political consciousness' developed, 'matured and strengthened steadily'.[30] Abdul Hamid dubbed it 'the early stirring of a national consciousness'.[31]

The Aga Khan firmly believed that, 'since we [the Muslims] had obtained separate electorate recognition, we must have a political organization too to make that separate representation effective.'[32] Soon, he was able to influence quite a few Muslim leaders, including some leaders associated with the earlier Simla Deputation. They met in Dacca (Dhaka) on 30 December 1906, after the conclusion of the annual session of the Muhammadan Educational Conference, and, after some thought and deliberations, decided to launch a Muslim political party. The meeting, chaired by Nawab Viqar-ul-Mulk and attended by delegates from different parts of India representing landed, commercial, and professional classes and groups, founded the All-India Muslim League, 'a logical culmination of the developments that had begun with the introduction of "representative" institutions in India.'[33]

The Aga Khan was elected the first President of the Muslim League (though he himself was unable to attend the meeting in Dacca), with Nawab Mohsen-ul-Mulk and Nawab Viqar-ul-Mulk as its Joint Secretaries. The Aga Khan remained President till his resignation in 1912. The Central Office of the League was set up at Aligarh (later, moved to Lucknow). The primary aim and objective of the League was to 'protect and advance the political rights and interests of the Muslims of India, and to respectfully represent their needs and aspirations to the government.'[34] This political development clearly suggested that the 'idea of a separate Muslim identity was built into the very rise of the new Muslim elite'[35] in the colonial era. This was a development that was not understood or appreciated well by the writers on the subject in general, and Indian writers in particular, prompting Jaswant Singh more recently to ask, 'why Partition [of India] and how are "Muslims a separate nation?"'[36] They need to delve deeper into the process of identity formation of the Muslims.[37]

The rising 'new Muslim elite', of course, looked up to the Aga Khan to lead them in the fast-changing political situation in the country, especially after the 1909 Act, granting them separate electorates and thus more space and scope for political activities to suit their particular interests. The separate electorates made them somewhat secure in the political system too, and, to boost their morale further, they now had their own political party—the Muslim League.

But, to their dismay, the Aga Khan was not prepared to play an active role in politics. He still wanted to keep it low and loyal to the British, lest they got offended and caused harm to Muslim interests. 'Caution verging on timidity', as one writer termed it,[38] was not only due to his own temperament and training, but also, to an extent, due to Syed Ahmad Khan's teachings and practice. He had urged the Muslims to stay away from active politics. But the Aga Khan did not realise that the objective conditions of India had radically changed since then. They were absolutely different now. Given the upsetting experience of the Partition of Bengal in 1911 and the British hostility towards the Ottoman Empire, during the Balkan Wars in 1912–13 in particular, the Muslims could no longer afford to remain loyal to the British rulers. They had to meet the new challenges and indeed take risks. One of these challenges was the rising tide of 'nationalism' and the associated demand for self-government. With the growing strength of the educated, urban middle classes in the Muslim League demanding 'self-government suitable to India', the leadership was left with no option but to pursue a different course. It had to be politically active and involved. The Aga Khan could not agree and adjust his position accordingly. Indeed, he decided to opt out and resigned from the presidentship of the Muslim League. In principle, he acknowledged, he had nothing against constitutional advance; but if the League, he warned, fell for 'a mere hasty impulse to jump at the apple when only the blossoming stage was over, then the day that witnessed the formulation of the ideal will be a very unfortunate one in the annals of their country.'[39] He did not want to deal with this 'formulation' or take responsibility for it. He wanted to be free from this burden of responsibility. As he wrote in his letter of resignation, 'Resignation frees me from that necessarily judicial character that attaches to presidency.'[40]

This withdrawal from the League politics did not mean that the Aga Khan was no more interested in political life and processes of India. In fact, this withdrawal, this stepping down, provided him an ideal opportunity to reflect upon the situation afresh and suggest a way out for India in this evolutionary phase of the British rule, particularly with regard to the Muslims' predicament. He wrote a masterpiece on Indian politics, *India in Transition: A Study in Political Evolution*, in 1918. He had already published a number of thought-provoking works, such as *Muslim Education in India* (1902), The *True Purpose of Education* (1904), *A Bill of Muslim Rights* (1906), *Some Thoughts on Indian Discontent* (1907), *Advice to the Muslim League*, and *The Problems of Minorities in India* (1909). All these publications clearly projected him 'as a leader among Muslims' and a call for 'their organization and unification in predominantly Hindu India.'[41] However, what distinguished *India in Transition* from his earlier works was his effort to present a wholesome roadmap for a democratic, modern India, through a federal compact for the benefit of all its people and its communal groups, especially the Muslim community. Some of the more relevant passages suggested:

> ... the Government of India needs radical change; that the time has come when it should be no more a government of fiat, however excellent that fiat, but an essentially modern State based on the cooperation of every community and of the Government, by giving to the people themselves the right to direct policy.
>
> ... for India, with her vast population, her varied provinces and races, her many sectarian differences (brought to the surface by the present search for the lines of constitutional advance), a unilateral form of government is impossible.
>
> ... the problem of a free India within the British Empire can only be solved by federalism and by facing this essential fact.[42]

Outlining his idea of a federal polity for India, he continued:

> ... for some years to come, each Indian province in the initial
> stages of federalism, must have a constitution that provides, on
> the one hand, for an independent and strong executive, responsible
> to the Viceroy and the Secretary of State for tenure of office and
> appointment; and, on the other hand, for elective assemblies to
> control finance and legislation. Thus will be built up [sic] the
> future of United States of India within the British Empire. This
> system, leaving the component members of the federation full
> local autonomy, will best conform to the varied needs of the great
> peninsula and to the facts of her evolution, and can most readily
> be adjusted to local conditions.[43]

However, the federal objective, the Aga Khan emphasised, must
take into account the communal make up and its representation in
politics, for 'it has a part to play in the life of the nation ...'.[44] There
was no denying it. As he elaborated it at some length:

> ... I maintain that communal representation should be accepted
> throughout. It must not be forgotten that the various races and
> regions of India each have a more or less complex social system of
> their own to which they attach great importance, that such matters
> as marriage and divorce, the rites and ceremonies of family or
> communal life, are settled and arranged by communal leaders
> on the basis of the sacred writings, traditions, and sometimes the
> environment of their peoples. This communal bond varies no
> doubt, in degree; frequently it is highly organized and powerful,
> but sometimes at the other end of the scale it is only held together
> like sand. Still, in all cases, it has a part to play in the life of the
> nation, and if the autonomy to be built up in India is to be a
> natural evolution it must take account of the internal and sectional
> governing methods which the congeries of India have historically
> developed.[45]

It was precisely because of this differentiation of communal groups,
races, and regions of India that, in the end, the Aga Khan felt
inclined to recommend the Switzerland model as an ideal type of
system of government for India. As he explained it:

One of the most successfully governed countries of the world, Switzerland, where you find the ideal combination of liberty and order, is ruled by small, freely elected parliaments over cantons of such compact dimensions that each citizen is a real participant in the affairs of the state. This illustration is especially important because Switzerland, on a small scale, like India, on a large one, consists of different nationalities grouped by political union.[46]

Ironically, two decades later, in October 1943, it was the British Secretary of State, L. S. Amery, claiming that 'the Swiss constitutional system might have a better chance of succeeding in an Indian province than the British.'[47] Amery even admitted that 'We should jettison the idea that ... a government [in India] can be established on conventional British parliamentary lines.'[48] But, by then, it was too late and irrelevant. The British had lost the will and the power to present any solution to the communal problem in India. They, indeed, were on their way out.

Apart from politics and political plans, one of the major concerns of the Aga Khan during this time was the uplifting of an educational project launched by Syed Ahmad Khan. He aimed to raise the status of Aligarh College to the status of a full-fledged university, and make it an institution of higher education and learning for all the Muslims of India. His inspiration, of course, came from his meeting with Syed Ahmad Khan at the College years ago. As he described the encounter:

> ... I met Sir Syed Ahmad and Nawab Mohsen-ul-Mulk. This was the origin of what was for many years one of the crucial concerns of my life—my interest in the extension and improvement of Muslim higher education, and especially the College and University at Aligarh.[49]

The Aga Khan had worked hard at it for a number of years, especially after the Muslim League session in Delhi in 1910, as 'a sort of one-man "ginger" on behalf of the project', as he himself put it.[50] The establishment of this university was a daunting task, given 'opposition' from 'that powerful British element whose argument was that a Muslim university would be undesirable and that its tendencies and teachings would be narrowly sectarian and particularist.'[51] But, fortuitously, due to the Aga Khan's 'support in high places', from Viceroy Lord Hardinge to members of the Viceroy's Executive Council like Sir Harcourt Butler, who understood 'Muslim position, and were aware of the fundamental differences in the social, cultural, and spiritual background of Muslim and Hindu',[52] some of this opposition could be checked. However, a case still had to be made that, in demanding a Muslim university, there was 'no narrow sectarian purpose in view'.[53] The Aga Khan, thus, prudently proposed that 'Sanskrit should be taught, and with it the history and evolution of Hindu civilization, religion, and philosophy, in order that our people should be able better to understand their neighbours.'[54] The Aga Khan's primary concern was that:

> If we [the Muslims] were to advance down the road towards independence and self-government—however distant that goal might seem—we must, as a community, possess the knowledge and the intellectual equipment to cope with the political responsibilities to which we were beginning to aspire.[55]

But then converting a college into a larger university also required funds, and plenty of them. The Aga Khan led by example. He became the head of a Central Foundation Committee and contributed '100,000 rupees, which was quite a sum in those days'. In 1911, he went on a whirlwind tour of India, along with Maulana Shaukat Ali, 'to great Muslim leaders, to the poor and to the rich, to princes and to peasants' asking for donations and indeed collecting 'more than three million rupees'.[56] The contributions came from far-off places. By 31 October 1911, the North-West Frontier Province (now Khyber Pakhtunkhwa), Baluchistan (Balochistan), Bengal, Bihar, Punjab, Sind (Sindh), and Bombay (Mumbai) had contributed significant amounts. The UP (United Provinces), including Rampur State, contributed the most—5,49,962 rupees. The UP Muslims naturally had the 'most to gain from the establishment of a Muslim university in their province'.[57] Such was the enthusiastic support of the Muslim masses for the proposed university. In the 1912 Coronation Durbar held in Delhi, apart from other important developments—such as shifting of the Indian capital from Calcutta (Kolkata) to Delhi, annulment of the partition of Bengal (announced by the Viceroy in December 1911)—Aligarh College was granted 'the status of a university'.[58] The university eventually came into being in 1920, under the Aligarh Muslim University Act, 1920. Expressing his 'satisfaction' and indeed happiness and pride over its subsequent progress over the years, the Aga Khan reminiscences in his *Memoirs*:

> Now when all is said and done, when I look back on all that the Muslim University of Aligarh has stood for and achieved ... this is without doubt one of the facts of my life which I can record and contemplate with real and abiding satisfaction. I do not want only to stress its political consequences, momentous as these have been. Where else than in a Muslim university would it have been possible to establish and maintain, alongside and fully integrated with the libraries, the laboratories and all the facilities essential for a full understanding of our world and of our time, a true centre of Islamic faith and culture, in which can be expounded and practiced the principles of our religion, its universality and its real modernity, its essential reasonableness, its profound spirit of tolerance and charity and respect for other faiths? That I played my part in establishing such a centre is for me one of the happiest, most consoling, and most fortifying thoughts ....[59]

The Aga Khan, however, soon had to deal with the 'the principles of our religion' up front, with the convulsions of the Khilafat Movement launched by the Indian Muslims to save the Khilafat (caliphate) in the Ottoman Turkish Empire. The fate of the Turkish Empire agitated the minds of the Muslims. In 1912, the Balkan states, encouraged by the British and other European powers, had invaded the empire. To make the situation worse, the Turks sided with Germany during World War I, and thus after its defeat at the hands of 'Allied' powers, the end of the empire—home of the Ottoman Khilafat—was but a foregone conclusion. Turkey, the core of the empire, would be punished; it would lose its major territories, and the Khilafat would be lost, particularly with regard

to its control of the areas of Hijaz, Syria, Palestine, and Iraq with
the holy places of Islam.

In March 1919, a Khilafat Committee was formed in Bombay,
with Seth Jan Muhammad Chottani as its president and, in July
1919, it was decided to form the nation-wide All-India Khilafat
Committee with branches all over the country to monitor and
oversee the worrying developments. In November 1919, the first
session of this committee was held, which called upon the British
to recognise and respect the religious authority of the Ottoman
Turkish Khalifa, that is the Caliph of Islam, and to treat Turkey
fairly in the armistice ending the war. The British, of course, were
not bothered by their entreaties or protests, as reflected in the
terms of the Treaty of Sevres, made public in May 1920. The treaty
dismembered the Ottoman Empire and forced Turkey to surrender
all its claims and interests, particularly in Arab lands. In August
1920, Turkey was left with no option but to sign the treaty.

Indian Muslims had already decided to launch a massive
movement and found a ready ally in the Congress, now led by
Mohandas Karamchand Gandhi, who had returned to India from
South Africa in 1915, and had established himself as its undisputed
leader—the 'Mahatma'. Leading a predominantly Hindu party,
Gandhi 'shrewdly seized' the opportunity[60] to win over the support
of the Muslims in his struggle against the British, especially after
the passage of the oppressive Rowlatt Act of 1919 and after the
brutal massacre at Jallianwala Bagh in Amritsar in April 1919,
leaving hundreds dead and thousands injured. The result of this
coming together was a formidable Hindu–Muslim alliance led by
Gandhi and the two Ali Brothers, Maulana Mohamed Ali and
Maulana Shaukat Ali, and a host of Muslim political and religious
leaders from all over India. It was armed with the 'non-cooperation'
methods, particularly the triple boycott of law courts, schools, and
legislatures, to advance the dual cause, both of the Khilafat and the
'Swaraj' (independence).

However, the Aga Khan and several prominent Muslim leaders
(including Syed Ameer Ali, Allama Muhammad Iqbal, and Quaid-
i-Azam Mohammad Ali Jinnah), refused to become part of the
agitational politics in spite of being committed and ready to save

the Khilafat. They preferred negotiations with the British to try to persuade them to appreciate and accept Muslim concerns. This was not an easy option, of course. There was a heavy price to pay for it. There was the threat of being isolated, of being cut off from mainstream Muslim politics, indeed from the Muslim leadership as a whole. As the Aga Khan explained this outcome:

> I found myself in a distressing difference of opinion with the majority of my Muslim brethren in India over our attitude to this conflict—a difference of opinion which, I am sorry to say, disrupted for some time to come the hitherto close and intimate associations, in thought and action, which had subsisted between myself and other Muslim leaders in India.[61]

He was, of course, convinced that 'Muslim concerns were profound and historic' and 'Turkey ... [being] the sole surviving independent Muslim nation; with all its shortcomings ... was a visible and enduring reminder of the temporal greatness of Islam's achievements.'[62] As for 'Muslim concerns', he elaborated further:

> What do the Muslims want? What do we plead for? Neither they nor we ask for any new status for Turkey. We consider it, however, our duty to urge, for the fair name of England, nay of the British Empire, that the pledge the Prime Minister in the name of England gave to the world, and in particular, to the world of Islam, should be maintained; and that the Turkish sovereign, as the Caliph of the vast Sunni congregation, should be left in absolute possession of Constantinople, Thrace, and Asia Minor stretching from the north of Syria proper along the Aegean coast to the Black Sea—a region predominantly Turkish in race. It would in our opinion be a cruel act of injustice to wrench any portion of this tract from Turkish sovereignty to satisfy the ambitions of any other people.[63]

Thus, to help uphold 'Turkish sovereignty', the Aga Khan generously contributed money to Turkey's 'war loans', and indeed 'donated a handsome amount' of 2,000 pounds. He also 'purchased bonds worth 25,000 rupees and invested another 90,000 rupees in Turkish bonds.'[64] More importantly, he kept regular contact with the British authorities to 'help obtain leniency for Turkey'.[65]

In this sense, his 'value to both sides of friendship between Great Britain and the Islamic world was of crucial importance.'[66] This is how his role was meant to be. However, the Aga Khan did not hesitate to warn the British authorities to do the right thing, for their own good. As he warned Edwin Montagu, then Secretary of State for India:

> Do not make any mistake. If Turkish rule came to an end no one in India will blame the French or Italians, rightly or wrongly[,] English Christianity and bigotry will be held responsible and the doctrine that the Turk must even after 500 years go away because he is a Moslem and Asiatic from the sacred soil of Europe will never be forgotten.[67]

In 1921, the Aga Khan led a delegation of the Indian Muslims to London, and had two important meetings with British Prime Minister Lloyd George (openly hostile to the Turks), on 12 and 24 March. He also submitted a written memorandum on the subject. In one meeting, according to Mushir Husain Kidwai (who was one of the delegates), after the delegation had made its case, Lloyd George,

> asked bluntly: 'Now that the Greeks are in military possession who will turn them out from there?' Unable to restrain himself, the Aga Khan jumped up, wagged a finger at Lloyd George and said: 'Well, Mr Prime Minister, old though I am, I will go sword in hand and turn them out ....' Mr Lloyd George was thunderstruck: 'No, no, we cannot do that!' he murmured.[68]

On 29 April 1921, Montagu, however, wrote to the Aga Khan saying that,

> In the final settlement you will be able to see that, even if all your requests have not been granted, your religious sentiments have been respected, and that the undoubted claims of India to special consideration in helping to determine the peace with Turkey have been abundantly recognized in the provisions of the peace.[69]

In 1923, the Aga Khan himself was present in Lausanne, on the eve of the Lausanne conference, 'holding "a watching brief" for the Muslims of India.'[70] But still, all said and done, Turkey was cut down to size. In the process, the Khilafat could not be saved and suffered, ironically, at the hands of none other than Mustafa Kemal Ataturk, a Turkish army commander, hero of the Gallipoli Campaign, and founder of modern Turkey. Ataturk abolished the Khilafat in March 1924, after proclaiming the Republic of Turkey earlier on 29 October 1923, a day celebrated as a national holiday there ever since.

According to some writers, including Naeem Qureshi, the abolition of Khilafat was 'precipitated by an innocuous letter' from the Aga Khan (and Syed Ameer Ali) from London in November 1923 to the Turkish Prime Minister, Ismet Inonu, 'entreating that the Turks reconsider their decision with regard to the Caliph and maintain "the religious and moral solidarity of Islam" by re-establishing the powers of the Sunni caliphate—imamate.' The letter, of course, reflected his 'personal anxiety over the fate of the caliphate, but the nationalists, in the prevailing atmosphere of suspicion, took it as part of a big British conspiracy. Thus, the fate of the caliphate was sealed.'[71]

The year 1924 also 'marked the conclusion of a phase' of the Aga Khan's 'public life'.[72] He retired, as he put it, 'devoted almost exclusively' to his 'own personal and private life'.[73]

However, at the end of 1928, the Aga Khan returned to active politics to help the Muslim cause which had suffered a severe setback in the wake of the Khilafat fiasco, and promote the Muslim separatist political movement which, too, had been put on the backburner during this period. The Khilafat Movement itself had met a violent end through the Mappila rebellion (1921) in Malabar district in Madras (Chennai) and the Chauri Chaura incident in Gorakhpur district in the UP, in 1922, with the burning of a number of police constables to death. The Muslims had failed to achieve their main objective of saving the Khilafat in Turkey and the Hindu–Muslim alliance forged for the purpose had given way to bloody Hindu–Muslim riots and conflict between the two communities like never witnessed before. Hindus, particularly the

Hindu Mahasabha leaders, such as Dr B. S. Moonje, had nothing but contempt for Muslim demands, including separate electorates, and considered them to be communal demands and opposed to the spirit of 'nationalism'. The harsh terms of the Nehru Report of 1928, calling for 'mixed electorates throughout India' demonstrated this feeling of ill-will and bias on the part of the Hindu majority community. The Muslims were being denied their hard-earned space in the political system.

The Aga Khan thus convened a meeting of prominent Muslim leaders under the banner of the newly formed All-India Muslim Conference, in 1929, attracting not only the traditional elite, comprising landlords, nawabs, and knights, but also the old prominent khilafatists, such as Maulana Mohamed Ali, Shaukat Ali, Maulana Hasrat Mohani, Maulana Abdul Qadir Azad Subhani, and Maulana Shafi Daudi to find a way out. Even some of the modernists, including Mohammad Yaqub, Deputy Leader of Jinnah's Independent Party in the Legislative Assembly, joined the proceedings. In the Aga Khan's own estimate, it was 'a vast gathering representative of all shades of Muslim opinion', making him 'the parent of its important and lasting political decisions'.[74] Some of these decisions were as follows:

> In view of India's vast extent and its ethnological ... divisions, the only form of government suitable to Indian conditions is a federal system with complete autonomy and residuary powers vested in the constituent states.
>
> The right of Muslims to elect their representatives in the various Indian legislatures is now the law of the land, and Muslims cannot be deprived of that right without their consent.
>
> In the provinces in which Muslims constitute a minority they shall have a representation in no case less than that enjoyed by them under the existing law (a principle known as weightage).
>
> It is essential that Muslims shall have their due share in the central and provincial cabinets.[75]

The Aga Khan even went on to 'warn' his 'co-religionists and compatriots of the perils of being too easily taken in by Congress' protestations of undefined goodwill.'[76] We are united because 'we now had our code-book, and we did not intend to deviate from it.'[77] However, this unity and thus 'unanimity'[78] of views, if at all, was not of much help, for it was the unanimity of views among themselves, among the Muslims. The Congress and the Hindu-majority community led by it, and the now ascendant Hindu Mahasabha, did not even register them. They did not care. In fact, in March 1930, the Congress, led by Gandhi, launched its Civil Disobedience Movement, without bothering to take the Muslims into confidence, thus complicating the already precarious situation not only for the Muslims but also, more importantly, for the British government. The much trumpeted Simon Commission had not helped at all; it was rejected by both the Congress and the Jinnah faction of the Muslim League. The British were forced to take a new initiative on constitutional development to the satisfaction of all the parties concerned.

The British government thus called a conference of the heads of all political parties, rulers of the princely states, community leaders, and prominent individuals, in London, to draw up a constitution acceptable to all, ultimately leading to self-government and freedom for India. Jinnah, President of the Muslim League at that time, had already asked the British Prime Minister, Ramsay MacDonald, in his letter of 19 June 1929 to invite the 'representatives of India who would be in a position to deliver the goods', to sit in such a conference for the purpose of reaching a solution that will have 'the willing assent of the political India'.[79] The Round Table Conference, as it was so called, was inaugurated by King-Emperor George V on 12 November 1930. In all, 57 delegates, including 18 Muslims, attended the conference. The Muslim representatives included stalwarts such as Jinnah, Mohamed Ali, and Mian Muhammad Shafi, among others, and were led by the Aga Khan who, indeed, deemed it 'an honour to be chosen to lead so notably a body of men including personalities of the calibre of Mr M. A. Jinnah, later to be the creator of Pakistan and the Quaid-i-Azam ....'[80] As for the conference itself, the Aga Khan saw it as

a remarkable assemblage of men and women of widely differing background and outlook, all genuinely anxious to discover a peaceful and honourable path to the independence and self-government which had explicitly been proclaimed to be the objective of Britain's rule in India.[81]

The conference, technically, had no fixed agenda or 'any definite scheme' to pursue.[82] On the other hand, there were, as the Aga Khan perceptively observed, 'deep and difficult rifts of sentiments and of outlook whose effect was bound to be felt from the outset.'[83] The major rifts, of course, were reflected in Hindu and Muslim positions. While the Hindus promoted

> the idea of a strong central government and the establishment of an immediate democracy, conceived solely in terms of numbers, in which religious differences counted as much and as nothing more, Muslim opinion had crystallized steadily in favour of a distribution of powers from the centre to virtually self-governing and autonomous provincial governments.[84]

The Aga Khan proposed a genuine All-India Federation, with statutory majorities in the Punjab and Bengal, a separate province of Sind, the introduction of a full-fledged constitutional government in the North-West Frontier Province and certain reserved seats for Muslims in the Army and the Civil Service as a way out of the impasse. But the Hindu leaders, under the influence of Mahasabha, refused to concede, much to the dismay of the Aga Khan. As he remarked later:

> I must formally record my solemn conviction that had my views been accepted then and there, later history would have taken a profoundly different course, and there would now [writing in the early 1950s] have long since been in existence a Federal Government of India, in which Muslims and Hindus would have been partners in the day-to-day administration of the country, politically satisfied, and contentedly working together for the benefit of India as a whole.[85]

But the 'continued stubbornness and intransigence of Hindu opinion',[86] even after the rulers of the princely states accepted the 'idea of federation', Indian federation, wrecked the conference beyond repair. It ceased to have 'much essential or practical importance'.[87] By the time the Second Round Table Conference convened, with Gandhi as 'the sole representative of the Congress' arriving in London in November 1931 after signing the Gandhi-Irwin Pact and suspension of the Civil Disobedience Movement, things had considerably deteriorated. The delegates had further hardened their positions, and Gandhi himself had no qualms about his indifferent, if not hostile, position either. As the Aga Khan recalled their meeting at the Ritz London one fateful night:

> Mahatmaji [Gandhi] turned to face me. 'I cannot in truth say,' he observed, 'that I have any feelings of paternal love for Muslims. But if you put the matter on grounds of political necessity, I am ready to discuss it in a co-operative spirit. I cannot indulge in any form of sentiment.'[88]

The Aga Khan described it as a 'cold douche',[89] with a 'chilly effect'[90] on his negotiations with Gandhi on behalf of the Muslim delegates. Indeed, difficult and 'certain basic points of difference: was India a nation or two nations?'[91] were involved. As the Aga Khan explained:

> Was Islam merely a religious minority, or were Muslims in those areas in which they were in a majority to have and to hold special political rights and responsibilities? The Congress attitude seemed to us doctrinaire and unrealistic. They held stubbornly to their one-nation theory, which we know to be historically insupportable. We maintained that before the coming of the British Raj the various regions of the Indian subcontinent had never been one country, that the Raj had created an artificial and transient unity, and that when the Raj went that unity could not be preserved and the diverse peoples, with their profound racial and religious differences, could not remain fellow-sleepers for all time, but that they would awake and go their separate ways. However close, therefore, we might come to agreement on points of detail, this ultimate disagreement on points of principle could not be bridged.[92]

While the Aga Khan's position reflected the 'separatist' creed enunciated by Syed Ahmad Khan and pursued by the Muslims ever since, through their separatist political movement, on the other end Gandhi, too, incredibly, was in a 'separatist' state of mind. He had made up his mind to separate the Muslims from the pursuit of the so-called 'Indian nationalism'. As he confided in Pattabhi Sitaramayya, his confidant and official Congress historian, upon his return from London, India must proceed 'only on the basis of Indian nationalism untainted by any communal considerations', clearly implying Muslim considerations.[93] This kind of thinking may have been helped by the ascendancy of the Mahasabha in politics at the time, with leaders like Pandit Madan Mohan Malaviya who was present at the Round Table Conference and influenced not only Gandhi but the entire spectrum of Hindu–Muslim relations between the delegates. But there still could be no denying that Gandhi's own attitude towards the Muslims and their interests was hardly positive or helpful. He had virtually taken the Muslims out of the equation. The result obviously was 'increased difficulty over the communal question'.[94] The Aga Khan could not have been more frustrated:

> As time went on the hair-splitting became finer and finer, the arguments more and more abstract: a nation could not hand over unspecified powers to its provinces; there was no constitutional way of putting a limit on the devices by which a majority could be turned into a minority—fascinating academic issues, but with little or no connection with the real facts and figures of Indian life.[95]

The Second Round Table Conference being inconclusive, the work of constitution-making for India had to wait for the third and final session in London, in November 1932. However, this session did not attract much attention. The number of invited delegates was less, with Jinnah, significantly, not invited and the Congress boycotting the session altogether. In addition, the agenda was quite limited. Primarily, the British government wanted 'to supplement the work so far accomplished' by 'filling in, in some detail, the more important gaps left by the discussions at two previous sessions.'[96] The only work accomplished and by the British government itself was its famous Communal Award, announced on 16 August 1932. One of the hallmarks of this award was, of course, the continuation of separate electorates for the Muslims, a long-standing aspect of the Muslim separatist political movement in India. Thus, while the Muslims were pleased on that account, the Hindus, led by the Congress and the Mahasabha, were up in arms, though the Congress eventually did not formally reject the award. But the award certainly had the effect of straining relations further between the two communities and their delegates in London.

The Third Round Table Conference remained in session for more than a month—from 17 November to 24 December 1932—without any significant advance on the constitutional front. Ultimately, the British government issued a White Paper in March 1933, based on the proceedings of all the three sessions of the conference and the Communal Award as modified by the Poona Pact of September 1932 (withdrawal of separate electorates for the Untouchable/Depressed/Scheduled Classes/Dalits—low caste Hindus) with regard to the method of elections and seats in the central legislature. A Joint Select Committee was formed to finalise its recommendations. The Aga Khan led the Muslim group. However, he could not help 'regret' the absence of Jinnah (not invited) in the committee and its deliberations:

> Looking back now on what happened in the course of this Committee, I think I regret Mr Jinnah's absence as much as that of Mahatmaji. It was, I think, extremely unfortunate that we Muslims did not insist on having Mr Jinnah with us ....[97]

But the die was cast. The joint memorandum failed to satisfy Indian aspirations be it the Muslims or the Hindus, compelling the British government to come up with its own scheme of things, the Government of India Act 1935. The Act merely went on to add constitutional woes to the communal situation of India.

The Aga Khan himself was convinced that the joint memorandum, as 'drafted by the delegation's brilliant official and myself', offered the best solution to India's constitutional problem, 'the penultimate step indeed before Dominion status'.[98] It provided 'the transfer to Indian hands of practically every power except certain final sections which would be reserved to the British Government.'[99] Indeed, he went on to claim: 'Had this constitution been fully established and an accepted and going concern, it would have been in due course a comparatively simple operation to lop off those reserve powers which in our draft marked the final stage of constitutional devolution.'[100]

But then, as pointed out earlier, the Hindus, and particularly the Congress, did not accept the memorandum and the British government too 'felt in their turn to reject it'.[101] The Aga Khan was distraught. He was not comfortable with the 1935 Act at all. In fact, he charged that 'it gave Britain too much influence (later he blamed it for taking India into the war).'[102] He even insisted that the Act 'ended all hopes of uniting India'.[103] In his opinion, as he stated in the course of evidence before the Joint Committee on the Government of India Act, the future constitutional plan should make India 'a congeries of great States' in a way 'akin to the American Federal Plan',[104] something that he had suggested earlier too, in 1918, in his *India in Transition*. But nobody paid any heed. Disillusioned, the Aga Khan called it 'parting of the ways',[105] and decided to end his 'own connection with Indian politics'.[106]

In 1934, he opted for 'a new line in public affairs'[107] and entered the international arena, already with an international presence, to represent India at the League of Nations (founded in January 1920 and dissolved in 1946, a forerunner of the present United Nations). He was an instant success, becoming the only Asian to be elected, in July 1937, as President of the League of Nations Assembly. However, his erstwhile Indian political party, the Muslim Conference, was lost. As Shafaat Ahmad Khan, one of its active leaders, lamented in November 1935:

> The Muslim Conference programme has been exhausted. It is empty of contents. I have been scratching my forehead for the last two years in a vain search for a new programme for Muslim India, but am like a blind man groping in the dark.[108]

By now, the Muslim League was beginning to emerge as the most representative party of the Muslims in India. Elected President in

1934, and upon his return to India from London in 1935, Jinnah had re-organised and rejuvenated it. Within a few years, it was a force to reckon with, indeed to the extent that the Aga Khan too went on to exclaim:

> The Muslim League, as it emerged under Jinnah's leadership, was an organization whose members were pledged to instant resistance— to the point of death—if Indian independence came about without full and proper safeguards for Muslim individuality or unity, or without due regard for the differences between Islamic culture, society, faith and civilization and their Hindu counterparts.[109]

But this importance of 'Muslim individuality or unity' was largely due to the Aga Khan's own relentless efforts and struggle of more than three decades to institutionalise the separate Muslim group life campaign of Syed Ahmad Khan through the Simla Deputation, the All-India Muslim League, and separate electorates for Muslims in the legislatures, as India embarked on its journey towards an elective, representative system of government in the early twentieth century. Indeed, following Syed Ahmad Khan, the Aga Khan consciously and carefully 'steered his efforts in the direction of separatist politics'[110] and helped the Muslim separatist political movement grow and eventually consolidate its gains under the leadership of his contemporary and close colleague, Syed Ameer Ali. This was a remarkable contribution to the separatist political movement at its nascent stage.

Notes

1. Aga Khan, *The Memoirs of Aga Khan: World Enough and Time*, with a Foreword by W. Somerset Maugham (London: Cassell and Company Ltd, 1954), 8. The Aga Khan's memoirs covered the entire spectrum of both his private and public life, and therefore it has been used in this chapter to highlight his political career in India.
2. Marc van Grondelle, *The Ismailis in the Colonial Era: Modernity, Empire and Islam* (New Delhi: Foundation Books, n.d.; first published London: C. Hurst & Co., 2009), 25.
3. Aga Khan, *The Memoirs*, xi.

4. Teena Purohit, *The Aga Khan Case: Religion and Identity in Colonial India* (Cumberland, US: Harvard University Press, 2012; Pro Quest ebrary [web], 24 July 2016), 18. The book focused on the case contested by the khojas challenging the Aga Khan's authority as a spiritual leader of the Ismailis.

5. Ibid., 111.

6. Grondelle, *The Ismailis*, 25.

7. Aga Khan, *The Memoirs*, 73.

8. Ibid., 74.

9. Ibid., 75.

10. Ibid.

11. Ibid.

12. Ibid.

13. Ibid.

14. Ibid.

15. Ibid.

16. Ibid.

17. Ibid., 76.

18. Ibid.

19. Ibid., 77.

20. Ibid., 76.

21. Ibid. (Italics added).

22. Purohit, *The Aga Khan Case*, 113.

23. Willi Frischauer, *The Aga Khans* (London: Bodley Head, 1970), 67.

24. Aga Khan, *The Memoirs*, 93.

25. Purohit, *The Aga Khan Case*, 111.

26. Desika Char, ed., *Readings in the Constitutional History of India, 1757–1947* (Delhi: Oxford University Press, 1983), 425–6.

27. Aga Khan, *The Memoirs*, 93. (Italics added).

28. Ibid., 94.

29. Ibid.

30. Ibid., 114.

31. Abdul Hamid, *Muslim Separatism in India: A Brief Survey, 1858–1947* (Lahore: Oxford University Press, 1967), 77.

32. Aga Khan, *The Memoirs*, 95.

33. M. Rafique Afzal, *A History of the All-India Muslim League, 1906–1947* (Karachi: Oxford University Press, 2013), 6.

34. Ibid.

35. Masood Ashraf Raja, *Constructing Pakistan: Foundational Texts and the Rise of Muslim National Identity, 1857–1947* (Karachi: Oxford University Press, 2010), xvii.

36. Jaswant Singh, *Jinnah: India—Partition—Independence* (New Delhi: Rupa & Co., 2009), 484.

37. See, Sikandar Hayat, *The Charismatic Leader: Quaid-i-Azam Mohammad Ali Jinnah and the Creation of Pakistan*, 2nd ed. (Karachi: Oxford University Press, 2014), 267–71.

38. Hamid, *Muslim Separatism*, 104.
39. Cited in Muhammad Noman, *Muslim India: Rise and Growth of the All India Muslim League* (Allahabad: Kitabistan, 1942), 135.
40. Hamid, *Muslim Separatism*, 105.
41. Grondelle, *The Ismailis*, 27.
42. Aga Khan, *India in Transition: A Study in Political Evolution* (Bennett, Coleman and Co., Ltd, 1918; Osmania University digital publication, 2005), 32, 37, 40.
43. Ibid., 41–2.
44. Ibid., 300.
45. Ibid.
46. Ibid., 36.
47. Nicholas Mansergh and E. W. R. Lumby, eds., *Constitutional Relations between Britain and India: The Transfer of Power, Vol. IV* (London: Her Majesty's Stationary Office, 1973), 402.
48. Ibid., 203.
49. Aga Khan, *The Memoirs*, 35.
50. Ibid., 114.
51. Ibid. But then there was opposition in Hindu quarters too. For instance, writers such as B. C. Paul 'identified the demand with a desire to establish a centre for the propagation of Pan-Islamism.' Hamid, *Muslim Separatism*, 94.
52. Aga Khan, *The Memoirs*, 115.
53. Ibid.
54. Ibid.
55. Ibid.
56. Ibid.
57. Francis Robinson, *Separatism Among Indian Muslims* (Cambridge: Cambridge University Press, 1974), 199.
58. Aga Khan, *The Memoirs*, 120. Razi Wasti was of the view that, 'The Muslim University at Aligarh could not have become a University without his complete, selfless and determined efforts.' S. Razi Wasti, 'The Role of the Aga Khan in the Muslim Freedom Struggle', in *Founding Fathers of Pakistan*, ed. Ahmad Hasan Dani (Lahore: Sang-e-Meel Publications, 1998), 145.
59. Aga Khan, *The Memoirs*, 116.
60. Ibid., 153.
61. Ibid., 128.
62. Ibid., 153.
63. Ibid., 154.
64. M. Naeem Qureshi, *Ottoman Turkey, Ataturk, and Muslim South Asia: Perspectives, Perceptions, and Responses* (Karachi: Oxford University Press, 2014), 34.
65. Ibid., 87.
66. Grondelle, *The Ismailis*, 37.

67. Ibid., 39.
68. Frischauer, *The Aga Khans*, 86–7.
69. Cited in S. M. Burke, *Landmarks of the Pakistan Movement* (Lahore: Research Society of Pakistan, 2001), 180.
70. Ibid., 181.
71. Qureshi, *Ottoman Turkey*, 65.
72. Aga Khan, *The Memoirs*, 168.
73. Ibid.
74. Ibid., 209.
75. Ibid.
76. Ibid.
77. Ibid., 210.
78. Ibid.
79. William Metz, *The Political Career of Mohammad Ali Jinnah*, ed. Roger D. Long (Karachi: Oxford University Press, 2010), 60.
80. Aga Khan, *The Memoirs*, 214.
81. Ibid., 213.
82. Ibid., 216.
83. Ibid., 215–16.
84. Ibid., 216.
85. Ibid., 218.
86. Ibid.
87. Ibid., 219.
88. Ibid., 227. Later, in 1940, almost a decade later, the Aga Khan 'reminded him of this', and Gandhi readily admitted that he 'completely recollected the episode', though he gave it an incredible spin. "I am very, very sorry,' he said, 'that you misunderstood that answer of mine. I didn't mean that I was aware of no emotional attachment, no feeling for the welfare of Muslims; I only meant that I was conscious of full blood *brotherhood*, yes, but not of the superiority that *fatherhood* would imply.' Ibid.
89. Ibid., 227.
90. Ibid.
91. Ibid., 228.
92. Ibid., 228–9.
93. B. Pattabhi Sitaramayya, *The History of the Indian National Congress, 1885–1935* (Madras: Working Committee of the Congress, 1935), 859.
94. Waheed Ahmad, *Road to Indian Freedom: The Formation of the Government of India Act 1935* (Lahore: The Caravan Book House, 1979), 127.
95. Aga Khan, *The Memoirs*, 229.
96. British Prime Minister's speech, cited in Ahmad, *Road to Indian Freedom*, 148.
97. Aga Khan, *The Memoirs*, 232.
98. Ibid.
99. Ibid., 233.

100. Ibid.
101. Ibid.
102. Frischauer, *The Aga Khans*, 116. Significantly, this criticism, sharp criticism, came from the so-called 'loyalist'. But then it showed the Aga Khan's loyalty to India over and above his loyalty to the British if a choice had to be made. He spoke for India. He was Indian representative, first and last.
103. Ibid.
104. Aga Khan, *The Memoirs*, 233.
105. Aga Khan's letter in the press, cited in Hamid, *Muslim Separatism*, 213.
106. Aga Khan, *The Memoirs*, 235.
107. Ibid.
108. Waheed Ahmad, ed., *Letters of Mian Fazl-i-Husain* (Lahore: Research Society of Pakistan, 1976), 470.
109. Aga Khan, *The Memoirs*, 295.
110. Purohit, *The Aga Khan Case*, 111–12.

4

Syed Ameer Ali and the Consolidation of the Muslim Separatist Political Movement in British India

Syed Ameer Ali, a contemporary of both Syed Ahmad Khan and the Aga Khan, played a brief but eventful role in Muslim politics of India. He was particularly helpful in securing for the Muslims the right of separate electorates—a critical constitutional safeguard for their rights and interests in the emerging Hindu-dominated system of government. The separate electorates remained the mainstay of Muslim politics and political development till the very end of British rule in India despite all the subsequent opposition from the Hindus and their representatives in the Indian National Congress and the Hindu Mahasabha.

Ameer Ali (1849–1928) also supported the All-India Muslim League and pursued its demands in Britain by establishing its London branch, London Muslim League, for the purpose. He, along with the Aga Khan, also worked for the Khilafat cause in Turkey, taking it to be the cause of the Indian Muslims. Indeed, he tried to do as much as he could to promote Muslim interests, demands, and concerns. In the process, he went on to consolidate the Muslim separatist political movement in India in an institutionalised, systematic way.

Ameer Ali was born on 6 April 1849 in Chinsurah, on the banks of Hooghly River in Bengal.[1] He traced his 'descent' from the Holy Prophet Muhammad [PBUH] through his daughter Hazrat Fatima [RA], as Syed, and claimed that his ancestors had moved to India and settled in a township in Oudh, Mohan, 'a prosperous township'.[2] His father, Saadat Ali, by his account, was 'a first class Arabic and Persian scholar' and towards the end of his life 'was engaged on a history of the [Holy] Prophet [PBUH]'.[3] According to him, they 'were not rich' but lived 'in comfortable circumstances'.[4]

Ameer Ali went on to attend Hooghly College and was one of the first Muslim graduates; he pursued his Master's degree in History, followed by a degree in law (LLB) which helped him win a government scholarship to go to London for his Bar-at-Law. He was called to the Bar on 27 January 1873.[5]

Upon his return to India, Ameer Ali got himself enrolled as an Advocate of the High Court of Calcutta (Kolkata), and started his practice primarily 'as an expert in Muslim law',[6] given his command over Arabic and Persian, having been tutored early in life by his scholarly father. This expertise even got him 'a part-time lectureship in Muhammadan Law' at the University of Calcutta.[7] However, he soon abandoned private practice, as, in 1877, he was 'persuaded' by the government 'to accept the permanent position of presidency magistrate',[8] at a hefty salary. In 1879, appreciating his hard work and merit, he was 'promoted to the [position] of officiating chief presidency Calcutta'.[9] In 1890, he was appointed judge of the Bengal High Court, the second Muslim High Court judge in India, after Justice Syed Mahmood (Allahabad Court, North-Western Provinces), son of Syed Ahmad Khan, to hold this coveted post. He retired from service in 1904.

Ameer Ali decided to move to England and settle in London, 'perhaps in deference' to his English wife, Isabella Ida Konstan's wishes, whom he had married in 1884 and who wanted to go back home.[10] This decision, according to his biographer, Muhammad Yusuf Abbasi, 'was a fateful decision of his career'. Henceforth:

[He] was [cut] off from the main current of Muslim political life. Perhaps he could have filled the gap in the Muslim leadership created by the death of Sir Syed by assuming the responsibility of Muslim leadership ... but he missed this historic opportunity.[11]

There is no denying that Ameer Ali's stay in India may have impacted Muslim politics in that crucial phase of Muslim struggle in more ways than can be imagined, for he was a man of immense talent and abilities, particularly 'political'. He had a knack for politics. In fact, he was more political than Syed Ahmad Khan. He demanded and pursued an active, organised political role for the Muslims. This was evident all through his life, even during his service in the judiciary in India. His contributions from England, through his London Muslim League, particularly the achievement of separate electorates for the Muslims—a significant achievement—went a long way in securing Muslim interests and demands, in fact, consolidating the separatist political movement founded by his forerunner, Syed Ahmad Khan, and shaped and strengthened by his contemporary and colleague, the Aga Khan.

Ameer Ali and Syed Ahmad Khan, of course, knew each other well, and had met both in England and India. As Ameer Ali recorded in his memoirs, they 'had frequent opportunities of discussing ... the position of the Muslims ... and of their prospects in the future.'[12] But they disagreed on the approach. As he elaborated their respective approaches:

> Syed Ahmad Khan pinned his faith on English education and academic training. I admitted their importance but urged that unless as a community, their political training ran on parallel lines with that of their Hindu compatriots they were certain to be submerged in the rising tide of new nationalism. He would at first not admit the correctness of my forecast, but I believe the birth of the National Congress [Indian National Congress] opened his eyes.[13]

Ameer Ali saw politics and a proper political organisation as its vehicle to be the only way out for the Muslims in the wake of Hindu resurgence and the so-called 'new nationalism' in India. He appreciated, therefore, that, in the end, Syed Ahmad Khan 'realized the danger of confining the intelligence and activities of the Muslims to a purely academic education [Aligarh College], and of keeping them aloof from political training.'[14] Indeed, he moved to establish the Muslim Defence Association for the purpose but, alas, 'the ground that had been lost could never be regained'.[15]

Whether the ground was 'lost' or was ultimately 'regained' is debatable; depending upon the larger perspective on the Muslim predicament at that point in time, this comment needs to be taken with caution. There was a perceptible political rivalry between the two leaders, both trying to lead the Muslims in their own ways and from their own separate and unique constituencies (Syed Ahmad Khan in the United Provinces [UP] and Ameer Ali in Bengal) and, thus, at times, not so much in harmony and accord with each other. As Ameer Ali put it:

> In 1877 indeed when I founded the Central National Muhammadan Association we respectfully invited him to give us his valuable support, but he declined. Twelve years later, however, he established the 'Muhammadan Defence Association' which I looked upon as rather than [sic] an unfortunate move, and likely to be considered provocative. But I am anticipating ....[16]

The year 1877 marked Ameer Ali's formal entry into Muslim politics in India, primarily through this Central National Muhammadan Association, a national political organisation devoted exclusively to the cause of the Muslims. Earlier, he was politically active through his membership of the Bengal Legislative Council. Even when he 'chose to give up his official appointment as chief presidency Magistrate' in 1881, he continued to serve on the council.[17] The government was so pleased with his work and contributions that, after his term expired in 1883, the Viceroy Lord Ripon went one step further and appointed him member of the Imperial Legislative Council. Ameer Ali played a 'notable role in the Ilbert Bill controversy and in the passing of the Bengal Tenancy Act'.[18]

In order to understand Ameer Ali's role and relevance in politics better, it is imperative that we first describe the conditions of Bengal, his home base. His position and perspective on national politics in general and Muslim politics in particular was largely shaped and determined by his response to the developments in Bengal. This may also explain why his perspective was so different from that of Syed Ahmad Khan in its emphasis on politics and political life for the Muslims. As Abbasi stated the Bengal case perceptively and at some length:

> In 1878, Bengal, the main scene of Ameer Ali's activities, was in ferment, which represented the general unrest in India. The discontent was more marked in Bengal than anywhere else in the sub-continent. Bengali Hindu elite mostly belonging to upper class were the pioneers in political awakening. Despite their English education they were stirred to no small degree by [the] contemporary Hindu religious revivalist movement. The political trends in Bengal, though predominantly Hindu, were a sign of the changing political temper of the country .... The rise of Hindu capitalism was in marked contrast to the backward agricultural structure of the Muslim society, and added another dimension to the Hindu–Muslim clash ... the Hindu press had developed a powerful instrument of Hindu politics .... The Bengali Hindu newspapers were in the vanguard of political agitation and commanded the monopoly of circulation among the rising bourgeoisie whose interests they served boldly. Contemporary Muslim journalism in Bengal or elsewhere was no match to this formidable array of well-organized Hindu journalism.[19]

This Bengal 'ferment' was, of course, deep-rooted. Bengali Muslims were 'the first to suffer from the impact of British rule' in India.[20] Indeed, since the advent of the British in Bengal, they were 'subjected to a policy of systematic deprivation of power, position and lands', so well described by W. W. Hunter in his influential work, *The Indian Musalmans*, in 1871.[21] This is not to suggest that there were no problems for the Hindus. They were distressed too because of their own reasons which were quite distinct from those of the Muslims, and understandably so. They were the larger and better educated community, and were more demanding and, thus, frustrated. For instance, unlike the Muslims, they were keen on entering the all-powerful Indian Civil Service (ICS). They, therefore, agitated against Viceroy Lord Lytton's restrictions on recruitment of Indians in the service. Abbasi thus compared the attitude of the two communities:

Where did the Muslims stand in the general discontent and how far did the Civil Service Agitation secure their interests? It is not difficult to determine that till then Muslims were too backward in English education, to make the Civil Service Agitation a serious issue ... the Muslim leaders gave their tacit or open support to the Civil Service Agitation, even though it was not in any way a real problem for the Muslims.[22]

The problem for the Muslims was indeed two-fold: educational and political. It required a 'concerted campaign for English-education; [*sic*] and giving an objective and positive direction to the Muslim politics vis-à-vis the Hindu politics and government policies.'[23] Politics, in turn, was conditioned largely by economic factors, especially in Bengal. The Muslim peasants (*ryots*) 'were persecuted by the Hindu landlords who had the English law-enforcing agencies on their side'[24], thanks to Lord Cornwallis' Permanent Settlement of Bengal with the zamindars in 1793. Indeed, the '*ryots* found themselves helpless in the stranglehold of the Hindu landlords who[,] by virtue of their wealth and influence[,] could tyrannize them with impunity.'[25] For instance, a local newspaper of the day, *The Pioneer Mail*, could not help but acknowledge that,

The Mahomedan *ryot* is more in debt of the village banker than his neighbours, the Mahomedan landholder is more impecunious and thriftless than a Hindu. The trades and to a great extent the professions are monopolised by Hindu, and in spite of the older Mahomedan families, they are gradually being pushed out of the public service by Hindu aspirants .... It is obviously a matter of great political as well as social concern.[26]

Thus the Muslims of Bengal had no choice other than 'channelising their economic discontent into self-reliant political action'[27] through a political organisation capable of aggregating and articulating their interests as a community as opposed to the more advanced Hindus who were already active under the banner of the Indian National Association, led by Surendranath Banerjee. While Ameer Ali quickly grasped the point, his erstwhile senior in Bengali politics, Nawab Abdul Latif, like Syed Ahmad Khan in the UP, kept on insisting 'on the pursuit of English education as the pre-requisite of any political activity' lest it may 'deflect the Muslims from the path of Education and Loyalty'.[28] No wonder, Abdul Latif 'failed to carry conviction in the milieu of 1878' and Syed Ahmad Khan, likewise, 'failed to make any deep impression on the Bengali Muslim',[29] leaving the political field to Ameer Ali to represent their interests and indeed, eventually, the entire Muslim community through his newly-founded National Muhammadan Association.

Still, it was not an open field for him. Both Abdul Latif and Syed Ahmad Khan continued to contest Ameer Ali's political stance and leadership. Abdul Latif represented the old guard, with influence and experience, having established 'the Mohammedan Literary Society into an influential nucleus of educated elite— mostly conservatives'.[30] He saw Ameer Ali and his Muhammadan Association as a threat to his leadership, even in the educational campaign. Thus, there emerged a kind of 'personal rivalry' between the two, to the extent that: 'Neither he nor his conservative and ultra-loyal friends had any sympathy for Anglicized Muslims like Ameer Ali who in their eyes had ceased to share the ways of life of the "mass of Muslim community".'[31] He even charged that Ameer Ali could not 'represent' the Muslims, 'for he was a Shia and they were Sunnis'.[32] The people in Bengal, of course, were 'above the sectarian issues' as they chose to follow Ameer Ali who 'represented the future', was 'a successful barrister [who] combined profound understanding of Islam with English Liberalism', and who was out to give 'a new direction to Muslim policies' and politics.[33] Syed Ahmad Khan's 'educational campaign' which 'had taken North India by storm failed to make any deep impression on the Bengali Muslim'.[34] Ameer Ali was able to carry the day with his Muhammadan Association.

The Association was launched on 12 May 1877, with Prince Mohammed Farrukh Shah, the great grandson of Tipu Sultan 'who wielded considerable influence among higher officials and the local Muslim community', as its first president.[35] Ameer Ali himself chose office of the secretary and remained in that position for more than twenty-five years, ensuring the growth and development of the Association into a representative organisation. The Association worked hard for the 'amelioration of the Muslims of India and until the turn of the century [nineteenth century] was the only de facto and de jure representative organization of Muslim India.'[36] That is, before the founding of the All-India Muslim League in 1906. Although the Association prided itself 'in being the sole Muslim political body', it was not against other communities, especially the larger Hindu community.[37] In fact, it 'eschewed public utterances and actions likely to strain Hindu-Muslim relations'.[38] The Association did not:

> overlook the fact that the welfare of the Mahomedans is intimately connected with the well-being of other races of India. It does not, therefore, exclude from its scope, the advocacy and furtherance of the public interests of the people of this country at large.[39]

The Association opened branches all over the country, in dozens, covering important cities of most of the provinces of India, and thus, pretty soon, it developed into an all-India organisation. The head office, of course, remained at Calcutta. On the educational front, it succeeded in securing some funding for Muslim students and providing them government jobs to whatever extent possible.[40] Some of these educated Muslims 'figured most prominently in the rank and file of the Association', transforming it truly into 'an organization of Muslim bourgeoisie'.[41] Impressed with its credentials, several like-minded Muslim societies operating at local/regional levels, such as Anjuman-i-Islam Amritsar, the Reform Association Lucknow, and the better-known Anjuman-i-Islam Bombay, responded favourably and offered their 'goodwill and cooperation' to it.[42]

Politically, the most significant contribution of the Association was its 'Memorial' of 1882, authored by Ameer Ali, and submitted to the Viceroy, Lord Ripon, embodying 'the various grievances of the Muslim community'.[43] Ripon had constituted a commission to suggest the reform of education and employment opportunities in the country. Ameer Ali, of course, expanded its scope 'to project Muslim demands and aspirations at a national level'.[44] The Memorial was debated and discussed thoroughly in the general meetings of the Association before it was 'approved for submission to the Government'.[45] In many ways, the Memorial was a 'monument' of Ameer Ali's 'political acumen and scholarly erudition'.[46]

It contended that 'Muslim education was not purely a matter of academic priorities but was complementary to Government policies.'[47] Highlighting 'the present impoverished condition' of the Muslims, it stressed that this condition 'deserves every commiseration. While every community has thrived and flourished under British rule, the Muhammadans alone have declined and decayed. Every day their position is becoming worse, and the call for urgent measures on their behalf more pressing.'[48] The Memorial explained at length that 'the Muslim decay was in no small degree a product of the political, economic and educational policies of the Government of India and should not be attributed alone to the Muslim apathy or intransigence.'[49] Indeed, it claimed that this 'myth' of blaming 'the Muslims entirely for their backwardness' had been 'propagated so assiduously by the British and Hindus' that some Muslim leaders too 'gave credence to it'.[50] The fact was that the 'Government policy was blatantly anti-Muslim', and the 'Muslims continued to be regarded with mistrust and suspicion'.[51] To make things more difficult for the Muslims, 'all avenues of public employment' were blocked by the Hindus despite the fact that they 'were not so backward in English education as they had been twenty years ago, but the progress in education did not bring about a corresponding change in their prospects in Government employment.'[52] Government employment was critical for the Muslims. The Hindus, Parsis, and other communities were 'not so hard-pressed' on this account since they 'could find avenues of fruitful employment in independent professions such as trade, law, and journalism'.[53]

The Memorial also touched upon the 'Urdu–Hindi controversy which had been raging with unabated bitterness' for the last decade or so, which had caused 'cultural tensions' between the Muslims and the Hindus, and which had become all the more pronounced with 'the spread of Hindu revivalism'.[54] In addition, the Memorial urged the need to improve the administration of Muslim law in the country, after the abolition of Qazi courts. The Muslims 'felt that their cases regarding marriages, divorces and dowry were not being decided in accordance with the Muslim Law' for want of Muslim officers in the judicial services.[55] This also accounted for difficulties in the execution of Muslim endowments. Indeed, the Memorial called for 'the appointment of a commission' to 'determine if the income from trusts, primarily endowed for religious education, could be utilized for the promotion of Muslim education in general under the present circumstances.'[56] In the end, the memorialists hoped that the government 'would not allow the Musalman race to continue in its present condition of decadence and depression—a condition which [they] believe, is alike injurious to the community as to the interests of the Empire.'[57]

In the ultimate analysis, as indicated above, the Memorial went way beyond the twin issues of education and employment for the Muslims. It not only 'crystallized their grievances' but also suggested 'the principles on which the Muslim rights were to be secured in future', and indeed 'epitomized the Muslim aspirations' and demands in the country.[58] Most of these demands found favour with the Education Commission, though their 'recommendations' to Viceroy Ripon 'fell short' of the expectations.[59] The Association and the memorialists 'still expected some useful results if "carried out fully by the Local Government".'[60] However, to their chagrin, the new Viceroy, Lord Dufferin, saw things differently, and not so sympathetically. He insisted that these recommendations 'were not of universal application' and that each province had its own 'particular conditions' and thus there was a need to map out a 'new policy' on education and employment for all, including the Muslims.[61] He even chided the memorialists, claiming that the Muslim case was built on 'various misconceptions'.[62] Despite this setback, Ameer Ali and his Association was 'highly successful in securing grants and scholarships for Muslim education and also Government service for them'.[63]

However, soon it was obvious that the Association, which was 'once a representative body, had now become ineffective and a powerful political organization was the crying need of the Muslims to fight for their existence.'[64] No one recognised or realised this better than Ameer Ali, the founder and architect of the Association himself. More so, he felt that 'Hindu nationalism is at present running in two channels', the Bharata Dharma Mandal, 'a purely indigenous growth, the outcome of genuine Hinduism' and the Indian National Congress, created by 'an Anglo-Indian official [A. O. Hume]—long retired from the public service' and the two, 'under stress of circumstances', might 'coalesce at any moment'.[65] He, like Syed Ahmad Khan and the Aga Khan before him, was particularly worried about the Congress in the sense that its 'juggernaut of majority' could well crush the Muslims 'out of the semblance of nationality'.[66] Indeed, he lamented that 'Whilst the non-official Anglo-Indian and the Hindu communities possess *powerful institutions* for safeguarding their rights and privileges and asserting their claims to consideration and fair play, the Indian Muslims are suffering acutely from political inanition.'[67]

Thus, Ameer Ali was pleased with the coming together of the Simla Deputation, led by the Aga Khan, and its 'approach' to the Viceroy, Lord Minto, on 1 October 1906, to highlight Muslim grievances and difficulties to the government, especially in view of the 'multiplicity of claims pressed upon its attention with unvarying persistency by more articulate sections of the Indian nationalities'.[68] Indeed, in his opinion:

> The resolve of the Muslims, after a lapse of twenty-three years [since 1882] again to approach the Viceroy personally points to a consciousness of the danger that lies before them, if they remain dormant and devoid of political life and activity much longer, of becoming entirely submerged under the rising tide of an exclusive [Hindu] nationalism.[69]

Ameer Ali was convinced that the Muslim demands 'were neither extravagant nor unfair to any other community', especially with regard to their 'representation in the Legislative Councils'.[70] He knew that 'further "enlargement" of the Councils and extension of the principle of election, with possibly a widening of their functions[,] are on the *tapis*.'[71] Therefore, he agreed that it was of 'vital importance to the Muslims to be properly represented in the Supreme and Provincial Councils.'[72] He also supported the deputationists in their demand that:

> the share accorded to the Muslim community should be commensurate, not merely with their numerical strength, but also with their political importance and the value of the contribution they make to the defence of the Empire; and ... the position which they occupied a hundred years ago, and of which the traditions have naturally not faded from their minds.[73]

Ameer Ali, however, emphasised that their 'eventual success' as a community required 'a central organisation' with 'association' in every province and district of the country. In his own words:

> To watch over the development of the Muslim people, to protect their interests, to see that their claims to equitable treatment are not neglected, to work loyally with the Government, and, in a spirit of fairness and compromise, with all other communities in the promotion of common welfare, they should have permanent and influential association in every district and in every province acting in conjunction with and under the guidance of a central organization located in some place like Aligarh, which focuses at this moment the intellectual life and political activity of the Muslims of India.[74]

Ameer Ali's plea for a central organisation of the Muslims found its fulfilment in the form of the All-India Muslim League founded on 30 December 1906 at Dacca (Dhaka). He not only welcomed it wholeheartedly, but to bring Muslims 'into touch with the leaders of thought in England' about its 'particular ideas', he hastened to form its London branch, the London Muslim League, which was formally launched on 6 May 1908.[75] He was fully settled in London by now. The London Muslim League went on to play a crucial role in securing for the Muslims the right of separate electorates in 1909, through the Morley–Minto reforms.

The reason why the London Muslim League and its president, Ameer Ali, had to work so hard for separate electorates was that, in spite of a favourable response to the demand by the Viceroy Minto in his meeting with the deputationists, the British government at home, led by Secretary of State John Morley, was not convinced. Morley insisted upon 'a new plan of a mixed electorate' which, of course, 'neither safeguarded Muslim rights nor satisfied the wishes of the Muslim community.'[76] Since this opposition came from London, it was but natural that the charge should be taken up by the London Muslim League. Indeed, Ameer Ali, ably supported by the Aga Khan, led the campaign relentlessly and, in the end, 'won this battle'.[77]

Ameer Ali, as K. K. Aziz summed up his range of efforts in this regard, 'sent articles to journals of opinion, wrote letters to the *Times* and other national newspapers, addressed meetings, and invited interested members of Parliament to meetings and get-togethers where they could be informed of the Muslim side of the question.'[78] In a lengthy letter to the *Times* on 9 January 1909, for instance, he argued:

> In asking for modifications [separate electorates] such as would probably safeguard their interests, they ask for no special privilege in derogation of just rights of any other class or community: they demand nothing more than that *their representation on the Councils and other representative bodies should under the projected reforms be real and not illusory, substantial and not nominal.* They are anxious to work in harmony with all sections of the population, but they will not consent to be dragged at the wheels of a majority along any course it may choose to take. This, if I interpret rightly the feelings and opinions of my people, is the position they have taken up.[79]

Ameer Ali opposed 'mixed electorates', especially on the following grounds. First, they would tend 'to divide Mahomedan votes' as the Hindu majority community would try 'to return to the electoral colleges and the Councils' only such Muslims that would be 'acceptable' to them.[80] Indeed, he claimed that 'not much exercise of imagination is required to understand the combination by which a Mahomedan unacceptable to the majority may be defeated.'[81] Secondly, the 'two communities', that is, the Muslims and Hindus, 'often differ greatly in material circumstances.'[82] The Muslim 'is less affluent than the Hindu' and thus he would not be able to compete in the system and his nominal representation would 'practicably' be 'of little value'.[83] Finally, all said and done, mixed electorate would not deliver anything to the Muslims. As he saw it:

> A Mahomedan brought in wholly or partly by Hindu votes would be pledged wholly or partly to the views of his political supporters; he would be used as a counterpoise to his Mahomedan colleague, and, to use a colloquialism, would often be putting a spoke in his wheel ... A nominee of the majority posing as a Mahomedan would often do more harm to Mussolman interests than if they were wholly unrepresented.[84]

Thus, he insisted, 'if Mahomedan representation is to have any meaning, it must be, as the Mahomedans urge adequate and substantial.'

Ameer Ali ended his letter with a subtle warning:

> The importance of a nation cannot always be adjudged on numerical considerations. Whatever may be the view regarding the historical and political position of the Mahomedans, to which the Government of India attaches some value, Mahomedan loyalty is an asset to the Empire which I venture to submit ought not to be lightly put aside.[85]

On 27 January 1909, Ameer Ali led a delegation of the London Muslim League to meet with Morley to convince him of the genuineness of the Muslim demand for separate electorates. In his introductory speech, he reiterated the position taken in his aforementioned letter to *The Times*, and went on to argue further that,

> in view of the fact that under these [proposed] reforms the privileges of the non-official members will be considerably extended, it is extremely important that our community should be represented in sufficient numbers to be able to exercise some weight, some influence on the Councils. My people will not be content with any representation which is less than adequate and substantial.[86]

He assured Morley that:

> I know the task you have undertaken is one of the most stupendous
> character which any Minister of the Crown in your position has
> undertaken, but our people feel sure that at this stage, which we
> consider to be the turning point in our national existence, the
> balance will be maintained fairly and equitably, and our interests
> will not be subordinated to that of any other community.[87]

The difficulty with Morley was that he was 'too enamoured of his
own scheme' to pay attention to the Muslim demand for separate
electorates.[88] In addition, and to complicate matters further, he was
afraid of 'Hindu annoyance'.[89] He did not want to upset them, the
majority community. Thus, only a day after he received Ameer Ali
and his delegation, he wrote to Minto, 'We have to take care that in
picking up the Musalman, we don't drop our Hindu parcels ....'[90]
However, in a speech in the House of Lords, on 23 May 1909, he
'gave his [word] that all Muslim demands would be met' including
separate electorates, only to back out in a while, writing to Minto
again on 6 August 1909 that the British Government never gave any
'pledge' to the Muslims.[91] He reiterated the government position in
another letter a week later, on 12 August 1909, that any departure
from mixed electorates would provoke 'reproach and dissatisfaction
among the Hindus'.[92] In November 1909, however, much to the
relief of the Muslims and Ameer Ali, the Aga Khan, and other
Muslim leaders involved, such as Syed Hasan Bilgrami, the 'Rules
and Regulations governing Muslim representation were published
and lo! they carried a scheme of (separate) electorates which the
Muslims had been demanding since the Simla Deputation' of
1906.[93] As K. K. Aziz described Ameer Ali's singular achievement:

> Almost single-handed he [Ameer Ali] had disarmed a stubborn
> and powerful Secretary of State who did not conceal his dislike of
> Muslim leaders. Without any strong organization behind him—
> the London Muslim League was small and still in its fancy—he
> forced the British Government to retreat on a vital issue. The All-
> India Muslim League loyally supported him, the Aga Khan put
> all his influence at [his] disposal, and his English friends carried

his messages to quarters beyond his own reach. His persistent hammering at the Whitehall doors, his closely-argued letters to *The Times*, his deputation to the India Office, his speeches at the London Muslim League, his conversations amid private circle of friends—all these added up to a formidable campaign. He knew that this was the first sure step leading to a secure future which the Indian Muslims must take …. The Muslims must have their own representatives, chosen by their own votes, sitting in their own seats, safeguarding their own interests. If this was separation, let it be so.[94]

This 'separation' was a major boost to the Muslim separatist political movement in India. Immensely pleased with his work, and the ultimate achievement of separate electorates, the All-India Muslim League invited Ameer Ali to preside its third annual session in Delhi in January 1910. However, Ameer Ali could not go to India because of his engagement with the Judicial Committee of the Privy Council. But he did send a message, which was read out by Mian Muhammad Shafi. In his address, Ameer Ali touched upon a host of issues and concerns—political, economic, and developmental—but, most importantly, spoke of the 'whole-hearted support to the Central League' and hoped that 'the solidarity that has existed so long will always be maintained … [and] that there should be absolute loyalty on all sides and the subordination of individual interests to the commonweal.'[95]

However, Ameer Ali himself could not maintain that 'loyalty' for long. He severed his connection with the All-India Muslim League in 1913, and for several reasons. For one, 'with the repeal of the partition of Bengal in December 1911 and the unhelpful British attitude towards Turkey in the Turco-Italian war the good old fabric of Muslim loyalty was beginning to crumble.'[96] Maulana Mohamed Ali, a Pan-Islamic leader, led the charge against the British in a defiant mood. More importantly, Mohammad Ali Jinnah's entry into the Muslim League, with the demand of 'self-government suitable to India', made the situation all the more precarious for him. Ameer Ali, like the Aga Khan, did not feel comfortable with this 'new policy' as he saw it 'rather "advanced", and, in part, even extremist'.[97] The result was that, in October 1913, after 'finding himself unable to work under the conditions now demanded', he resigned from the presidentship of the London Muslim League and also ceased to be an active representative of the All-India Muslim League in London. He might still have been associated with the Muslim League, but only in 'his personal capacity' and in a limited sense.[98] His 'relations' with that organisation 'were never the same again'.[99] As far as the London Muslim League and his association with it is concerned, we have no idea. In fact, after his resignation, 'we hear no more of the London body; we do not even know at what point it ceased to exist'.[100]

While Ameer Ali took a break from the Muslim League, his interest in the affairs of Muslims in general and that of India in particular never ended. He continued to be interested and involved. In fact, he 'pleaded the cause of Muslims when he found their interests unrepresented' at any point in time.[101] The Turco-Italian war and the 'unprovoked' attack on Tripoli had moved him to write 'an angry letter' to The Times, asserting that Italy had no right 'to provoke a war of creeds and races by spoliation of Turkey'.[102] In order to help the affected Muslims, he went on to establish the 'Red Crescent Society'. The British Red Cross was not willing or prepared to help 'the sick and distressed Turkish soldiers and civilians', especially the 'sick, the wounded, and starving'.[103] As president of the Red Crescent Society, Ameer Ali was 'in charge of constituting the units and dispatching relief' which was collected from its three branches in India.[104] In this endeavour, he was, of course, helped by 'the generosity' of his old colleague, the Aga Khan.[105] The Red Crescent Society continued to alleviate the 'misery, suffering and distress' of the Indian troops during World War I, based on the recommendations of their regimental officers.[106]

During the war, especially towards its end, 'the Turkish problem arose in its full gravity and significance', forcing Ameer Ali to stand up 'as the defender of his faith and the protector of Turkey'.[107] He wrote a host of articles in the press, making 'a case for a sober and objective study of the problem, for shedding old animosities and the bitter memories of the war' and, more importantly, 'for trying to understand the importance of the Khilafat [Caliphate] for the world of Islam, and for doing justice to Turkey.'[108] He was deeply aware of British Prime Minister Lloyd George's 'anti-Turk animus and general British hostility to Turkey'.[109] This hostile policy, 'in a real and personal sense', was the policy of Lloyd George who had 'an unbounded zeal for the Greek cause and a deep hatred for the Turk'.[110] Thus, in June 1919, together with the Aga Khan, he wrote to *The Times* suggesting 'the terms on which peace with Turkey should be made' along with the proviso that the Khalifa (Caliph) should be left 'in absolute possession' of Constantinople, Thrace, and Asia Minor—a region that Lloyd George himself had admitted was 'predominantly Turkish in race'.[111] In August 1919, writing to *The Times* again, both the leaders reiterated their position. In November 1920, Ameer Ali signed a petition to the Assembly of the League of Nations demanding 'a review' of the Treaty of Sevres, and claimed that it 'pressed too hardly upon Turkey, and, by its unfairness to a Muslim State, had aroused Muslim sentiment against Great Britain'.[112]

The Indian Muslims having launched the Khilafat Movement— led by Maulana Mohamed Ali and other Muslim leaders, and soon joined by Mohandas Karamchand Gandhi and other Congress leaders through the Khilafat-non-cooperation movement—were deeply concerned with the fate of Turkey, Ottoman Turkey, because the institution of Khilafat rested in that country, with the Khalifa being the spiritual head of the Muslims, especially the Sunni Muslims. Although himself a Shia, Ameer Ali 'subscribed to the Sunni theory of the caliphate',[113] and thus was keen to protect and preserve it for the good of all Muslims. As Abbasi observed, he was a man of:

> moderation and judicious balance [and thus] remarkably free from any outcomes of extreme Sunnism or Shiaism. He was able to construct that golden bridge of understanding and amity between the two major Muslim sects which enabled them later to stand shoulder to shoulder in their struggle against the Hindus and the British. In this respect, he was the true precursor of Muhammad Ali Jinnah ....[114]

Realising that the future of the Khilafat lay in the hands of the leaders of the 'rejuvenated Turkey', led by Mustafa Kemal Ataturk and his Prime Minister, Ismet Inonu, Ameer Ali (along with the

Aga Khan) wrote a letter to Inonu on 24 November 1923, 'urging that "the religious leadership of Sunni world should be maintained intact"', that is the Khilafat, for:

> any diminution in the prestige of the Caliph or the elimination of the Caliphate as a religious factor from the Turkish body politic would mean the disintegration of Islam and its practical disappearance as a moral force in the world.[115]

Inexplicably, copies of the letter were simultaneously sent to some leading Turkish newspapers, which published it right away, with Inonu reading it in the press 'before the original was put before him'.[116] He was rightly offended but went too far in his reaction. In 'a harshly worded statement', he attacked both Ameer Ali and the Aga Khan by emphasising that both 'were foreigners, and therefore incompetent to discuss the constitution of Turkey. They were also Shias and[,] therefore[,] disqualified to pontify on Sunni institutions.'[117] The situation was complicated further by an 'impression' in Turkey that they 'had been instigated by the British Government which was anxious to see the Republican Government overthrown and the old Ottoman dynasty restored to power.'[118] Nothing could be farther from the truth. The Aga Khan and Ameer Ali were, no doubt, pro-British leaders but then, as an erudite scholar on the subject claimed, 'No evidence in support of this has yet turned up.'[119] But the damage was done. The Turkish government moved to abolish the Khilafat. On 27 February 1924, a resolution to that effect was moved in the Grand National Assembly. On 3 March 1924, it stood approved and adopted. The Khilafat was abolished, with the Khalifa sent into exile. Muslim India was 'stunned'.[120] The Khilafat Movement in India petered out. Ameer Ali himself was 'shocked', calling the abolition 'a disaster both to Islam and to civilization'.[121]

The fact was that, as Naeem Qureshi explained, 'Despite being a Shia Muslim, Ameer Ali subscribed to the Sunni theory of the caliphate and because of his writings on Islamic history, he had earned the respect of all ....'[122] As early as 1873, and as young as 24 years old, he had authored A *Critical Examination of the Life and*

Teaching of Mohammad (pbuh), which was 'the first book ever on the [Holy] Prophet [pbuh] and Islam in English by a Muslim author' which was later revised and expanded into *The Spirit of Islam* (1891).[123] The book, of course, went on to exercise 'a much wider influence on the international audience',[124] ran several editions, and became one of the most authoritative works on the subject. In 1899, Ameer Ali's popular book on Islamic history, *A Short History of the Saracens*, was published. Above all, Ameer Ali was considered an authority on what was then called Muhammadan Law (Islamic Law), and authored two volumes on the subject; 'the first draft of his *Personal Law of the Muhammadans*, which was later amplified and still later formed the second volume of his work on Muhammadan Law', was written during his stay in England in 1879–80.[125] In fact, it was due to his command over the Islamic laws that he, in his early career, was offered that teaching position at the University of Calcutta,[126] which he held for a while before launching his judicial career as presidency magistrate leading up to his appointment as judge of the Bengal High Court. Thus, Ameer Ali was an accomplished and accepted scholar of Islam. He understood Islam and its institutions, such as the Khilafat, very well. In this sense, Inonu's remark that he was 'disqualified to pontify on Sunni institutions' was not only 'an act of folly but also one of discourtesy' to a leading scholar of Islam.[127] Both Ameer Ali and the Aga Khan 'were genuinely concerned about Turkey's welfare and in this connection had rendered useful services behind scenes.'[128] In addition, it can hardly be overemphasised that Ameer Ali's 'pan-Islamic activities were also inextricably woven with his older commitment to the cause of the Indian Muslims.'[129]

This cause necessitated promoting and pursuing the Muslim separatist political movement, indeed consolidating separate Muslim interests in any way possible. Khilafat and its preservation represented separate Muslim interest, separate from those of the Hindus, in spite of their alliance with the Muslims during the Khilafat-non-cooperation movement. However, the abolition of the Khilafat in Turkey brought Ameer Ali back to his primary constituency, the Muslims and their separate interests in India.

Here Ameer Ali, like Syed Ahmad Khan, was committed to the advancement of Muslims under British rule, thinking like him that there will be 'a long British innings in India' and it was 'good for the country'.[130] He apprehended that 'India's weakness and disunity were a guarantee that the British withdrawal would inevitably lead to the arrival of some other foreign power'.[131] Like Syed Ahmad Khan, again, Ameer Ali was convinced that 'without education the community would never make their mark in India'.[132] He also 'appreciated' Syed Ahmad Khan's 'concern for social reforms' for uplifting the Muslims.[133] More importantly, he also agreed with Syed Ahmad Khan that Muslims had separate interests and must pursue separate group life and thus not join the Indian National Congress, which essentially represented the Hindu-majority community and its demands. Indeed, Syed Ahmad Khan felt that the Muslims should shun politics as a whole. But that is where 'the two leaders had different points of view'.[134] Ameer Ali favoured— rather, urged—Muslim participation in politics. In fact, as one writer noted: 'Ameer Ali was the first Muslim leader in India to publically state that the Muslim ... community should organize themselves politically', and form a political organisation:

> to negotiate with the Government, to demand and receive concessions, to express their opinions and to present their grievances, to make suggestions for reforms and to take advantage of constitutional advance, and to safeguard the community against Hindu aggression as well as British indifference ....[135]

He was so convinced of the need for a political organisation that even Syed Ahmad Khan's 'opposition to it could not stop him from proceeding to establish the first Muslim political body in India', the Central National Muhammadan Association.[136]

The major thrust of the activities of this Association and later the London Muslim League, as discussed earlier, remained much in line with Syed Ahmad Khan's main thesis, that the Muslims were a separate community, separate from the Hindus and other communities of India. Both organisations 'repeatedly emphasized the extent and degree of this separateness'[137] in all spheres of life. They insisted that the Muslims 'had separate interests in politics, in society, in religion, in law; in short, in all that made up the life of a people[,] they were different from others.'[138] It was precisely on this basis that Ameer Ali (and the Aga Khan) pursued a relentless campaign for separate electorates and secured them against all odds. Ameer Ali knew that the Muslims were a 'minority' in India and would remain so for good, and thus 'inevitably every new move in the direction of a so-called democracy', that is, representative rule, 'would damage rather than improve their prospects'.[139] They would be on the receiving end. The system was inherently biased against them. Still, unlike Syed Ahmad Khan, Ameer Ali readily 'upheld elections as the best insurance of Muslim rights and the real source of strength' than 'nominations'.[140] He was willing to pursue Muslim interests through the electoral, representative system of government, though with safeguards, such as separate electorates at the time.

In this sense, by 'formulating the twin principles of separate representation and elections into a political credo', Ameer Ali 'laid the cornerstone of Muslim nationalism'.[141] He was reported to be 'the first Muslim to use the English word "nation" for the Muslims of India'.[142] In the process, Ameer Ali helped the Muslim separatist political movement come a long way, confident and consolidated. Maulana Mohamed Ali, of course, went on to desist and derail this movement and thus any claim on Muslim nationhood, through the Khilafat-non-cooperation movement. But he soon returned to the fold, realising the futility of a Hindu–Muslim alliance for the benefit of Muslims. The Hindus, he found out, would not be obliging or helpful. He then took it upon himself to revive the separatist political movement with conviction and clarity, paving the way for Allama Muhammad Iqbal and Quaid-i-Azam Mohammad Ali Jinnah to strive for the separate state of Pakistan.

Notes

1. K. K. Aziz, *Ameer Ali: His Life and Work* (Lahore: Research Society of Pakistan, 2006), 2.
2. Syed Razi Wasti, ed., *Memoirs and Other Writings of Syed Ameer Ali* (Lahore: Peoples Publishing House, 1968), 5–7.
3. Ibid., 12.

4. Ibid., 10.
5. Ibid., 15, 34.
6. Ibid., 38–9.
7. Aziz, *Ameer Ali*, 7.
8. Ibid.
9. Ibid.
10. Muhammad Yusuf Abbasi, 'Syed Ameer Ali (Pioneer of Muslim Politics)', in *Founding Fathers of Pakistan*, ed. Ahmad Hasan Dani (Lahore: Sang-e-Meel Publications, 1998), 74.
11. Ibid.
12. Wasti, *Memoirs*, 33.
13. Ibid., 33–4 (Italics added).
14. Ibid., 62.
15. Ibid.
16. Ibid., 34.
17. Aziz, *Ameer Ali*, 10.
18. Ibid.
19. Abbasi, 'Syed Ameer Ali', 75–7.
20. Muhammad Yusuf Abbasi, *The Political Biography of Syed Ameer Ali* (Lahore: Wajidalis, 1989), 59.
21. Ibid.
22. Abbasi, 'Syed Ameer Ali', 78–9.
23. Ibid., 85.
24. Abbasi, *The Political Biography*, 59.
25. Ibid.
26. Abbasi, 'Syed Ameer Ali', 82.
27. Abbasi, *The Political Biography*, 61.
28. Abbasi, 'Syed Ameer Ali', 85.
29. Ibid.
30. Abbasi, *The Political Biography*, 71.
31. Ibid., 72.
32. Ibid.
33. Ibid., 73.
34. Abbasi, 'Syed Ameer Ali', 85.
35. Abbasi, *The Political Biography*, 75.
36. Aziz, *Ameer Ali*, 8.
37. Abbasi, *The Political Biography*, 77.
38. Ibid., 79.
39. Ibid., 80.
40. Shan Muhammad, 'Introduction', in *The Right Hon'able Syed Ameer Ali: Political Writings*, ed. Shan Muhammad (New Delhi: Ashish Publishing House, 1989), vi.
41. Abbasi, *The Political Biography*, 81.
42. Ibid.
43. Ibid., 115.

44. Ibid.
45. Ibid.
46. Ibid.
47. Ibid.
48. Muhammad, 'Memorial of the National Muhammadan Association...', in *Political Writings*, 297–8.
49. Abbasi, *The Political Biography*, 117.
50. Ibid.
51. Ibid., 117–18.
52. Ibid., 119.
53. Ibid.
54. Ibid., 120.
55. Ibid., 123.
56. Ibid., 126.
57. Muhammad, 'Memorial of the National Muhammadan Association....', in *Political Writings*, 314.
58. Abbasi, 'Syed Ameer Ali', 90.
59. Ibid., 98.
60. Ibid.
61. Ibid., 100.
62. Ibid.
63. Muhammad, 'Introduction', in *Political Writings*, vi.
64. Ibid., vii.
65. Muhammad, 'India and the New Parliament', in *Political Writings*, 74–5.
66. Ibid., 75.
67. Ibid. (Italics added).
68. Ibid., 89.
69. Ibid.
70. Ibid., 98–9.
71. Ibid., 100.
72. Ibid.
73. Ibid.
74. Ibid., 104.
75. Ibid., 184–5.
76. Aziz, *Ameer Ali*, 68.
77. Ibid.
78. Ibid.
79. Muhammad, 'Letter of Syed Ameer Ali to the Times....', in *Political Writings*, 229 (Italics added).
80. Ibid., 230.
81. Ibid.
82. Ibid., 231.
83. Ibid.
84. Ibid.
85. Ibid., 233.

86. Ibid., 194.
87. Ibid., 195.
88. Aziz, *Ameer Ali*, 70.
89. Ibid.
90. Cited in Aziz, *Ameer Ali*, 71.
91. Ibid.
92. Ibid.
93. Ibid. Also see, M. R. Kazimi, *A Concise History of Pakistan* (Karachi: Oxford university Press, 2009), 90, 94.
94. Aziz, *Ameer Ali*, 72.
95. Muhammad, 'Presidential Address to the Third Session of the All-India Muslim League Held at Delhi in January 1910....', in *Political Writings*, 210.
96. Aziz, *Ameer Ali*, 53.
97. Ibid.
98. Ibid., 55.
99. Ibid.
100. Ibid.
101. Shan, 'Introduction', in *Political Writings*, xviii.
102. Aziz, *Ameer Ali*, 84.
103. Ibid., 86–7.
104. Ibid., 87.
105. Syed Razi Wasti, 'Introduction', in Wasti, *Memoirs and Other Writings*, 3.
106. Ibid.
107. Aziz, *Ameer Ali*, 88.
108. Ibid.
109. Ibid., 87.
110. Ibid., 92.
111. Ibid., 89.
112. Ibid., 90.
113. M. Naeem Qureshi, *Ottoman Turkey, Ataturk, and Muslim South Asia: Perspectives, Perceptions, and Responses* (Karachi: Oxford University Press, 2014), 34.
114. Abbasi, *The Political Biography*, 285.
115. Aziz, *Ameer Ali*, 95.
116. Ibid. Apparently, its translation into Turkish language took time before it could be placed before the Prime Minister.
117. Ibid., 96.
118. Ibid., 97.
119. Ibid.
120. Ibid., 98.
121. Ibid., 99.
122. Qureshi, *Ottoman Turkey*, 34.
123. Abbasi, *The Political Biography*, 12–13.
124. Ibid., 13.
125. Aziz, *Ameer Ali*, 9.

126. Ibid., 10.
127. Ibid., 97.
128. M. Naeem Qureshi, *Pan-Islam in British India: The Politics of the Khilafat Movement, 1918–1924* (Karachi: Oxford University Press, 2009), 281.
129. Abbasi, *The Political Biography*, 307.
130. Aziz, *Ameer Ali*, 107.
131. Ibid., 109.
132. Ibid., 43.
133. Ibid.
134. Ibid.
135. Ibid., 44.
136. Ibid., 44, 49.
137. Ibid., 116.
138. Ibid.
139. Ibid.
140. Abbasi, *The Political Biography*, 239.
141. Ibid.
142. Aziz, *Ameer Ali*, 116.

5

Maulana Mohamed Ali and the Revival of the Muslim Separatist Political Movement in British India[1]

Syed Ahmad Khan's Muslim separatist political movement in British India—given the difficult circumstances that befell Muslims in the wake of the dismal failure of the Revolt of 1857—based on the principles of 'loyalty' to British rule and a separate group life in the emerging Indian polity provided the pivot around which Muslim politics in India came to revolve and rest.[1] Both Aga Khan and Syed Ameer Ali, his successors, followed suit, though conditioned by their respective challenges and difficulties they encountered. In essence, these principles remained their guiding principles and pursuits. They shaped, sustained, and indeed strengthened the Muslim separatist political movement to advance Muslim interests and demands. The Muslim community at large supported the movement.

However, their support to the Muslim separatist movement suffered from the Hindu–Muslim 'entente cordiale' of the early 1920s, during the Khilafat-non-cooperation movement—ironically enough at the hands of Maulana Mohamed Ali, a man reared and trained in the Aligarh tradition of Syed Ahmad Khan. In fact, the political situation in India—worsened by the Rowlatt Act of 1919, Jallianwala Bagh massacre, and hostile policies of the British government towards the Ottoman Turkish Empire during World War I, as well as the fate of the empire and, more importantly, that of the Khilafat—directed and determined the course of events. Mohamed Ali, nonetheless, went on to revive and eventually pursue

136

the separatist movement after fully exploring the potential of Hindu–Muslim unity, and learning a valuable lesson in the process. The Hindus would not help secure Muslim interests and demands.

In this chapter, an attempt will be made to recount those events and influences that forced Mohamed Ali first to accept a divergent—though futile—course to enter into an alliance with the Hindus, and then to repudiate and advance the Muslim cause in a situation that, he eventually realised, was bound to be Hindu-dominated as India moved towards self-government. Indeed, his critical role in the revival and reinforcement of the Muslim separatist political movement in India will be discussed at some length.

Born into a family associated with the court of the princely state of Rampur, Mohamed Ali (1875–1931) entered public life by joining the efforts to establish the All-India Muslim League in Dacca (Dhaka) in December 1906. He attended the inaugural session of the Muslim League as a delegate from the United Provinces (UP). He supported the main resolution seeking the formation of the Muslim League, and was included in the Provincial Committee which was formed to frame the constitution of the new political party. Mohamed Ali was also involved in the movement for separate electorates for the Muslims. It was, however, only after launching the English weekly, *Comrade*, in 1911, first from Calcutta (Kolkata) and then from Delhi, that Mohamed Ali, a journalist-turned-politician, rose to the pinnacle of fame and glory in the Muslim politics of India. The *Comrade* was not only a journalistic success but also a major force in moulding public opinion of the Muslims. Educated at Aligarh and Oxford,[2] Mohamed Ali knew well how to reflect the political aspirations of the Western-educated classes as well as those of the masses. To reach the latter still more effectively, Mohamed Ali started the Urdu newspaper *Hamdard*, in 1913.

Mohamed Ali, like his predecessors Syed Ahmad Khan, the Aga Khan, and Syed Ameer Ali, was 'loyal' to the British rule. He called it:

a dispensation of providence sent to an afflicted and distraught country for enlarging its views and ambitions, and bringing it within the orbit of modern thought and action, so that it could combine all that was good in the East with the best that the West had to offer.[3]

A series of events in 1911–13, however, portended a break and aroused Muslim anger and frustration with the British in general, leaving Mohamed Ali disenchanted with the old policy of 'loyalism'. He no longer found it relevant or realistic. In fact, he claimed that in 1913, 'I was precipitated into open conflict with the official world ....'[4] The first event was the British reluctance to agree to the Muslim demand to raise the level of the Aligarh College, a Muslim marker, to the status of a full-fledged Muslim University. To Mohamed Ali, it was:

> not so much as a memorial to the great man to whom we owe our existence today as an important and respected portion of the Indian Empire, as on account of its being the culmination of Sir Syed Ahmad's life-long efforts, that we are attached to the idea of a Muslim University.[5]

The second event, and a touchy one again, which influenced Mohamed Ali's attitude was the annulment, in December 1911, of the partition of Bengal; the partition had come into effect in 1905 to create a Muslim-majority province of East Bengal and Assam, on administrative grounds, and the Muslims had come to regard it as clearly beneficial to them. In fact, at the League session held in Calcutta in 1912, Mohamed Ali condemned the British move to annul the partition as a 'blunder'. The third event, with much religious sensitivity and thus explosive, was the decision of the Municipality of Kanpur, in 1913, to demolish a portion of the Machli Bazar Mosque. While the Governor, James Meston, dismissed the Muslim grievance as 'imaginary' because the portion to be demolished was a bathing enclosure and not a part of the mosque, the Muslims were offended. Mohamed Ali explained to the governor that the 'part used for ablutions [was] always considered [an] integral portion of [the] mosque',[6] but to no avail. The last, and perhaps the most distressful event was the now self-evident onslaught on Ottoman Turkey during World War I.

Ottoman Turkey was the home of the Khilafat and thus symbolised 'not merely a Turkish question' but also, more importantly, as Mohamed Ali explained:

> ... an Islamic question, an Indian question, an Algerian question, and a Tunisian question. It is [a] question of the preservation of the Khilafat. The Khilafat is the most essential institution of the Muslim community throughout the world. A vast majority of the Muslims of the world recognizes the Sultan of Turkey to be the Commander of the Faithful, and the Successor and the Khalifa of their Prophet. It is an essential part of this doctrine that the Khalifa, the Commander of the Faithful, should have adequate territories, adequate military and naval resources, adequate financial resources .... Not for aggression, nor even for the defense of Turkey, but for the defense of our Faith.[7]

The British were not impressed. Their indifference and apathy bordering on hostility towards the Muslims in India and abroad heightened the Muslim sense of anger, frustration, and despair. Mohamed Ali, still basically one of the 'loyal and devoted subjects', decided to intervene and, in 1913, personally led a Mission to England to help explain the situation. In a letter to the British Prime Minister, H. H. Asquith, he desperately sought,

> ... an opportunity for explaining in some detail the point of view of Indian Muslims with reference to some of the events and measures of government agitating the minds of Indian Muslims. This is all the more necessary because ... ideas and aspirations have been attributed to our people which are of such a preposterous character that they constitute a libel [sic] on a numerous and great community of loyal and devoted subjects of His Majesty, and contrary to our expectations ... to create a misunderstanding between [the] government and Indian Muslims.[8]

Mohamed Ali's pleas failed to evoke any sympathy or understanding, or any response for that matter. The Prime Minister, the Secretary of the State, and other leading members involved with Indian affairs ignored his letter and even refused to see him. The 'suspicious and cynical officials'[9] in India went further and, upon return, interned him on 15 May 1915.[10] This was in spite of the fact that Mohamed Ali, in an article, 'The Choice of Turks', published in the *Comrade* of 26 September 1914, had categorically stated that if Turkey took the 'fateful step' of going to war with England, 'the Muslims would stand by their government and would not in any way add to the embarrassment of their rulers.' In the same vein, Mohamed Ali went on to warn the Turks that 'they must not be lured by the blandishments of those opposed to England and her allies. They must remember that "War is Deceit".' He did not mince words about the dilemma of Indian Muslims in case Turkey opted for a war. As he put it:

> But if, by some evil chance, they engage in hostilities against our own government, we shall ask them to pray for us also, for they can hardly imagine the mental anguish and the heart-pangs that will be ours. We shall be torn between two passions, or rather the same passion will be warring with itself within us. When in a household the parents fall out, whichever of them may be at fault the children are bound to suffer. That will be our plight and we shall deserve all the sympathy that we may secure.[11]

The long and lonely years of internment and the chagrin over the fate of Turkey left a marked impact on Mohamed Ali's mind and relationship with the British government. He 'discovered the "evil" character of British rule, recognized the futility of the politics of mendicancy so forcefully advocated by Syed Ahmad Khan, and realised the necessity of agitational methods for redressal of grievances.'[12] The old 'ardent and sustained pro-British policy' of Syed Ahmad Khan[13] lost its appeal to him. He could not pursue it any further. This is not to suggest that Mohamed Ali doubted the wisdom of this policy in the first place. Indeed, as late as 1923, Mohamed Ali admitted:

> Reviewing the actions of a bygone generation today when it is easier to be wise after the event, I must confess I still think the attitude of Syed Ahmad Khan was eminently wise, and much as I wish that somethings which he had said should have been left unsaid, I am constrained to admit that no well-wisher of Muslims, nor of India

as a whole, could have followed a very different course in leading the Muslims ....[14]

But then Syed Ahmad Khan, he recalled, had also suggested that 'our attitude towards the Government established in this country must be governed only by one consideration—the attitude of that Government towards ourselves. Every other consideration is foreign to the subject ....'[15] Now, since the British gave them no more 'opportunities of attaining spiritual salvation and temporal prosperity'[16] and indeed had 'challenged Islam in India to do what it can in defence of the faith',[17] there was no reason for the Muslims to remain loyal and faithful. In fact, Mohamed Ali had lamented in a letter to the Viceroy, Lord Chelmsford, on 24 April 1919 that 'for all this loyalty and support, that, without any effective protest, and often with the concurrence of His Majesty's Government, blow after blow after blow was aimed at the temporal power of Islam.'[18]

Mohamed Ali's shift from the loyalist policy of Syed Ahmad Khan reflected not only the futility of the policy of reliance on the British but also indicated that the Indian National Congress, a party dominated by the Hindu-majority community, no longer aroused the kind of hostility it did earlier. A new generation of Muslim leaders had emerged who had received much the same Western education as their Hindu counterparts, and who were equally keen on finding a place for their community in the new political life and processes of India and thus had no problem working with the Congress if it helped their interests or cause. They had established the All-India Muslim League as a vehicle of their political interests and demands, and had even shifted its central office from Aligarh to Lucknow to save it from what was called the policy of 'caution verging on timidity'.[19] In the treatment meted out to Turkey, they saw clear 'Western imperialism', and the British, in particular, bent upon 'conquering and destroying' Muslim culture and identity.[20] They, therefore, began to feel at home with Congress' active, even violent, opposition to the government, notwithstanding its predominantly Hindu character and aspirations. Mohamed Ali, who represented this radical shift in Muslim attitude, thus claimed: 'we will not lose by conferring with the Hindus as to the future, but by sitting with folded hands and allowing others to settle the future for us.'[21] This stood in sharp contrast to what he had been advocating until recently. In not-too-distant a past, he had chided the proponents of Hindu–Muslim alliance and the Congress–League concord in these harsh words:

> Soft-headed and some self-advertising folk have gone about proclaiming that the Muslims should join the Congress because the government had revoked the Partition of Bengal or because Persia and Turkey are in trouble. We are simply amused at this irresponsible fatuity. But when a responsible body like the London Branch of the All-India Muslim League [of Syed Ameer Ali] talks of close cooperation between the Hindus and Muslims because the Muslims of Tripoli and Persia have been the victims of European aggression, we realize for the first time that even sane and level-headed men can run off at a tangent and confuse the issues. What has the Muslim situation abroad to do with the conditions of the Indian Muslims? Either their interests come actually into conflict with those of the Hindus, or they have been all along guilty of a great political meanness and hypocrisy. Has the Indian situation undergone a change? Are the Hindu 'communal patriots' less militant today and have they grown more considerate and careful about Muslim sentiments? Have the questions that really divide the two communities lost their force and meaning? If not, then the problem remains exactly where it was at any time in recent Indian history ... An attempt to impose artificial unity is sure to end in failure, if not in disaster.[22]

How prophetic Mohamed Ali's final words were was only a matter of time and truism. He would soon be at the head of the Muslim separatist political movement, strengthening and reinforcing it, both with his experience of working with the Congress and the hostile attitude of the Hindu-majority community in the aftermath of the Khilafat-non-cooperation movement. For the present, however, he and the Muslims he led had decided to turn a new leaf in Indian politics. Political frustrations at home, exacerbated by the hostility of the British towards Turkey, pushed them towards an alliance with the Hindus and the Congress and an open break with the British. Not that Syed Ahmad Khan's 'clean-cut logic' had lost its force but because they, as Muslims, had to commend themselves first to the 'logic of God'. Mohamed Ali exhorted:

> ... we would advise everyone who wished to know what a Musalman may do or must do, and what he may not and must not, to read the 9th chapter of the [Holy] Quran on 'Repentance'. The limits of all contracts, legal and social are clearly laid down and no territory is more justly or unmistakably demarcated than that of right and wrong in the dealings of Moslems with non-Moslems.[23]

The Khilafat, Mohamed Ali insisted, enjoined upon the Muslims to 'become loyal to God before they are loyal to his creatures'.[24] Muslims, he indeed warned,

> ... can obey only such laws and orders issued by their secular rulers as do not involve disobedience to the commandment of God, who, in the expressive language of the Holy Quran is 'the All-ruling Ruler'. These very clear and rigidly definite limits of obedience are not laid down with regard to the authority of non-Muslim administrations. On the contrary, they are of universal application, and can neither be enlarged nor reduced in any case ... We owe a duty to God, and we owe a duty to the Empire; and in the last resort when the demands of the Imperial Government came into direct conflict with the demands of the Universal Government of God, as Musalmans we could only obey God, and are endeavouring to do so ... [so long as] the Musalmans of India had not been forcibly driven to believe that the British Government was the enemy of God and the enemy of Islam, they remained loyal to it ....[25]

As the institution of Khilafat rested in Turkey, Mohamed Ali and the Indian Muslims obviously called for the safety and security of the Ottoman Turkish Empire first. In a 'three-fold claim', Mohamed Ali explained their position at some length:

> The first claim of the Indian Muslims ... is that the Khilafat should be preserved with temporal power adequate for the defence of the Faith, and the irreducible minimum that is the restoration of the territorial *status quo ante bellum*, while taking guarantees from Turkey consistently with her independence and dignity as a

sovereign state for security of life and property and opportunities of autonomous development of all races, Christian, Muslim and Jew. This is a region in which compromise was possible …. Our second claim is that the Island of Arabia, the fourth boundary being the Euphrates and the Tigris, should remain in exclusive Muslim control, and since it would be idle to suggest [British] handing over some other territory to the Khalifah, for the preservation of the Khilafat, that main claim of ours necessitates that this entire region which includes Syria, Palestine and Mesopotamia should remain within the scheme of Ottoman Sovereignty … Our third claim is that the Holy Places, namely, the three Sacred Harems of Mecca, Medina and Jerusalem, and the Holy Shrines in Mesopotamia, should remain in the custody and under the wardenship of the Khalifah himself. The claim with regard to the exclusive Muslim control of the Island of Arabia is based on the dying injunction of the [Holy] Prophet [PBUH] and this claim with regard to the wardenship of the Holy Places rests on a series of injunctions to be found in the [Holy] Quran and the Prophet's [PBUH] traditions.

In short, Mohamed Ali's demands were:

The Khilafat shall be preserved, there shall be no Christian mandate over any part of the Island of Arabia, and the Khalifa shall remain as before the war, the Warden of the Holy Places.[26]

Indian Muslims' concern regarding the fate of the Turkish Empire was clear from the moment Italy attacked Tripoli in October 1911. The Balkan wars of 1912 and 1913 caused considerable reaction and resentment among them. They expressed it in public agitation as well as in their writings in the newspapers. Within a year of the breaking out of the first Balkan war, they organised a medical mission for the Turkish army headed by Dr Mukhtar Ahmad Ansari.[27] In May 1913, they established the *Anjuman-i-Khuddam-i-Ka'ba* or Society of Servants of the Ka'ba to help secure and preserve the sacred character of the Holy Places. When Turks, despite their entreaties, joined the war on the side of Germany,[28] they prayed for the safety of the Turkish Empire. Turkey was the greatest Muslim empire and its ruler, the Khalifa (Caliph), was the defender of their faith, Islamic faith.

Interestingly, the British authorities in India understood the significance and value of the Khilafat to the Indian Muslims very well. They, in fact, exploited more than once the emotional attachment of these Muslims to the Khalifa to mobilise support for their rule in India. As early as 1799, they had sought the help of the Khalifa to impress upon Tipu Sultan, the fiery ruler of Mysore, the need to establish peace with the British authorities. Even during the Revolt of 1857, the British had hastened to obtain a proclamation from the Khalifa advising the Indian Muslims to be loyal to their British rulers. Indeed, the British had consciously projected the institution of Khilafat and the office of Khalifa during the years that followed the Crimean War (1853–6). Above all, the Indian Muslims after the 1840s, under the influence of Shah Muhammad Ishaq, the grandson of Shah Waliullah, had come to recognise and proclaim publicly the Ottoman Turkish title to the 'universal' Khilafat. By the 1870s, the position of the Khalifa was widely accepted and his name was read in the Friday *khutba* (sermon) in India.[29]

The Viceroy, Lord Chelmsford, therefore, felt obliged to assure the Muslims, on 3 September 1919, that their 'feelings have been given the fullest representation'.[30] He assured them again, in January 1920, that 'no effort has been spared, no stone left unturned, to place before those with whom the decision will rest, the plea of Indian Musalmans for the most favourable possible treatment of Turkey.'[31] There was no denying that 'the Muslim unrest was the chief worry of the Government of India and India Office'.[32]

Ironically, these assurances were being violated at the time they were being given as the British troops were already on the move in Mesopotamia. It did not take long to become quite evident that the British assurances were no more than attempts 'to dispel Muslim uneasiness, and moreover, to soothe their agitated minds'.[33] However, whether the assurances were made out of 'expediency or good intentions or both',[34] there was no doubt that Turkey would not receive fair treatment at the hands of the British authorities. Not only that, the Greeks, with the encouragement of Lloyd George, the British Prime Minister and a friend and admirer of the Greek Prime Minister Venizelos, went on to attack Turkey. Lloyd George,

Arthur Balfour, and almost all leading British politicians were openly prejudiced against the Turks. Otherwise men of 'sanity and moderation', they spoke with 'great indiscretion' when they chose to discuss Turkey and gave the impression that they were thirsting for some kind of 'revenge'. General Allenby, who captured Palestine was, in fact, called 'the victor of the last crusade'.[35] Indeed, there were all indications that the British government was determined to make sure that a vanquished Turkey 'when it is driven to take refuge in some decayed city of Asia Minor, will no longer afford a fulcrum by which apostles of pan-Islamism may hope to move the world.'[36] As Naeem Qureshi pointed out,

> The fact of the matter [was] that ever since the reversal of the pro-Turkish policy by the Marquess of Salisbury (1830–1903) in the 1870s, British public opinion had been ill-disposed towards the Ottoman Empire. Mild at first, this hostility had become extremely aggressive since the First World War. As time passed, the clamour for vengeance intensified.[37]

However, Mohamed Ali and other Indian Muslims who felt strongly about the Khilafat, went ahead to mobilise public opinion to force the British to keep Viceroy Chelmsford's word once the war was over. In a public meeting held in Bombay (Mumbai) on 20 March 1919, and attended by thousands of Muslims, they set up a Khilafat Committee and appealed that Khilafat Day be observed on 17 October 1919. Encouraged by the enthusiastic response to the Khilafat appeal, they held the first All-India Khilafat Conference on 23–24 November 1919[38] in Delhi with Mohandas Karamchand Gandhi, the rising Congress leader, as a prominent participant. The Muslim mood at the conference could be gauged from the resolutions adopted:

1) The Muslims of India should not participate in the celebration of Armistice to register their anger over the excesses committed against the holy places in Iran and Turkey.

2) The Muslims would be forced to adopt a non-cooperative stance against the government if Turkey was treated unfairly in the Armistice.

3) They would boycott British goods in case Turkey was treated unjustly.

4) A delegation was to be formed to keep abreast the British government about the feelings of the Muslims on the question of Khilafat.[39]

Interestingly, Gandhi's support to the Khilafat Movement has been a matter of considerable speculation and controversy among writers on the subject. Some are of the view that Gandhi joined the movement to enhance his own status and standing in the Congress and the Indian political system.[40] Others are of the opinion that Mohamed Ali and his Muslim colleagues needed Gandhi's support to bolster their campaign, and they, in fact, dragged him into the Khilafat Movement for that purpose. Gandhi was capable of ensuring the backing of the bulk of the Hindu community to the Khilafat cause.[41] The truth was that both Mohamed Ali and Gandhi needed each other's support,[42] though for different reasons. For Mohamed Ali and the Muslims, it was the Khilafat and their Islamic duty. For Gandhi, it was the need to mobilise the Muslims in his fight, the Congress' fight against the British, necessitated by the Amritsar massacre of 1919 and other disturbing developments in the Punjab, popularly referred to as the 'Punjab Wrongs'.[43] This is not to suggest that the Muslims would not have launched the movement on their own without Gandhi's support. They were deeply distressed over the turn of events affecting the Khilafat and were particularly annoyed with the terms of the Treaty of Sevres, signed on 10 August 1920,[44] which marked the beginning of the dismemberment of the Turkish Empire by depriving it of its Arab possessions, including sacred places such as Hijaz, Palestine, and Mesopotamia. The majority of the Muslims were thus prepared to struggle and suffer for the Khilafat, with or without Gandhi. They had lost their patience and trust in the so-called British assurances. As some years later (in 1925), Mohamed Ali bluntly put it in a rejoinder to Lala Lajpat Rai, a prominent leader of the Hindu Mahasabha:

> ... let Lalaji remember that even if the Mahatmaji [Gandhi] had not come so generously and warmheartedly to Muslim help, the Muslims, or rather such of them as really took it up, would not have given up the Khilafat cause.

He went on to assert that:

> ... it was principally the Khilafat movement that vitalized the Congress and led to non-co-operation. The Punjab wrongs are still unredressed, but far fewer Punjabis seem to have remembered them during the last two years than the Muslims who remember even today the unredeemed Jazeerat-ul-Arab. There is an undying vitality in the cause as long as there is any vitality in Islam, but there seems to be far less vitality in the cause of redressing Punjab wrongs ....[45]

The Muslim enthusiasm for the Khilafat can also be gauged from the fact that a major leader, Maulana Abdul Bari, in 1921, when apparently the movement for Khilafat was in full swing, was still not satisfied with the pace of the struggle. He, along with his associates and followers, demanded more aggressive tactics for the redressal of their grievances. He was wary of Gandhi's 'policy of caution and moderation', and even publicly expressed 'dissatisfaction with the limited vigour with which he prosecuted the Khilafat agitation.'[46] Indeed, by the end of 1921, as the governor of UP, Spencer Butler, informed the higher authorities, 'the matter is now largely in the hands of the *Mussulmans*, and they are determined to go through with it ....'[47]

There is little doubt that Gandhi saw in this Khilafat Movement 'a way to gain Muslim adherence to the drive for self-government', or what he called *Swaraj*.[48] The efforts to bring about cooperation and unity between the two communities in the common cause of India had, of course, been taking shape since the Lucknow Pact of December 1916, agreed between the Muslim League and the Congress, led by Mohammad Ali Jinnah. But then there were some Hindu leaders who were not willing to go as far as the Khilafat issue. In order to bring these recalcitrant leaders over to support the Khilafat, Gandhi took almost a year before he could assure them, at a special Congress session in Calcutta on 8 September 1920, that the overall aim of the Khilafat Movement was none other than the pursuit of *Swaraj*. Referring to the tragic events of the Punjab in general and Amritsar in particular, he told them that the only way a repetition of such 'wrongs' could be averted was by seeking the cooperation of Muslims through Hindu support of the Khilafat. Indeed, in a broader appeal to Hindu sentiment, he implored them: 'The way to save the cow is to die in the act of saving the Khilafat without mentioning the cow.'[49]

Mohamed Ali was convinced that the support of Hindus was critical, indeed decisive. He had already failed in his mission to persuade the British authorities in London to desist from tampering with the Turkish Empire's pre-war frontiers, especially the Hijaz and Palestine. Despite all 'the lucidity and moderation' with which he credited Mohamed Ali and the members of his Khilafat delegation,[50] Lloyd George was not prepared to concede. In fact, he was quite hostile and blunt in his response. He told Mohamed Ali and his entourage:

> I do not understand Mr Muhamed Ali to claim indulgence for Turkey. He claims justice, and justice she will get. Austria has had justice, Germany has had justice—pretty terrible justice. Why should Turkey escape? ... Is there any reason why we should apply a different measure to Turkey to that [*sic*] which we have meted out to the Christian communities of Germany and Austria? I want the Muhammadans in India to get it well in their minds that we are not treating Turkey severely because she is Muhammadan; we are applying exactly the same principles to her as we have applied to Austria which is a great Christian community.[51]

Mohamed Ali thus had no option but to join hands with Gandhi. He even helped Gandhi carry the all-important resolution on the non-cooperation movement, in support of the Khilafat, in December 1920 at the Nagpur Congress.[52] 'A choice', he felt, is being forced on Musalmans between obedience to the clearest commandments of God and obedience to the dictates of mundane governments, and in such a case Musalmans can only act on the dictum of their [Holy] Prophet [PBUH] that 'no obedience is due to the creature of God which involved disobedience towards the Creator'.[53]

Mohamed Ali assumed the leadership of the Khilafat movement, reinforced with the support of Gandhi. He was assisted by his brother Maulana Shaukat Ali, Maulana Abul Kalam Azad, Maulana Abdul Bari, Maulana Hasrat Mohani, Sayyid Sulaiman Nadvi, Maulana Zafar Ali Khan, Hakim Ajmal Khan, Dr Mukhtar Ahmad Ansari, and Saifuddin Kitchlew, to name but a few of the more important ones. The movement, in fact, turned out to be a popular, unifying movement with which most Muslim leaders— Aligarh or ulema,[54] loyalists or agitators, traditional or modernists, young or old—agreed. Indeed, as Mohamed Ali saw it:

> The temporal misfortunes of Islam, therefore, drew the Muslims to their religion as if inevitably and the wedge that Western education had seemed to insert between the ranks of the religious, and of the men of the "New Light" vanished as if by magic. The orthodox and the anglicized were drawn together ....[55]

The movement attained support of the masses in no time. Mohamed Ali and other leaders went on a whirlwind tour of the country, mobilising support for the Khilafat. In addition, they developed a network of alliances ranging from religious centres and educational institutions to social strata, political groups, classes, and interests. They established close links with seminaries in Deoband, Nadwa, and, of course, Firangi Mahal of Maulana Abdul Bari. Aligarh also became one of the important centres of the Khilafat Movement. The focus of political activities shifted from the upper classes and intelligentsia to the middle and lower classes and the bulk of the masses. Students came out from the government-aided schools and colleges, and lawyers stayed away from the courts. British goods were boycotted[56] and, in certain cases, British cloth was burnt in bonfires, and *khaddar*—the coarse cloth made from hand-spun yarn—became the material of choice. Many thousands of Indians, Hindus and Muslims, courted arrest and about 30,000 people were interned during the two months (December 1921–January 1922).[57] A new dimension was added to the movement by a fatwa (religious edict) issued by Maulana Abul Kalam Azad and Maulana Abdul Bari declaring India as a Dar-al-Harb (Abode of War), implying that it was incumbent upon Muslims to migrate to Dar-al-Islam, a Muslim country. 'When a land', Mohamed Ali told the Viceroy in a letter on 24 April 1919,

> is not safe for Islam a Moslem has only two alternatives—*Jihad* or *Hijrat*. That is to say, he must either make use of every force God has given him for the liberation of the land and the ensurement of perfect freedom for the practice and preaching of Islam, or he must migrate to some other and free land with a view to return to his motherland when it is once more safe for Islam ... In view of our weak condition, migration is the only alternative for us ....[58]

Thousands of Muslims responded to the fatwa and left India for Afghanistan. Many were refused entry, with some of them dying on the way back home. Those who were able to return safely to India found themselves penniless and homeless—their property which they had sold at throw-away price was in the hands of others and they were not willing to oblige them.[59] It took them quite a while to settle down. The ulema who issued the fatwa and 'decreed it to be mandatory and the politicians who developed it into a campaign, ignored all economic and political realities'.[60] In their 'anti-British temper they had closed their eyes to its consequences.'[61]

In addition to these sufferings and sacrifices, a number of events caused severe setbacks to the movement. In August 1921, Muslims of Malabar, called Mappila, challenged the local administration and declared Khilafat in India.[62] In their zeal, the Mappila also committed 'atrocities' against some Hindus, particularly those Hindu landlords who had oppressed them in the past and were now suspected of providing information to the British on their activities.[63] The Mappila rebellion was brutally crushed by the end of the year but a serious dent had been made in the Khilafat-non-cooperation movement. There were now feelings of bitterness and, indeed, loathing between the two communities. The Hindus were disturbed by the reports of violent incidents which, according to a Hindu leader of the Congress himself, were 'undoubtedly exaggerated'.[64] Still, the overall impact was devastating for Hindu–Muslim relations. There were disturbances and unrest in various parts of the country. The unrest reached its climax on 5 February 1922 at Chauri Chaura, a village in Gorakhpur district in UP, where an unruly mob set fire to a police station, along with 22 policemen and a few guards who were present inside the building. Gandhi, calling this tragedy the 'index finger' of further troubles to come, and without consulting the Muslims, abruptly called off the movement.[65]

The abrupt forsaking of the movement shocked Indians, particularly the Muslims. They found it difficult to understand why the movement had been called off at a point when its effect was clearly being felt by the British authorities.[66] The movement was generally peaceful and there were very few isolated incidents of violence and bloodshed like the one at Chauri Chaura. The movement, however, received a major setback a few months later when, on 21 November 1922, the Turkish Parliament decided to separate the Khilafat from the Sultanate (rulership). The fate of the Khilafat was eventually sealed by Mustafa Kemal Ataturk, president and founder of modern Turkey, who sent Khalifa Abdul Majid II into exile and abolished the institution of Khilafat on 3 March 1924. This marked the end of a centuries-old institution of Islam and, for all practical purposes, the Khilafat Movement in India. Mohamed Ali was completely lost. He called it an 'irreligious' act.[67] His brother, Shaukat Ali, 'sent a telegram to Mustafa Kemal [Ataturk] pleading with him to revise the decision.'[68] But, of course, 'the Turkish President had no intention of either rescinding his decision or assuming the title of caliph for himself. To him the caliphate had ceased to have any relevance for Turkey.'[69] Apparently, 'the majority of the Indian Muslims', including Mohamed Ali and their present leadership, 'did not comprehend the dynamics of change in post-war Turkey' or, for that matter, correctly 'interpret the Kemalist motives ....'[70] The Khilafat Movement lingered on for a while but the Turkish decision regarding Khilafat had taken the wind out of its sails.

The petering out of the Khilafat-non-cooperation movement deeply affected efforts at Hindu–Muslim unity. There were riots during the next few years, resulting in the loss of many lives on both sides.[71] The alarming increase in the number of riots in fact encouraged both Hindu and Muslim partisans to organise more systematic attacks against one another. Strangely, Gandhi, the apostle of 'non-violence' and, by now, undisputed leader of the Hindu majority community and the Congress, did not even raise a finger to stop the bloodshed. He was content to comment, 'let Hindus and Mussalmans fight one another and fight to their heart's content. Let them break each other's heads and let them flow a stream of blood out of it.'[72] Gandhi, as Qureshi described him, now 'was certainly not the Gandhi of 1919–22. He had ceased to be an impartial leader of India'.[73]

The resultant Hindu–Muslim conflict was not surprising at all. As mentioned earlier, there was a marked difference in the concerns of Gandhi and Mohamed Ali in the course of the movement and this difference was too pronounced to augur well for the future. Mohamed Ali and his followers had joined hands with the Hindus, after a bitter experience at the hands of the British, to save the sole surviving independent Muslim empire, which to them represented the temporal greatness of Islam and whose ruler was the Khalifa of the Muslim world. They were not seeking a 'political or psychic fusion' with the Hindu community.[74] They merely sought a check to:

> the transfer of their Holy Land to non-Muslim control, to the destruction of the temporal power of the Khilafat to the position of a petty Emir controlled in every direction by the enemies of Islam, and living on the sufferance of Christian Powers.

Mohamed Ali saw the freedom of the Jazeerat-ul-Arab from 'non-Muslim control' and maintenance of the necessary degree of 'temporal power of the Khilafat' as 'two of the principle religious obligations of the Muslims of the world'.[75]

The Khilafat-non-cooperation movement was primarily an alliance between 'bed-fellows in adversity'.[76] The Muslims needed the support of Hindus, particularly Gandhi,[77] and Gandhi, in turn, realised that his *Swaraj* depended on 'the strength and emotional intensity' of the Khilafat Movement.[78] The two needed each other to forge a common front against the British rulers. The cause of Indian freedom happened to coincide with the cause of Islam in the Muslim World situation.[79] Beyond that, the two leaders and their respective communities did not have a clear picture of the future; in fact, very few knew what would actually happen if the British—which is who they clearly knew they were fighting against—were removed from the scene.[80]

Things were further aggravated by Gandhi's use of 'you' and 'we' epithets. 'If you Muslims,' he would say, 'are in the right, we shall offer you unconditional help. This is a hereditary privilege of the Hindus.'[81] He differentiated between Hindus and the Muslims to the extent that he even suggested on a number of occasions that the latter, like Hindus, need not be 'non-violent' for there were for them, he claimed, 'special Koranic obligations' on the subject.[82] Gandhi also saw it fit to remind the Muslims off and on that they were not only a community different from the Hindus but also a 'minority' community. 'How can twenty-two crore Hindus,' he emphasised, 'have peace and happiness if eight crore of their Muslim brethren are torn in anguish?'[83]

Some eminent writers have thus claimed that the Khilafat Movement was essentially a Muslim movement 'in relation to a feeling of insecurity in the midst of Hindu majority', and indeed an effort to find space and security in a future independent India.[84] The idea, Gail Minault argued, was to:

> ... offset their minority status by their ability to bargain from a position of strength .... The Congress, needing Muslim support to strengthen the campaign for self-government at this critical period, would have to listen to Muslim desires, recognize minority rights and make some political concessions.[85]

The argument, though plausible on the face of it, is not supported by evidence. By the time the Khilafat Movement was formally launched in 1919, the so-called 'minority–majority' issue had not become a functional concern of Indian politics, both for the Hindus and the Muslims. Many Muslims, of course, were conscious of their weak, minority status in the political system since the days of Syed Ahmad Khan, and had, in fact, asked for and gained the right of separate representation through separate Muslim electorates in 1909, which was in turn duly acknowledged by the Congress–League Lucknow Pact in 1916. But the 'minority–majority' syndrome was still not a dominant condition of politics and political life. The very fact that the Hindus, under the banner of the Congress, conceded this right to the Muslims in 1916 without much reluctance only goes to prove that even they, in spite of a longer and more intense experience at politics than their Muslim counterparts in the Muslim League, did not consider it to be a matter of much interest. It was only after the operation of the Montagu–Chelmsford Reforms and the so-called principle of 'dyarchy' envisaged in it that the question of 'minority' or 'majority' community began to assume importance not only in the provinces but also, to a considerable extent, in the national set-up. No wonder, the Congress was bitterly opposed to the principle of separate electorates in subsequent years, as exemplified by the Nehru Report of 1928. In 1919, when the Montagu–Chelmsford Reforms were introduced, not only the Khilafatists and other politicians in general boycotted these reforms but many among them appeared blissfully ignorant of its impact on future developments. Besides, one should not forget that most of the heat that powered the Khilafat Movement and set it on its momentous course had started to gather force from events of 1911–13 when the Muslims had just begun to shed their old distrust of the Hindu community and were willing to work with them for 'self-government suitable to India'.

Again, one might ask, if the Muslims had launched the Khilafat Movement to 'offset' their minority status, why did the various Muslim groups and interests involved with it not persist in their unity of purpose and action once the movement had ceased, leaving them in a much more precarious situation. After all, if one were to follow the argument to its logical end, there was more reason now to unite and meet the challenge of Hindu majority on the political plane than ever before. Not only did the ulema, Western-educated groups and classes, and other interests in general part company with each other, but two of the most important votaries of the institution of Khilafat, Maulana Azad and Mohamed Ali, along with their followers, took clearly different and indeed divergent paths. While Azad chose to join the Congress and its brand of 'Indian nationalism', Mohamed Ali went on to uphold the separatist tradition of Syed Ahmad Khan and indeed turned out to be a fierce critic of the Congress and its creed in the years ahead. Besides, one wonders, why would Jinnah, the architect of the Lucknow Pact, have stayed away from the Khilafat Movement if it was about Muslim rights and interests in a Hindu-dominated India?

The Indian Muslims did not pursue the Khilafat issue to secure their political interests in India. Indeed, in the heyday of Hindu–Muslim unity, they did not bother to seek any 'political concessions' from the Hindu majority community.[86] They were not politically motivated. As for Mohamed Ali benefitting from the movement personally, as has been claimed by some writers,[87] there is plenty of evidence to suggest that he was already on the rise much before the formal launch of the Khilafat Movement. As indicated earlier, he was one of the founder members of the Muslim League in 1906. In 1912, he was the principal organiser of the Medical Mission sent to Turkey under Dr Mukhtar Ansari. In 1913, he was the chief spokesman of the Muslim community on the Kanpur Mosque tragedy and also the leader of the delegation to England, the same year, to express Muslims' grievances in India. The argument, therefore, that the Indian Muslims, or Mohamed Ali, for that matter, had to gain something out of this movement politically hardly stands credible or convincing.

But this is also not true, as has been suggested by some writers, that the Khilafat Movement was essentially 'an adventure in altruism' undertaken to save their Muslim fellows on other lands of bondage to Europe.[88] The Khilafat Movement was not a movement merely to help secure the interests and welfare of the Turks in their fight against the hostile advance of the West. It was a movement for the realisation of the Islamic ideal of the Khilafat. Its temporal content was essentially dictated by the spiritual force of Islam. 'Temporal power', as the Khilafat Conference in its address to the Viceroy on 19 January 1920, explained, 'is of the very essence of institution of the Khilafat'.[89] Mohamed Ali himself pressed the point in one of his speeches delivered in London in connection with the Khilafat campaign on 22 April 1920:

> The claim put forward is a simple claim. It says that it is one of the fundamental doctrines of Islam, absolutely unalterable, that there should always be a Khalifa, and that the Khalifa should have power at all times adequate for the defence of the faith ....[90]

Indeed, Mohamed Ali's interest in the Khilafat was primarily religious and political only secondarily. Political realities of the Turkish situation (based on their nationalist aspirations leading to the abolition of Khilafat by Kemal Ataturk) or, indeed, for that matter, of the Indian situation, concerned him little. As for India, it was only after the failure of the Khilafat-non-cooperation movement that he turned his full attention to the political fate of Muslims in the country.[91]

Religion was, in fact, rooted in his social consciousness. As his biographer, Afzal Iqbal, described him: '[Mohamed Ali] was clearly smitten by God. The fire of faith had completely consumed him. The message had permeated through the innermost depths of his being.'[92] Mohamed Ali himself admitted that he was 'bitten by religion'[93] and was a 'fanatic', and indeed claimed that 'there is a so-called "fanatical" side to every Muslim'.[94] However, there is no denying the fact that his 'fanaticism' was the outcome of much thought, reflection, and scholarship. He had made his first acquaintance with the meaning of the Holy Quran through the teachings of Maulana Shibli Nomani at Aligarh College. At Oxford University, fascination with the Quran was 'such that once I took it up, I could not be induced to close it for some hours'. In subsequent years, he, along with his brother, Shaukat Ali, turned more and more to the Quran to 'thoroughly soak ourselves [in] that perennial fountain of truth that the gathering dust of thirteen centuries has not been able to choke or dry'.[95] This deeply religious disposition had a lot to do with his stand on the Khilafat. He was convinced about the necessity of the institution of Khilafat and especially for the safety of the holy places and welfare of the Muslims at large.

In this sense, the Khilafat had a role and relevance for the Muslim community in India. It was to this end that Mohamed Ali spoke of the Khalifa as defender of their faith, as a man who could 'stand before the world as the leader of the Muslims in this cause, and whenever the liberty of conscience of the Muslim in any part of the world is placed in jeopardy, he should at least be able to say to the aggressor, "you shall not do that with impunity".'[96]

The failure of the efforts to save the Khilafat, however, convinced Mohamed Ali that the time had come for the Indian Muslims to concentrate on their own affairs and secure their own interests as a separate political community. His 'deep-rooted loyalties' to the Muslim group that had been dormant for a while emerged 'irresistibly'.[97] Although he was President of the Indian National Congress in 1923, he defended the principle of separate electorates for Muslims, an integral aspect of the Muslim separatist political movement, arguing that a 'community that failed to get its representative elected would have inevitably borne a yet deeper grudge against its successful rival.'[98] But he did not become a 'separatist' or proponent of the Muslim separatist political movement itself as such, not yet. He was still keen to work for Hindu–Muslim unity. He, along with Jinnah who called and presided that meeting,[99] emerged as one of the leading architects of the Delhi Muslim Proposals of March 1927, willing and even ready to abandon separate electorates and 'accept a joint electorate' provided the Muslims got some palpable share of power through the creation of a separate province of Sind (Sindh), political reforms in the North-West Frontier Province (now Khyber Pakhtunkhwa) and Baluchistan (Balochistan), Muslim representation in the Punjab and Bengal according to their population, and one-third representation in the central legislature.[100] In fact, he subsequently claimed that 'he alone was responsible for getting the proposal for joint electorates under certain conditions (Delhi Muslim Proposals) accepted by both the Muslim and the Hindu leaders ....'[101]

In addition, Mohamed Ali, like Jinnah, advised the Muslims to boycott the all-white British Simon Commission and, instead, work with the Congress to help frame an agreed constitution for India. The ultimate goal, after all, he insisted, was the same—self-government and freedom of India.

But to his utter dismay, the Congress, in spite of its acceptance (May 1927) and ratification of the Delhi Muslim Proposals in December 1927, refused to oblige. It rejected all the proposals, including the bartering of separate electorates for the Muslims in the future constitution of India. It called for 'mixed joint electorates'. Mohamed Ali was incredulous but not in despair. Like Jinnah at this point in time, he still had some faith left in the Congress and the Hindu-majority community. In an impassioned plea to their sense of fair play and justice, he entreated the Hindus:

… a minority is after all a minority and no matter what you do for it, 'suffering is the badge of the tribe'. To deprive it even of minority representation by swamping it is to play the bully and the tyrant, and that is far less compatible with nationalism than communal representation of minorities secured to them through separate communal electorates.[102]

Mohamed Ali indeed warned the Hindu majority community that 'abhorrence of the communal representation' would not help. It could be 'rid of', eventually, if the minorities were treated well after the establishment of 'Swaraj'. As he explained it:

It does not increase a minority's faith in the majority's sincerity if a community enjoying the comfortable position of security that its majority gives it behaves as if it enjoyed a monopoly of the abhorrence of the communal representation. With all the abhorrence that we feel with regard to communal representation, we cannot pretend to think that if it is allowed to continue for a short period after Swaraj is established, we shall never be rid of it. That would depend upon the treatment that the majority metes out to the minorities and we cannot help thinking that morbid mistrust of communal representation argues on the part of the majority some mistrust of itself.[103]

However, Mohamed Ali's appeal to communal harmony and majority–minority understanding for the sake of its own Swaraj did not move the Congress leadership. His desire to deal justly with difficulties in Hindu–Muslim relations did not make any difference. Gandhi, his old ally in the Khilafat-non-cooperation movement, did nothing to stop the eventual estrangement in Mohamed Ali and his Muslim followers towards himself, the Congress, and its political creed.

Mohamed Ali's differences with Gandhi and the Congress had become known after the Kohat riots of 1924. Gandhi, who was incidentally staying in Delhi as a guest of Mohamed Ali at that time, not only condemned the Muslims but also went on to encourage the Kohat Hindus to fight back, without waiting to ascertain the facts. When Mohamed Ali's brother, Shaukat Ali, issued a statement in 1925, suggesting that both Hindus and Muslims were responsible for the riots, Gandhi disagreed, and vehemently claimed that only the Kohat Muslims were to be blamed. The trouble lay in the offensive pamphlet circulated by Lala Jiwandas, Secretary of Sanatan Dharma Sabha, and the matter was aggravated by the alleged abduction of a married Muslim girl by one Sardar Makhan's son, coupled with the general resentment felt by the Muslim traders of Kohat over the Hindu monopoly of trade in the area. Gandhi himself, in his paper, *Young India*, acknowledged these factors and, yet, insisted that the Muslims were 'responsible' for the whole affair.[104] Thus, the relationship between the Ali brothers and Gandhi was publicly strained. Mohamed Ali went on to blame him for 'giving free reins to the communalism of the majority'.[105]

However, Mohamed Ali was still keen on cultivating good relations with the Hindu majority community. He saw no other way out for the Muslims. He admitted that the non-cooperation movement had failed and that cooperation with Hindus was 'a vain hope, a snare and a delusion'. But then, he wondered, what alternative did the Muslims have? Should the Muslims, he asked,

... 'progress backwards' till we begin to walk on all fours? Shall we cooperate with our foreign rulers and fight with our non-Muslim countrymen as we used to fight before? And if we do that[,] what hope [do] we have of any better results than we achieved for ourselves in the settlements after the Tripoli and the Balkan wars, or, nearer home, in the unsettlement of a 'settled fact' in Bengal? No, friends, that book is closed and into it we shall look no more. You have no alternative better than non-cooperation with the foreigner and cooperation with our neighbours, nor have I. And it is futile to waste our time over the impossible.[106]

Mohamed Ali's persistent and bold efforts to woo the Hindu community were, in fact, 'futile'. The significant success of the Hindu Mahasabha in the 1923–4 elections and the growing strength of 'Hindu nationalism'[107] had made the Hindus all the more indifferent and insular. The Muslims had become irrelevant to their scheme of things for the future. The 'objective conditions' of India, as Jawaharlal Nehru put it,[108] had created a new situation. It was not that Mohamed Ali could not see the winds of change but, apparently, he needed a surer index to measure the intensity of the change. The Nehru Report of 1928,[109] which openly confronted the Muslims with the challenge of a scheme of government for India in which Muslims' particular rights and interests were dismissed and indeed their 'minority' status was challenged,[110] did just that. Mohamed Ali could not believe that the Congress, Gandhi, and the Hindu community in general, would stand up as 'open enemies of Muslims'. 'The Nehru Constitution,' he charged,

... is the legalized tyranny of numbers and is the way to rift and not peace. It recognized the rank communalism of the majority as nationalism. The safeguards proposed to limit the highhandedness of the majority are branded as communal.[111]

The Nehru Report proved to be the most critical point in Mohamed Ali's political career, pushing him now, finally and irrevocably, towards the Muslim separatist political movement. Indeed, he arrived, convinced through practical experience and the hard way, at the conclusion that the Congress, the so-called champion of 'Indian nationalism', was primarily the instrument of Hindu nationalism. Its leaders did not care about the Muslims. It was not only Gandhi who, under the influence of the Mahasabhites, such as Madan Mohan Malaviya and Lajpat Rai, had no interest in the Muslims any more, but the so-called 'liberals' like Motilal Nehru were also prepared to 'denationalize' the Congress and India by their 'blatant and unremitting efforts to placate the Hindu Mahasabha'.[112] Mohamed Ali, thus, publicly snapped ties with the Congress and its brand of nationalism. He felt sure that these ties had completely betrayed the Muslim cause. Mohamed Ali now advised the Muslims, much like Syed Ahmad Khan, the Aga Khan, and Syed Ameer Ali earlier, not to participate in the Congress meetings or get involved with its activities. He also appealed to the Muslims not to participate in the Congress non-cooperation movement (of 1930).[113] 'We refuse to join Mr Gandhi,' he declared, 'because his movement is not a movement for the complete independence of India but for making the seventy millions [sic] of Indian Musalmans dependent of the Hindu Mahasabha ....'[114]

Mohamed Ali increasingly began to find ways and means to promote separate Muslim identity in India by asserting its separatist claims and reviving and reinforcing the separatist political movement. The proposed Round Table Conference in London provided him an opportunity to further this objective. In spite of his failing health and much against the wishes of his doctors, he put his life at stake for what he called his 'religious duty' to go to the conference and 'proclaim the truth both to the tyrannical ruler and the misguided subjects ...'.[115] Addressing the fourth plenary session of the conference on 9 November 1930, Mohamed Ali proclaimed:

Many people in England ask us why this question of Hindu and Muslim comes into politics, and what it has to do with those things. I reply, 'it is a wrong conception of religion that you have, if you exclude politics from it. It is not dogma, it is not ritual! Religion to my mind, means the interpretation of life.' I have a culture, a polity, an outlook on life—a complete synthesis which is Islam. Where God commands I am a Muslim first, a Muslim second, and a Muslim last and nothing but a Muslim. If you ask me to enter into your Empire or into your nation by leaving that synthesis, that polity, that culture, that ethics, I will not do it. My first duty is to my Maker, not to H. M. the King, nor to my companion Dr Moonje [Hindu Mahasabha leader]; my first duty is to my Maker, and that is the case with Dr Moonje also. He must be a Hindu first, and I must be a Muslim first, so far as that duty is concerned. But where India is concerned, where India's freedom is concerned, where the welfare of India is concerned, I am an Indian first, an Indian second, an Indian last, and nothing but an Indian.

Mohamed Ali went on to highlight this paradox thus:

I belong to two circles of equal size, but which are not concentric. One is India, and the other the Muslim world ... We belong to these two circles, each of more than 300 millions [sic], and we can leave neither.[116]

There can be no doubt that Mohamed Ali gave full vent to his Muslim group identity, based on religion, though in sync with his loyalty to India. He was not prepared to break loose. He did not think of Muslims as a separate nation. In fact, he was not enamoured of 'nationalism' as such which, he thought, was divisive and 'cruel' in its manifestations. As he chided the British government:

We are not nationalists but supranationalists, and I, as a Muslim, say that 'God made man and the Devil made the nation.' Nationalism divides; our religion binds. No religious war, no crusades, have seen such holocausts and have been so cruel as your last war, and that was a war of your nationalism, and not my *jehad*.[117]

For Mohamed Ali, as has been emphasised all along, it was primarily his commitment to his religion, to Islam, which inspired him to secure and support Muslim interests wherever they were threatened or in danger, be it in Turkey or in India. Realising the impending threat to the Muslim community in India, Mohamed Ali was now determined to secure for them a share of power, political power, in the Indian polity. 'Luckily, however,' he pointed out, 'there are Muslim majorities in certain provinces ....'[118] Thus, in a letter to the British Prime Minister, Ramsay Macdonald, on

164   A LEADERSHIP ODYSSEY

1 January 1931, when he was bed-ridden and in critical condition, Mohamed Ali articulated the Muslim case at length:

> The real problem before us is to give fuller power to Muslims in such provinces as those in which they are in a majority, whether small or large, and protection to them in such provinces as those in which they are in a minority, and in order to be absolutely fair to the Hindu community also, precisely the same thing must be done with the Hindus. What is needed is to give power to a community which is in majority in any province no matter how small or how large it may be and protection to it in a province, no matter how large or small it may be. The Muslims desire ... that there should be federal government so that the central unity government with a permanent Hindu majority should not override them everywhere; that they should have at least a third of the British Indian representative in the Federal Government, that in the provinces of the Punjab and Bengal where they have small majorities in the population which are unorganized, and greatly controlled by the banyas [Hindu money-lenders] and the Sikhs and the Hindu landlords, as in Bengal, those majorities should be reserved (personally I shall be satisfied if for a number of years only such as 20); that in the NWFP and in Baluchistan (which is only nominally a province) where there are clearly huge Muslim majorities, full reforms should be extended to the Muslims which have so far been denied by the combination of British, military and civil domination and Hindu narrowness characteristically supporting it, and that Sind should be made a separate small province like Assam; and that the Muslims should be allowed to have their majorities in all these as the Hindus have everywhere else. Unless in these few provinces Muslim majorities are established by the new constitution, I submit, not as a threat, but as a very humble and friendly warning, *there will be civil war in India. Let there be no mistake about that.*[119]

The threat of 'civil war' had indeed come a long way—from Syed Ahmad Khan to Mohamed Ali. The Hindus and Muslims not only stood as two separate political communities in India but Mohamed Ali and the Muslims, like Syed Ahmad Khan and his followers in his days, were also alienated from the Hindu community and the Indian National Congress and equally wary of the representative system of government introduced by the British in India. Indeed, reaffirming Syed Ahmad Khan's prognosis, Mohamed Ali admitted that '*a territorial electorate in India of the type of England is an absurdity.*' In such provinces of India, he pointed out:

> Where the minority communities number only 4 and 7 per cent, respectively, the minorities have no chance of getting their true representatives elected even if 20 seats were reserved for them, if 96 per cent or 93 per cent of the rival community are to be allowed to choose their representatives. Men of straw, men who are merely religious Hindu or Muslim, but not *politically* so, will be returned by the votes of *politically* Muslim and Hindu majorities.[120]

In fact, Mohamed Ali had a plan of his own to serve the two communities equitably and fairly. He suggested:

> Let the seats be reserved for the two communities but let no candidate be declared elected unless he secures: (1) at least 40 per cent of votes cast of his own community; (2) at least 5 per cent of the votes cast of other communities wherever he is in a minority of 10 or less per cent and 10 per cent where he is in a larger minority or in a majority.

This, he explained, would serve three purposes:

> In the *first* instance, every candidate will have to go cap in hand to both the communities as in the Minto-Morley Reforms which he does not do today; and the rank abuse of sister communities which goes on today since the Montagu-Chelmsford Reforms, which had [*sic*] ruined Indian politics, and even social life, will cease. *Secondly,* no man would be returned to represent any community who does not represent at least a fair percentage of that community though not necessarily its majority as in the separate electorates today. The *third* purpose which is no less important is that ordinarily no person who is not in the least a *persona grata* to a sister community will be able to get returned even if he secures election from his own community.[121]

However, Mohamed Ali insisted that the Muslims were not a 'minority' in the sense there were some other minorities in India. In the right faithful exposition of Syed Ahmad Khan's ideas, again, Mohamed Ali highlighted the historical importance of the Muslim community in India. The Muslims had 'ruled over India in one way or another from the 8th to the middle of 19th century in some part of the country or another and that no other community has anything like that record [sic].' But then, more importantly, he stressed:

> A community that in India alone must now be numbering more than 70 millions [sic] cannot easily be called a minority in the sense of Geneva minorities, and when it is remembered that this community numbers nearly 400 millions [sic] of people throughout the world ... who claim and feel a unique brotherhood; to talk of it as a minority is a mere absurdity.[122]

Mohamed Ali died soon after this long, painstaking plea and could not see the response of the British authorities one way or another. He breathed his last on 4 January 1931, two days after the letter was written. In accordance with his wishes, he was buried in the courtyard of Masjid-al-Aqsa in Jerusalem. He kept his allegiance with the Muslim world intact, both alive and dead. In the process, Mohamed Ali 'gave his life for India but denied her his body'.[123]

Mohamed Ali had dominated Muslim politics since the establishment of the All-India Muslim League in December 1906. He had been 'in the centre of every melee, as reformer and social radical, as crusader for the Turkish cause, and as champion of Muslim political interests.'[124] He was a devout Muslim and indeed claimed that he was Muslim first and last. Islam was his motive and mode of conduct in every act. In leading the Khilafat Movement, he was convinced of espousing and advancing the cause of Islam. Though it failed to realise its ostensible objective of saving the Khilafat, the movement did succeed in leaving behind 'a pattern of politics which the Muslims of British India later tried to follow.' It was 'the first India-wide agitation' of the Muslims, and thus helped them not only learn the art of 'political agitation' but also made them 'conscious of their potentialities'.[125] It also showed the British and the Hindus that the Muslims were not there for the asking.

The Khilafat Movement also impressed upon the Muslims the need to give up the idea that they could depend on the British or the

Hindus to secure their political rights and interests. It convinced them that the British would not hesitate to leave them in the lurch if it suited them and the Congress could not give them anything more than submergence of their 'separate political identity into the fathomless ocean of India, and more specifically Hindu, nationalism'.[126] Their only hope lay in relying upon themselves, their own 'inherent strength', and working out their destiny by themselves.[127] The period of 'entente' or rapprochement, if at all, between the Muslims and Hindus could not evolve a permanent platform for the reconciliation of separate and, in many ways, conflicting interests of the two communities. The movement had, no doubt, served as a unifying force for a while, but even in this venture, as mentioned again and again, there were inherent conflicts of interests between the two communities and their leaders. With its eventual collapse, this artificial, pretended, and misleading unity gave way to mutual antipathy and separateness; indeed a spate of communal riots followed like never before. Both Hindus and Muslims took to their separate paths and their separate destinies. As Halide Edib, a Turkish writer, perceptively noticed, 'the Khilafat Movement had "two curiously contradictory results in India: that of uniting the Muslims and Hindus around a common activity; and that of dividing them."'[128] This division, of course, helped 'the Muslims to strengthen the case for Muslim nationalism as distinct from Indian nationalism.'[129]

Mohamed Ali's efforts to promote and pursue Muslim interests revived the moribund Muslim separatist political movement of the Khilafat days. It regained strength and momentum, and got a new lease of life. Indeed, Mohamed Ali and the separatist political movement had come full circle. However, Mohamed Ali was still not ready to abandon his Indian connection and thus help charter a clear, separate, course for the Muslims, with their separate national goal. Maybe he would eventually have, had he lived longer and experienced further political developments such as the Congress rule of provinces in 1937-9. His trajectory certainly suggested that. But then, as the turn of events showed, it was left to Allama Muhammad Iqbal, 'the poet of Islam's reawakening in India in the 20th Century', as Mohamed Ali himself described him,[130] to reinforce Muslim separatism and lead and secure the separatist political movement through Muslim nationalism and the formulation of the idea of a separate state in India.

Notes

1. For a detailed discussion of this perspective on Syed Ahmad Khan, see, Sikandar Hayat, 'Syed Ahmad Khan and the Foundation of Muslim Separatist Political Movement in India', *Pakistan Journal of Social Sciences*, Vol. VIII, No. 1 and 2 (Jan-July-Dec, 1982): 33–47. For a revised and updated version, see Chp. 2 of this book.
2. In his autobiographical account, *My Life: A Fragment*, Mohamed Ali explained his learning 'at Oxford, where I took an Honours Degree in Modern History [was] an excellent opportunity of acquainting myself with a portion of the history of my co-religionists as the period of general history that I selected ... covered the rise and growth of the Muslim power ....' Afzal Iqbal, ed., *My Life: A Fragment, An Autobiographical Sketch of Maulana Mohammad Ali Jauhar* (Islamabad: National Press Trust, 1987), 32.
3. Quoted in Afzal Iqbal, *Life and Times of Mohamed Ali* (Lahore: Institute of Islamic Culture, 1974), 159.
4. Iqbal, *My Life*, 40.
5. Mushirul Hasan, *Mohamed Ali in Indian Politics: Select Writings* (Delhi: Atlantic Publishers, 1982), 77.
6. Ibid., 151–2.
7. Afzal Iqbal, ed., *Select Writings and Speeches of Maulana Mohamed Ali*, Vol. II (Lahore: Sh. Muhammad Ashraf, 1969), 4.
8. Hasan, *Mohamed Ali in Indian Politics*, 181.
9. Ibid., xxiv.
10. The official position regarding the arrest of Mohamed Ali and his brother Shaukat Ali, as communicated by the Viceroy to the Secretary of State was: 'Mohamed Ali leaves trouble wherever he goes. Recently, he was in Lahore and addressed the students in the Medical College, the result being that a few days later, 14 or 15 students went off to Afghanistan nominally to raise the tribes against us. Mohamed Ali also went to Aligarh College and created trouble, the result being that the Lieutenant Governors of the Punjab and United Provinces asked the Government of India to prevent these two agitators from entering their provinces. This was in my opinion, sufficient reason for their internment.' Quoted in Iqbal, *Life and Times*, 113. Mohamed Ali himself believed, as he wrote to Ramsay Macdonald, a leading British politician, in a letter which was withheld by the British authorities at that time, 'The Kanpur controversy and my somewhat successful trip to England were the particular counts of the charge.' Hasan, *Mohamed Ali in Indian Politics*, 231. The researchers and scholars, in

general, strangely enough, always considered publications of the article, 'The Choice of Turks' to be the main cause of Mohamed Ali's arrest. See, for instance, Hasan, *Mohamed Ali in Indian Politics*, 'Introduction', xxviii. See the article in Afzal Iqbal, ed., *Select Writings and Speeches of Maulana Mohamed Ali*, Vol. I (Lahore: Sh. Muhammad Ashraf, 1969), 179–217.

11. Iqbal, *Select Writings and Speeches*, Vol. I, 209–12.

12. Hasan, *Mohamed Ali in Indian Politics*, xxxv-vi.

13. Wilfred Cantwell Smith, *Modern Islam in India: A Social Analysis* (London: Victor Gollacz, 1946), 24.

14. Iqbal, *Select Writings and Speeches*, Vol. II, 112.

15. Iqbal, *Select Writings and Speeches*, Vol. I, 213.

16. Iqbal, *Select Writings and Speeches*, Vol. I, 64.

17. Rafique Akhtar, ed., *Historic Trial: Maulana Mohamed Ali and Others* (Karachi: East and West Publishing Co., 1971), 54.

18. Hasan, *Mohamed Ali in Indian Politics*, xxxiv.

19. Abdul Hamid, *Muslim Separatism in India: A Brief Survey, 1858–1947* (Lahore: Oxford University Press, 1967), 103–4.

20. Smith, *Modern Islam*, 196.

21. Cited in Gail Minault, *The Khilafat Movement: Religious Symbolism and Political Mobilization in India* (New York: Columbia University Press, 1982), 56.

22. Iqbal, *Select Writings and Speeches*, Vol. I, 81.

23. Ibid., 215.

24. Akhtar, *Historic Trial*, 64.

25. Ibid., 60–1. Syed Ahmad Khan, on the contrary, believed that the ruler of Turkey was a Muslim King and not their *Khalifa* and thus could not claim their temporal and spiritual allegiance. Their religious duty was quite clear: 'to obey our rulers and remain quite loyal to them.' Syed Ahmad Khan, *Akhri Mazameen* (Lahore: Matba Rafai Aam Press, 1898), 32–3.

26. Iqbal, *Select Writings and Speeches*, Vol. II, 21–3.

27. Dr Ansari was a physician at Delhi. Earlier, he was resident medical officer at the Charing Cross Hospital in London. The mission comprised 26 members including seven doctors, five pharmacists, twelve medical attendants, and two managers catering to a 'hundred-bed mobile-hospital, with ten thousand pounds sterling at hand'. M. Naeem Qureshi, *Ottoman Turkey, Ataturk, and Muslim South Asia* (Karachi: Oxford University Press, 2014), 35.

28. According to Mustafa Kemal Ataturk, however, 'those who had dragged the nation and the country into the Great War had thought only of saving their own lives and had fled abroad. Vahideddin, who occupied the position of Sultan and Caliph, was a degenerate who, by infamous means, sought only to guard his own person and throne. The Cabinet, headed by Damad Ferid Pasha, was weak, cowardly and without dignity, subservient to the will of the Sultan, and ready to agree to anything that might protect him as well as their person'. Bernard Lewis, *The Emergence of Modern Turkey*

(Lahore: Oxford University Press, 1967), 240–6. Quoted in Iqbal, *Life and Times*, 166.

29. See, for instance, Aziz Ahmad, *Studies in Islamic Culture in the Indian Environment* (London: Oxford University Press, 1964), 63; Ziya ul-Hassan Farooqi, *The Deoband School and the Demand for Pakistan* (Bombay: Asia Publishing House, 1963), 19, n.1, and 24–5; and M. Naeem Qureshi, *Pan-Islam in British India: The Politics of the Khilafat Movement, 1918–1924* (Karachi: Oxford University Press, 2009), 7.

30. K. K. Aziz, ed., *The Indian Khilafat Movement, 1915–1933: A Documentary Record* (Karachi: National Publishing House, 1972), 72.

31. Ibid., 73.

32. M. Naeem Qureshi, 'The Indian Khilafat Movement (1918–1924)', *Journal of Asian History*, Vol. 12, No. 2 (1978), 165.

33. Sharif al Mujahid, 'The Khilafat Movement', in *Mohammad Ali: Life and Work* (Karachi: Pakistan Historical Society, 1978), 108–9.

34. M. Mujeeb, *The Indian Muslims* (London: George Allen & Unwin, 1967), 434.

35. Hamid, *Muslim Separatism*, 134. It was indeed Lloyd George himself who credited General Allenby with having 'won the last and most triumphant of the crusades'. Iqbal, *Select Writings and Speeches*, Vol. II, 38.

36. Secret Memorandum by Political Department, India Office, on War with Turkey. Cited in Iqbal, *Life and Times*, 164.

37. Qureshi, *Ottoman Turkey*, 81.

38. For the constitution of the Khilafat Conference see, Aziz, *The Indian Khilafat Movement*, Appendix II, 228–348.

39. Ahmad Saeed and Kh. Mansur Sarwar, *Trek to Pakistan* (Lahore: Al-Fouzi Publishers, 2012), 127.

40. See, for instance, Z. A. Suleri, *My Leader* (Lahore: Lion Press, 1945), 52; and A. B. Rajput, *Muslim League Yesterday and Today* (Lahore: Sh. Muhammad Ashraf, 1948), 37.

41. Minault, *The Khilafat Movement*, 56; Judith Brown, Chp. 6, 'Khilafat', in *Gandhi's Rise to Power: Indian Politics, 1915–1922* (Cambridge: Cambridge University Press, 1977), 190–230; and Francis Robinson, *Separatism among Indian Muslims* (Cambridge: Cambridge University Press, 1974), 35. Hamza Alavi, a noted sociologist, in a review article claimed that 'it was Gandhi who played a key role in organizing the *Khilafat* movement … Maulana Abdul Bari, Abul Kalam Azad, Dr Ansari, Maulana Mohammad Ali, Maulana Shaukat Ali and all the principal leaders of the *Khilafat* movement committed themselves, only too readily, to follow Gandhi's dictates.' Hamza Alavi, 'Pan-Islam in British Indian Politics', Review Articles, *Pakistan Perspectives*, Vol. 7, No. 2 (July–December 2002): 153.

42. Incidentally, Gandhi on meeting Mohamed Ali for the first time in 1915 at Delhi observed: 'it was a question of love at first sight between us.' M. K. Gandhi, *The Collected Works of Mahatma Gandhi*, Vol. XV (Delhi: Publications Division, Ministry of Information, 1979), 265.

43. 379 were killed and some 1,200 were wounded when General Dyer, without any apparent reason and without any warning to the crowd assembled at Jallianwala Bagh on 13 April 1919 to protest against the Rowlatt Act, ordered his troops to open fire. The Government was initially silent about this tragedy for a period of eight months, but then appointed a Commission of Inquiry. The commission did no more than criticise General Dyer, the architect of the massacre in such mild terms as 'unfortunate' and 'injudicious'. For some of the discussion on the subject and its impact on Indian politics, see particularly, Reginald Coupland, *India: A Re-Statement* (London: Oxford University Press, 1945), 50; Annie Besant, *The Future of Indian Politics* (London: Theosophical Publishing House, 1922), 243. Michael O'Dwyer, *India As I Knew It, 1885–1925* (London: Constable, 1925); and Michael Edwards, *the Last Years of British India* (London: Cassell, 1963), 52–4.

44. Text of the Treaty given in Aziz, *The Indian Khilafat Movement*, 149–65.

45. Iqbal, *Select Writings and Speeches*, Vol. II, 270.

46. Mushriul Hasan, *Nationalism and Communal Politics in India: 1916–1928* (Delhi: Manohar, 1979), 187.

47. John Gallagher, 'Nationalism and the Crisis of Empire, 1919–1922,' in *Power, Profit and Politics*, eds. Christopher Baker, Gordon Johnson and Anil Seal (Cambridge: Cambridge University Press, 1981), 364.

48. Minault, *The Khilafat Movement*, 68.

49. M. K. Gandhi, *The Collected Works of Mahatma Gandhi*, Vol. XX (Delhi: Publications Division, Ministry of Information, 1979), 2.

50. Iqbal, *Select Writings and Speeches*, Vol. II, 29.

51. Aziz, *The Indian Khilafat Movement*, 111. Important 'Labourites', however, helped Mohamed Ali and the delegation 'individually and through their Party workers who thronged to the Khilafat meetings, and had even provided Mohamed Ali with an opportunity to speak at the twentieth annual conference of the Labour Party at Scarborough in June 1920. However, as a collective, the Labour Party could not be won over.' Qureshi, *Ottoman Turkey*, 100.

52. *The Indian Annual Register, 1921* (Calcutta: Annual Register Office, 1921), Part III, 106–8.

53. Aziz, *The Indian Khilafat Movement*, 147.

54. While initially the ulema's participation in the Movement was on an individual basis and mostly the result of the efforts of Maulana Abdul Bari and his Farangi Mahal group, the *ulema* subsequently decided to act in concert and founded *Jamiat-i-Ulema-i-Hind*. See Mohammed Mian, ed., *Jamiyat-ul-Ulama Kiya Hai* (Delhi: Jamiat-ul-Ulama, 1946), 16. Also see Qureshi, 'The Khilafat Movement in India 1919–1924,' 80; Minault, *The Khilafat Movement*, 72, 79–82; Farooqi, *The Deoband School*, 76; Mushir-ul-Haq, *Muslim politics in Modern India; 1857–1947* (Meerut: Meenakshi Parakshan, 1970), 116; and Peter Hardy, *Partners in Freedom and True Muslims: The Political Thought of Some Muslim Scholars in British India,*

1912–1947 (Lund: Student Literature Scandanavian Institute of Asian Studies, 1971).

55. Iqbal, *My Life*, 46.

56. This should not be confused with the Swadeshi movement of 1905, which was a boycott of British goods for different reasons.

57. Jawaharlal Nehru, *An Autobiography* (London: Bodley Head, 1958), 80.

58. Quoted in Iqbal, *Life and Times,* 139.

59. T. Morrison, in Sir John Cumming, ed., *Political India, 1832–1932* (London: Oxford University Press, 1932), 97. Also see, Waheed-uz-Zaman, *Towards Pakistan* (Lahore: United Publishers, 1969), 28. Others, who did not return to India, found refuge in Turkey and Russia.

60. Qureshi, 'The Indian Khilafat Movement (1918–1924)', 157.

61. Ibid.

62. R. C. Majumdar, *History of the Freedom Movement*, Vol. III (Calcutta: Firma K. L. Mukhopadhyay, 1962), 191.

63. Mujahid, 'The Khilafat Movement', 130–1.

64. Rajendra Prasad, *India Divided* (Bombay: Hind Kitab, 1977), 123.

65. M. K. Gandhi, *The Collected Works of Mahatma Gandhi*, Vol. XXII (New Delhi: Publications Division, Ministry of Information, 1979), 418.

66. Ainslie T. Embree, *India's Search for National Identity* (New York: Alfred A. Knopf, 1972), 81. R. P. Dutt, *India Today* (London: Victor Gollancz, 1940), 233; Michael Breeher, *Nehru: A Political Biography* (Boston: Beacon Press, 1962), 43, and Abdul Hamid, *On Understanding the Quaid-i-Azam* (Islamabad: National Committee for Birth Centenary Celebrations of Quaid-i-Azam Mohammad Ali Jinnah, 1977), 74.

67. Speech on the abolition of Khilafat at Aligarh on 8 March 1924. Similarly, Syed Ameer Ali was distressed. 'The Khilafat' he said, 'is not a national institution, the property of a single State to "abolish" it at its free will…'. Aziz, *The Indian Khilafat Movement*, 289, 292. Allama Iqbal, however, saw it differently. 'Personally', he remarked, 'I believe the Turkish view is perfectly correct. It is hardly necessary to argue this point. The republican form of government is not only thoroughly consistent with the spirit of Islam, but has also become a necessity in view of the new forces that are set free in the world of Islam.' Muhammad Iqbal, *The Reconstruction of Religious Thought in Islam* (Lahore: Sh. Muhammad Ashraf, 1965), 157.

68. Qureshi, *Ottoman Turkey*, 149.

69. Ibid.

70. Qureshi, *Pan-Islam in British India*, 287.

71. For some of the details on these riots see, B. R. Ambedkar, *Pakistan, or the Partition of India* (Bombay: Thacker & Co., 1946), 153–66; Mujeeb, *The Indian Muslims*, 437; and Sharif al Mujahid, 'Communal Riots', *A History of Freedom Movement*, Vol. IV, Part II (Karachi: Pakistan Historical Society, 1970), 142–89.

72. M. K. Gandhi, *The Collected Works of Mahatma Gandhi*, Vol. XXVI (Delhi: Publications Division, Ministry of Information, 1979), 215.

73. Qureshi, *Pan-Islam in British India*, 303.
74. Hamid, *Muslim Separatism*, 147.
75. Iqbal, *Select Writings and Speeches*, Vol. II, 271.
76. Hamid, *Muslim Separatism*, 147.
77. Robinson, *Separatism among Indian Muslims*, 35.
78. S. K. Majumdar, *Jinnah and Gandhi: Their Role in India's Quest for Freedom* (Lahore: Peoples Publishing House, 1976), 63.
79. Keith Callard, *Pakistan: A Political Study* (London: George Allen & Unwin, 1968), 34.
80. Smith, *Modern Islam*, 201.
81. M. K. Gandhi, *The Collected Works of Mahatma Gandhi*, Vol. XVI (Delhi: Publications Division, Ministry of Information, 1979), 308 (Italics added).
82. M. K. Gandhi, *The Collected Works of Mahatma Gandhi*, Vol. XVII (Delhi: Publications Division, Ministry of Information, 1979), 100.
83. M. K. Gandhi, *The Collected Works of Mahatma Gandhi*, Vol. XVI, 306.
84. Aziz Ahmad, *Islamic Modernism in India and Pakistan* (London: Oxford University Press, 1967), 123. Also see F. Rahman, 'Muslim Modernism in the Indo-Pakistan Sub-continent', *Bulletin of the School of Oriental and African Studies* (London, 1958): xxi, 1, 89; Khalid bin Sayeed, *Pakistan: The Formative Phase, 1857–1948*, 2nd ed. (Karachi: Oxford University Press, 1994); and Minault, *The Khilafat Movement*, 2–3.
85. Ibid.
86. This point is amply supported by the text of the Central Khilafat Committee Statement of April 1930. The Khilafat workers, it said, 'continued the struggle without pressing for any safeguards for the Muslim minority.' See Aziz, *The Indian Khilafat Movement*, 325.
87. Robinson, in particular, is convinced that Mohamed Ali was exploiting the Khilafat sentiment for political and financial gains. Robinson, *Separatism Among Indian Muslims*, 184–5, 189. Robinson fails to appreciate the hold of Islam on Mohamed Ali's personal and public life. That made him what he was, in the eyes of the Muslims. All else about him was secondary.
88. See, for instance, Ishtiaq Husain Qureshi, *The Muslim Community of the Indo-Pakistan Subcontinent (610–1947); A Brief Historical Analysis* (Hague: Mouton & Co., 1962), 318.
89. Aziz, *The Indian Khilafat Movement*, 67.
90. Iqbal, *Select Writings and Speeches*, Vol. II, 41.
91. See in particular Mohamed Ali's response to Gandhi's Presidential address to the Congress at Belgaum in January 1925. Iqbal, *Select Writings and Speeches,* Vol. II, 205–30.
92. Iqbal, *Life and Times*, 156.
93. Iqbal, *My Life*, 147.
94. Mohamed Ali in a letter to Ramsay Macdonald on 18 February 1916, in Hasan, *Mohamed Ali in Indian Politics*, 227–8.
95. Iqbal, *My Life*, 29, 76. This autobiographic work, 'originally entitled "Islam: Kingdom of God"', completed during the internment period of

Mohamed Ali is, in fact, 'a detailed explanation of the author's religious antecedents and his attitude towards Islamic Theology'. The original purpose was to compile a study of the Holy Prophet (PBUH) more or less on the lines of Shibli's famous *Sirat-un-Nabi*. This could not be done 'for want of necessary books and facilities for communicating with the outside world.' For a useful background information on the book see, Afzal Iqbal's 'Introduction' to the volume. Ibid.

96. Iqbal, *Select Writings and Speeches*, Vol. II, 4.
97. J. Coatman, *Years of Destiny: India, 1926–1932* (London: Jonathan Cape, 1932), 105.
98. Iqbal, *Select Writings and Speeches*, Vol. II, 117.
99. Mohamed Ali not only supported Jinnah in his efforts to reorganise the League after the Khilafat Movement was over but also projected that he would 'lead the Muslims in [the] future if [the] great God puts in his head to take up the job.' A. A. Ravoof, *Meet Mr. Jinnah* (Lahore: Sh. Muhammad Ashraf, 1955), 225.
100. See the details of 'Delhi Muslim Proposals, 1927', in Sharif al Mujahid, *Quaid-i-Azam Jinnah: Studies in Interpretation* (Karachi: Quaid-i-Azam Academy, 1981), Appendix 8, 466–7.
101. See Maulana Muhammad Ali, Editorial, *Hamdard*, 15 January 1929. Cited in Mujahid, *Studies in Interpretation*, 387.
102. Iqbal, *Select Writings and Speeches*, Vol. II, 240.
103. Ibid., 237–8.
104. For a detailed analysis of the Kohat riots and their bearing on Hindu–Muslim relations in general and Gandhi–Ali relations in particular see, Mujahid, *Studies in Interpretation*, 194–8, 382.
105. Iqbal, *Life and Times*, 360.
106. Iqbal, *Select Writings and Speeches*, Vol. II, 153.
107. Coupland, *A Re-Statement*, 135.
108. Nehru, *Autobiography*, 119.
109. For 'Nehru Report' on Minority Representation see Mujahid, *Studies in Interpretation*, Appendix 9, 468–72.
110. Coatman, *Years of Destiny*, 105.
111. Cited in Iqbal, *Life and Times*, 360.
112. Hamid, *Muslim Separatism*, 185.
113. For the text of the Central Khilafat Committee Statement on the issue see, Aziz, *The Indian Khalifat Movement*, 324–8.
114. Address to the All-India Muslim Conference, 1930. Quoted in Coupland, *A Re-Statement*, 136.
115. Cited in Iqbal, *Life and Times*, 376.
116. Iqbal, *Select Writings and Speeches*, Vol. II, 356–7.
117. Ibid., 357.
118. Ibid., 358.
119. Ibid., 372. (Italics original).
120. Ibid., 376–7. (Italics original).

121. Ibid., 377.
122. Ibid., 367.
123. Afzal Iqbal, 'Introduction', in Iqbal, *Select Writings and Speeches*, Vol. II, xix.
124. Hasan, *Mohamed Ali in Indian Politics*, xxvii.
125. Qureshi, 'The Indian Khilafat Movement (1918–1924)', 168–9.
126. Mujahid, *Studies in Interpretation*, 343.
127. Rajput, *Muslim League: Yesterday and Today*, 42.
128. Qureshi, 'The Indian Khilafat Movement (1918–1924)', 166.
129. Qureshi, *Pan-Islam in British India*, 326.
130. Iqbal, *My Life*, 177. Also see, Mohamed Ali's 'Appreciation of Iqbal', in *Selections from Maulana Mohamed Ali's Comrade*, ed. Syed Rais Ahmad Jafri (Nadvi) (Lahore: Mohamed Ali Academy, 1965), 307.

6

Allama Muhammad Iqbal and the Formulation of the Idea of a Separate State in India

Allama Muhammad Iqbal's role in Muslim politics in India hardly needs to be emphasised. Not only did he promote the Muslim separatist political movement—founded by Syed Ahmad Khan[1] and strengthened and reinforced by the Aga Khan, Syed Ameer Ali, and Maulana Mohamed Ali in their own ways—but, more importantly, he formulated the idea of a separate state for Muslims as a separate 'nation'. In the process, he also played a crucial role in persuading Quaid-i-Azam Mohammad Ali Jinnah to accept and pursue the idea, and thus helped the Muslim separatist movement reach its ultimate goal.[2]

Allama Iqbal (1877–1938) was born on 9 November 1877 in Sialkot (Punjab) to a family of middle class origins.[3] He started his schooling in Sialkot, at Scotch Mission College, and then attended Government College Lahore, a reputed institution, for higher studies. He obtained his Master's degree in Philosophy in 1899, mentored by Professor Thomas Arnold, 'a loving teacher who combined in himself [*sic*] a profound knowledge of western philosophy and a deep understanding of Islamic culture and Arabic literature.'[4] During this period, Iqbal indulged in poetry, started reciting poems, and soon emerged 'as a promising young poet in the literary circles of Lahore'.[5] However, inspired by Professor Arnold, Iqbal sailed for Europe in 1905 to seek further education and, in addition to securing a Bachelor of Arts degree from Cambridge University and completing his doctorate in Philosophy at Munich

University,[6] he also did Bar-at-Law at Lincoln's Inn, London,[7] before returning in 1908 a changed man—both personally and professionally. Interestingly, he started 'his professional career as an attorney, college professor, and poet—all at once.'[8] However, the legal profession did not interest him much and he did not pursue it for long. It was philosophy and poetry that really absorbed his attention and efforts, and soon he came to be known more as a poet 'proclaiming and elaborating his message of dynamic activism, of a potentially glorious future, and of the supreme value of Islam'.[9]

Iqbal also started taking interest in politics, particularly Muslim politics of India. He was quite favourably disposed to the activities of the All-India Muslim League since its inception[10] but more so after 1910.[11] He chose the Punjab, his home province, as his 'political arena'.[12] He became Joint Secretary of the Punjab Muslim League and was elected Chair of the Public Relations Committee of the important League session to be held in 1919 at Amritsar. But, while he did attend that session, he did not act as chair of that committee. He was not keen enough![13] In 1920, he even refused to serve on the Khilafat Committee in Punjab.[14]

While this reluctance to serve on the Khilafat Committee may also be attributed to his strong reservations, like Jinnah, on the non-cooperation method employed for launching the Khilafat-non-cooperation movement,[15] the fact was that Iqbal was probably not ready for a political life and career. Many reasons can be deduced. First, Iqbal possessed a temperament—a philosophical temperament—which encouraged him to prefer a life of calm and contemplation rather than the hubbub of the political world.[16] Secondly, Iqbal was deeply involved with his poetic-philosophic works. He had already produced *Asrar-i-Khudi* (1915) and *Rumuz-i-Bekhudi* (1918), and was busy completing his stirring work *Payam-i-Mashriq* (1923).[17] His message in *Asrar-i-Khudi, Rumuz-i-Bekhudi, Payam-i-Mashriq*, and indeed in all his subsequent works, such as *Bang-i-Dara* (1924), *Zabur-i-Ajam* (1927), *Javid Nama* (1932), *Bal-i-Jibril* (1935), *Zarb-i-Kalim* (1936), and *Armughan-i-Hijaz* (1938), published posthumously, was to help Muslims awaken their 'soul' from deep slumber and to realise their true potential through a life of action and dynamism, in line with the demands of the fast changing world. He exhorted the Muslims not to lose hope in the wake of their political setbacks at the time. They were a great community as their past showed, and with a little more initiative, drive, determination, and will to move forward, they could make their twentieth-century destiny as promising as it was in the past. Iqbal, in fact, argued that the spiritual force of Islam was not dependent on its temporal power. As he put it:

> The history of Islam tells us that the expansion of Islam as a religion is in no way related to the political power of its followers. The greatest spiritual conquests of Islam were made during the days of our political decrepitude. When the rude barbarians of Mongolia drowned in blood the civilization of Baghdad in 1258 A.D., when the Muslim power fell in Spain and the followers of Islam were mercilessly killed or driven out of Cordova by Ferdinand in 1236, Islam had just secured a footing in Sumatra and was about to work the peaceful conversion of the Malay Archipelago.[18]

Finally, it must be remembered that until 1925, Iqbal was teaching at the Punjab University and was thus barred from taking part in active politics. This, according to many writers, seemed to be 'a more accurate reason' for his cautious, hesitant approach towards political developments.[19]

However, soon after, in 1926, Iqbal was prepared to get actively involved in politics,[20] and for a good reason. While Muslims, in the aftermath of the Khilafat Movement, were at a loss, Hindus, led by Gandhi and under the guidance of the Congress, were emerging from their struggle with a newfound confidence in their future. Their 'political ideals', indeed their concept of nationalism, Iqbal felt, could 'affect' India's 'original structure and character' beyond redemption. He, therefore, decided to join practical politics.[21] However, understandably, a 'poet whose primary aim was to egg on his co-regionalists into concerted worldly action in defence of their religion did not find it easy to translate his own ideals into political practice.'[22]

Still, Iqbal took his cue from Syed Ahmad Khan's political lead. In fact, according to Hafeez Malik, 'Iqbal followed Sir Sayyid

Ahmad Khan's school of political thought',[23] which helped him publicly acclaim the separatist course chartered by him. Indeed, he felt that it was only after the bitter experiences of the present that the Muslims had come to realise the soundness of his policy.[24] 'We tried the majority community', he lamented, 'and found them unwilling to recognize the safeguards which we can forego only at the risk of complete extinction as a nation determined to live its own life'.[25] He stood for elections to the Punjab Legislative Council in 1926, defeated his opponent convincingly,[26] and got involved in legislative politics by 1927. At the time, the Muslim League was moribund in Punjab. Major parties in Punjab were Mian Fazl-i-Hussain's Punjab Nationalist Unionist Party, a grand alliance of rural Muslim, Hindu, and Sikh landowning classes, and the Swaraj party, which included a few die-hard Khilafatists. The Swarajists were more 'pro-Hindu than nationalist' and were 'more urban' in their orientation.[27] There were, of course, the Indian National Congress and the Hindu Sabha parties. Thus, sensing 'the Unionist alliance as a lesser evil, Iqbal joined it.'[28] Although he realised that he was 'only an odd man in their alliance', and he 'maintained a nominal membership among the Unionists',[29] he saw no other platform. For Iqbal and other like-minded Muslims,

> the alternative was equally unpleasant. By forming a separate bloc in the [legislative] council, they would have reduced the Unionist strength, making the rule of Hindu Sabha and the Congress group a distinct possibility. The latter were publicly committed to annul the separate electorates in all shapes and forms and to repeal the Land Alienation Act [to the detriment of the Muslim landowning classes]. To Iqbal both were necessary to protect Muslims' interests.[30]

Iqbal's ideas on the Muslim predicament had been taking shape since 1905–8, during the course of his three-year stay in Europe. Before leaving India for Europe, like many educated Muslims of his day, he was a votary of the idea of nationalism—Indian nationalism. His early poems, such as 'Himalaya', 'Niya Shiwala', and quite a few others were 'expressive of his patriotism', convinced that 'religion was not a barrier' between the Hindus and the Muslims and their 'unity'.[31] Although he shared Syed Ahmad Khan's view of Muslim separatist group life in India, he still did not believe in isolating Muslims from other communities 'on the grounds that the representatives of the various religious communities in India allegedly had no common national interest'.[32] He saw a common interest and, indeed, was convinced that the freedom of India was not possible without a joint national consciousness and effort, transcending all religious lines of differentiation and differences.[33]

The European experience and the maturity of ideas over a period of time, however, brought home to Iqbal the harsh realities of the nationalist creed and nationalism.[34] He saw a materialistic outlook of life and an obsession with territory, and, along with it, a tendency to negate the best values in individuals and humanity at large. 'I am opposed to nationalism as it is understood in Europe,' he proclaimed,

> ... because I see in it the germs of atheistic materialism which I look upon as the greatest danger to modern humanity. Patriotism is a perfectly natural virtue and has a place in the moral life of man. Yet that which really matters is a man's faith, his culture, his historical tradition. These are the things which in my eyes are worth living for and dying for, and not the piece of earth with which the spirit of man happens to be temporarily associated.[35]

In Iqbal's estimate, nationalism was essentially a materialistic creed, devoid of any spiritual or ethical content. It was a Western concept,[36] rooted in the conception of Christianity as a monastic order separating the world of matter from the world of spirit, and thus accentuating the separation of Church and State. The Islamic ideal was totally different. In Islam, Iqbal explained:

> ... the spiritual and temporal are not two distinct domains. In Islam it is the same reality which appears as Church looked at from one point of view and State from another. It is not true to say that Church and State are two sides or facets of the same thing. Islam is a single unanalysable reality which is one or the other as your point of view varies.[37]

Islam, according to Iqbal, united religion and state, matter and spirit, ethics and politics. It was an integrated 'religio-political system'.[38] Was it possible then, Iqbal asked, 'to retain Islam as an ethical ideal and to reject it as a polity, in favour of national polities in which the religious attitude is not permitted to play any part?' His answer was in the negative. The experience of Islam, Iqbal insisted, was not:

> mere experience in the sense of a purely biological event, happening inside the experiment and necessitating no reaction on its social environment. It is individual experience creative of a social order. Its immediate outcome is the fundamentals of a polity with implicit legal concepts whose civic significance cannot be belittled merely because their origin is revelational.[39]

These 'fundamentals', Iqbal believed, were of special importance to India where the Muslims happened to be a 'minority'. The case of Muslim countries was different. They were practically wholly Muslim in their population. They were Muslim-majority countries. The minorities there, he pointed out:

> belong in the language of the [Holy] Quran, to the 'people of the Book'. A Jew or a Christian or a Zoroastrian does not pollute the food of a Muslim by touching it, and the law of Islam allows inter-marriage with the 'people of the Book'. Indeed the first practical step that Islam took towards the realisation of a final combination of humanity was to call upon peoples possessing practically the same ethical ideal to come forward and combine.[40]

Iqbal, therefore, argued that in Muslim countries where nationalism did not countenance the separation of the spiritual from the temporal, it was not necessarily in 'conflict' with Islam. It came into conflict with Islam only when it began to play the role of:

> a political concept and claims to be a principle of human solidarity demanding that Islam should recede to the background of a mere private opinion and cease to be a living factor in the national life. In Turkey, Persia, Egypt and other Muslim countries the Muslims constitute an overwhelming majority and their minorities, i.e. Jews,

Christians and Zoroastrians, according to the law of Islam, are either 'people of the Book' or 'like the people of the Book', with whom the law of Islam allows free alliances.[41]

Thus, nationalism, Iqbal insisted, became a problem in a country where the Muslims happened to be in a minority, and where religion was supposedly a private affair of the individuals and had nothing to do with their temporal existence, demanding their 'complete self-effacement'. In the Muslim-majority countries, Islam not only accommodated nationalism but indeed complemented it.[42] In fact, 'nationalism is not an issue in a Muslim country... [and] nationalisms may flourish, for they pose no threat to the Muslim personality of the people concerned.'[43] In this qualified sense, then, 'if Muslims are politically dominant[,] Islam has no quarrel with modern territorial nationalism.'[44]

In this assessment, Iqbal was also helped by the Turkish experience. The abolition of Khilafat, in particular, convinced Iqbal that 'Islam is neither Nationalism nor Imperialism but a League of Nations which recognizes artificial boundaries and racial distinctions for facility of reference ....'.[45] The 'new ideal' of Islam, in fact, suggested that:

> For the present every Muslim nation must sink into her own deeper self, temporarily focus her vision on herself alone, until all are strong and powerful to form a living family of republics.[46]

Iqbal commended the Turks for initiating 'the trend of modern Islam'. He appreciated the way the Turkish National Assembly had exercised the power of ijtihad (independent reasoning) with regard to the institution of Khilafat and the form of government in modern Turkey. Indeed, he stressed that, 'If the renaissance of Islam is a fact, and I believe it is a fact, we too one day, like the Turks, will have to re-evaluate our intellectual heritage.'[47]

Iqbal's stress on ijtihad was clearly reflected in his scholarly lectures delivered in 1928–9 at Madras (Chennai), Hyderabad, and Aligarh, and later published under the title of The Reconstruction of Religious Thought in Islam (1930).[48] In these lectures, Iqbal emphasised the need for 'fresh interpretation' of the Islamic principles in the light of changed circumstances. He defined ijtihad as 'the principle of movement in the nature of Islam' and argued that ijtihad was fully capable of solving the present problems confronting the Muslims.[49] He lamented that *ijma*, or consensus of the orthodox schools of Islamic law, through ages had remained 'practically a mere idea, and rarely assumed the form of a permanent institution' in any Muslim country. This, he thought, was due to the 'political interests' of the kind of 'absolute monarchy' that arose in the Muslim world immediately after the fourth Caliph (Hazrat Ali [RA]), which could only 'leave the power of *ijtihad* to individual *mujtahids* rather than encourage the formation of a permanent assembly, which might become too powerful for them'. However, he was convinced that: 'The transfer of power of *ijtihad* from individual representatives of schools to a Muslim Legislative Assembly ... [was] the only possible form *ijma* can take in modern times ....'[50]

Iqbal realised that a non-Muslim legislative assembly in India could not exercise the power of ijtihad.[51] He, therefore, warned that the construction of a polity in India on national lines, with the Hindu-majority domination, would indeed mean 'a displacement of the Islamic principle of solidarity ...'. This, he insisted, was 'unthinkable to a Muslim.'[52] Besides, Iqbal, like Syed Ahmad Khan before him, maintained that:

> India is a continent of human groups belonging to different races, speaking different languages and professing different religions. Their behaviour is not at all determined by a common race-consciousness. Even the Hindus do not form a homogenous group. The principle of European democracy cannot be applied to India without recognizing the fact of communal groups.[53]

Iqbal thus brought the Muslim separatist political movement of Syed Ahmad Khan to its higher end by expressing the 'ethical ideal' of Islam emphatically and boldly in his now famous presidential address at the Allahabad session of the Muslim League in 1930. It cannot be denied, he declared, that Islam, as:

... an ethical ideal plus a certain kind of polity[—]by which expression I mean a social structure regulated by a legal system and animated by a specific ethical ideal—has been the chief formative factor in the life-history of the Muslims of India. It has furnished those basic emotions and loyalties which gradually unify scattered individuals and groups, and finally transform them into a well-defined people, possessing a moral consciousness of their own. *Indeed it is no exaggeration to say that India is perhaps the only country in the world where Islam, as a people-binding force, has worked at its best.*[54]

Islam in India, in fact, Iqbal went on to claim, made the Indian Muslims something more than a homogenous community—a nation. 'We are', he pronounced:

... far more homogenous than any other people in India. *Indeed the Muslims of India are the only Indian people who can fitly be described as a nation in the modern sense of the world.* The Hindus, though ahead of us in almost all respects, have not yet been able to achieve the kind of homogeneity which is necessary for a nation and which Islam has given you [Muslims] as a free gift. No doubt they are anxious to become a nation, but the process of becoming [a] nation is a kind of travail, and in the case of Hindu India, involves a complete overhauling of her social structure.[55]

Iqbal, thus, like Syed Ahmad Khan and Maulana Mohamed Ali[56] before him, warned the British that 'to base a constitution on the concept of a homogenous India or to apply to India principles dictated by the British democratic sentiments is unwittingly to prepare her for a civil war.' There would be no peace until the various communities in India were 'given opportunities of free self-development'. This demand for 'self-development', he elaborated,

is not inspired by any feeling of narrow communalism. There are communalisms and communalisms. A community which is inspired by a feeling of ill-will towards other communities is low and ignoble. I entertain the highest respect for the customs, laws, religious and social institutions of other communities. Nay, it is my duty, according to the teachings of the [Holy] Quran, even to defend their place of worship, if need be. Yet I love the communal group which is the source of my life and behaviour, and which has formed me what I am by giving me its religion, its literature, its thought, its culture, and thereby recreating its whole past as a living operating factor, in my present consciousness.[57]

In demanding a 'redistribution' of India thus calculated to secure 'a permanent solution of the communal problem' and to allow the Muslim community in particular 'full and free development' of its 'own culture and tradition', Iqbal formulated the idea of 'a consolidated North-West Indian Muslim State', comprising the Punjab, North-West Frontier Province (now Khyber Pakhtunkhwa), Sind (Sindh) and Baluchistan (Balochistan) as 'the final destiny of Muslims, at least of North-West India'.[58] He argued and justified this by insisting that: 'The life of Islam as a cultural force in this living country very largely depends on its centralization in a specified territory.'[59]

Iqbal, thus, went on to draw a clear distinction between a concept of nationalism necessitated by the peculiar conditions of India and subjected to the will of Islam and the all-pervasive concept of nationalism that was in vogue in Europe at that time. This was a crucial distinction. The Indian Muslims were faced with an existential threat—the threat of being altogether wiped out as a distinct religio-cultural political group or community in the emerging pattern of self-government in India that was based on numbers and thus inherently biased in favour of the Hindu majority community, with the Hindus always in power. Since these 'seventy millions of Muslims', in the country, he claimed,

> constitute a far more valuable asset to Islam than all the countries of Muslim Asia put together [*sic*], we must look at the Indian problem, not only from the Muslim point of view, but also from the standpoint of Indian Muslims as such.[60]

L. R. Gordon-Polonskaya, in a study titled, 'Ideology of Muslim Nationalism', in fact, saw this 'standpoint' supported and sustained by 'political separatism' along the way. As she put it: 'In India, where the ideology of Muslim nationalism was the ideology of a religious and cultural minority, it inevitably harbored from the very beginning the seeds of political separatism.[61]

'Political separatism', and indeed the idea of a separate state for the Muslims in British India, in one form or another, was quite old. A number of Muslims, individually and collectively, had already worked along these lines from time to time and a number of regional/zonal schemes had been presented and promoted.[62] What made Iqbal's idea different from the earlier ones was that it was based on the philosophical content of Islam rather than being a territorial solution, claim, or demand. Iqbal was convinced that Islam did not approve of the separation of the spiritual from the temporal. The idea that religion was merely a private affair and thus it had nothing to do with the public sphere, particularly politics, was a European idea, not an Islamic one. The religious aspect of Islam was 'organically related to the social order which it has created. The rejection of the one will eventually involve the rejection of the other.'[63] Islam 'admitted of no *modus vivendi* and is not prepared to compromise with any other law regulating human society.'[64]

Here it also needs to be stressed, as Hafeez Malik has perceptively argued, that while in his Allahabad address of 1930, and a couple of years later, Iqbal favoured 'autonomy' for the Muslims, 'not partition', in later years, 'by 1936–8, he had swung to the position of a demand for a sovereign and independent state'.[65] This is well articulated in his letters to Jinnah in 1936–7, which will be discussed later. Hopefully, this explanation should help clarify Iqbal's position and end unnecessary debate and controversy about his demand. One must also bear in mind that, as Ayesha Jalal pointed out, 'Iqbal may have been the originator of the idea of a separate state in north-western India but by 1937 the notion was coming to acquire a life of its own.'[66]

Iqbal's demand for a separate state was not simply to secure a national homeland for the Muslims of India but, more importantly, also to serve as 'a means to higher and nobler end',[67] in the best interests of Islam. The Indian Muslims 'had to live on some territory ... to realize the ideal values of Islam ....'[68] Iqbal did not believe in territorial nationalism as such, for its own sake.

Indeed, in a long and intense debate with Maulana Hussain Ahmad Madani of Jamiat-i-Ulema-i-Hind, who, in a statement, had contended that 'nations are formed by countries', and hence the Muslims could live in unity with other communities of India, as *umma wahida* (singular community), Iqbal could not be more emphatic. He strongly rejected 'the idea of territorial nationality, for on the one side it subordinates the distinction of Muslim and non-Muslim and on the other it impinges on the universalistic character of Islam.'[69] Iqbal differentiated between 'patriotism and nationalism' and readily acknowledged that 'historically nations had been associated with countries and countries with nations' and, thus, there 'was nothing wrong with loving one's land of birth and residence' and being patriotic about it.[70] But he objected to Maulana Madani's 'proposition when it was urged upon Indian Muslims as a political concept, implying that they should put aside their faith, stop thinking of themselves as a separate nation, and sink their identity to a larger Indian nationhood.'[71]

Iqbal explained to Maulana Madani that 'nationalism' as such, would 'shatter the religious unity of Islam to pieces.' It was Islam and Islam alone, he reminded the Maulana, that gave humanity a message that 'religion was neither national and racial, nor individual and private, but purely human and its purpose was to unite and organize mankind, despite all its natural distinctions.' He made it clear in his discussion that 'distinction' between *millat* and *qaum* is no distinction. The Muslims, as a nation, cannot be other than what they are as *millat*. Those who embraced Islam became 'part and parcel of the Muslim or Muhammadan community, irrespective of the fact whether they belonged to his own nation or other nations.' Had the Maulana, he wondered,

> sought evidence from the [Holy] Quran, I am confident, the solution of this problem would have automatically suggested itself to him... Has not the word 'qaum' been used hundreds of times in the Quran? And has not the word 'millat' occurred repeatedly in the Quran? What do *qaum* and *millat* mean in the Quranic verses? Are these words to denote the follower of the [Holy] Prophet [PBUH]? Are these words so divergent in meaning that because of this difference one single nation can have different aspects, so much

so that in matters of religion and law, it should observe the divine code, while from the viewpoint of nationality it should follow a system which may be opposed to the religious system? ... [S]o far as I have been able to see, no other word except *ummat* has been used for Muslims in the Holy Quran. If it is otherwise I would very much like to know it. *Qaum* means a party of men, and this party can come into being in thousand places and in a thousand forms upon the basis of tribes, race, colour, language, land and ethnical code. Millat, on the contrary, will carve out of the different parties a new and common property. In other words, *millat* or *ummat* embraces nations but cannot be merged in them.[72]

Iqbal, thus, articulated the idea of a separate Muslim nation in India, with a difference. His nationalism was 'territorial' only to the extent of the Indian Muslims who, as a 'minority' in India, were bound to lose the 'life of Islam' in a Hindu-dominated political system. There was no way out except to seek a separate state for the preservation and promotion of their own culture, traditions, and values. This rationale, this motivation, in fact, not only strengthened the Muslim separatist political movement but, indeed, became the main inspiration of the subsequent nationalist Pakistan Movement under the charismatic leadership of Quaid-i-Azam after the adoption of the Lahore (Pakistan) Resolution in March 1940. Jinnah, of course, given his own political experience and the failure to reach an accord with the Hindu community and, thus, achieve Hindu–Muslim unity for the common good of India, readily agreed with Iqbal. He went on to state publicly that: 'His views were substantially in consonance with my own and have finally led me to the same conclusion as a result of careful examination and study of constitutional problems facing India ...'.[73]

Iqbal and Jinnah had known and respected each other for a long time, although not without some anxiety in the beginning. It was primarily on two issues of vital concern to the Muslims—separate electorates and the 1927 Simon Commission.[74] While Jinnah, like Maulana Mohamed Ali[75] and other leading Muslims of the day, was not averse to the idea of joint electorates under certain clear conditions (Delhi Muslim Proposals of 1927),[76] Iqbal was strongly committed to separate electorates, no matter what.[77] He saw it as an inalienable right of the Muslims for their survival, let alone progress, as a political community in India. In fact, he saw separate electorates as an integral 'principle of Muslim national identity'.[78] Iqbal and his colleagues' (such as Mian Muhammad Shafi and Mian Fazl-i-Hussain) opposition to the surrendering of separate electorates 'seriously weakened Jinnah's bargaining position with the Congress'[79] in his efforts to settle the Hindu–Muslim problem.

While Jinnah was opposed to the Simon Commission as he believed it was not a sincere effort on the part of the British government to advance constitutional reforms in India, Iqbal (now Secretary of the split Muslim League, Shafi League, led by its president, Mian Muhammad Shafi) felt that nothing could be lost by way of cooperation with the commission provided the Muslims could use the opportunity to their advantage.[80] So, much to the chagrin of Jinnah, he cooperated. The result was that Iqbal and Jinnah found themselves in opposite camps. The memorandum submitted by Iqbal (and Mian Shafi), however, failed to impress the commission. Iqbal also appeared in person before it but his pleas did not help much. While some of the Muslim demands, such as the retention of separate electorates, which was a critical demand, were accepted, the final Simon Commission report, published in May 1930, failed to secure Muslim interests as a whole. It left the Muslims disappointed and 'aggrieved'.[81]

However, the hostile Nehru Report of 1928, as far as the Muslims were concerned, brought the two leaders together and for good, as they became convinced that the Hindus did not care about Muslim interests and demands, and that the Muslims had to pursue their interests themselves, with their own efforts and plans. Thus, from now onwards, especially after the Simon Commission report, Iqbal and Jinnah, carefully and consciously, took almost identical positions on all matters related to Muslims. Iqbal indeed came to appreciate that Jinnah not only understood the Muslim predicament in India well but also perceived correctly the nature of the tussle between the British and the Hindus.[82]

Iqbal opposed the civil disobedience campaign launched by the Congress in 1930. How can a minority, he asked, 'join a campaign which is directed as much against itself as against the Government?'[83] He was certain that the Hindu-majority community was not interested in seeking a political solution to the communal problem in India. In a rejoinder to Pandit Jawaharlal Nehru, in which he attacked the attitude of the Muslim delegation at the Round Table Conference in London ('reactionism') in the early 1930s, Iqbal asked him pointedly, without mincing any words:

> How is India's problem to be solved if the majority community will neither concede the minimum safeguards necessary for the protection of a minority of 80 million people, nor accept the award [Communal Award] of a third party; but continues to talk of a nationalism which works out only to its own benefit?[84]

Iqbal was now convinced that the Hindu-majority community believed in 'a nationalism theoretically correct, if we start from Western premises, belied by fact, if we look to India.' But here was the rub. The real parties in India were not Britain and India, 'but the majority community and the minorities of India which [could] ill-afford to accept the principle of Western democracy until it is properly modified to suit the actual conditions of life in India.'[85] But since the majority community was not interested in any modification or concessions whatsoever to accommodate the minorities and share power with them in spite of their representative status, the situation warranted that:

> Either the Indian majority community will have to accept for itself the permanent position of an agent of British imperialism in the East or the country will have to be redistributed on a basis of religious, historical and cultural affinities so as to do away with the question of electorates and the communal problem in its present form.[86]

Iqbal was not satisfied with the Communal Award of 1932 announced by the British government at the end of the Round Table Conference.[87] He could see that the British did not mean to act 'as an impartial holder of balance in India', and were indeed driving the Hindus and Muslims to 'a kind of civil war'.[88] The Award, he maintained, attempted to vindicate two political principles: one, no majority should be reduced to a minority and two, the interests of the minorities should be protected through suitable safeguards. In the application of both these principles, he charged, 'it is the Muslim who suffers'.[89] This is not to suggest that Iqbal suffered any complex because Muslims were a minority in India. He did not. On the contrary, he firmly believed that:

> The fate of the world has been principally decided by minorities. The history of Europe bears ample testimony to the truth of the proposition. It seems to me that there are psychological reasons why minorities should have been a powerful factor in the history of mankind. Character is the invisible force which determines the destinies of nations and an intense character is not possible in a majority. It is a force, the more it is distributed, the weaker it becomes.[90]

In 1933, Iqbal's health began to deteriorate, making it difficult for him to remain politically active. Thus, he decided to withdraw from public life. He had played his part in the most formative phase in Muslim politics of India, and a very productive and useful one, from 1926 to 1933:

> As an elected president of the Muslim League he delivered the historic Allahabad Address. Twice he went to England to participate in the Second and Third Round Table Conferences. Also, he presided over the All Parties Muslim Conference session in Lahore; and until the last day of his life he remained deeply involved in the future political prospects of the Muslims. But never again [did] he ever think of fighting in another provincial or central legislative election.[91]

Iqbal was, however, keen to help another champion of Muslim rights and interests in his efforts to secure for the Muslims a safe future. Thus, in 1936, when Jinnah started his campaign to re-organise the Muslim League and to fight the coming elections to save Muslims from the impending threat to their survival as a political community, Iqbal readily joined hands with him. He was re-elected President of the Punjab Muslim League. In addition, Jinnah appointed him President of the Punjab Parliamentary Board and entrusted him with the task of organising the League for the success of League candidates in the province. Iqbal worked hard to organise the League and even 'urged the Muslims to sever relations with other Muslim and non-Muslim parties in order to create a united front.'[92] He was determined to make the League a 'mass party' of the Muslims.[93] He was encouraged by 'Jinnah's integrity and political judgement' and felt confident that his 'organizational endeavors would shatter illusory leadership of the selfish leaders, because the Muslims would now elect their true representatives in the forthcoming elections.'[94] However, to his utter dismay, the League could not do well—particularly in Punjab, where it failed miserably. It was able to elect only two representatives out of 175 seats available in the Punjab Legislature. Sikandar Hayat Khan, having succeeded Fazl-i-Hussain as head of the Unionist Party, secured a clear majority, with 89 seats.[95] He, of course, subsequently joined Jinnah and the League, under the Jinnah–Sikandar Pact, in Lucknow, in October 1937. But the election results proved 'disastrous for the growth of the League' in the Punjab,[96] at least in the short term.

Although the League in the Punjab, despite Iqbal's untiring efforts to instil new life into its activities,[97] failed in the elections for a variety of reasons,[98] the personal bonding between him and Jinnah went on to serve the Muslim cause at a very critical state in Indian politics. There was so much at stake. The most productive manifestation of this bonding was underscored in the private letters exchanged between the two leaders, in 1936–7, especially in Iqbal's persistent efforts to impress upon Jinnah the *raison d'état* of the Muslim demand for a separate homeland.

Iqbal's letters to Jinnah made it abundantly clear that he supported a separate homeland, not as an integral part of the Indian Federation[99] but as 'a free Muslim state or states', constituting a 'separate Federation of Muslim Provinces'. In a letter dated 20 March 1937, he appealed to Jinnah to declare 'as clearly and as strongly as possible the political objective of the Indian Moslems as a distinct political unit in the country'. In another letter of 28 May 1937, he told Jinnah that *'the enforcement and development of the Sharia of Islam is impossible in this country without a free Muslim state or states'*. 'This,' he stated, 'has been *my honest conviction for many years* and I still believe this to be the only way to solve the problem of bread for Moslems as well as to secure a peaceful India'.[100] Again, pointing out the inadequacy of the Government of India Act of 1935 as far as the Muslims were concerned, he, in another letter, dated 21 June 1937, observed that 'the new constitution is devised only to placate the Hindus.' He wondered, *'why should not the Moslems of North-West India and Bengal be considered entitled to self-determination just as other nations in India and outside India are?'* He stressed in clear and categorical terms that, 'To my mind *the new constitution with its idea of a single federation is completely hopeless. A separate Federation of Muslim provinces ... is the only course by which we can ... save Muslims from the domination of non-Muslims.'*[101]

The demand for a separate federation of Muslim provinces was, of course, a 'reaffirmation of Iqbal's earlier idea of a consolidated Muslim State in the much broader sense' of the term.[102] It also reaffirmed that, for Iqbal,

> the Indian Muslims were not a political minority, but constituted a separate political nationality, and as such had no other option except either to demand full autonomy in the Muslim majority provinces within a very loose federal structure or to carve out a separate sovereign Muslim state.[103]

Either way, Iqbal was articulating the need and rationale for a separate homeland for the Indian Muslims on the one hand and prompting Jinnah on the other. Jinnah, he reckoned, was 'the only Muslim in India today to whom the community has a right to look up for safe guidance through the storm which is coming to North-West India and perhaps to the whole of India.'[104] He had watched Jinnah for a long time, and 'he believed in Jinnah's integrity, because Jinnah was the only Muslim leader with an unchallenged national status, and because Jinnah had no provincial or regional ties of any kind.'[105] And this was no small trust in Jinnah's qualities of leadership. A few years back, in 1930, Iqbal, in his Allahabad address, had 'frankly' lamented the dearth of leadership, genuine leadership, among the Muslims, in these words:

> Let me tell you frankly that, at the present moment, the Muslims of India are suffering from two evils. The first is the want of personalities [leaders] .... By leaders I mean men who, by Divine gift or experience, possess a keen perception of the spirit and destiny of Islam, along with an equally keen perception of the trend of modern history. Such men are really the driving force of a people, but they are God's gift and cannot be made to order. The second evil from which the Muslims of India are suffering is that the community is fast losing what is called the herd instinct. This makes it possible for individuals and groups to start independent careers without contributing to the general thought and activity of the community ....[106]

Iqbal was now happy that the Muslims had discovered a leader, a political leader, whose 'genius will discover some way out of our present difficulties'.[107] But Iqbal also realised that it was not going to be an easy task. There would be huge challenges and difficulties. The proponents of Indian nationalism, as he saw it, possessed by their 'political idealism', would not let the Muslims have their way as determined by them. As he put it, 'The Indian nationalism whose political idealism has practically killed his sense for fact is intolerant of the birth or a desire for self-determination in the heart of north-west Indian Islam.'[108]

Jinnah, however, did not disappoint Iqbal. Not only did he define Muslim nationhood in his now well-known 'two-nation theory' and spell out in clear terms the demand for Pakistan by insisting upon the partition of India, simple and pure, on the basis of Muslim-majority areas, in March 1940, Jinnah also re-organised the Muslims under the banner of the Muslim League just as Iqbal had wanted, at the grassroots level. Commenting upon the moribund state of the League in the 1930s, Iqbal had exhorted the League leadership to decide finally whether the League:

will remain a body representing the upper classes of Indian Muslims or Muslim masses who have so far, with good reason, shown no interest in it. Personally I believe that a political organization which gives no promise of improving the lot of average Muslims cannot attract our masses ....[109]

Iqbal was convinced that Jinnah alone was capable of transforming the League into a mass party.[110]

Jinnah not only brought together the Muslim masses, social groups, and classes—especially the aspiring, ambitious, and educated urban middle classes—into the fold of the League but also, demanding the unity of the Muslim nation, succeeded in making the British and the Congress concede the demand for Pakistan. With the League's enormous electoral victory in the 1945–6 elections, and convinced, in the wake of World War II, that the British could not hold India for long, Jinnah called for 'Direct Action' to achieve Pakistan. In the process, and largely because of the communal riots that followed, the partition of India emerged as the only alternative to civil war and bloodshed in the country. The writ of the state had already been increasingly compromised during the war years. The British were indeed willing to envisage a 'national government' including the Indians. There were a number of mutinies in the armed forces at Bombay (Mumbai) and Karachi in particular. Independence and partition was the only way out. On 3 June 1947, the British government was constrained to announce the partition plan, and on 14 August 1947 Pakistan came into being as a separate, sovereign state. Iqbal's idea of a separate state for the Muslims had become a concrete reality.

Iqbal, unfortunately, did not live long enough to see this reality for himself. He breathed his last on 21 April 1938, after a protracted illness, even before the historic Lahore Session of the League adopted the separate state resolution on 23–4 March 1940. But Jinnah did not fail to acknowledge his debt to Iqbal for his contributions. He told his political biographer, M. H. Saiyid: 'Iqbal is no more amongst us ... but had he been alive he would have been happy to know that we did exactly what he wanted us to do.'[111] This was no small compliment from the man who was the then undisputed leader of the Muslims, indeed their charismatic leader, and who was also proverbially a man of very few words.

There can be no denying that Iqbal's formulation of the idea of a separate state largely influenced the thinking of Jinnah and the turn of events leading to the demand for Pakistan.

> [His] philosophical conceptions led him to the conclusion that his ideals of equality and freedom could be embodied only in an Islamic state, and that consequently the Muslims of India had no other course but self-determination and the creation of Pakistan.[112]

Indeed, the creation of Pakistan was the final embodiment of Iqbal's ideals of Islam in the difficult, distressful conditions of India. Rejecting European nationalism based on material considerations, Iqbal helped evolve a concept of Muslim nationalism, emphasising the unity of religion and state in Islam. The idea was to secure the integral relationship between Islam and its social structure, and eventually its polity. A Hindu-dominated body politic could not help achieve this objective. It was, therefore, necessary that the Muslims in the Muslim-majority areas of India established a separate state. This was Iqbal's distinct contribution to Indian Muslim nationalism and the idea of a separate state for the Muslims in India.

The more scholars and researchers will delve into the history of modern India, the more they will be convinced of the crucial role played by Iqbal in securing a separate state for the Muslims, much in line with their historical separatism and the Muslim separatist political movement founded by Syed Ahmad Khan. Iqbal eventually passed on this separatist movement over to Jinnah to launch a determined and decisive movement for Pakistan in the early 1940s, appropriately named the Pakistan Movement, for the achievement of Pakistan. As Saleem M. M. Qureshi succinctly put it: 'The vision of one [Iqbal] and the leadership of the other [Jinnah] led to an act of political creation—the State of Pakistan.'[113] How Jinnah's political leadership emerged, worked, and achieved its goal of Pakistan needs to be carefully and comprehensively analysed.

Notes

1. See, Sikandar Hayat, 'Syed Ahmad Khan and the Foundation of Muslim Separatist Political Movement in India', *Pakistan Journal of Social Sciences,* Vol. VIII, Nos. 1 and 2 (Jan–July–Dec 1982), 33–47. For a revised and updated version, see Chp. 2 of this book.

2. 'Even without Jinnah', wrote Ishtiaq Husain Qureshi, 'Pakistan would have come but it would have been delayed for decades and would have entailed much greater conflict and travail'. Ishtiaq Husain Qureshi, *The Struggle for Pakistan* (Karachi: Karachi University, 1969), 302. Such was the importance of the personal leadership of Quaid-i-Azam Jinnah in the creation of Pakistan. For some aspects of this discussion also see, Penderel Moon, 'Jinnah's Changing Attitude to the Idea of Pakistan', in *World Scholars on Quaid-i-Azam Mohammad Ali Jinnah,* ed., A. H. Dani (Islamabad: Quaid-i-Azam University, 1979), 270; Altaf Hussain, 'Memories of the Quaid-i-Azam' in *Quaid-i-Azam As Seen by His Contemporaries,* ed. Jamil-ud-Din Ahmad (Lahore: Publishers United, 1966), 73; H. V. Hodson, *The Great Divide* (London: Huchinson, 1969), 38; and Sharif al Mujahid, *Quaid-i-Azam Jinnah: Studies in Interpretation* (Karachi: Quaid-i-Azam Academy, 1981), 315, 371, 403–8.

3. Abdul Majid Salik, *Zikr-i-Iqbal* (Lahore: Bazm-i-Iqbal, 1955), 7–16 and Mohammad Abdullah Chughtai, *Iqbal ki Suhbat Mein* (Lahore: Majlis-i-Taraqi-i-Adab, 1971), 6–14.

4. Hafeez Malik and Lynda P. Malik, 'The Life of the Poet-Philosopher', in *Iqbal: Poet-Philosopher of Pakistan,* ed. Hafeez Malik (Lahore: Iqbal Academy Pakistan, 2005), 12. The two authors provide a very informative and interesting biographical information on Iqbal in this chapter.

5. Ibid.

6. See its publication as Allama Muhammad Iqbal, *The Development of Metaphysics in Persia: A Contribution to the History of Muslim Philosophy* (Lahore: Sang-e-Meel Publications, 2004).

7. Malik, *Iqbal: Poet-Philosopher of Pakistan,* 20.

8. Ibid., 25.

9. Wilfred Cantwell Smith, *Modern Islam in India: A Social Analysis,* (London: Victor Gollacz, 1946), 102.

10. There is indeed evidence to suggest that Iqbal was associated with the London branch of the All-India Muslim League, founded by Syed Ameer Ali, during his stay in London in 1908 (*Archives of Freedom Movement,* Karachi University, Vol. 23). Also see Syed Razi Wasti, *Lord Minto and the Indian Nationalist Movement, 1905 to 1910* (Oxford: Clarendon Press, 1964), 227.

11. Syed Abdul Vahid, *Studies in Iqbal* (Lahore: Sh. Muhammad Ashraf, 1976), 251.

12. Malik, 'The Man of Thought and the Man of Action', in *Iqbal: Poet-Philosopher of Pakistan,* 76.

13. Ibid., 252. Almost all the writers on Iqbal are convinced that he actually took no part in active politics between 1910 and 1925. See, for instance, Parveen Shaukat Ali, *The Political Philosophy of Iqbal* (Lahore: Publishers United, 1978), 708; Mohammed Ahmad Khan, *Iqbal Ka Siyasi Karnama* (Lahore: Iqbal Academy, 1977), 78; and Abdus Salam Khurshid, *Sarguzashat-i-Iqbal* (Lahore: Iqbal Academy, 1977), 197.

14. Even Maulana Mohamed Ali's personal visit to Lahore to mobilise support for the Khilafat Movement in the Punjab could not move Iqbal. Vahid, *Studies in Iqbal*, 252.

15. 'Even if non-cooperation', Iqbal confided in a letter, 'is considered a religious duty, the method adopted for carrying it out is, in my opinion, against the spirit of Islamic *Shariat'*. Cited in Vahid, *Studies in Iqbal*, 253. Also see, Ali, *The Political Philosophy of Iqbal*, 317; Khan, *Iqbal Ka Siyasi Karnama*, 83–4; and Salik, *Zikr-i-Iqbal*, 18. For a more detailed explanation of Iqbal's role in the Khilafat-non-cooperation movement see, Javid Iqbal, *Zinda Rood* (Lahore: Sang-e-Meel Publications, 2014).

16. Also see Ali, *The Political Philosophy of Iqbal*, 8.

17. Khan considered this to be the most important reason. See, Khan, *Iqbal Ka Siyasi Karnama*, 78. For a historical analysis of Iqbal's early poems see, Bashir Ahmad Dar, *Articles on Iqbal* (Lahore: Iqbal Academy Pakistan, 1997), 55–98. Here, one can see Iqbal's steady shift away from nationalism. He blamed Europe's 'concept of territorial nationalism' for instigating 'the Turks to abolish Khilafat, the Egyptians to raise slogans in favour of Egypt' and conjuring up 'the ghost of Pan-Indian democracy before the Indians'. Ibid., 85.

18. Allama Muhammad Iqbal, 'Islam as a Moral and Political Ideal', in *Thoughts and Reflections of Iqbal*, ed. Syed Abdul Vahid (Lahore: Sh. Muhammad Ashraf, 1973, rep.), 47.

19. Muhammad Saleem Ahmad, 'Iqbal and Politics – Part I', *Pakistan Studies*, Vol. II, No. 3 (Winter 1983/4): 68–9.

20. Also see Khan, *Iqbal Ka Siyasi Karnama*, 142.

21. Vahid, *Thoughts and Reflections of Iqbal*, 196.

22. Ayesha Jalal, *Self and Sovereignty: Individual and Community in South Asian Islam since 1850* (Lahore: Sang-e-Meel Publications, 2007), 179.

23. Hafeez Malik, *Iqbal in Politics*, adopted from Iqbal, *Zinda Rood*, Biography of Allama Iqbal by Dr. Javid Iqbal (Lahore: Sang-e-Meel Publications, 2009), 28.

24. See Iqbal's address to the All-Parties Muslim Conference, 29 December 1928–1 January 1929, in *Guftar-i-Iqbal*, ed. Rafique Afzal (Lahore: Research Society of Pakistan, 1969), 73.

25. Vahid, *Thoughts and Reflections of Iqbal*, 205.

26. Salik, *Zikr-i-Iqbal*, 133–4. Still, Iqbal entered the political arena very reluctantly, and in the fond hope that, 'I might be able to render useful services to the cause of our nation—which consumes all of my daily efforts'. Cited in Malik, *Iqbal in Politics*, 31.

27. Malik, 'The Man of Thought and of Action', in *Iqbal: The Poet-Philosopher of Pakistan*, 82.
28. Ibid.
29. Ibid., 82–3.
30. Ibid. Interestingly, as Hafeez Malik wrote elsewhere, Iqbal's participation in the Unionist politics 'gave him a window of opportunity to examine closely the machinations of this party.' Malik, *Iqbal in Politics*, 41.
31. Manzooruddin Ahmed, 'Iqbal and Jinnah on the "Two-Nations" Theory', in *Iqbal, Jinnah and Pakistan: The Vision and the Reality*, ed. C. M. Naim (Lahore: Vanguard Books, 1984), 45.
32. Hafeez Malik, *Iqbal: The Poet-Philosopher of Pakistan* (New York: Columbia University, 1971), 110.
33. Rizwan-ul-Islam, 'Iqbal's Concept of Muslim Nationalism (Millat)', in *Contributions to Iqbal's Thought*, ed. Mohammad Maruf (Lahore: Islamic Book Service, 1977), 109.
34. 'There is no doubt', Iqbal acknowledged, 'that my ideas about Nationalism have undergone a definite change. In my college days, I was a zealous Nationalist which I am not now. The change is due to my mature thinking'. B. A. Dar, ed., *Letters and Writings of Iqbal* (Karachi: Iqbal Academy, 1967), 58–9. For a useful discussion on the change and the sources of change in Iqbal's ideas on nationalism and nationality see, in particular, Waheed Qureshi, *Iqbal aur Pakistani Qaumiyat* (Lahore: Maktaba-e-Aliya, 1977), 52–77.
35. Vahid, *Thoughts and Reflections of Iqbal*, 196–7. Also see, Aziz Ahmad, 'Iqbal's Political Theory', in *Iqbal As a Thinker: Essays by Eminent Scholars* (Lahore: Sh. Muhammad Ashraf, 1973), 216–44.
36. There are some who claimed that 'Iqbal repudiated nationalism because nationalism was a western concept, and that he was opposed to all things Western'. Riffat Hassan observed that, 'This is palably untrue; he has given many reasons for his attitude, and there is no reason to doubt them'. For one, she thought that 'Iqbal also saw nationalism as a weapon of European imperialism'. But, more importantly, she felt, 'The narrowness of the political concept of nationalism was Iqbal's greatest difficulty in accepting it'. Riffat Hassan, 'The Development of Political Philosophy', in *Iqbal: Poet-Philosopher of Pakistan*, 146. For those accusing Iqbal of a bias towards West and 'things Western' see, in particular, Jan Marck, 'Perceptions of International Politics' and Freeland Abbott, 'View of Democracy and the West', in *Iqbal: Poet-Philosopher of Pakistan*. These authors failed to take into account Iqbal's charge that 'the imperial powers of Europe tried to employ this weapon [of nationalism] in order to weaken and destroy the unity and solidarity of the Muslim peoples of the world'. Dar, *Articles on Iqbal*, 85.
37. Muhammad Iqbal, *The Reconstruction of Religious Thought in Islam* (Lahore: Sh. Muhammad Ashraf, 1965), 154. Iqbal's son, Javid Iqbal, a scholar in his own right, went on to argue that 'Hence "Secularism" is

an integral part of Islam and it is for this reason that the Islamic State assimilates the qualities of an ideal "Secular State".' Javid Iqbal, *Ideology of Pakistan* (Lahore: Ferozsons, 1971), 4.

38. Ibid., 154. Thus, as L. R. Gordon-Polonskaya noted, 'Islam emerges in this ideology as a form of national unity and (in essence) absorbs political thought.' L.R. Gordon-Polonskaya, 'Ideology of Muslim Nationalism', in *Iqbal: Poet-Philosopher of Pakistan*, 114.

39. Allama Muhammad Iqbal, 'Presidential Address, Allahabad Session, December 1930'. Also available in *Speeches, Writings and Statements of Iqbal*, 3rd ed., ed. Latif Ahmad Sherwani, (Lahore: Iqbal Academy, 1977), 6–7.

40. Sherwani, *Speeches, Writings and Statements of Iqbal*, 23.

41. Vahid, *Thoughts and Reflections of Iqbal*, 287–8.

42. Ibid., 288.

43. Anwar H. Syed, 'Iqbal and Jinnah on Issues of Nationhood and Nationalism', in *Iqbal, Jinnah and Pakistan*, 79.

44. Ibid., 84.

45. Iqbal, *The Reconstruction of Religious Thought in Islam*, 159. Also see Ahmad, 'Iqbal's Concept of an Islamic State', in Maruf, *Contributions to Iqbal's Thoughts*, 91.

46. Ibid., 159.

47. Ibid., 153, 157, 59.

48. Only three lectures were given on the tour. Three were prepared later. The seventh lecture, 'Is Religion Possible?', was delivered in London at the request of the Aristotle Society. This intellectual effort kept Iqbal engaged in studies and reflections from 1924 to 1932. Mohammad Abdullah Chughtai, *Iqbal Ki Suhbat Mein* (Lahore: Majlis-i-Taraqi-i-Adab, 1977), 319–44. According to Muhammad Munawar, another writer on the subject, Iqbal's six lectures which he delivered at Madras (Chennai), Hyderabad, and Aligarh, were first published from Lahore, in 1930, and then by Oxford University Press in 1934. Muhammad Munawwar, *Dimensions of Iqbal* (Lahore: Iqbal Academy Pakistan, 2003), 5.

49. Iqbal, *The Reconstruction of Religious Thought in Islam*, 63, 148. Also see Aziz Ahmad, *Studies in Islamic Culture in the Indian Environment* (Lahore: Oxford University Press, 1970), 68; and Peter Hardy, *The Muslims of British India* (Cambridge: Cambridge University Press, 1972), 240.

50. Iqbal, *The Reconstruction of Religious Thought in Islam*, 173–4. However, Iqbal suggested that 'a Board of Ulema could be nominated by the government and it could guide, help or assist the elected members in the process of Islamic law-making in Parliament'. Javid Iqbal, *Intellectual Legacy* (Lahore: Iqbal Academy Pakistan, 2012), 73.

51. Ibid., 174. For a detailed, scholarly work on the subject see, Khalid Masud, *Iqbal's Reconstruction of Ijtihad* (Lahore: Iqbal Academy Pakistan, 2009).

52. Sherwani, *Speeches, Writings and Statements of Iqbal*, 7.

53. Ibid., 8.

54. Ibid., 3. (Italics added).
55. Ibid., 23. (Italics added).
56. See Maulana Mohamed Ali's 'last letter' written to Ramsay Macdonald, the British Prime Minister, on 1 January 1931, when Maulana was attending the Round Table Conference in London. Afzal Iqbal, ed., *Select Writings and Speeches of Maulana Mohamed Ali*, Vol. II (Lahore: Sh. Muhammad Ashraf, 1969), 372.
57. Sherwani, *Speeches, Writings and Statements of Iqbal*, 8–9, 22.
58. Ibid., 8, 10, 19. Iqbal, Hafeez Malik thought 'was torn apart by a dilemma: if partition was a "solution" for the Muslims of the northwestern provinces of India, it was bound to be devastating to the interests and security of Muslims as a minority in the Hindu dominated provinces of India. They would be, in the eventuality of partition, at the mercy of the Hindu majority. Iqbal was mostly silent about East Bengal ....' It was much later, during his correspondence with Jinnah in 1937 that he mentioned Bengal along with 'northwest India'. Malik, *Iqbal in Politics*, 24.
59. Sherwani, *Speeches, Writings and Statements of Iqbal*, 10.
60. Ibid., 25. Also see Hafiz Abdullah Farooqi, 'Iqbal's Concept of State', in *Studies in Iqbal's Thought and Art*, ed., Saeed Sheikh (Lahore: Bazm-i-Iqbal, 1972), 379.
61. Gorden-Polonskaya, 'Ideology of Muslim Nationalism', in *Iqbal: Poet-Philosopher of Pakistan*, 114.
62. For details on these schemes see, *The Indian Annual Register, 1939* (Calcutta: Annual Register Office, 1939); Maurice Gwyer and A. Appadorai, eds., *Speeches and Documents on the Indian Constitution, 1921–1947.* Vol. II (Bombay: Oxford University Press, 1957), 455–62; Reginald Coupland, *The Indian Problem, 1833–1935* (London: Oxford Universty Press, 1968), 203–4; Syed Sharifuddin Pirzada, *Evolution of Pakistan* (Lahore: All-Pakistan Legal Decisions, 1963); and Y. B. Mathur, *Growth of Muslim Politics in India* (Lahore: Book Traders, 1980), Appendix, 293–329.
63. Sherwani, *Speeches, Writings and Statements of Iqbal*, 7.
64. A. R. Tariq, ed., *Speeches and Statements of Iqbal* (Lahore: Sh. Ghulam Ali, 1973), 231.
65. Malik, *Iqbal in Politics*, 22.
66. Jalal, *Self and Sovereignty*, 383.
67. Waheed-uz-Zaman, *Towards Pakistan* (Lahore: United Publishers, 1969), 144.
68. Saleem M. M. Qureshi, 'Iqbal and Jinnah: Personalities, Perceptions and Politics', in *Iqbal, Jinnah and Pakistan*, 22.
69. Ibid., 15.
70. Syed, 'Iqbal and Jinnah', in *Iqbal, Jinnah and Pakistan*, 78.
71. Ibid.
72. Sherwani, *Speeches, Writings and Statements of Iqbal*, 31–2, 35, 42. Manzooruddin Ahmad, however, argued that Iqbal, 'in enunciating the

theory that Indian Muslims were truly a nation in the modern sense, did not discard his original theory of Muslim *millat*; he simply gave it a new name—Muslim nation—in the political context of India ... in fact translated the idea of Muslim community into the vocabulary of modern political science as the true basis of Muslim nationalism'. Ahmad, 'Iqbal and Jinnah on the "Two-Nations" Theory', in *Iqbal, Jinnah and Pakistan*, 55.

73. *Letters of Iqbal to Jinnah* (Lahore: Sh. Muhammad Ashraf, 1968), Preface by M. A. Jinnah.

74. Ahmad Saeed, *Iqbal Aur Quaid-i-Azam* (Lahore: Iqbal Academy, 1977), 26–7, 52.

75. Maulana Mohamed Ali, in fact, claimed that he alone was responsible for getting the proposals for joint electorates accepted by the Muslim leaders. See his 'Editorial', *Hamdard*, 15 January 1929, in Mujahid, *Studies in Interpretation*, 387.

76. Sir Muhammad Shafi who was the President of the Punjab Muslim League with whom Iqbal was associated as its General Secretary at that time, however, felt that 'Mr Jinnah has, in his individual capacity agreed to the introduction of joint electorate and has undertaken to carry that settlement, opposed to the overwhelming majority of Indian Muslim opinion ...'. *Civil and Military Gazette*, 5 March 1928, 6.

77. Afzal, *Guftar-i-Iqbal*, 52.

78. Malik, *Iqbal in Politics*, 55.

79. Maik, *Iqbal: Poet-Philosopher of Pakistan*, 88.

80. In the end, however, Iqbal was not satisfied with the recommendations of the Simon Commission, and expressed his disappointment clearly in his 1930 Allahabad address. Sherwani, *Speeches, Writings and Statements of Iqbal*, 13, 19.

81. Waheed Ahmad, *Road to Indian Freedom: The Formation of the Government of India Act 1935* (Lahore: Caravan Book House, 1979), 178–9.

82. Iqbal paid Jinnah this tribute on 24 January 1938. Syed Nazir Niazi, *Iqbal Kay Hazoor* (Karachi: Iqbal Academy, 1971), 104.

83. Vahid, *Thoughts and Reflections of Iqbal*, 203.

84. Ibid., 367.

85. Ibid., 211.

86. Ibid., 367.

87. Iqbal, as Hafeez Malik put it, 'was not a very active participant in discussions. Even in the proceedings of the Minority Sub-Committee Iqbal remained silent by and large'. Malik, *Iqbal in Politics*, 207.

88. Ibid., 205.

89. Ibid., 347.

90. Ibid., 79.

91. Malik, *Iqbal in Politics*, 82.

92. Malik, *Iqbal: Poet-Philosopher of Pakistan*, 94.

93. Ibid., 95.

94. Ibid., 96.
95. Ibid., 98.
96. Ibid., 100–1.
97. For some of the details of Iqbal's painstaking efforts see, Ashiq Hussain Batalvi, *Iqbal Kay Akhri Do Saal* (Karachi: Iqbal Academy, 1961).
98. Only two candidates of the League were elected, Malik Barkat Ali, who barely won, and Raja Ghazanfar Ali Khan, who defected to the Unionists as soon as he was elected to the Punjab Legislature. Hence, for all practical purposes, the League had only one member on the electoral rolls of the legislature. For details see, Malik, *Iqbal: Poet-Philosopher of Pakistan*, 98. For some discussion of the difficulties in the way of the League during the elections see, in particular, Vahid, *Studies in Iqbal*, 275, 280; and Ali, *The Political Philosophy of Iqbal*, 345–6. The main difficulty was the attitude of the Unionists who left no stone unturned to hamper the cause of the League in the province. Iqbal kept Jinnah informed of the activities of the Unionists. See, for instance, Iqbal's letter to Jinnah on 25 June 1936, in *Letters of Iqbal to Jinnah*, 9–10.
99. Many writers, thus, felt unsure whether Iqbal supported the idea of a separate state or 'a Muslim block in an Indian Federation'. See, for instance, K. K. Aziz, *The Making of Pakistan* (London: Chatto & Windus, 1970), 81. Also see H. V. Hodson, *The Great Divide*, 81; Hafeez Malik, *Moslem Nationalism in India and Pakistan* (Washington D.C: Public Affairs Press, 1963), 240–1; Beni Prasad, *India's Hindu-Muslim Questions* (London: George Allen & Unwin, 1946), 77; Marietta Stepaniants, 'Development of the Concept of Nationalism: The Case of Muslims in the Indian Subcontinent', *The Muslim World*, Vol. LXIX, No. 1 (January 1979), 35; and Muhammad Saleem Ahmad, 'Iqbal and Politics Part-2', *Pakistan Studies*, Vol. II, No. 4 (Summer 1984), 79.
100. Also remember the speech Iqbal made on 15 December 1932 in London stating: 'Four or five years ago as President of All-India Muslim League (1930?), I suggested as a possible solution the formation of large West-Indian Muslim State'. Dar, *Letters and Writings of Iqbal*, 75. Since Shariah could 'only be applied in a Muslim state which could be established only in Muslim majority areas', Iqbal suggested to Jinnah 'that the Muslims of North-West India and Bengal ought at present to ignore Muslim minority provinces. This is the best course to adopt in the interests of both Muslim majority provinces'. Qureshi, 'Iqbal and Jinnah: Personalities, Perceptions and Politics', in *Iqbal, Jinnah and Pakistan*, 27–8.
101. *Letters of Iqbal to Jinnah*, 12, 16, 21–2 (Italics added for emphasis).
102. Ahmad, 'Iqbal and Jinnah on the "Two-Nations" Theory', in *Iqbal, Jinnah and Pakistan*, 61.
103. Ibid., 68.
104. *Letters of Iqbal to Jinnah*, 19.
105. C. M. Naim, 'Afterword', in *Iqbal, Jinnah and Pakistan*, 171.
106. Sherwani, *Speeches, Writings and Statements of Iqbal*, 24.

107. *Letters of Iqbal to Jinnah*, 18.
108. Vahid, *Thoughts and Reflections of Iqbal*, 258.
109. *Letters of Iqbal to Jinnah*, 17–19.
110. Niazi, *Iqbal Kay Hazoor*, 298.
111. M. H. Saiyid, *Mohammad Ali Jinnah: A Political Study* (Karachi: Elite Publishers, 1970), 231. 'Would Iqbal have supported the idea of Pakistan as a sovereign state?', wondered Riffat Hassan. 'It is almost certain', she hastened to add, however, 'that he would have done so. The question for him (had he been alive in 1947) would not have been to choose between nationalism or antinationalism. It would have been the preservation of Islamic culture in India'. Hassan, 'Development of Political Philosophy', in *Iqbal: Poet-Philosopher of Pakistan*, 146.
112. Gordon-Polonskaya, 'Ideology of Muslim Nationalism', in *Iqbal: Poet-Philosopher of Pakistan*, 132.
113. Qureshi, 'Iqbal and Jinnah', in *Iqbal, Jinnah and Pakistan*, 11.

7

Quaid-i-Azam Mohammad Ali Jinnah, the Pakistan Movement, and the Achievement of the Separate State of Pakistan

A ll writers, past and present, agree on one thing, no matter how they approach it: 'Pakistan in 1947 would have proved impossible had it not been for the role played by Mohammad Ali Jinnah.'[1] As Lawrence Ziring explained at some length:

> It was Jinnah who persuaded the British that Partition was both necessary and morally correct. It was Jinnah who took the measure of the Congress leaders and who deftly frustrated their hopes to rule over a united India. It was Jinnah who pressured dissident Muslim leaders in the Punjab, Sind [Sindh] and on the North West Frontier [now Khyber Pakhtunkhwa] to fall in line behind him and the Muslim League [All-India Muslim League]. Above all it was Jinnah who embodied the desires and aspirations of those Indian Muslims who could not reconcile themselves to Hindu government [in united India].[2]

Another American scholar and Jinnah's biographer, Stanley Wolpert, in the opening lines of his 'Preface' in *Jinnah of Pakistan* (1984),[3] went on to claim that:

> Few individuals significantly alter the course of history. Fewer still modify the map of the world. Hardly anyone can be credited with creating a nation-state. Mohammad Ali Jinnah did all three. Hailed as 'Great Leader' (*Quaid-i-Azam*) of Pakistan and its first governor-

general, Jinnah virtually conjured the country into statehood by
the force of his indomitable will.[4]

Indeed, Wolpert described him as 'one of recent history's most
charismatic leaders'.[5] In a similar vein, I, in an earlier edition of
my book, *The Charismatic Leader: Quaid-i-Azam Mohammad Ali
Jinnah and the Creation of Pakistan* (2008),[6] compared Jinnah with
other charismatic leaders, and concluded:

> In the end, Jinnah was not only a founder of a state like [Kemal]
> Ataturk or an architect of a political movement like [Kwame]
> Nkrumah or proponent of change like [Vladimir] Lenin, but
> he was also maker of a nation, the Muslim nation of India (and
> Pakistan). This Muslim nation recognized him as a charismatic
> leader, revered him as the *Quaid-i-Azam*, and indeed nominated
> him to the highest office of the Governor-General of Pakistan.[7]

In reaching this remarkable status and stature, Mohammad Ali
Jinnah (1876–1948), of course, faced many challenges, difficulties,
setbacks, ups and downs, and twists and turns. It was neither an
easy journey, nor a straight path. Jinnah had to make necessary
compromises, adjust and readjust his position and priorities, and
indeed explore and secure ways and means to eventually meet his
ultimate goal of a separate state of Pakistan in 1947, after having
exhausted all other avenues for a reasonable, realistic share of
power for the Muslims, a 'minority' community, in India.

In order to pursue a detailed analysis of this endgame of Muslim
separatism in India, of this leadership odyssey, Jinnah's political
life and career may analytically be divided into several discernible,
distinct phases. Jinnah, for most part, was 'an "Indian Muslim",
never only an Indian and never only a Muslim, though some of his
pronouncements were subjected to one-sided interpretations'.[8] In
the post-1940 period, however, 'Muslims would not have heeded
him if he had not spoken to them as a Muslim'.[9]

In the first phase (1906–13), Jinnah started off as an 'Indian
nationalist', a member of the Indian National Congress like
most educated, urban middle class aspirants—both Hindus and
Muslims—especially under the influence of stalwarts, such as

Dadabhai Naoroji, Gopal Krishna Gokhale, Pherozeshah Mehta, Badruddin Tyabji, and other moderate, constitutionalist Congress leaders and nationalists. In the second phase (1913–16), realising the political situation of the Muslims and their particular demands and interests, he joined the newly formed All-India Muslim League, hoping to be able to reconcile India's national interests with Muslim interests. In the process, he supported and secured the Muslim demands for separate electorates, weightage, etc. through the Congress–League Lucknow Pact of 1916. Hailed as the architect of this pact, he emerged as the 'Ambassador of Unity'. In the third phase (1916–23), Jinnah reached the pinnacle of his political career through the Home Rule League and the anti-Willingdon protest in Bombay (Mumbai) and then, soon after, lost it with Mohandas Karamchand Gandhi's entry into politics and the launching of the Khilafat–non-cooperation movement, with its extra-constitutional, even 'unconstitutional nature'. The situation was complicated further with the Rowlatt Act and the Jallianwala Bagh (Amritsar) massacre, keeping him out of constitutional, legislative politics. The so-called Hindu–Muslim unity turned out to be a farce, and counterproductive, leading to a spate of communal riots. This was a period of political turmoil and uncertainty, with Jinnah, in the end, fighting for his own political survival and relevance more than anything else.

In the fourth phase (1923–31), after having taken a back seat during the Khilafat–non-cooperation movement in the early 1920s, Jinnah now made efforts to reconcile Muslim interests with the overall Indian national interests (after the revival of the Muslim League) through the Delhi Muslim Proposals of 1927 (withdrawing the demand for separate electorates for certain concrete concessions from the Congress) and amendments to the Nehru Report of 1928. But it was to no avail. His representative status, too, was challenged. Consequently, Jinnah decided to aggregate and articulate Muslim interests, and demands, first and foremost, through his 'Fourteen Points' presented in 1929 but, again, without much success. The Congress did not pay any heed to these points at that time or later during the Round Table Conference in London (1931) and, thus, frustrated at the hands of not only the Congress and the British government but also the Muslims, Jinnah decided to leave India and take residence in London. His stay in London during 1931–5, essentially introspective in nature, constituted an important fifth phase in his political career. Some contacts with political leaders back in India helped him understand and re-assess the Indian situation and his own role, if any.

In the sixth phase (1935–40), after returning to India on what he called, a 'grand mission', after sensing the 'greatest danger' the Muslims faced as they confronted the constitutional and political challenges ahead, and without a clue, he once again chose to reconcile Muslim interests with India's national interests by rekindling the spirit of 1916. But the Congress, and the Hindu-majority community it represented, was not interested at all. The 1937 elections had helped them attain power in several provinces and they refused to share it with the Muslims. The Congress rule of the provinces in 1937–9 left no one in doubt about its Hindu character and Hinduising tendencies, especially Jinnah and the Muslim League. In the seventh and penultimate phase (1940–6), Jinnah was left with no choice but to fall back, fully and forcefully, on the Muslim separatist political movement of Syed Ahmad Khan and his successors and seek a separate, safe, and secure destiny for the now Muslim 'nation' (not a 'minority' anymore) in a separate state of Pakistan through the Lahore Resolution of March 1940. During the WWII years, with the British vulnerable due to the Congress' non-cooperation, indeed 'rebellion', Jinnah took full advantage of the situation to make 'Pakistan' the main issue of politics in India. The August Offer (1940), Cripps Proposals (1942), and the Cabinet Mission Plan (1946), all went on to accept the validity of the demand for Pakistan, though in different ways and to different extents. In the eighth and final phase (1946–7), Jinnah, disillusioned and distressed at the British 'duplicity' in the pursuit of the Cabinet Mission Plan, which he reluctantly, but tactically, accepted, added the extra-constitutional 'Direct Action' method to his decades-old constitutional struggle, to wrest Pakistan both from the British and the Congress despite their opposition to the partition and Pakistan.

In all these phases, from 1906 to 1947, one must remember that Jinnah was a Muslim representative, representing the Muslims of Bombay through separate electorates, entering the Imperial Legislative Council in 1910 and remaining a legislator till the very end (1947) as member of the Central Legislative Assembly; he was always elected, once unopposed and even in absentia. Yet he did not promote or lead the Muslim separatist political movement in the early phases of his political career; in fact, he even opposed the demand for separate electorates and the formation of the All-India Muslim League. He remained committed to Hindu–Muslim unity in the service of the so-called 'Indian nationalism'. It was only after his long and frustrating experience of the system of government in India, inherently biased in favour of the Hindu-majority, and the indifferent, haughty, and hostile attitude of the Congress (and Hindu Mahsabha) towards the Muslims and their interests that, in the late 1930s, he found a paradigm shift inevitable and decided to take up and lead the separatist movement, transformed into Pakistan Movement (after the demand for Pakistan), to its logical, historic end, that is, the separate state of Pakistan. He realised that the Congress was a 'Hindu party', pursuing 'Hindu nationalism' in the garb of Indian nationalism. We will discuss all of this at some length in the subsequent pages.

But first, let us have a look at Jinnah's family life, early career, and those formative influences which went on to cause and shape his political role in Indian politics in general, and Muslim politics in particular. This will also lead us to the first phase of his political life and career, the 1906–13 period.

According to his sister, Mohtarma Fatima Jinnah, Mohammad Ali Jinnah was born in Karachi on Sunday, '25th of December in the year 1876'.[10] His father, Jinnah Poonja, an Ismaili Khoja, seeking better business prospects, had moved to Karachi from Gondal, a princely state in Kathiawar in the Bombay Presidency, and had taken up residence in the Kharadar area 'which was the business heart of the city'.[11] He must have felt at home here as 'numerous business families, some of them having come from Gujrat and Kathiawar' lived in this locality.[12] He worked closely with one

British firm, Graham Trading Co., which was 'one of the leading import and export houses in Karachi'.[13]

Helped by this trading company, Mohammad Ali Jinnah, 'a boy of sixteen, unaccompanied and unchaperoned in those far off days of the early 1890s, when voyage to England was an out of the ordinary event in the life of an Indian', arrived in London in 1892, to gain some practical experience and training as apprentice.[14] Jinnah, however, with tremendous foresight at that young age, opted 'for law, abandoning his initial business training plans'.[15] He joined the Lincoln's Inn, and in April 1895, 'qualified' the Bar examination, 'the youngest among the fifty-three students who had qualified'.[16] On 11 May 1896, Jinnah petitioned the Inn 'for a "certificate" attesting his "Admission Call to the Bar and of his deportment"'.[17] With that certification, Jinnah could practice in Britain and British India.

During his four-year stay (1892–6), Jinnah 'developed a penchant for politics' through the debates of 'great British liberal stalwarts in the House of Commons' and thus 'got himself bathed in the Liberalism of Lord Morley which was then in full sway'.[18] In fact, as he himself acknowledged later, 'I grasped that Liberalism, which became part of my life and thrilled me very much.'[19] That liberalism 'which stayed with him till the end', Sharif al Mujahid thought, 'led him to opt for law, abandoning his initial business-training plans.' This decision, among other things, 'highlights his independence and decision-making power, even at this initial stage.'[20] Interestingly, Jinnah 'made the transition' to London 'with remarkable speed and aplomb. He took to the English language, western dress and western mode of living, and felt perfectly at home.'[21] He even anglicised his name from 'Mohammad Ali Jinnahbhai' to Mohammad Ali Jinnah. In fact, Mujahid claimed, his 'Anglicism was uninhibited and permanent. He aspired to the lifestyle of an upper-class Englishman, achieved it, and revelled in it.'[22]

Initially, however, upon his return to India in 1896, his lifestyle was anything but 'upper-class'. His father's business was down. His young wife, Emi Bai, whom he had married 'at the dictates of parental authority', and his mother, Mithibai, both had passed away during his absence. Sadly, thus, Jinnah 'had already lost his mother, his wife, and was aware that [the] prosperous family business, so painstakingly built up by his father, was on the verge of collapse'.[23] Realising that Karachi had little to offer him under the circumstances, he decided to move to cosmopolitan Bombay and the same year, in 1896, got himself enrolled as an Advocate of the Bombay High Court. At 20 years of age, 'his briefless interlude in Bombay was very trying; he could hardly make ends meet.'[24] He would go from his apartment to the court daily, only to return without a brief—but not without attracting attention. In 1900, John MacPherson, Advocate-General of Bombay, 'took a liking to the young, smart Khoja barrister, who behaved and even looked like a young Englishman', and gave him a job as Third Presidency Magistrate against a leave vacancy.[25]

Jinnah made an 'excellent impression' and soon was approached by Sir Charles Olivant, Law Member of the Governor's Council, who 'offered him a permanent place in the judicial service on a salary of Rs 1,500 a month, a princely salary in those days', but, Jinnah, confidently and so sure of himself, declined the good offer, saying 'he hoped to earn that much in a single day.'[26] Indeed, in 1936, at the peak of his legal career, he received Rs 1,500 a day for a case. M. C. Chagla, his apprentice (and later Chief Justice of India), who worked with him for a number of years, recalled his ability:

> What impressed me most was the lucidity of his thought and expression. There was no obscure spot or ambiguities about what Jinnah had to tell the Court. He was straight and forthright, and always left a strong impression whether his case was intrinsically good or bad.[27]

In the end, even his political rival and the main contender for leadership in Indian politics, Gandhi, could not help but admit that he (along with Sir Tej Bahadur Sapru) was one of the most distinguished lawyers of India. His command over law and growing practice helped Jinnah to launch a political career like most successful lawyers of the day did. His friends and foes both would later insist that, 'apart from law and politics, he had no other interests'.[28] Law, in fact, was a means to politics. As William Metz perceptively remarked, Jinnah:

regarded neither his law career nor the money it made him as
ends in themselves. Rather, he regarded them as the means to the
economic independence and the personal prestige he needed in
order to play a significant role in India's nationalist movement.[29]

Together, law and politics were 'sufficient to satisfy him'.[30]

Jinnah formally joined mainstream politics in 1906 at the
Calcutta (Kolkata) session of the Congress as Secretary to Dadabhai
Naoroji who presided this session. This 'Grand Old Man of
India' had specially come to India for the purpose. Naoroji had
'a significant influence' on Jinnah who readily 'acknowledged'
that he had 'learned his particular brand of politics "at the feet of
Dadabhai Naoroji".'[31] But there was another 'dominant influence'
too, and that was that of Pherozeshah Mehta, 'a leading light of
the Congress' and leader of the Bombay Presidency Association.[32]
Jinnah, soon after the end of his short tenure as Presidency
Magistrate, had joined the 'Mehta group of lawyers'.[33] Under
Mehtas' 'patronage', Jinnah made his first political appearance
and eventually emerged as 'a prominent member' of the Bombay
Presidency Association. In fact, it was this Association that helped
Jinnah join the Congress and launch his political career at the
aforementioned Calcutta session.[34] But then, 'Jinnah's political
direction' was truly set by yet another moderate leader 'within
the Mehta circle', Gopal Krishna Gokhale, who happened to meet
Jinnah in 1904 and made an 'immediate impression' on him.[35]
Gokhale, like Naoroji and Mehta, firmly believed 'in achieving
political advance through constitutional methods'.[36] The result was,
as Ian Bryant Wells suggested: 'As Jinnah's political apprenticeship
drew to a close, he was solidly implanted in the moderate wing of
Indian nationalism as a strong ally and confidante of Gokhale, and
of constitutional politics.'[37] His 'social and educational background'
promoting 'Liberal nationalism',[38] coupled with the guidance of
these moderate, liberal nationalists, made the Congress a natural
vehicle for the promotion of his political ideas and ideals.

However, in one respect, and in a very important respect,
Jinnah was unique, and indeed was closer to a Muslim moderate
nationalist, Badruddin Tyabji who, as judge of the Bombay High

Court, had earlier mentored Jinnah and whose 'politics differed from those of Mehta and Naoroji'.[39] While Tyabji 'maintained the same tone of moderate nationalism, he attempted to project the aims of the Muslim community from within Congress.[40] In this sense, he was also different from Syed Ahmad Khan, the most influential leader of the Muslim community at that time for he was convinced that the 'Muslims had a place within Congress and should not rely for all their political aspirations on the British.[41] He believed that the Muslims should become part of the Congress movement 'so that the needs of the Muslim community would not be overlooked in the haste to win concessions from British'.[42] Jinnah, in fact, 'soon came to reflect very similar views',[43] indeed, not only reflect but promote and pursue them in practice. An early indicator, of course, was Jinnah's hostile reaction to the Simla Deputation, a manifestation of the separatist legacy of Syed Ahmad Khan and a major building block of the Muslim separatist political movement.

Jinnah not only attacked its representative character but even questioned the purpose of the deputation. He charged: 'It is such a pity that some people are always assuming the role of representatives without the smallest shadow of ground or foundation for it …. May I know what is the object of the deputation [sic]?[44] Interestingly, this 'bold criticism', contained in a letter to the editor of the Times of India to be published on 1 October 1906, the day of the deputation, led by the Aga Khan, waited upon by the Viceroy Lord Minto, did not see the light of the day. However, it was published in a Gujarati local newspaper of Bombay. Soon after, Jinnah signed a memorandum, sponsored by the Bombay Presidency Association, and sent it to the Viceroy, 'opposing separate electorates for Muslims'.[45] Subsequently, at the Calcutta session of the Congress in 1906, Jinnah opposed a resolution moved by a Muslim delegate which demanded 'a reservation for the educationally backward classes', implying the Muslims.[46] Jinnah insisted that: 'The Foundation upon which the Indian National Congress is based, is that we are all equal, that there should be no reservation for any class or community and … that the reservation should be deleted.'[47]

Similarly, Jinnah was opposed to the formation of a separate political organisation of the Muslims, another essential, defining characteristic of the Muslim separatist political movement, in opposition to the entire efforts of Syed Ahmad Khan, the Aga Khan, and Syed Ameer Ali. In fact, Syed Ahmad Khan's political lead rested on opposition to the Congress and the creation of a separate political organisation for the benefit of Muslims. The Aga Khan helped establish that separate political organisation, All-India Muslim League. Ameer Ali supported and, indeed, extended its scope further through his London Muslim League. But Jinnah would have none of it. As stated earlier, for him, the Congress, like for Tyabji, was good enough to secure Muslim rights and interests. He believed that 'Muhammadans can equally stand on this common platform and pray for our grievances being remedied through the programme of the National Congress.'[48] His 'disdain' for a separate Muslim political organisation, such as the Muslim League, was in line and 'consistent with the moderate leadership of Congress, who pointed to the representative character of Congress when arguing against the need for a second organization.'[49] In fact, a few days after the foundation of the League on 30 December 1906 at Dacca (Dhaka), Jinnah not only criticised the League but joined and was 'elected Vice President of the newly formed rival organization, the Indian Mussalman Association'.[50]

However, in the first phase of Jinnah's political career (1906–13), in spite of all the formative influences, things began to change fast because of the change in the objective conditions of India. Jinnah had to make amends. This remained true not only for this phase but all subsequent phases in his career. He had to respond and thus adjust and re-adjust to political dynamics. That is what made him such a resilient and formidable leader in the end, the undisputed leader of the Muslims, indeed their charismatic leader.[51]

The Morley–Minto Reforms, embodied in the Act of 1909, granted Muslims the right to separate electorates, providing Jinnah an opportunity to start his long, illustrious parliamentary career. In 1910, he was elected Member of the Imperial Legislative Council, representing Muslims of Bombay, defeating Maulvi Rafiuddin

Ahmad, President of the Bombay Muslim League. During this tenure, he 'became the "first non-official Muhammadan member" to get his Mussalman Wakf Validating Bill passed by the Imperial Legislative Council.'[52] He had introduced this bill to help the Muslims whose right to make *wakf* (trust) to their families and descendants was affected by the British interference in the Muslim Personal Law. Introduced in 1911, the bill was passed in 1913.

While Jinnah's willingness to represent a 'Muslim reserved seat' reflected his 'pragmatism', there was no doubt that he 'strongly believed in the probability of a "union of the two great communities [Hindus and Muslims] in India". He considered it necessary for the Hindus and Muslims "to combine in one harmonious union for common good".'[53] Indeed, this was 'the problem of all problems that the statesmen in India had to solve before any true advance or real purpose can be achieved'.[54] A sensible, fair, and just 'solution' of this problem was 'the primary political objective' during this phase of his political career.[55]

Jinnah, like 'several other Muslim leaders' at the time, believed that 'in advancing the Indian nationalist cause, he was simultaneously advancing the cause of the component units of the Indian nation', Muslims being one major, integral component.[56] 'Indeed,' as Mujahid argued, 'the fact that he worked for Hindu-Muslim unity, not for Indian unity as such, presupposes his belief in Muslims being one of the two major components in the Indian body-politic.'[57] It is no wonder then that, during 1910–12, he remained in touch with the Muslim League leadership, particularly its Secretary, Syed Wazir Hassan, and attended its many meetings, acknowledging its role and relevance in Muslim affairs. In 1911, he was even 'prepared to concede that the League represented "a great volume of Mussalman opinion"' in Indian politics.[58] In 1912, he helped the League change its constitution and adopt the goal of 'self-government suitable to India', and indeed congratulated it for 'going ahead, even of the Congress, in the formation of the ideal'.[59] It meant, he explained, a demand for 'government of the people by the people.'[60]

Jinnah was ready now to enter the second phase of his political career (1913–16), to shift gears and help accommodate Muslim interests and demands into the mainstream nationalist agenda for the common cause of India—indeed, to place the burden of responsibility essentially upon the shoulders of the Hindu-majority community.

In 1913, sponsored by Maulana Mohamed Ali and Wazir Hassan, Jinnah formally joined the Muslim League, without severing his connections with the Congress—in those days it was permissible to belong to two or more parties simultaneously. In 1915, he was willing to accept the League 'as "the only political organisation" the community had, and of which it could feel proud'.[61]

This fundamental shift in Jinnah's 'attitude towards the Muslim League was also reflected in his attitude towards separate electorates'.[62] This 'doughtiest opponent' of the separate electorates, according to the Aga Khan, now 'came to realize and recognise', given his intimate exposure to 'Muslim problems and to the main body of Muslim opinion in northern India—to Nadwa, to Aligarh and to the Muslim League', that the Muslims 'had certain special interests and certain particular [sic] needs which must be catered to if they were not to be left behind'[63] in the greater cause of Hindu–Muslim unity and Indian nationalism.

In October 1916, in his presidential address to Bombay Provincial Conference, a non-communal organisation,[64] Jinnah declared that:

> This question of separate electorates … has been before the country ever since 1909 and rightly or wrongly the Mussalman community is absolutely determined for the present to insist upon separate electorates. To most of us the question is no more open to further discussion or argument as it has become a mandate of the community … the demand for separate electorates is not a matter of policy but a matter of necessity, to the Mahomedans who require to be roused from the coma and torpor into which they had fallen so long.[65]

He continued:

> I would, therefore, appeal to my Hindu Brethren that in the present state … they should try to win [the] confidence and trust of the

Mahomedans who are, after all in the minority in the country.
If they are determined to have separate electorates, no resistance
should be shown to their demand.[66]

Jinnah thus clearly called upon the Hindu-majority community and
its representative organisation, the Congress, 'to make concessions
to the Muslim community for the greater good of India'.[67] Indeed,
the Congress made a few concessions, including the all-important
acceptance of separate electorates which, according to an analyst,
was understandable for the simple reason that the '1916 session of
both the Muslim League and Congress was dominated by a young
emerging educated elite, steeped in the principles of democracy
and sharing common experiences and interests.'[68]

The resultant 'Congress–League Joint Scheme of Reforms' or,
as it was more popularly known, the Lucknow Pact—given that
both the League and Congress sessions were held at Lucknow—
was 'made possible by the "signal service" of Jinnah to the cause
of unity'.[69] Indeed, the Lucknow Pact turned out to be 'the high
watermark of Jinnah's career ... the only leader who wielded
influence in both the communities'.[70] More importantly, the
pact helped resolve 'the dilemma which had tormented him
since the incorporation of separate electorates in [the] Minto-
Morley Reforms. His Muslim identity no longer clashed with his
nationalist identity.'[71] He was able to reconcile the Indian national
movement with particular Muslim demands and interests, a
hallmark of this most successful phase of his career. The discord
over the separate electorates was no more and this fundamental
Muslim demand had been clearly conceded by the Congress and
its leadership. Jinnah had been able 'to remove the danger of Hindu
and Congress opposition to separate Muslim electorates' and thus,
very importantly, assure the British government that 'there was no
opposition from anyone in India'.[72]

But that did not mean that the Muslims had gained all, despite
the separate electorates, and the so-called 'weightage'—a greater
share for Muslim representation in Muslim-minority provinces,
such as United Provinces (UP), Bombay, Bihar, etc. The 'weightage'
was achieved at the expense of losing statutory majorities in the

Muslim-majority provinces of the Punjab and Bengal, which caused quite a bit of resentment among the provincial leaders of the two provinces at a later stage. In fact, Jinnah, throughout his political career, 'had to balance the claims of Muslims in the provinces in which they were in a minority with those of Muslims in the provinces in which they were in majority.'[73]

For now, however, Jinnah, by 'uniting Hindus and Muslims … achieved all he had hoped for'.[74] Sarojini Naidu, an ardent Indian nationalist leader, extended Gokhale's view of Jinnah as 'the best ambassador of Hindu-Muslim unity', and even published a selection of his speeches and statements titled *Mohammad Ali Jinnah: Ambassador of Unity* (1918). Indeed, as Jaswant Singh in his recent book-length study of Jinnah noted, 'In politics now all factions gave him recognition—the Extremists [led by Bal Gangadhar Tilak], the Moderates, the Muslims, the Hindus, the Parsis and others.'[75] It was all because Jinnah stood for constitutional politics, following his political mentors, to bring about Hindu–Muslim unity and thus strengthen the national movement for the benefit of both the communities—Hindus and Muslims. It was obvious enough for all to see that as '1916 drew to close, the advocates of constitutional politics were firmly in control of the Indian political scene'.[76]

This was about to change in the third difficult phase of Jinnah's career (1916–23) with the entry of Gandhi, a quiet spectator at Lucknow in 1916, with his extra-constitutional non-cooperation methods. Ironically, his entry into Indian politics was due to 'approbation from the British Government through the good offices of Gokhale', one of Jinnah's mentors, who 'exerted the full weight of his prestige and influence upon the Viceroy, Lord Harding … to bring the Government of India solidly behind Gandhi.'[77] But first, let us examine further Jinnah's rise and role in Indian politics, particularly the peak period.

In June 1917, Jinnah joined the Home Rule League founded by Annie Besant to press for the attainment of self-government for India and, within days of her internment, was elected its president. Although the Secretary of State, Edwin S. Montagu, charged 'that "ambition" was the driving force behind Jinnah', the fact was that his joining the League 'reflected the widespread reaction to repressive government policies at a time when most Indians were expecting reforms'.[78] Being a major political force in Bombay at the time, Jinnah indeed 'brought the "whole legal profession in Bombay to the Home Rule League"'.[79] But Jinnah's aggressive political campaign for reforms, along with his signature and support of the Memorandum of Nineteen submitted to governments, both in Britain and India, got him in trouble. The Memorandum boldly stated:

> We cannot ask young men to fight for principles [during the course of WWI] the application of which is denied to their own country. A subject race cannot fight for others with the heart and energy with which a free race can fight for the freedom of itself and others. If India is to make great sacrifices in the [defence of the] Empire, it must be as a partner in the Empire and not a dependency ....[80]

The government, of course, saw this document as 'an act of gross disloyalty at a time of war', reinforcing its 'view of Jinnah as an "extremist" and "agitator" who should be carefully watched'.[81] This hostile view was 'confirmed by his role in the agitation against a proposed memorial to [Lord] Willingdon', the retiring Governor of Bombay, in December 1918.[82] Jinnah appeared at the venue, Town Hall, leading hundreds of his supporters and told Willingdon 'to his face that the people of Bombay were not party to commemorating or approving' his services as governor.[83] It could not be clear whether the memorial was carried through or not as 'an assault by the police caused the meeting to end in pandemonium'.[84] However, Jinnah was 'instantly recognized by the people as their hero' and funds were raised for a lasting memorial in his honour, which was aptly named '"Jinnah Peoples Memorial Hall" in the compound of the Bombay office of the Congress in recognition of his brave fight against the "combined forces of bureaucracy and autocracy"'.[85] The Hall was inaugurated by Besant in 1919, but then Jinnah was out of India and, hence, he was telegraphed in these words: 'A prophet is honoured in his own country in his own times.'[86] On the other end, Willingdon did not hesitate to recommend to his successor, Lord Lloyd, 'his [Jinnah's] "deportation" to Burma [Myanmar]'.

Jinnah's 'antipathy to Willingdon', according to some writers on the subject, continued, and may have been 'part of the reason for his decision to stay in England' after Willingdon became Viceroy in 1931.[87]

Thus, the years 1916–18, including the anti-Willingdon protest, 'represented the high point in Jinnah's nationalist career'.[88] In the estimate of B. R. Nanda, a noted Indian historian and prolific writer, at this time:

> Jinnah's reputation was built on solid foundations. He was one of the leading lights of the Bombay Bar. He was a member of the Imperial Legislative Council. He was the president of the Home Rule League in Bombay and the Chairman of the Board of Directors of the *Bombay News Chronicle*, the main nationalist newspaper in Bombay. He was the only political leader in the higher echelons of both the Indian National Congress and the All India Muslim League. At the age of 42, he was in front rank [sic] of India's leaders.[89]

Jinnah, once again, demonstrated courage of conviction by opposing the newly introduced draconian law, the Rowlatt Act, which empowered the government to deport or imprison Indians for any number of years, and, in March 1919, resigned from the Imperial Legislative Council in protest. As he put it in his letter of resignation:

> The passage of the Rowlatt Bill by the Government of India, and the assent given to it ... against the will of the people has severely shaken the trust reposed by them in British justice .... In my opinion, a Government that passes or sanctions such a law in time of peace forfeits its claim to be called a civilized government ....[90]

'Ironically', and inexplicably, 'the Rowlatt Bill was passed in an era' depicted by Reginald Coupland, a prominent British historian, 'as a "new angle of vision" reflecting British appreciation of India's contribution to the war efforts.'[91] More than one and a half million Indians, with eight hundred thousand troops 'eventually engaged on all fronts' had willingly 'volunteered to fight alongside their colonial masters', the governments of India and Britain.[92] In a way, this 'support for the war also helped ensure that Indian security was never a serious British wartime concern.'[93] And yet, the British government did not hesitate to let loose terror on a peaceful meeting at Jallianwala Bagh, Amritsar, leaving hundreds dead and more than a thousand injured, 'with no warning or order to disperse' to 'produce "moral effect" from a military point of view, on those present and elsewhere'.[94] These brutal, extra-constitutional acts damaged 'the credibility of not only the Government of India but also of those Indian politicians advocating a constitutional approach to nationalist politics.'[95]

But then, some of the Indian politicians too, especially Gandhi, opted for extra-constitutional methods to advance their agenda. Taking advantage of the Muslim sentiment over the Khilafat and the fate of the Ottoman Turkish Empire in the aftermath of WWI, Gandhi prevailed upon the Muslim leadership, particularly Maulana Mohamed Ali, to launch a movement of non-cooperation to force the government to concede the Muslim case that, 'The Khilafat shall be preserved, that there shall be no Christian mandate over any part of the Island of Arabia, and that the Khalifa shall remain, as before the war, the Warden of the Holy places.'[96] In turn, Gandhi sought Muslim 'support to remedy the "Punjab wrongs", the situation in the Punjab after the Jallianwala Bagh massacre, and to put maximum pressure on the British authorities to grant "responsible government" to India.'[97]

Jinnah, being 'essentially a constitutional politician' could not approve the non-cooperation movement, though he was 'neither indifferent to the fate of the Khilafat (caliphate) in Turkey nor unmindful of the Punjab situation'.[98] He 'condemned the British government for its "Punjab atrocities" and "the spoliation of the Ottoman Empire and the Khilafat"'.[99] Indeed, he claimed, 'The one attacks our liberty, the other our faith.'[100] On 19 January 1920, he insisted that the British government 'in concluding any settlement to which they attach any degree of finality ... should take into the fullest consideration the most binding religious obligations and the most highly cherished sentiments of 70 millions of Indian Musalmans'.[101]

What Jinnah 'disagreed with' were the non-cooperation methods adopted for the purpose 'which, among other things, called for the triple boycott of law courts, schools, and legislatures.'[102] He had 'only recently led the agitation against Lord Willingdon' and, thus, 'was not afraid of taking on the government. However, he believed that the non-cooperation movement must be launched after due deliberation.'[103] Otherwise, it will be disastrous. Thus, he told Gandhi bluntly:

> Your extreme programme has for the moment captured the imagination mostly of the inexperienced youth and the ignorant and the illiterate. All this means complete disorganization and chaos. What the consequences of this may be, I shudder to contemplate ....[104]

The Chauri Chaura incident of 5 February 1922, where 'an unruly mob set fire to a police station and burnt twenty-two policemen who at the time were inside the building', forced Gandhi to call off the non-cooperation movement 'abruptly, and without consulting the Khilafat leaders', leaving them 'bewildered and indeed shocked'.[105] Jinnah thus stood 'vindicated', but 'this could not help him regain his former status in national politics instantly.'[106] He had lost his standing in the masses, both Muslims and Hindus, and, as his early biographer, Hector Bolitho, put it, 'the graph of Jinnah's career showed a downward trend.'[107] In addition, 'elevation of provincial politics [through dyarchy] under the reforms of 1919 [Montagu–Chelmsford Reforms] ... made his position all the more precarious', for:

> Jinnah did not have a power base at the provincial level. He was essentially an all-India leader, operating at the national level, and for good reason. Self-government and freedom could only come with responsibility at the centre. The only provincial office Jinnah ever held was that of the Bombay Home Rule League, and that too for a limited period of time, and ... for all-India purposes.[108]

But, more importantly, Jinnah's setback was also a setback for Hindu–Muslim unity which he had cultivated for more than a decade, and quite successfully, as expressed in the aforementioned Lucknow Pact. The Khilafat–non-cooperation fiasco roused communal animosities like never before, and there were violent riots all over the country. The so-called 'spirit behind the Hindu-Muslim unity of the Khilafat days had long been dead and forgotten.'[109] M. R. Jayakar, a leading Hindu Mahasabha leader, even blamed Gandhi for trying for 'a most artificial and unreal unity between Hindus and Muslims.'[110] But there was no denying the fact that Gandhi was the main beneficiary of this entire episode, demonstrating to one and all, including Jinnah, that 'there was no place within the Congress for a politician of Jinnah's type', a constitutionalist and then a Muslim.[111] In fact, as Wells explained it, 'The ease with which Gandhi had displaced him in Congress and the rising star of Jawaharlal Nehru also demonstrated to Jinnah the limitation of a Muslim in Congress.'[112] Jinnah was told to think and act as a Muslim leader and no more. Jinnah, of course, left the Congress after the Nagpur session in 1920.

In the fourth phase (1923–31), Jinnah was left with no option but to act as a Muslim leader, no doubt, pressing Muslim rights and interests and hoping to reconcile them with the national interests of India collectively as an all-India leader. Jinnah would not give up his national stance despite having left the Congress, the so-called instrument of the nationalist movement. He would now operate through the Muslim League to settle the Hindu–Muslim problem and advance the common cause of self-government and freedom.

But settling the Hindu–Muslim problem was no easy undertaking under the circumstances. As Pandit Motilal Nehru told his son, Jawaharlal Nehru, on 20 May 1926:

> The Hindu-Muslim problem is now getting more and more acute. No sooner a riot is suppressed in one town than there is an outburst in another.... Almost all public men have now taken sides.[113]

The reason it was not 'all public men' was, Jinnah. He still was determined to resolve this problem fairly and equitably. Only this time, he wanted to go through the League route. That is, he 'aimed to re-establish the Muslim League as the primary representative of the Muslims of India' first, and then 'negotiate an agreement with Congress on an equal basis'.[114] At the personal level, too, having left the Congress in 1920 and resigned from the Home Rule League at the same time, Jinnah saw 'the Muslim League as the vehicle of his political career' and, indeed, 'actively sought to control it'.[115] Thus,

> in contrast to his earlier position where his membership in the Muslim League and his representation of a Muslim constituency in the Imperial Council were offset by his Congress and Home Rule League affiliations, his formal associations were now exclusively Muslim.[116]

And, although quite a few Muslim leaders had disagreed with him on non-cooperation and Khilafat issues, many Muslims generally 'respected him as a man of integrity, courage, and great political ability'.[117] In fact, he was ideally suited to lead the League into the future. In 1923, he had returned, unopposed, to the newly formed Central Legislative Assembly, and had assumed the leadership of the 'Independent Party', a vibrant legislative party comprising 16 legislators, and only second in strength to Motilal Nehru's main Swaraj party, in the assembly.

Jinnah's most important qualification to lead the League, however, was the fact that he had emerged unscathed from the Khilafat–non-cooperation movement. In May 1924,[118] he was elected president of the League session at Lahore, and, soon after, was elected its president, unopposed, for three years. Although, as Naeem Qureshi argued, old Khilafat leaders were:

> indignant at the prospect of the leadership slipping out of their hands ... they had no solution for the new situation. Jinnah at the head of the All-India Muslim League seemed to be more suited to take up the challenge.[119]

Jinnah started off by trying to persuade the Congress and 'the Hindu brethren that, in the present state ... they should try to win the confidence and trust of the Mohammadans who are, after all, in the minority in the country.'[120] He told them that 'if we, the two communities, can settle our differences, it will be more than half the battle for responsible government won.'[121] He even suggested that separate electorates, which, only a few years back, he had stoutly defended and called 'a settled fact',[122] were negotiable. The important thing, he felt, was to safeguard Muslim rights and interest through a give-and-take agreement with the Congress and indeed the Hindu Mahasabha for the sake of Hindu–Muslim unity in the long run and thus be able to promote and pursue the national cause. In March 1927, he called a representative meeting of Muslim leaders in Delhi, including Maulana Mohamed Ali, Raja Sahib of Mahmudabad, Nawab Muhammad Ismail Khan, Dr Mukhtar Ahmad Ansari, and Mian Muhammad Shafi, among several other prominent leaders,[123] to agree to surrender separate electorates under certain reciprocal concessions to Muslims. His idea was to secure 'five stable Muslim provinces', with the addition of three new provinces of Sind (Sindh), North-West Frontier Province (now Khyber Pakhtunkhwa), Baluchistan (Balochistan) to 'balance the remaining six Hindu provinces coupled with one-third Muslim representation at the centre' for 'a modus vivendi' between the two communities leading to the final settlement of the problem.[124] These proposals, which later came to be known as the Delhi Muslim Proposals were 'unique products of Jinnah's ingenious constitutional lawyer's mind'.[125] In essence, they were 'a meeting ground upon which the more unity-minded elements of both the Congress and Muslim League' could agree.[126]

Although the Delhi Muslim Proposals 'elicited a positive response' from the Congress in its Madras (Chennai) session in December 1927, the then influential Mahasbha refused to concede Muslim demands as a *quid pro quo*, and thus struck a 'discordant note'.[127] This was a major blow. Jinnah tried to explain and indeed 'appeal to political India to approach the proposals with an open mind ... "within a spirit of toleration".' After all, he argued, 'the real issue is how to give a real sense of confidence and security to the minorities. Other questions ... can, I think, be solved if the major proposal contained in the offer be agreed upon.'[128] But the Mahasabha was not moved, except for obviously accepting the joint electorate part of the proposals as it suited them, in spite of Jinnah's reminder that 'the offer to give up separate electorates in return for the Delhi Proposals was "inter-dependent and can only be accepted or rejected in its entirety".[129] The Mahasabha also went on to attack Jinnah in person 'as being unrepresentative of Muslim India and, therefore, inconsequential in any negotiations between the two communities'.[130] While the Mahasabha was least qualified or, indeed, relevant a party to determine Jinnah's status as representative of the Muslims, the die was cast. Seeing the Mahasabha opposition, the Muslim leaders of the UP, Bengal, and the Punjab, including some signatories of the proposals, such as Shafi, backed out 'citing the reaction of the Mahasabha as exemplifying the approach of Hindu politicians'.[131] The rejection of the proposals was not only 'a significant defeat for Jinnah' but also went on to 'widen rather than diminish the breach between the two communities.'[132]

More significantly, it was a defeat of Jinnah's sincere, relentless efforts to pursue the cause of Indian nationalism in concert with the Muslims. As A. G. Noorani aptly put it, Jinnah had 'tried, on the one hand, to bring Muslims closer to the nationalist movement of India's freedom, and, on the other, to urge the leaders of the movement to reckon with Muslims' insecurities and demands for proper safeguards.'[133] But the Mahasabha, and, more importantly, the Congress, with its apathy and indifference (or, maybe, collusion), let him down. Jinnah's 'bold and patriotic initiative which had interjected a ray of light into the encircling gloom'[134] went begging.

Still, Jinnah, a 'compulsive nationalist that he was', and 'keen as ever to advance the national struggle' did not hesitate to 'set aside his personal grievance and decided to cooperate with the Congress rather than with the British Government, which had already announced the formation of the all-British Simon Commission in November 1927.'[135] Interestingly, this all-White, Simon Commission was formed at the insistence of the Punjab Governor, Malcolm Hailey who, in turn, was advised by 'the Indians themselves, divided as they are at present on communal lines…'.[136] This soon became evident with the support of the Muslim leadership of Punjab, including Shafi and Allama Muhammad Iqbal, 'leaving Jinnah high and dry' and the Muslim League split into two, with the

Shafi League going its separate way.[137] The split, of course, 'reduced the political effectiveness of both the League as an organization and Jinnah himself.'[138] But Jinnah did not relent in his opposition to the Commission. He saw it as 'an affront to Indian nationalism'.[139] In one of his 'rare angry outbursts' he went on to charge: 'Jallianwala was physical butchery, the Simon Commission is the butchery of our soul.'[140] He became a leading opponent of the commission and, indeed, leader of its boycott all over the country. He called a session of the League at Calcutta and 'was able to draw a large and representative gathering of delegates from all parts of India, including the Punjab and Bengal.'[141] He even invited Mahasabha leaders, particularly its top leader, Pandit Madan Mohan Malaviya, to the meeting and went on to exclaim:

> I welcome ... the hand of fellowship extended to us by Hindu leaders from ... the Congress and the Hindu Mahasabha. For, to me this offer is more valuable than any concession which the British Government can make. Let us grasp the hand of fellowship.[142]

The session duly 'confirmed Jinnah's leadership and his policies by re-electing him as working president [of the League] for the next three years.'[143]

The Simon Commission visited India twice, in 1928 and 1929, and were generally met with protests and hostile slogans of 'Simon Go Back'. Its long-awaited report was published in May 1930, and had little to offer to the Indians or, for that matter, to the Punjab Muslims who had enthusiastically supported the commission. The report rejected their principal demand of statutory majorities in Punjab and Bengal. Iqbal publicly expressed his disappointment in the 1930 Allahabad Address for failing to 'recognize' the Muslims 'as a distinct' political entity;[144] Jinnah, of course, was furious. 'So far as India is concerned,' he lambasted the report, 'we have done with it'.[145] The British, too, soon realising the futility of this exercise, decided to hold fresh consultations with Indian leaders at the proposed Round Table Conference in London.

But for Jinnah the major shock was the report prepared by the Motilal Nehru-led committee, formed by the All-Parties

Conference in 1928—comprising a number of Indian political parties opposed to the Simon Commission—to frame an agreed and acceptable constitution of India. The committee included a couple of Muslim members. It completed its task with some difficulties and, eventually, its report, dubbed the Nehru Report, came out in August 1928. Though the Muslim League had initially participated in the conference in the hope that the Congress was willing to discuss the Delhi Muslim Proposals, it was not part of the later proceedings, especially of the committee. Jinnah was out of the country at the time. In fact, a 'number of prominent Indian leaders', including Motilal Nehru, 'saw Jinnah's presence as vital' and even 'supported an adjournment of proceedings until his return'.[146] But Jinnah could not be available any time soon because of his wife's (Rattanbai 'Ruttie' Jinnah) illness, treatment, and stay in Europe. Jinnah returned in October 1928, after the report was published. Soon after his arrival, Motilal Nehru 'wrote him a very cordial letter, urging him to give favourable consideration to the report', but Jinnah refused to commit.[147] He 'refused to express his views' before consulting his party, the League.[148] Jinnah felt that the report was a mere 'proposal from the Congress which needed to be discussed and changed as needed'.[149]

Jinnah, indeed, 'found several aspects of the Nehru Report unacceptable',[150] and, as explained by Wells at some length,

Specifically, he did not think the 25 per cent representation in the central government, given to the Muslims, significant. He was concerned with maintaining the Muslim position at the centre and avoiding the domination of the central government by one religious community. The Nehru Report's advocacy of a strong central government made this even more important. Regardless of its Muslim component, Jinnah was opposed to the concept of an all-powerful central government. He endorsed a federal system of autonomous provincial governments .... Jinnah also saw the existence of autonomous provinces as a second-tier safeguard for the rights of the Muslim community he represented. As such, he disagreed with the Nehru Report's endorsement of residual powers to the central government. Under the Nehru Report the central government was given excessive power and the needs of his own community were not recognized.[151]

More shockingly, the report:

repudiated the principle of separate electorates ... [and] called for 'joint mixed electorates' for all assemblies. The Muslim demand for reservation of seats in the Punjab and Bengal legislatures was dismissed as opposed to 'the principles on which responsible government rests'. The Muslims were to get proportional representation in the central legislature and not one-third of representation, as recommended in the Delhi Muslim Proposals ....[152]

Indeed, for these reasons, Jinnah chided Motilal Nehru, saying,

In my opinion the proposals formulated by you relating to Hindu-Muslim settlement may be treated as counter-proposals to those known as the Delhi Muslim proposals which were substantially and practically endorsed by the Congress of Madras ... in December 1927.[153]

The League, thus, 'rejected the Nehru Report as it stood' but to help mobilise Muslim support in the common cause of India, proposed 'a number of amendments', which, in turn, were systematically 'incorporated in six points' to be presented at the forthcoming convention to ratify the report.[154] Three points were particularly important: 'reservation of seats for Muslims in the legislatures of the Punjab and Bengal, vesting of residual powers in the provinces instead of at the centre, and the reservation of one-third seats in the central legislature for Muslims'.[155]

Jinnah spoke at the All-Parties Convention of Calcutta on 22 December 1928, and, again, on 28 December, in 'a determined effort yet again to reach an amicable settlement with the Congress, Mahasabha, and other involved parties.'[156] He made a fervent appeal, more as an Indian than a Muslim to help 'seven crores of Mussalmans to march along with us in the struggle for freedom'.[157] But there was hardly any support for Jinnah or his proposals.[158] Worse, 'no Congress leader spoke' at the meeting, making it 'clear to Jinnah that he was addressing an unsympathetic audience'.[159] The most unsympathetic, indeed hostile, 'comments', however, were made by Jayakar, the Mahasabha leader, who even 'questioned Jinnah's credentials', claiming that he 'spoke for only a small minority of Mohammedans ....'[160] Nothing could have 'hurt' Jinnah more,[161] but there was still more at stake. Indeed, as Wells noted, 'Jinnah was offended by Jayakar's criticisms, there can be no doubt', but he was 'more concerned with the implications of the conference's rejection of his amendments' as he 'had been a consistent advocate of Hindu-Muslim unity on the grounds that such unity would greatly enhance India's chance of political advance ....'[162]

The trouble was that the Hindu-majority leadership did not see 'the Hindu-Muslim question "as a national problem and not a communal dispute"' in spite of all the efforts made by Jinnah for so long in this regard.[163] More ominously, this Hindu leadership 'misjudged Jinnah's resilience, however, by underestimating his powers ... a fatal error, not only for [the Nehru] report, but for his [Jinnah's] hopes of retaining India as a united entity.'[164] Prakash Almeida insisted: 'The Nehru Report episode was the real turning point that launched Jinnah on the path of becoming what he became—the Quaid-i-Azam.'[165] Jinnah, indeed, left Calcutta, with 'tears in his eyes' as he told his friend, Jamshed Nusserwanjee, who had come to see him off at the railway station, 'Jamshed, this is the parting of the ways'.[166] One perceptive writer, Patrick French, could not help but suggest that 'From now on he [Jinnah] came to believe, quietly at first, in separation, either in the form of powerful, autonomous, provinces within a federal system, or ultimately in an independent state.'[167]

While the Delhi Muslim Proposals were an effort on Jinnah's part to persuade the Muslims to offer a scheme of things likely to be acceptable to the Congress and Hindu leadership, his amendments to the Nehru Report were aimed at Hindus to help accommodate Muslim demands and interests. Both approaches were meant to conciliate, to forge Hindu–Muslim unity for the good of India. The strategic goal remained the same. Only tactics were different. The intransigent Hindu leadership, particularly that of the Mahasabha, failed him on both occasions, given the lack of foresight or, more accurately, political prescience. Jinnah, therefore, decided to try another approach, to speak for the Muslims alone, and hoped that the Hindus would recognise and respect Muslim demands for their own sake. He presented his now famous 'Fourteen Points'. This was:

> a definite departure from the spirit which motivated Jinnah's political activities up to the All-Parties National Convention. They were a challenge, a reaction against the failure of the conciliatory policy; and they represented ... Jinnah's ultimate decision that if he could not unite Hindus and Muslims, he should at least unite Muslims ....[168]

This move, of course, did not mean that Jinnah had 'become a communalist', though 'he could no longer be called the Ambassador of Unity in the same sense as that title had been applied to him theretofore.'[169] He continued to make attempts at 'Hindu-Muslim unity until late in the 1930s as opportunities which seemed to justify such attempts occasionally presented themselves to him.'[170] There was no denying however that, for the present, 'Jinnah's belief in the possibility of unity and in his ability to bring it about was seriously shaken.'[171]

Jinnah's 'Fourteen Points' were essentially aimed at diffusing the powers of the central government through a 'federal constitution, with residuary powers vested in the provinces, Muslim majority in the Punjab, Bengal and the North-West Frontier Province (NWFP), a new province of Sind, and political reforms in the NWFP and Baluchistan on the same footing as in other provinces of British India.'[172] The idea indeed was to protect the Muslim community in an 'Indian Federation', with 'a maximum number of Muslim-majority provinces, with full provincial autonomy to guard against the threat of Hindu domination at the centre.'[173] This federal objective made a lot of sense in view of the operation of the Government of India Act 1919, with the centre having a central legislative assembly, and the provinces, with some kind of autonomy through 'dyarchy'—the division of executive power and responsibilities between the governors and elected ministers—

in the provincial legislatures. In this way, provinces had become 'major centres of political activities and government'.[174] 'Provincial autonomy' as such, had to come much later in the Government of India Act 1935. In addition to the several constitutional safeguards, the Fourteen Points also included a critical communal safeguard:

> No Bill or resolution, or any part thereof, should be passed in any legislative or any other elected body, if three-fourths of the members of any community in that particular body oppose such a bill or resolution or part thereof, on the ground that it would be injurious to the interest of that community or, in the alternative, such other method is devised as may be found feasible and practicable to deal with such cases.[175]

This safeguard was meant to supplement the 'separate electorates',[176] which Jinnah had already included in the main points of his formulation. In effect, then, the Fourteen Points provided 'the Muslims with a sense of participation and belonging.'[177] In fact, it would be no exaggeration to state that these points presented a 'comprehensive Charter of Muslim demands for constitutional safeguards which incorporated every possible demand that could be made on the majority community and could satisfy every section of the Muslim community.'[178]

The Fourteen Points indeed brought Jinnah closer to the ideas and ideals of the Muslim separatist political movement, though they 'received a lukewarm reception from the Muslim community' at that time.[179] The Muslims, of course, 'wanted all of his fourteen points' later at the Round Table Conference in London in 1930–2, though 'none of which [Mahasabha leaders] Jayakar or [B. S.] Moonji would fully accept',[180] and thus would not receive 'a serious consideration in official circles' like the Nehru Report earlier, which, the British Government held, did not represent united voice of political India.[181] The Fourteen Points 'only elevated in status when Jinnah's star began to rise again in the late 1930s'.[182]

But not before Jinnah went through a lean period, in the early 1930s, ironically at the Round Table Conference, the idea for which was largely floated by Jinnah himself. In a letter to the British

Prime Minister, Ramsay MacDonald, he had suggested 'to invite "representatives of India, who would be in a position to deliver the goods", to sit in a conference with the British authorities to reach a solution that may have the "willing assent of the political India".'[183] The British Prime Minister, of course, called the conference in London on 12 November 1930, and the main Indian political parties showed up except the Congress which, in the wake of the Nehru Report, had launched its Civil Disobedience Movement to press for a dominion status for India. Jinnah did his best to persuade the Congress to attend the conference and make good 'use of the opportunity in London for what it was worth', but it refused to budge. Led by Gandhi, who Jinnah now thought 'was "mentally and constitutionally incapable of learning things", the Congress preferred the Civil Disobedience Movement to the Round Table Conference.'[184]

The Congress, with Gandhi as its sole representative, did attend the Second Round Table Conference in 1931 but, by then, considerable damage had been done to Hindu–Muslim unity and the cause of India. Hindu and Muslim representatives had taken hard and divergent positions on a host of important issues, including federation, provincial autonomy, representation, weightage, etc. On top of it, Gandhi not only 'compromised the representative character of the whole Indian delegation', but also, in effect, 'proved to be chief wrecker of the conference'.[185] He was not interested in any Hindu–Muslim settlement and constitutional advance, particularly a 'genuine' federation, with maximum provincial autonomy, the main Muslim demand. All he could commit was that, 'the residuary powers shall vest in the federating units, unless on further examination, it is found to be against the best interests of India.'[186] The 'unless' part did not help at all. It was neither here nor there. To complicate matters further, the Mahasabha proved to be 'the major stumbling block to a Hindu-Muslim accord', with Moonji, in particular, 'hostile to the Muslim demands and to Jinnah personally'.[187] Thus, there was no progress, and as Jinnah expressed in exasperation, 'we went round and round in London ... without reaching the straight path that would lead us to freedom.'[188]

Jinnah himself championed self-government and freedom for India and told the Prime Minister point blank:

> I am glad, Mr. President that you referred to the fact that 'the declarations made by British sovereigns and statesmen from time to time that Great Britain's work in India was to prepare her for self-government was plain'... But I must emphasize that India now expects translation and fulfilment of these declarations into action.[189]

In this regard, Jinnah bitterly opposed the 'federal scheme' being prepared by the British government. He was convinced that this scheme 'would never materialize in a manner which would satisfy the legitimate aspirations of India.'[190] His opposition to the federal scheme indeed cost him an invitation to the Third Round Table Conference in 1932.[191] He was not invited, and the official leader of the Muslim delegation, the Aga Khan, did not make an issue out of it. Later, however, he lamented in his book, *The Memoirs of Aga Khan* (1954), that, 'we Muslims did not insist on having Mr. Jinnah with us'.[192]

Jinnah was not only hurt by the attitude of the British and the Congress leadership which, in his opinion, did not have 'the necessary courage',[193] he was equally disappointed with the Muslims who failed to rise to the occasion and 'realize their precarious position'. As he recalled:

> The Muslamans were like dwellers in the no-man's land; they were led either by the flunkeys of the British Government or the camp-followers of the Congress. Whenever attempts were made to organize the Muslims, toadies and flunkeys on the one hand and traitors in the Congress camp on the other frustrated the efforts. I began to feel that neither could I help India, nor change the Hindu mentality, nor could I make the Musalmans realize their precarious position.[194]

Jinnah, indeed, felt 'so disappointed and so depressed' that he 'decided to settle down in London'[195] and seek a new life for himself there.

This happened to be the fifth phase (1931–5) in his political career. He bought himself a 'large mansion' in London, and started legal practice at the Privy Council which 'earned him "great admiration for his legal skill and the judgement with which he conducted his cases".'[196] But being an Indian to the core, he could not stay away from India and Indian politics. He remained in regular correspondence, particularly with one of his former colleagues and member of the Legislative Assembly, Abdul Matin Chaudhury of Assam, even assuring him that his stay in London would be beneficial for India. As he explained it to Chaudhury on 25 March 1931, 'the centre of gravity is here and in the next two or three years London will be the most important scene of Indian drama of constitutional reforms.'[197] On 2 March 1932, he gave him advice and guidance: 'The Musalmans must stand united and I agree that there should be one organization'[198] for them, meaning the Muslim League, which was in disarray and division since he left India. He was confident that, 'If the Muslim leaders knew how to play their cards, I am sure the community will get what they want and after all it is not much.'[199]

The trouble was that the only Muslim leader who could play the 'cards' best, Jinnah, was not in India. Inevitably, a host of Muslim leaders, such as Liaquat Ali Khan, Raja Sahib of Mahmudabad, and Abdullah Haroon, to name a few more important ones, wrote letters to him to return to India and lead the Muslims. Liaquat Ali Khan and Allama Muhammad Iqbal even visited him. The Muslim League Council, after deliberating upon the uncertain, difficult situation arising out of the 'White Paper', and the imminent constitutional advance, following recommendations of the Round Table Conference, sent him 'an urgent telegram to return and lead the Muslims in this hour of crisis'.[200] Indeed, the Muslims, as one of his ardent followers and journalist, Z. A. Suleri, put it, were 'Charterless on the sea of India's most crucial years'.[201] They needed a leader, and they needed Jinnah.

The Muslims were badly 'divided into numerous groups, motivated by narrow, parochial interests, and engaged in mutual acrimony and hostilities.'[202] The Muslim League, too, since Jinnah left it in 1930, was divided, at least in two major groups, holding

League sessions at different places, and with little impact. There was no lead or leadership for that matter. The Muslims were at a loss. Indeed, as one Muslim leader explained their predicament in these words: 'The closing scene of the Round Table Conference has left the Muslims in the cold. We are unable to judge the real position, and there is no one else to give correct lead and take up the command'.[203]

Jinnah came to realise the gravity of the situation with the passage of the time. In his own words, 'I found that the Musalmans were in the greatest danger'.[204] In March 1934, he agreed to become the President of the Muslim League under Matin Chaudhury's 'amalgamation scheme', meant to amalgamate all factions into one, unified Muslim League.[205] Later that year, he was elected member of the Indian Central Legislative Assembly, in absentia and unopposed, from his Bombay Muslim constituency. In 1935, he made a couple of visits to India to assess the situation on the ground before deciding to return finally, since 'I could not do any good from London'.[206] Eventually, he left London on what he himself called, 'a grand mission to India'.[207]

Thus started the sixth eventful and momentous phase of his political career, from 1935 to 1940; it was a phase that saw him break from Indian nationalism and the associated Indian nationalist movement to lead the Muslim separatist political movement and indeed lay the foundation of Muslim nationalism through his 'two-nation' theory and the demand for the partition of India and the separate state of Pakistan for the Muslims.

The 'grand mission' did not mean that Jinnah wanted to break with Indian nationalism right away. He joined the 'Muslim camp' and, by implication, became a part of the separatist movement but—and that is important—he still stood for 'national' self-government for India. The difference now was that he was not prepared 'to allow nationalist interests to develop at the expense of Muslim interests'.[208] He insisted that Muslim interests were genuine, necessary interests, and, therefore, should be accommodated in any future constitutional set-up for the country. He was not happy with the 1935 Act nor with the Communal Award of 1932.

The Communal Award did not concede the main Muslim demand for statutory majorities in the Punjab and Bengal. The 1935 Act fell 'considerably short of the federal objectives' pressed by the Muslim leadership for a long time now.[209] In fact, the Act 'promoted a federation with a strong unitary structure'[210] which Jinnah had strongly opposed in the Round Table Conference earlier. The Act 'not only empowered the centre to legislate the "Federal" list of subjects but also the "concurrent" list, if it so desired. In addition, the Act failed to protect the autonomy of the provinces.'[211] Jinnah indeed held the Act to be 'totally unacceptable' and 'devoid of all the basic and essential elements and fundamental requirements which are necessary to form any federation'.[212] He, however, in order to secure those provisions in the Act which were beneficial to the Muslims, helped pass it in the Legislative Assembly in February 1935 which was 'not only "a personal triumph" for Jinnah as a legislator and political leader but [also] a clear message to the Congress and the British that the Muslims "would refuse to support any measure" that ignored their interests.'[213]

In the hope that this deliberate approach would work better once their representative party, the Muslim League, was strong enough, Jinnah decided to concentrate his attention on reorganising it afresh and instilling new life into its activities and plans. He was convinced that, 'The Hindus and Muslims should be organized separately and once when they are both organized they will understand each other better and then we will not have to wait for years for an understanding.'[214]

But the task of organising the League was daunting. As Mujahid summed up its state:

> The League was still dormant. Even its annual session had in the past few years failed to generate any interest among Muslims, with attendance so meagre as to warrant the reduction of quorum from 75 to 50 [attendees]. Primary organization it had none. Even its provincial bodies "lived on paper", being for the most part ineffective and nominally under the control of the central organization. Nor did the central body have any coherent policy of its own.[215]

On top of these difficulties, there was a host of pro-British leaders under the influence of British officials, such as Sir Mian Fazl-i-Husain, Sir Muhammad Ahmad Said Khan Chhatari (Nawab of Chhatari), Sir Ghulam Hussain Hidayatullah, Sir Abdullah Haroon, and Sir Abdul Qaiyum, to mention a few leading ones, who 'refused to have any truck with Jinnah at this juncture'.[216] They did not want to upset the government and the bureaucracy in their respective provinces. Also, there were several pro-Congress leaders and, of course, those 'torn as they were largely by personal, parochial, and regional loyalties and ambitions.'[217] In general, provincial leaders of the Muslim-majority provinces, mainly driven by 'personal rivalries, provincial jealousies, and an overriding desire to make quick political profit', posed the most serious and formidable challenge.[218] To compound Jinnah's difficulties, following the passage of the 1935 Act, the provincial elections were due shortly. He had to act fast.

Jinnah began by restructuring the League in a number of ways. He helped establish district and primary leagues. He set up a central parliamentary board and encouraged the formation of provincial parliamentary boards, though with halting success due to personal feuds, factionalism, and provincial myopia. For instance, Fazl-i-Husain, who had 'welcomed his return to India',[219] now conveyed a message to him to keep 'his fingers out of the Punjab pie'.[220] Some provinces failed to constitute parliamentary boards under pressure, especially because of 'attempts by the British and the Congress to mould Muslim thinking' to serve 'their interests'.[221] However the central parliamentary board and provincial parliamentary boards, wherever and whenever formed, prepared their manifestos for election campaigns. The League's constitution was amended to make it more representative of its organisational units. A committee was formed to mobilise support for the League and to expand its membership. The annual subscription was drastically reduced, from four rupees to two annas. The League had meagre finances for a national party but this was done to attract the masses who had, so far, remained indifferent and aloof from its activities. These were bold, refreshing, and enthusiastic initiatives but, as the results of the 1936-7 elections showed, a little too late, if not too little.

Jinnah led the election campaign on a conciliatory note. The League's election manifesto (June 1936) had recalled 'the Lucknow Pact of 1916 as "one of the greatest beacon lights in the constitutional history of India".'[222] He felt that, 'if Muslims would speak with one voice, a settlement between Hindus and Muslims would come quicker'.[223] But then, he had no idea that a spoiler, Jawaharlal Nehru, who was now president of the Congress would insist that 'there are only two parties in India—the [British] Government and the Congress—and others must line up'.[224] Jinnah was taken aback:

> I refuse to line up with the Congress. I refuse to accept this proposition. There is a third party in this country and that is Muslim India ... We are not going to be the camp followers of any party .... We are willing as equal partners to come to a settlement with our sister communities in the interest of India.[225]

But that did not help. Nehru was still insistent: 'I come into greater touch with the Muslim masses than most of the members of the Muslim League'.[226] This, of course, was ridiculous, forcing Jinnah to retort that:

> his claim that he has got a large body of Muslim followers cannot be accepted by any intelligent man .... I would request him to come to earth ....[227]

This sharp exchange set the tone for what was to follow after the elections, indeed till the very end—the Partition of India and the creation of Pakistan. Increasingly, Nehru's 'marked dislike of Jinnah' became too strong to auger well for Hindu–Muslim unity or any national cause for that matter.[228]

The 1936-7 elections proved to be a mixed bag for the League. It did not do well enough in 'numerical terms'. But it did not fare that bad either, especially if one keeps in mind the performance of the other major party, Congress, with regard to Muslim seats. The League secured 110 seats (excluding those won by pro-League independent candidates who could not contest through the provincial parliamentary boards one way or the other) out of 496 reserved for the Muslims.[229] This was a creditable performance given that the League had 'come into the field from almost nonexistence in the middle of 1936 and completed its preparations with practically no experience in collective electoral politics in a short period of six months'.[230] The Congress, with Nehru and his 'Muslim masses', on the other hand, could bag only 27 seats, 15 out of them in the NWFP, thanks to the Khudai-Khidmatgars, led by its ally, Adbul Ghaffar Khan. Its 'claim to represent Muslim opinion had been badly tarnished.'[231] According to Salesh Kumar, the League emerged as the only 'organization that could reasonably claim to represent the Muslims on an all-India basis'.[232] Jinnah himself was elated: 'In each and every province where the League Parliamentary Board was established and the League parties were constituted we carried away about 60 and 70 per cent of the seats that were contested by the League candidates'.[233]

Thus, Jinnah, after the elections, 'hoped that the Congress would treat the League with respect for its healthy support among the Muslims, and thus it would not be difficult to secure an accord between the two parties for the greater cause of India.'[234] This, he believed, was the only way to win 'complete freedom and self-government for this country'.[235] The Congress, however, led by Nehru, remained hostile, and decided to form governments on its own, without sharing power with the League even in a province such as the UP (United Provinces), where it had won almost half of the seats—29 out of 64. The Congress' later 'negotiations',[236] so to speak, with the local leadership simply demanded 'absorption'.[237] The UP was home of the League and its absorption would have virtually ended the Muslim League in India. Nehru, thus, knowingly, demanded 'absorbing it into the Congress to "free field for our work without communal troubles"'.[238] In fact, he had forewarned all provincial Congress committees that, 'With other groups we can form no alliances'.[239] During the election campaign, he had described the Congress as a 'national forum' and parties like the Muslim League as 'social and religious groups',[240] which said a

lot about his understanding and grasp of politics and the political
situation in India.

However, this short-sighted, self-serving, and haughty approach
by its leadership 'proved too costly for the Congress and for the
cause of Indian unity'.[241] Maulana Abul Kalam Azad, who was
involved in the failed negotiations with the League, later described
the whole development as 'a most unfortunate development', for
it gave the 'League in the UP a new lease of life'.[242] In fact, he went
on to conclude: 'All students of Indian politics know that it was
from the UP that the League was reorganized. Mr. Jinnah took full
advantage of the situation and started an offensive which ultimately
led to Pakistan.'[243]

The 'offensive' was launched at Lucknow on 15 October 1937,
ironically the place of the 1916 'Lucknow Pact' between the
League and the Congress that brought the two communities,
Hindus and Muslims, together on one national platform. The
offensive, of course, was led by Jinnah, but now at the head of
the Muslim separatist political movement, accusing Congress
governments of alienating the Muslims, and indeed generating a
'general feeling' among them that 'Hindu Raj' had arrived.[244] Even
a Muslim minister of the Congress government in Bihar, a Hindu-
majority province, could not help complain to Nehru that, 'The
Congress is full of provincialism, caste prejudices and [Hindu]
revivalism'.[245] That was to be the hallmark of the Congress rule
of provinces in 1937–9.

The Lucknow session of the League was attended by a host of
Muslim leaders all over India, including the premiers of three
Muslim-majority provinces, Sikandar Hayat Khan (Punjab), Maulvi
A. K. Fazlul Haq (Bengal), and Mohammad Saadullah (Assam),
who now felt threatened by the prospects of a Hindu-majority
government at the centre in the future and the resultant impact on
their provinces. The session turned out to be what Jinnah described
as 'one of the most critical that has ever taken place during its
[League's] existence for the last more than [sic] thirty years.'[246]
With 'a record attendance of nearly 5,000, including 200 women',[247]
it represented 'the first breakthrough' in the League's efforts to
mobilise public support at the grassroots level.[248] But, more

importantly, this Lucknow session also reflected a radical shift in Jinnah's own political thinking and standing. He had moved 'far from his classical position in politics'.[249] There was 'no longer confusion in his mind as to the aims of the Congress or the possible fate of the Muslims' in a Hindu majority-dominated polity.[250] The Congress, he was now convinced, was 'pursuing a policy which is exclusively Hindu'.[251] He, therefore, was particularly critical of the Muslims aligned with the Congress for they were 'making a great mistake when they preach unconditional surrender' and throw themselves 'on the mercy and goodwill of others'.[252] Indeed, he made a fervent appeal to all the Muslims to come together on the League platform to the 'exclusion of every other consideration'.[253] This was the only way, he insisted, to reach a 'settlement with the Hindus', for settlement, he explained, 'can only be achieved between equals'.[254] 'Politics', he exhorted the Muslims, 'means power and not relying only on cries of justice or fair play or good will.'[255] In the end, he galvanised them:

> There are forces which may bully you, tyrannise over you and intimidate you and you may even have to suffer. But it is by going through this crucible of fire of persecution ... tyranny ... threats and intimidations that may unnerve you, and it is by resisting, by overcoming, by facing these disadvantages, hardships, and by suffering and maintaining your true convictions and loyalty that a nation will emerge worthy of its past glory and history .... Eighty millions of Musalmans in India have nothing to fear. They have their destiny in their hands ....[256]

This was indeed a different, charged, and completely transformed Jinnah, inspiring and leading the Muslims and the Muslim separatist movement like never before. He had come to Lucknow dressed in a different attire and in a different state of mind. He had come dressed in the traditional Muslim dress, shedding his lifelong Western suit, to clearly and consciously express 'his Muslim cultural identity'.[257] He had come to represent Muslim India and to promise the Muslims a 'future' in which 'neither the British nor the Congress would be arbiters of their destiny but they themselves'.[258] The present delegates were 'electrified and enthused' by his appeal, and indeed one of the delegates, Maulana Zafar Ali Khan, a prominent Muslim politician and editor of the Urdu newspaper *Zamindar*, moved a resolution to bestow upon Jinnah the title of *Quaid-i-Azam*,[259] a title that 'stuck',[260] and stayed with him for the rest of his life.[261] This honorific title was, in fact, indicative of his emergence as a charismatic leader of Muslim India as well.[262] He remained the charismatic leader of Muslim India in the crucial decade of 1937–47, and beyond: in Pakistan, in 1947–8, as its first Governor General, till his death on 11 September 1948.

Jinnah's appeal to the Muslims to join the Muslim League started paying off pretty soon. In fact, the League–Congress clash polarised Hindu–Muslim relations to such an extent that it made exceedingly 'difficult for Muslim elites to remain outside the League'.[263] This was clearly 'reflected both in the strength and composition of the delegates at the [future] annual sessions and in the membership' of the party.[264] A surer indicator, of course, was provided by the by-elections in the post-Lucknow period. In 61 by-elections for Muslim seats between 1937 and 1943, the League won an overwhelming number of 47 seats.[265] Clearly, the League had fast become the party of the Muslims.

Jinnah 'felt confident that the increased strength of the League would help dispel doubts and misgivings about Muslim interests and demands and will make the Congress better appreciate its position.'[266] He decided to seek, once again, negotiations with the Congress leadership to resolve the Hindu–Muslim problem and 'proceed further' on the road to self-government and freedom for India. However, given his past experience of the Congress and its tendency, of late, to dismiss the League offhand, he believed these negotiations could be successful only if the Congress was prepared to recognise the League as 'the authoritative and representative organization of the Indian Muslims'.[267] He got in touch with Subhas Chandra Bose, the then Congress president, as well as Nehru, to seek recognition for the League, but to no avail. In March 1938, he, finally, turned to Gandhi to apprise him:

We have reached a stage where no doubt should be left that you recognize the All-India Muslim League as the one authoritative and

representative organization of the Muslims of India .... It is only
on that basis that we can proceed further and devise a machinery
of approach.[268]

Gandhi was equally indifferent. However, upon Jinnah's insistence,
he agreed to meet him eventually. They met in Bombay but
failed to resolve the issue. The Congress was not ready to 'accept
either explicitly or implicitly, the status of the League as the
"authoritative" Muslim organization of India'.[269] Obviously, such
an acceptance would have been the end of its so-called national
pretence in politics. Soon, however, Jinnah was able to derive 'his
strength and representative status from the support of the Muslim
masses, not the Congress recognition'.[270] By the middle of July 1939,
Nehru confided in Rajendra Prasad, the Congress president that,
they had been 'unable to check the growth of communalism and
anti-Congress feelings among Muslim masses'.[271] But, again, Nehru
failed to understand the situation well. It was not 'communalism'
as such. At this point in time, it was more than that. It was the rise
of Muslim nationalism.

In his speeches since 1936, Jinnah had referred to the Muslims
as a 'nation' several times, indeed calling for 'a settlement with
the Hindus as two nations, if not as partners'.[272] Allama Iqbal,
in his letters to Jinnah during 1936–7, had assured him that 'the
Muslims of India are the only Indian people who can fitly be
described as a nation in the modern sense of the word.'[273] In his
address to the Karachi Conference of the League in October 1938,
Jinnah thus warned: 'If the Musalmans are going to be defeated in
their national goal and aspirations, it will only be by the betrayal
of the Musalmans against us ....'[274] The Conference obliged by
adopting a resolution which, 'in the interest of an abiding peace of
the vast [sic] Indian continent and in the interests of unhampered
cultural development, the economic and social betterment and
political self-determination of the *two nations*, known as Hindus
and Muslims', recommended to the League 'to review and revise
the entire conception of what should be the suitable constitution
for India which will secure [an] honourable and legitimate status
to them'.[275] Interestingly, the original resolution had called for

'full independence in the form of a federation of their own'.[276] Jinnah, of course, did not encourage that idea at this stage. He felt that the Muslims had 'yet to develop a national self and national individuality'.[277] They still had to work for it.

But Jinnah was troubled by the inherent and increasing bias against the Muslims in the working of the representative system of government introduced by the British in India, based on numbers. The system had 'definitely resulted in a permanent communal majority government ruling over minorities'.[278] More significantly, however, he also insisted that the Muslims were not a:

> minority in the ordinary sense as understood in the West. They are in a majority in the North-West and in Bengal, all along the corridor stretching from Karachi to Calcutta. That part of the Indian continent alone has double the population of Great Britain and is more than 10 times in area.[279]

He, therefore, called upon the Congress to 'come down to earth and face realities' for, failing that, 'they will be wholly responsible for blocking the progress of India'.[280]

Jinnah, of course, welcomed the resignation of Congress ministries in October/November 1939, and called upon the Muslims to observe a 'Day of Deliverance' on 22 December 'as a mark of relief ... from the unjust Congress regime'.[281] But still, to help work out a just and mutually beneficial solution for the Hindu–Muslim problem for the 'progress' of India,[282] Jinnah wrote to Gandhi again on 1 January 1940, indeed commending him:

> More than anyone else, you happen to be the man today who commands the confidence of Hindu India and are in a position to deliver the goods on their behalf. Is it too much to hope and expect that you might play your legitimate role ...? Action and statesmanship alone will help us in our forward march.[283]

Gandhi was not moved. He did not care. He had no consideration for Jinnah or his plea to 'play your legitimate role'. Thus, in an indifferent, imprecise, and indeed condescending manner, he wrote back: 'I do not mind your opposition to the Congress', and went on to suggest:

If you succeed you will free the country from communal incubus,
and, in my humble opinion, give a lead to the Muslims and others
for which you will deserve the gratitude not only of the Muslims
but of all other communities.[284]

Jinnah was not amused. Indeed, this kind of attitude alienated him
from Gandhi, the Congress, and the whole system of government
in the hands of the Hindu community for good. He saw no future
in persisting with the system. In fact, in his interview with Viceroy
Linlithgow, in March 1939, before the war, he had already stressed
'that the system of government was more a part of the problem than
a solution', and that those who had 'advocated a reformed system
of government' were now convinced 'that the present system would
not work and that a mistake had been made in going so far'.[285] In
his opinion, 'the escape from this impasse lay in partition'.[286]

In an article that he wrote for the *Time and Tide* of London, on
19 January 1940, Jinnah publicly vented out this frustration with
the system, demanding that 'a constitution must be evolved that
recognizes that there are in India two nations who both must share
the governance of their common motherland'.[287] This, of course,
was the beginning of the end of united India, a prelude to Jinnah's
more radical demand for the partition of India and a separate 'state'
for the Muslim 'nation' on 22 March 1940 in the Muslim League
session at Lahore.

This also led to the seventh and the most crucial phase of
Jinnah's political career, from 1940–6/7. That phase ultimately
determined his place in history, for presenting and pursuing the
demand for Pakistan through what has come to be known as the
Pakistan Movement. This movement was the ultimate culmination
of the Muslim separatist political movement, from Syed Ahmad
Khan through Allama Iqbal.

In his lengthy, historic presidential address[288] to a large gathering
of about 100,000 Muslims from all over India, definitely the largest
Muslim gathering so far at any session, Jinnah offered the final
'solution' of the Hindu–Muslim problem in a reasoned, logical,
and persuasive manner. First, and foremost, he explained that the
Muslims and Hindus,

notwithstanding a thousand years of close contact, nationalities, which are as divergent today as ever, cannot at any time be expected to transform themselves into one nation merely by means of subjecting them to a democratic constitution and holding them forcibly together by unnatural and artificial methods of British Parliamentary Statute.[289]

In fact, he found it 'extremely difficult to appreciate why our Hindu friends fail to understand the real nature of Islam and Hinduism' and their impact upon the two communities.[290] Islam and Hinduism, he elaborated,

are not religions in the strict sense of the word, but are, in fact, different and distinct social orders, and it is a dream that the Hindus and Muslims can ever evolve a common nationality, and this misconception of one Indian nation has gone far beyond the limits and is the cause of most of [our] troubles and will lead India to destruction if we fail to revise our notions in time.[291]

'The problem in India', thus Jinnah claimed, 'is not of an inter-communal character but manifestly of an international one, and it must be treated as such.'[292] He stressed,

If the British Government are really in earnest and sincere to secure peace and happiness of the people of this sub-continent, the only course open to all is to allow the major nations separate homelands by dividing India into 'autonomous national states'.[293]

'History', he pointed out, provided 'many examples' where 'geographical tracts, much smaller than the sub-continent of India, which otherwise might have been called one country ... have been divided into as many states as there are nations inhabiting them.'[294] Indian Muslims, he insisted, 'are a nation according to any definition of a nation, and they must have their homelands, their territory, and state.'[295] They 'cannot accept any constitution which must necessarily result in a Hindu majority government ... Hindu raj.'[296]

But, most importantly, Jinnah emphasised:

We wish our people to develop to the fullest our spiritual, cultural, economic, social and political life in a way that we think best and in consonance with our own ideal and according to the genius of our people. Honesty demands and the vital interests of millions of our people impose a sacred duty upon us to find an honourable and peaceful solution, which would be just and fair to all.[297]

The League session fully endorsed Jinnah's 'honourable and peaceful solution' on 23 March 1940, and in a resolution adopted on 24 March, resolved 'that the areas in which the Muslims are numerically in a majority as in the North-Western and Eastern zone of India, should be grouped to constitute Independent States in which the constituent units shall be autonomous and sovereign.'[298] The minorities, Hindus or Muslims (in other parts of India), should be provided 'adequate, effective, and mandatory safeguards' for 'the protection of their religious, cultural, economic, political, administrative and other rights and interests in consultation with them.'[299]

Apparently two Muslim states, not one independent state, were indicated at this moment in time, for tactical reasons. Jinnah wanted to maintain and mobilise the new converts, the powerful provincial leaders of the Punjab and Bengal, Sikandar Hayat Khan and A. K. Fazlul Haq (mover of the resolution), respectively, for his cause. Soon dubbed as 'Pakistan Resolution' by the Hindu press and politicians, he needed their support more than anybody else's to popularise the resolution among the Muslim masses, at least till such time that the League could stand on its own feet in these two major Muslim-majority provinces. He was a rational, realistic leader, and thus had 'the ability to see things through realism and pragmatism, to be able to see things as they are'.[300] He could wait for the opportune time. With greater political mobilisation and support for the League, especially in the 1945–6 elections, he went on to modify and declare in clear, unambiguous terms that 'our formula is based on the territory of this sub-continent being carved into two sovereign states of Hindustan and Pakistan'.[301]

Apart from this ambiguity about the number of states, a few other 'ambiguities' have also been pointed out in the resolution but have been addressed elsewhere at length,[302] and thus they need not be discussed here. Suffice it to say that the Lahore resolution 'lowered the final curtain on any prospects for a single united independent India .... The ambassador of Hindu-Muslim unity had totally transformed himself into Pakistan's great leader.'[303] Jinnah had come to learn from experience—and the hard way—that:

> the Congress party was a Hindu organization, dedicated to the establishment of Hindu Raj in India, and that it had no intention of developing a non-sectarian, genuine liberal polity which might value the diversity of religious and cultural expressions in the country. Hindu leaders had made it abundantly clear that 'Hindustan is for the Hindus' ....[304]

The consequences were but a foregone conclusion.

The Muslim separatist political movement, from Syed Ahmad Khan all the way to Jinnah, now developed into a Muslim nationalist movement—the Pakistan Movement—demanding the partition of India and the creation of separate state of Pakistan for the Muslim nation. Muslim separatism, at the hands of Jinnah, who had been a reluctant separatist for most part earlier on, had morphed into Muslim nationalism in direct opposition to the erstwhile Indian nationalism led by the Congress, 'a Hindu party'.[305] Jinnah had tried to 'resolve the communal problem in India in the Indian context, but after all his efforts were frustrated, he was left with no option but to ask for the establishment of a separate homeland.'[306] In this sense, clearly, 'Muslim separatism was not a given or a priority thing as far [as] Jinnah was concerned.'[307] Jinnah's 'conversion' to Muslim separatism, however, 'was to prove a turning point not only in his own political career, but in the history of India'.[308] This conversion also showed that the Pakistan movement did not spring up abruptly and out of nowhere. It was the end product of the separatist political movement for a long time and Jinnah evolved into its votary and ultimate leader.

How Muslim nationalism was to prevail over Indian nationalism and overcome the British aversion to partition of India was to be

Jinnah's main, vital task in this most crucial phase, 1940–6, leading up to the achievement of Pakistan in 1947. A lot has been written on this phase—probably the most documented phase in the British colonial history of India—by academics of all persuasions and places, including myself,[309] and needs not be recounted here at length. A brief summary of the main events and developments will serve the purpose.

The first and most demanding aspect of Jinnah's task, of course, was to unite the Muslims behind the demand for Pakistan. He had to reorganise the League to help mobilise Muslim support before he could force the British, primarily, and the Congress, secondarily, to concede to the demand of Pakistan. The British held the reins of power, not the Congress which, like the League, sought freedom. The only difference was that the Congress sought freedom from the British only; Jinnah sought freedom from both the British and the Congress. He wanted freedom for India but also wanted the Muslims to be free to live their lives separately with all the powers and security of a sovereign, separate state.

As I have discussed elsewhere at great length, Jinnah based his strategy for re-organisation of the Muslim League and 'political mobilization of the Muslims on a number of systematic, planned moves'.[310] These moves did not necessarily follow one another. They were pursued independently and, more often than not, simultaneously, reinforcing and strengthening one another. The first move pertained to the restructuring of the League to make room for new social groups and classes readily willing and attracted to the idea of Pakistan. A special effort was made to accommodate the educated, urban middle classes (professionals, lawyers, journalists, students, etc.), who had come to realise, more than any other class or group, that the Congress was promoting 'Hindu nationalism', instead of the so-called Indian nationalism, and thus there was going to be no place for them under the Indian sun. Only Pakistan could provide them opportunities for growth and development. The League amended its constitution (in 1940), and expanded its organisational structure to make room for the new entrants from primary, tehsil, and district leagues all the way up to the Working Committee, Council of the League, and the office of the President to be elected every year by the Council from amongst the nominees of different tiers of the party.[311] The support of the middle classes not only balanced the preponderant influence of the old, traditional groups, such as the landowners and tilted gentry, but also transformed the League into a genuine nationalist movement representing major groups and classes of the Muslim community involved, both old and new, traditional and modern.[312] The idea was to help the League concentrate 'its creed, its propaganda, and its strategy on one objective: a separate Muslim state'.[313]

Having expanded its organisational structure, Jinnah moved on to 'make the League a well-knit and disciplined organization of the Muslims'.[314] He was mindful of the fact that, 'If Wardha [Gandhi's ashram retreat] makes any decision and issues orders tomorrow, millions of Hindus will follow and obey. I ask you, suppose the Muslim League were to issue any order, what will happen to it?'[315] Thus, Jinnah helped strengthen the office of the President of the League through an amendment in its constitution (in 1940). In fact, he empowered that office in successive constitutions of the League in 1941, 1942, and 1944, the last stipulating that the:

> President shall be the principal head of the whole organization, shall exercise all the powers inherent in his office and be responsible to see that all the authorities work in accordance with the constitution and rules of the All-India Muslim League.[316]

Jinnah, indeed, needed these enhanced powers to discipline the recalcitrant provincial leaders of the Punjab and Bengal who had joined the League in 1937 more for tactical gains against the Congress than any genuine loyalty and commitment to the party or its cause. These leaders were hesitant to yield control to the centre and Jinnah. But Jinnah kept up the pressure through his enhanced authority by forcing them into 'alliances', such as with Sikandar Hayat Khan in the Punjab, through the 'Jinnah–Sikandar Pact'. The result was that soon, in 1942, Sikandar Hayat Khan was not only 'reluctant' to 'stand up to Jinnah' but, more tellingly, realised that 'unless he walked wearily and kept on the right side of Jinnah he would be swept away'.[317] His successor, Khizar Hayat Khan Tiwana, tried to defy, and was routed in the 1945–6 elections.

Jinnah, of course, was not content working through the League alone. He was the charismatic leader of Muslim India since the 1937 Lucknow session of the League and his charisma had been validated in the Lahore session of 1940, especially after the passage of the Lahore (Pakistan) Resolution. Thus, he also had his personal charisma to add and employ in the cause of Pakistan. There was a:

> large number of Muslims [who] owed their allegiance to Jinnah and Jinnah alone. They were not interested in the League or party politics for that matter. And because of Jinnah, they were ready and willing to support the League without being formally associated with it. In this sense, the League was a charismatic movement rather than a political party in the conventional sense.[318]

That is why, according to one 'American Witness', the overwhelming victory of the League in the 1945–6 elections, 'inadequately measured' its 'influence' and appeal.[319] Jinnah's 'charisma was the real measure'.[320] Jinnah drew huge crowds, 'even larger crowds than those seen at the height of the Khilafat campaign as he travelled the length and breadth of the subcontinent popularizing the League's demands.'[321] In fact, as time went by, 'hundreds of thousands of Muslims joined processions, demonstrations and strikes as the Pakistan movement gained momentum.'[322] No wonder, at the end of the day, when the movement had accomplished its goal, and the state of Pakistan had been achieved, Jinnah was deemed to be 'the personification of the state'.[323]

In addition to his personal charisma and following, certain acts of omission and commission on the part of his opponents, the British and the Congress, during the war years, also helped Jinnah's cause immensely. The British had declared war (World War II) on behalf of India without taking the Indian political parties, particularly the main parties—Congress and the League—into confidence. The Congress reacted and resigned from its ministries, without realising the long-term implications of its decision, leaving 'the field entirely to the Muslim League'.[324] Jinnah, already weary of the Congress rule in the provinces, promptly declared a 'Day of Deliverance' on 22 December 1939, and went on to take full advantage of this gross miscalculation. He was further helped, of course, by Gandhi's other, ill-advised, Civil Disobedience Movement launched on 8 August 1942 to force the British to 'Quit India'. This was 'a serious, almost inexcusable miscalculation.'[325] The result of these rash moves on the part of the Congress was that both British and Indian governments were 'left with no choice but to woo the non-Congress parties and leaders in the country, and especially Jinnah', for two very important reasons:

> Jinnah was the leader of a party which was second only to the Congress at all-India level, and as a leader of the Muslims, he had a special clout. Although the Muslims were a 'minority' in India, they contributed as much to the army as the Hindu majority, a fact known to responsible British authorities both in Britain and India. They contributed 37.65 per cent soldiers against 37.50 percent contributed by the Hindus.[326]

Interestingly, more than half of the armed forces were 'deployed' in the Muslim-majority areas 'now constituting Pakistan'.[327] Thus, the Muslim factor was very important for the British during the war.

Unlike the Congress leadership, Jinnah understood the war situation and the British stakes in it very well. While Gandhi advised the British to 'fight Nazism without arms ... [and] invite Herr Hitler and Signor Mussolini to take what they want of ... your possessions ... [and] allow yourself, man, woman and child to be slaughtered',[328] Jinnah knew that the British would fight to win the war at all costs. He even reckoned, in 1943, almost accurately, that 'the war would last another three years or so', and, again, amazingly, that at the end of it, the British would be left 'in a state of exhaustion', leaving it easy for us to 'wrest' Pakistan from their 'unwilling hands'.[329] Thus, Jinnah, 'a superb strategist', who always 'realized his own strengths and weaknesses', knew the strength of the League at that time as well, and needing 'all the help it could get', decided to cooperate with the British in their war effort.[330] But on his own terms, and to his own advantage. He insisted 'that where aid to the war effort conflicted with League policy, there, League policy must prevail.'[331] He agreed to cooperate at the provincial level only (not at the centre), and went on to replace Congress ministries in all the provinces included in his Pakistan scheme, that is, Assam, Sind, Bengal, and the NWFP; Punjab, a non-Congress province, was already allied with the League. Baluchistan was not a full-fledged province then. Jinnah had 'seized the opportunity of the Congress eclipse to strengthen the position of the League, with great success'.[332] The support of Muslim-majority provinces reinforced his standing for, 'without it, his credibility in any post-war negotiations' would have been 'severely limited'.[333] Indeed, as Jaswant Singh observed:

> By playing his cards adroitly [during the war] he was able to secure for the League a status equal to that of the Congress. The Congress, on the other hand, displayed poverty of forethought, lack of statesmanship and absence of flexibility, [sic] in consequence it could simply not regain its earlier position of primacy.[334]

The British, of course, saw this whole development as 'a further example of Jinnah's skill in consolidating his position'.[335] But, under the prevailing circumstances, it suited them fine. They needed political governments to run these provinces. In the process, however, 'they did not fully gauge the impact of [Jinnah's] wartime strategy upon the future course of politics in India'.[336] They failed to realise how Jinnah was going to capitalise on this cooperation to strengthen and consolidate the Pakistan demand during the war years and, more importantly, confront them at the end of the war with a fait accompli, a united demand of Muslim India to deal with.

While the British suffered under the illusion that there was 'going to be nothing doing with either the Congress or the Muslim League while the war lasts',[337] Jinnah's whole wartime strategy was to keep things moving till the British agreed to concede his demand for Pakistan. In fact, he pursued a brilliant strategy in ensuring that he 'neither antagonized the British by attempting to extract too many concessions [at one time] nor adopted the opposite course of unconditional support in the war effort.'[338] The result soon became evident in his well-considered plea to the British government on 27 June 1940 that: 'No pronouncement should be made by His Majesty's Government which would in any way militate against, or prejudice the "two nations" position which had become the universal faith of Muslim India.'[339] Indeed, he sought 'a definite assurance' from the government that 'no interim or final scheme of constitution would be adopted ... without the previous approval and consent of Muslim India.'[340]

The British could not help but respond positively to conciliate Jinnah. This was the early phase of the war, with the Japanese on the offensive against their empire in the east in Malaya, Singapore, etc. They found it difficult 'to stand still',[341] and thus, in their so-called 'August Offer', assured Jinnah and the Muslims, as the League Working Committee meeting on 1 September 1940 appreciated, 'that no future constitution, interim or final, should be adopted by the British Government without their approval and consent'.[342] This was a major breakthrough in the realisation of the Pakistan demand. The British had publicly admitted the Muslim position in any future constitutional set-up. The League, however, rejected a reference in the Offer to the 'unity of national life' in India 'as historically inaccurate and self-contradictory'.[343] Apparently, this reference was meant for the Congress, to keep them interested and involved. As Jinnah confided in Liaquat Ali Khan,

> the British have not yet definitely made up their mind to displease the Congress as there is still lingering hope on their part and much more so with His Majesty's Government in England that the Congress would still fall in line with them.[344]

Jinnah could not be more correct as, in 1942, an old friend of the Congress, particularly of Nehru,[345] Stafford Cripps, was in India:

> as the British War Cabinet's representative, to meet with the Congress leaders to persuade them to support the British war effort. The westward advance of Japan and the precarious situation developing in India forced the British to launch a fresh political initiative.[346]

This was the making of the Cripps Proposals.

Cripps entered into negotiations with the Congress leaders, ignoring Jinnah, essentially promising them 'a new Indian Union', like any British dominion, after the war. In the meanwhile, he expected the Congress to join the government and participate in the affairs of the country except in defence, which, for the present, was to remain in British hands. However, to neutralise Jinnah, indeed to waylay him, and simultaneously pressurise the Congress to accept his proposals, Cripps proposed that if any province refused to accept the 'new constitution', the British Government would be constrained 'to grant such "non-acceding Provinces" the same status as that of the Indian Union.'[347] He even warned the Congress politely but as firmly as he could, that:

> if this scheme was not accepted, they would find that those who had been their best friends in British political circles in the past were no longer able to do anything to assist them towards the aim which they had.[348]

Jinnah, of course, saw through the non-accession clause in the proposals. The vote was to be exercised by the whole population of the province, not Muslims alone. This amounted 'to rejecting the Pakistan claim, since the League could not obtain necessary majorities in Bengal and Punjab.'[349] Jinnah spelt it out clearly in his Allahabad address on 4 April 1942:

> the alleged power of the minority in the matter of secession suggested in the document is illusory, as Hindu India will dominate the decision in favour of one All-India Union in all the provinces, and the Muslims in Bengal and the Punjab will be at the mercy of the Hindu minority in those provinces who will exert themselves to the fullest extent and length for keeping the Musalmans tied to the chariot wheel of Hindudom. Thus the Musalmans will be doomed to subjection in all the provinces.[350]

Though Jinnah agreed that the Cripps proposals offered considerable advance over the August Offer in the sense that the 'principle of partition' was conceded, Pakistan still was 'a remote possibility' as there was a 'definite preference for a new Indian Union which is the main objective'.[351] Jinnah, thus, refused to 'play the game with loaded dice', and rejected the proposals. The Congress, of course, rejected them too, but for their own reasons. They were upset with the non-accession clause more than anything else but rejected them primarily because they thought the British had offered them too little and too late. In the wake of the British military setbacks in the region, they, in fact, saw the British irrelevant and inconsequential to the future of India. Indeed, Gandhi advised Cripps to take the 'first plane home'.[352] Soon after, the Congress launched 'an open rebellion'.

While the Cripps Proposals were gone, things could never be the same for all the parties involved. Jinnah had made a huge strategic gain. He had the British recognise 'the principle of partition', and thus, the case for Pakistan. As the British writer H. V. Hodson saw it, the proposals offered Jinnah 'a hole in the dyke' which he was bound to extend as such opportunities came his way in the future.[353] And that did not take long. More importantly, it was the Congress now, ironically enough, in 1944, providing him an opportunity to breathe new life into the demand for Pakistan.

Gandhi and Jinnah entered into some of the most intricate and detailed discussions on the demand through 9–27 September 1944 in Bombay—at Jinnah's residence of all the places. Gandhi could not help but recognise Jinnah's enhanced status and standing in politics. He proposed that two 'life servants of the nation' should meet and resolve this 'communal tangle', as he put it, 'which had hitherto defied solution'.[354] 'The fact', thus wrote Nanda, 'that Gandhi, who had once described the division of India as a sin, had relented so far as to discuss ... the right of self-determination by the Muslims was a feather in Jinnah's cap.'[355] In fact, he maintained: 'Viewed in the long-term strategy of the campaign for Pakistan, the Gandhi-Jinnah talks were another milestone marking further progress from the offer of Lord Linlithgow in August 1940 [August Offer] and the Cripps Mission in 1942.'[356] Here, it needs to be pointed out that a proposal, called the 'Rajaji [Rajagopalachari] formula' and approved by Gandhi, was presented to Jinnah earlier in April 1944, along the same lines as proposed by Cripps, calling for 'a district-wise plebiscite to be taken in the [Muslim-majority] Pakistan provinces, the test being the recording of an absolute majority of adults in favour of separation or against it.'[357] The idea, like in the case of Cripps' proposals, was 'to sabotage the whole scheme' of Pakistan[358] in a subtle, insidious way.

Jinnah, of course, was not pleased with the Rajaji formula. He believed that the formula had the same 'fundamentals' as that of the Cripps' Proposals which 'were not open to any modification, and that was the reason why he failed'.[359] In fact, he claimed that Rajagopalachari and Gandhi were 'out-heroding Herod'.[360] While Gandhi initially (during the negotiations) insisted on that formula, he was eventually forced by Jinnah to concentrate 'on the Lahore Resolution in the hope of finding a ground for mutual agreement'.[361] However, Jinnah soon found out that Gandhi did not accept 'the basis and fundamental principles of the Lahore Resolution', including the fact that the Indian Muslims are a 'nation' and they have 'an inherent right of self-determination' and 'they alone are entitled to exercise this right of theirs for self-determination'.[362]

Jinnah, therefore, very candidly, told Gandhi that 'As a result of our correspondence and discussions I find that the question of the division of India as Pakistan and Hindustan is only on your lips and it does not come from your heart'.[363] If you were sincere and willing to accept its 'concrete consequences', he asked, 'why not then accept the fundamentals of the Lahore Resolution and proceed to settle the details?'[364] Gandhi, of course, never wanted to accept these 'fundamentals' as they were. He never wanted the partition of India and the creation of Pakistan as a separate, sovereign state. He let out his 'inner voice' in a press statement, after the failure of talks, on 28 September 1944:

the Lahore Resolution is quite sound—where there is an obvious Muslim majority they should be allowed to constitute a separate State by themselves and that has been fully conceded in the Rajaji formula or my formula. There is not much distinction between them. That right is conceded without the slightest reservation. But if it means utterly independent sovereignty so that there is to be nothing in common between the two, I hold it is an impossible proposition. That means war to the knife.[365]

'Here is an apostle and a devotee of non-violence', a shocked Jinnah responded on 4 October 1944, 'threatening us with a fight to the knife', and wondered, 'what kind of separate States does he then concede to the obvious Muslim majorities in their national homelands?'[366] Obviously, not based 'on the two nation theory'.[367] But then, the question was, why these long, tedious and testing negotiations? According to K. H. Khurshid, Jinnah's Private Secretary at the time, 'Mr Gandhi was anxious to stretch the negotiations, probably because he expected some move from the Viceroy's House.'[368] Gandhi wanted to project these talks as 'a threat of "united opposition" to the British Government, so that it would yield to the Congress.'[369] If so, it was truly lamentable. A genuine, fair, and agreed settlement on the Lahore Resolution and the associated demand for Pakistan between Jinnah and Gandhi would have been more acceptable to both communities, Muslims and Hindus, and also by implication to the Sikhs. India could have avoided 'violence' and 'the phenomenal extent of the killing during partition',[370] which came about through the British 3 June Partition Plan and its by product, the Radcliffe Award, on 17 August 1947. But that was not to be.[371] Gandhi, indeed the whole Congress leadership, failed to rise to the occasion. A historic moment went begging.

The failure of the Jinnah–Gandhi talks, of course, brought the British back at the centre-stage of constitutional negotiations. Viceroy Wavell felt that the political 'deadlock' could be 'broken only by a *demarche* by the third party'.[372] He organised a conference of leading political parties and their leaders in Simla on 24 June 1945. But like Gandhi, he too failed to notice how serious Jinnah was about progress with his demand for Pakistan. Indeed, Jinnah sought, right at the start, a 'declaration' accepting the Muslim 'right of self-determination', with a pledge that 'after the war, or as soon as it may be possible, the British Government would establish Pakistan having regard to the basic principles laid down in the Lahore resolution'.[373] Wavell, of course, was more interested in expansion of the Viceroy's Executive Council, an interim short-term proposal to help the government. But, for Jinnah, the long-term and short-term proposals were interrelated, indeed intertwined, and had to be pursued together and simultaneously. He apprehended that this:

> interim or provisional arrangement will have a way of settling down for an unlimited period and all the forces in the proposed Executive plus the known policy of the British Government and Lord Wavell's strong inclination for a united India, would completely jeopardize us ....[374]

While, in the end, Wavell claimed that the Simla Conference broke down on the issue of the Executive Council, with Jinnah demanding 'parity' with the Congress and the exclusive right of Muslim representation, and some historians supported this contention,[375] the fact was that Jinnah, first and foremost, was keen on 'a long-term settlement to be made with the Muslims on Pakistan. The Wavell proposals did not say anything specific on this crucial point.'[376] He could not forgo a long-term settlement for the sake of a short-term gain, if at all.

Jinnah wanted the British government to deal with the 'inevitable issue of Pakistan' clearly and upfront, and he succeeded to a great extent.[377] Wavell could not 'evade' it. He admitted:

> The object of the Simla proposals was to bypass the Pakistan issue and to get the parties [League and the Congress] working together in the Central Government in the hope that after some inside experience they would take a more realistic view. As things are now we cannot evade the issue.[378]

Wavell also acknowledged that Jinnah 'spoke for 99 per cent of the Muslim population of India in their apprehensions of Hindu domination ... that fear might or might not be well-founded but of its existence and reality there could be no question.'[379]

The Simla Conference, then, brought the Pakistan issue to the front, like never before. While the British officials 'expected' that its 'failure would weaken Jinnah's power over the League', Jinnah's position grew 'stronger', and 'the demand for Pakistan gained credence among Muslim masses across the land'.[380] The British were forced to deal with the demand, seriously and systematically. They, of course, did this in the Cabinet Mission Plan, proposed by a cabinet mission comprising Pethick Lawrence, Secretary of State for India, Stafford Cripps, President of the Board of Trade, and A. V. Alexander, the First Lord of the Admiralty in May–June 1946. They had come to realise that 'interim settlements were not the answer, and that time had come to find final solutions.'[381] In this sense, wittingly or unwittingly, they were following Jinnah's lead in the matter.

The Cabinet Mission Plan, again, had two sets of proposals: short-term and long-term. The short-term proposals were related to the formation of an interim government. For, as the Cabinet Mission emphasised: 'While the Constitution-making proceeds, the administration of India had to be carried on. We attach the greatest importance to the setting up at once of an interim government'.[382] This was an important part of the 16 May statement and was reiterated in the next (16 June) statement. The long-term proposals included in the 16 May statement concentrated on the constitution-making process. The main thrust of the process was:

to offer India a three-tiered constitutional structure in which provinces were grouped to form 'sections' which, in turn, would determine themselves what subjects would be under the jurisdiction of their respective sectional government.[383]

Three sections were made. Section A had Madras, Bombay, UP (United Provinces), Bihar, Central Provinces (CP), and Orissa—a section primarily comprising Hindu-majority provinces. Section B comprised the Muslim-majority provinces of the Punjab, NWFP, and Sind (with a representative of British Baluchistan included). Section C was a mix of Muslim-majority and Hindu-majority provinces of Bengal and Assam. All three sections of the Constituent Assembly 'had to come together along with representative of the Indian States, to settle the Union constitution after the provincial constitutions had been formed.'[384] Significantly, once the Union Constitution had come into operation, 'the provinces could "opt out" of their assigned groups/sections'.[385] This, the Mission contended, would help 'bring about a stable and practicable form of constitution for All-India'.[386] The Mission ruled out the Pakistan scheme pressed by Jinnah during his lengthy negotiations with them, insisting that 'neither a larger nor a smaller sovereign state of Pakistan would provide an acceptable solution of the problem.'[387]

Jinnah was, of course, disappointed with the whole approach of the Mission for having 'thought fit to advance commonplace and exploded arguments against Pakistan' and thus 'hurt the feelings of Muslim India'.[388] He pointed out numerous areas where the Mission had ignored Muslim concerns taken up during the negotiations, and particularly lamented that they did not agree to their proposals of 'two constitution-making bodies' (not one) and the 'right to secede from the [Indian] Union after an initial period of ten years'.[389] All this, he insisted, 'was done by the Mission to appease and placate the Congress'.[390]

Still, Jinnah accepted the Cabinet Mission Plan and relented, so to speak, on his demand for Pakistan despite an overwhelming victory in the 1945–6 elections he fought based precisely on this demand. The League had won all 30 Muslim seats in the Central Legislative Assembly, with some candidates elected unopposed, securing 86.6 per cent of the votes polled in Muslim constituencies. Except for the NWFP, where it bagged 17 and the Congress 19 Muslim seats, it swept all the Muslim-majority provinces. In Bengal, it won 116 out of 122 Muslim seats (about 96 per cent). In Punjab, it secured 79 out of 88 Muslim seats (about 90 per cent). In Sind, the League secured 28 out of 34 Muslim seats (about 82 per cent).[391] The question is, why did Jinnah, in spite of a clear, convincing verdict on Pakistan, accept the Cabinet Mission Plan? It becomes more pertinent a question in view of Jinnah's later rejection and call for 'Direct Action' to achieve Pakistan.[392] And, of course, he did not accept the plan in a rush. He made it after due deliberation and thought. As he acknowledged: 'I have thought much ... and have prayed for guidance, because the decision I was called upon to make would mar or make the destiny of our nation.'[393]

There are quite a few explanations, but, as already stated elsewhere, the most plausible ones are the following:

1) [The] war was over, and it was no longer easy to reject British offers at will. The British were not obliged to woo the League any more ... the Congress had re-entered mainstream politics.[394]

2) Viceroy Wavell gave Jinnah his 'personal assurance that we do not propose to make any discrimination in the treatment of either party; ... if either party accepts ....' This "assurance" from the Viceroy was "one of the most important considerations" with the League Working Committee in their acceptance of the statement of 16 May'.[395]

3) Jinnah knew that 'the foundation and the basis of Pakistan are there in their own scheme'. Sections B and C, comprising essentially the Muslim-majority areas, with the entire Punjab and Bengal provinces, ensured that the Muslims could 'reach [their] goal and establish Pakistan'.[396]

4) Jinnah knew that the plan was 'cryptic with several lacunas', out of touch with the realities of Hindu-Muslim politics, and thus 'unworkable'.... Jinnah had no doubt whatsoever that the constitutional package had serious problems and was not workable.[397]

5) Jinnah did not want the Congress to have a free hand in the formation of the interim government. A Congress government could badly hurt his efforts to create Pakistan .... That is why Jinnah made strenuous efforts to seek an 'assurance' from the Viceroy and the Mission on the formation of the interim government before announcing his response.[398]

6) Finally, Jinnah reckoned that some proposals in the plan were not, and could not, be acceptable to the Congress leadership. The Congress would 'sabotage' the plan sooner than later. For instance, Jinnah knew that the grouping clause, which formed the 'crux' of the long-term proposals as far as he understood, was not acceptable to the Congress.[399]

The above explanations, separately or taken together, explained Jinnah's acceptance of the Cabinet Mission Plan essentially as a tactic, a means to reach his strategic goal of Pakistan. Some, of course, were compelling, such as 'the foundation and the basis of Pakistan' in the plan, its being 'unworkable', and the grouping clause being unacceptable for the Congress leadership. But what ultimately 'sabotaged' the plan, as anticipated by Jinnah, and thus paved the way for his 'goal' of Pakistan, was Congress' refusal to accept the grouping clause, as an essential, integral part of the long-term proposals. This was in spite of the fact that, on 25 May 1946, the Cabinet Mission was constrained to publicly declare that 'the reasons for the grouping of the Provinces are well known and this is an essential feature of the scheme and can only be modified by agreement between the parties'.[400] But Gandhi and the Congress leadership would not agree, though they had, apparently, accepted the plan as a whole. In his article in the *Harijan* (a weekly newspaper in English) on 17 May, Gandhi insisted that, 'No province could be forced against its will to belong to a group even if the idea of grouping was accepted.'[401] The fact was that Gandhi was 'frontally opposed to Assam and NWFP being placed, without their approval in "Pakistan" area'.[402] Indeed, he called upon the provincial leadership in Assam 'to offer *satyagraha*'.[403] Nehru went one step further and 'wrecked' the plan by announcing in his fateful press conference of 10 July that:

> the big probability is that from any approach to the question, there will be no grouping .... I can say, with every assurance and conviction there is going to be finally no grouping there, because Assam will not tolerate it under any circumstances whatever. Thus ... this grouping business approached from any point of view does not get on at all.[404]

The problem was, as Ayesha Jalal noted, 'Grouping ... had brought him [Jinnah] to Simla [venue of the Cabinet Mission meetings]. He had been denied a sovereign Pakistan and offered grouping instead. Now Congress wanted to take away grouping'.[405]

All this clearly showed that the Congress' acceptance of the plan was more apparent than real, and not in line with the long-term proposals in particular. It was only interested in the short-term proposals, the interim government part, as Nehru indicated to Lord Wavell in his meeting on 16 May, 'immediate control of the Centre, so that they can deal with Muslims and Princes and then make at leisure a Constitution to suit themselves'.[406] To complicate matters further, the British Prime Minister Clement Attlee's government was favourably inclined towards the Congress and the Cabinet Mission was more than willing to help them attain power now. They 'were "obviously bent on handing over India to their Congress friends as soon as possible".[407] A responsible member of the Mission, Secretary of the State Pethick Lawrence, was even prepared to seek an 'agreement' with the Congress, beyond the original plan, to give them 'some concessions' in Assam and the NWFP.[408] While he described this proposal as 'both dishonest and cowardly',[409] Wavell could not help conclude in the end that throughout the negotiations, the Mission was 'living in the pocket of the Congress' and, thus, was 'unable to remain impartial'.[410]

Jinnah, who had put his ultimate goal of Pakistan and, indeed, his entire political career at stake, found the trickery and somersaults offensive and unacceptable. So far, his 'legal adroitness proved more than Pethick-Lawrence, Cripps, or Alexander could outwit, though all these wise British brains tried their best.'[411] But he was now fully convinced that the 'Congress had accepted their [Cabinet Mission's] proposals conditionally', and, worse, the Cabinet Mission and the Viceroy 'had committed a flagrant breach of faith'.[412] His two major adversaries that he had fought off and on, separately,[413] had finally joined hands to deny him his Pakistan by retaining united India at all costs. He had no doubt left that 'in the final phase of his struggle, he was to have both the Congress and the British as his adversaries'.[414]

Jinnah thus convened a meeting of the Muslim League Council on 27 July to review and plan the future course of action. He explained to the Leaguers in clear, categorical terms that the British had 'gone back on their plighted word', and now there was 'no room left for compromise'.[415] We must mobilise 'the Muslim Nation', he declared, for 'the only solution of India's problem is Pakistan'.[416]

On 29 July, the League endorsed Jinnah's stand, rejected the Cabinet Mission Plan, and indeed resolved that 'the time has come for the Muslim nation to resort to Direct Action to achieve Pakistan'.[417] Jinnah called for the 'Direct Action Day'. This was a historic moment in many ways, and especially in the sense that Jinnah, for the first time in his long political career spanning four decades, had opted for extra-constitutional methods to achieve his political goal. He explained it:

> We have been attacked on two fronts—the British front and the Hindu front. Today we have said good bye to constitutions and constitutional methods ... the two parties with whom we bargained held a pistol at us; one with power and machine-guns behind it, and the other with non-cooperation and threat to launch mass civil disobedience. This situation must be met. We also have a pistol. We have taken this decision ... with full responsibility and all the deliberations possible for a human being, and we mean it.[418]

Henceforth, the eighth, final, and the most intense phase of Jinnah's political career in British India started with 'extra-constitutional' methods supplementing and, indeed, strengthening his essentially constitutional struggle, from 1946 to 1947, leading to the ultimate achievement of the separate state of Pakistan.

Jinnah, as our discussion has suggested all along, was a constitutionalist to the core, in theory and practice, and by training, temperament, and conduct. Constitutional rules provided the means for politics and political advancement, with the rules of the game set by the rulers. But now that the colonial order was under severe strain and eroding after the war, with the British apparently on their way out, Jinnah could well afford to add extra-constitutional manoeuvres to press for his demands and goal. In this sense, they were a tactical choice, not a strategic imperative as in the case of Gandhi all along.[419] The extra-constitutional measures were meant to supplement, not to overtake or override, his constitutional moves and counter-moves. In fact, Jinnah thrived on these moves. His 'penchant for detail gave him an enormous edge over both his political colleagues and opponents in discussions and negotiations.[420] But Jinnah certainly had the capacity, too, to prove the Congress 'wrong' in its sarcasm that 'the League had no stomach for fight'.[421]

The Direct Action Day was observed on 16 August 1946, with Jinnah appealing to the Muslims to come out and 'conduct themselves in a peaceful manner'.[422] But, in spite of that appeal, the strike (hartal) 'revived the animosities' of the past, which 'exploded' in Calcutta, 'resulting in immense loss of human lives'.[423] In four days (16–19 August), according to the official estimates, '4,000 humans lost their lives and 10,000 were injured'.[424] Dubbed the 'Great Calcutta Killing', another estimate placed figures at 4,400 dead, 16,000 injured and more than 100,000 homeless, with casualties shared almost equally between the Muslims and the Hindus.[425] These estimates were revised upward from time to time as more and more Muslim casualties were discovered. The fact, however, remained that, 'No communal riot in British Indian history had ever reached such dimensions.'[426]

While the Muslims and Hindus accused each other for the bloody riots, there was no way the Muslims could have started or even provoked them. In Bengal, the League 'was in power', and, on top of it, the Muslims 'constituted a minority in the Calcutta city'.[427] It did not suit them at all. Ultimately, of course, the 'hooligans of the Calcutta underworld of the two communities' were blamed for the bloody, brutal riots.[428] More riots followed in other provinces, mostly Hindu-majority provinces, Bombay, UP, and Bihar, led by the Hindus, with even Gandhi admitting in one case, at least, that 'the conduct' of the Congress government in Bihar was 'shameful and disgraceful'.[429] Eventually, the rioting affected princely states of India too. For all practical purposes, it appeared to be the making of 'civil war in an odious and horrible form' in the country.[430]

This civil war-like situation was further aggravated by Wavell's ill-advised invitation to the Congress to form a government at the centre—an interim government—in spite of its repudiation of the Cabinet Mission Plan where it mattered the most, the long-term grouping scheme. Wavell did this under pressure from Cripps who, indeed, threatened that he 'would resign if this was not done'.[431]

The interim government was formed and installed on 24 August 1946. More riots and violence followed, especially in Bombay and Ahmedabad. Gandhi could not help but declare now that, 'we are not yet in the midst of civil war but we are nearing it.'[432] Even Wavell was alarmed and saw the worsening situation as a kind of 'tragic ending of rule in India'.[433] He, indeed, warned Secretary of the State Pethick Lawrence on 27 August: 'I am afraid we are in for a very great deal more violence all over India unless I can find some means of changing the present attitude of Jinnah and the League.'[434] In the meanwhile, the Congress' indifferent, hostile government 'reaffirmed the Leaguers' faith in a fully sovereign Pakistan'.[435] The distressed Leaguers and the Muslims at large,

> rallied around Jinnah like never before raising his charisma to a new, unprecedented level. They were now ready and willing to follow him to the bitter end. They realized that he was the man who could lead them into the 'promised land', into Pakistan.[436]

While Lawrence, an ardent Congress supporter, still wanted to persist with the Congress government, leaving it to find a way out of the volatile situation,[437] Wavell, the man on the ground, could not hold it any more. He knew that the situation was increasingly getting out of control. Thus, he wanted a 'settlement at the centre' right away.[438] He decided to persuade Jinnah to join the interim government. Jinnah finally agreed, but under certain conditions. One, he did not want anything to do with the long-term proposals at this stage. As he put it:

> The question of the settlement of the long-term plan should stand over until a better and more conducive atmosphere is created and an agreement had been reached ... and after the interim Government had been re-formed and finally set up.[439]

Two, he would join the government on the basis of 'parity' with the Congress and, as before at the Simla Conference in 1945, with an exclusive right to nominate Muslim members.

Wavell conceded on the issue of long-term proposals in the hope that 'the League Council will meet at a very early date' to reconsider its rejection of the Cabinet Mission Plan and call for Direct Action.[440] He also assured him that,

> he was prepared to honour the demand for parity (though in a modified form: six members, including one Scheduled Caste representative, nominated by the Congress, five members nominated by the League ...), [but] he could not guarantee that the Congress' list of nominees would not include a Muslim.[441]

Jinnah who, for the sake of his Pakistan, thought it 'fatal to leave the entire field of administration of the Central Government in the hands of the Congress',[442] did not press the matter further. On 14 October, he forwarded five names—topped by his 'right hand' and General Secretary of the Muslim League, Liaquat Ali Khan, and including, much to the consternation of the Congress, Jogendra Nath Mandal of the Schedule Caste—to represent the League in the newly formed interim government. However, in a press conference a month later, on 15 November, he publicly declared that the League ministers would essentially work 'as sentinels who would watch Muslim interests in the day-to-day administration of Government' and thus would 'resist every attempt which would directly or indirectly militate or prejudice our demand for Pakistan'.[443] He also made it clear that the interim government was neither a 'cabinet' nor a 'coalition'; it was simply the Executive Council of the Governor General.[444]

Jinnah, indeed, not only rejected,

> the interim government as a legitimate source of authority, but also went on to reject the bona fides of the Constituent Assembly, insisting that since the Cabinet Mission had failed to win the support and approval of the two major political parties, the Congress and the League, the Assembly could not come into existence.[445]

The Congress had never accepted the long-term proposals of the plan. Thus, Jinnah refused to attend the Constituent Assembly on 9 December 1946, again on 20 January 1947, and 3 February 1947:

in spite of the fact that he had joined the Interim Government, and the Congress was insisting that the 'League must either get out of the Interim Government or change its Karachi decision', that is, the decision to reject the Cabinet Mission Plan.[446]

But Jinnah would not budge. He remained committed to pursuing his goal of an independent, sovereign Pakistan. He would not embrace the Indian Union. Congress' threat to quit the government created a very difficult and challenging situation for the British authorities. They could not ask for the withdrawal of the League either. They were really in a fix:

> [The League withdrawal] would have serious repercussions in India and in the Muslim countries of the world. To allow the Congress to resign would lead to even more disastrous consequences .... In further communal disorders, it was doubtful if the loyalty of the Army and the Services could be relied upon.[447]

Wavell was already worried about the deteriorating law and order situation in the country. As he saw it, 'police in many parts of India were affected with communalism and were no longer to be relied on for firm action against their own community.'[448] The Army, he believed, 'had so far escaped any taint of communalism and was carrying on its duties in loyalty to the orders of its officers', though this, he conceded, 'would not last indefinitely, if troops continued to be employed in the suppression of civil disturbances'.[449] However, in 1946, 'mutiny' in quite a few places such as Bombay and Karachi, to name the two more serious ones, had exposed that 'loyalty'. Indian soldiers were being influenced by the INA (Indian National Army) propaganda, and Wavell himself had conveyed his 'Breakdown Plan' to the British government for a calculated, phased withdrawal from India.[450]

On 20 February 1947, Clement Attlee, the British Prime Minister, was left with no choice but to declare that the 'present state of uncertainty is fraught with danger and cannot be indefinitely postponed', and thus, it was necessary to take 'steps to effect the transference of power to responsible Indian hands by a date not later than June 1948'.[451] Wavell was sacked, and 'Admiral the Viscount Mountbatten' was appointed new Viceroy to bring about this transfer, ensuring 'the future happiness and prosperity of India'.[452] How far Mountbatten succeeded in that regard is a different story. The Radcliffe Award (announced a few days *after* the Partition, and thus leaving the opposing communities exposed and vulnerable) and the resultant Partition violence across the borders (especially in Punjab) speak for themselves. Suffice it to say, for our purpose here, that Mountbatten did all he could to deny Jinnah his Pakistan largely due to his close personal relationship with Nehru. He even brought forward the date of transfer of power to August 1947 at his behest.[453] Nehru, of course, helped appoint him as the first Governor General of independent India for further patronage and support of the British government, as the later events were to demonstrate, including on the issue of Kashmir.

The most obvious move by Mountbatten was to deny Jinnah his full provinces of Punjab and Bengal by insisting upon their division along communal lines. The whole idea was to force Jinnah to accept the Cabinet Mission Plan even at this late stage or, eventually, settle for a 'truncated, moth-eaten Pakistan', the 'smaller Pakistan', so to speak, which he had frowned upon in his negotiations with the Cabinet Mission earlier. This was in spite of the fact that Jinnah tried to explain to Mountbatten, again and again, that the division of these two major provinces will make his Pakistan 'economically very difficult if not impossible to function'.[454] As Nirad C. Chaudhuri, a prolific Indian writer, noted, the two provinces were 'indivisible geographically and economically as also culturally if culture is seen as a pattern of behaviour combined with [a] particular outlook on life'.[455] In religion, too, he maintained,

> which in this case meant social identity, they were indeed divided into three communities in Punjab [Muslims, Sikhs, and Hindus] and two [Muslims and Hindus] in Bengal. But even these distinct collective personae were like Siamese twins which could not be separated without making them bleed to death.[456]

Jinnah, thus, had no doubt that the division of these two provinces was meant to force him to abandon his demand for Pakistan. But

Mountbatten, pressed by the Congress which demanded a 'division' of these provinces,[457] tried to justify the division, ostensibly on the high moral ground that since 'the division of India is being planned at Mr Jinnah's insistence, he cannot be allowed to impose his will on the minorities'.[458] In the case of Punjab in particular, he claimed that it was:

> necessitated by the Sikh case. The Sikhs cannot and will not be dominated by the Muslims and no partition will meet the ends of justice if it does not exclude from the Muslim area as large a percentage of Sikh population as possible.[459]

Jinnah tried his best to persuade the Sikhs to stay in Pakistan. He told them that, 'if they were divided, they could not play the part they might hope to do [sic] if they stayed together—in Pakistan.'[460] But they were not moved. Unionist Premier Khizar Hayat Tiwana's resignation, under pressure from the League, accompanied by violent clashes between the Muslims and the Sikhs and 'the overall charged communal atmosphere in the Punjab [had] made any understanding between the two communities over Pakistan or the fate of the Punjab exceedingly difficult, if not impossible.'[461] To save the division of Bengal, Jinnah even agreed to its League Premier Huseyn Shaheed Suhrawardy's scheme of a 'Socialist Sovereign State of Bengal', an independent state. Sarat Chandra Bose, a Congress leader (and elder brother of Subhas Chandra Bose) in Bengal, too, favoured a 'United Independent Bengal'. But Mountbatten insisted on the division of the province, like in the case of Punjab: 'I simply could not visualize being so inconsistent as to agree to the partition of India without also agreeing to partition within any province in which the same problem arose' for a minority.[462]

The Partition Plan of 3 June confirmed the division of Punjab and Bengal, thus forcing Jinnah to accept 'a truncated, moth-eaten Pakistan', that is 'the minimum territorial extent', as Ian Talbot described it.[463] But then, the issue was not that Jinnah 'achieved a moth-eaten Pakistan, the real wonder is that he achieved any Pakistan at all. No freedom fighter in history was ever faced with such awesome odds as he was.[464] Besides, as Alan Whaites curtly put it, 'the logic of Pakistan was self-determination for minorities and this meant a truncated Pakistan, whatever the problems of seeking immediate independence'.[465]

The process of achieving Pakistan was completed after a host of difficult, complex steps, bringing together the provinces of East Bengal, West Punjab, Sind, Baluchistan, NWFP, and the district of Sylhet into the new nation-state,[466] leading finally to Mountbatten's announcement that, 'We can now look upon the creation of Pakistan on 15 August as legally decided upon'.[467] On 14 August 1947, Mountbatten came down to Karachi to legally transfer power and welcome Pakistan to the British Commonwealth. On 15 August, Jinnah assumed the office of the first Governor General of Pakistan, having been nominated by the Muslim League for this office as early as 4 July 1947. Jinnah's decision to become the Governor General himself was well thought out, indeed 'essential to consolidate power as fast as possible if Pakistan was not to be swept back into the powerful new Indian union and that with Mountbatten as Governor General his own control would be reduced.'[468]

With this official position, Jinnah's long and chequered political career in British India concluded, 'capped by a lasting achievement, namely the creation of Pakistan'.[469] His range of 'political achievements', as Patrick French summed up his career, 'had been colossal, and more remarkable than that of his opponents in Congress'.[470] But, most remarkably, Jinnah had brought the odyssey of Muslim separatist political leaders from Syed Ahmad Khan to Aga Khan to Syed Ameer Ali to Maulana Mohamed Ali to Allama Muhammad Iqbal to a systematic, successful end. India was partitioned to make room for a separate state.[471] Jinnah achieved the separate state of Pakistan.

Notes

1. Lawrence Ziring, 'The Phases of Pakistan's Political History', in *Iqbal, Jinnah and Pakistan: The Vision and the Reality*, ed. C. M. Naim (Lahore: Vanguard, 1984), p. 139. See, for instance, some Indian writers, academic

and non-academic. Tara Chand, *History of the Freedom Movement in India*, Vol. 4 (Lahore: Book Traders, 1972), 541; B. R. Nanda, *Road to Pakistan: The Life and Times of Mohammad Ali Jinnah* (New Delhi: Routledge, 2010), 333; V. P. Menon, *Transfer of Power in India* (Princeton: Princeton University Press, 1957), 437; Narendra Singh Sarila, *The Shadow of the Great Game: The Untold Story of India's Partition* (New Delhi: Harper Collins, 2005), 277; and Jaswant Singh, *Jinnah: India—Partition—Independence* (New Delhi: Rupa & Co., 2009), 485. One Indian writer, however, claimed that Mohandas Karamchand Gandhi, Jawaharlal Nehru, and Sardar Vallabhbhai Patel 'were equally responsible for creating a feeling of separatism in Jinnah's mind and subsequently they kept on strengthening it by their utterances.' Sheshrao Chavan, *Mohammad Ali Jinnah: The Great Enigma* (New Delhi: Authorpress, 2006), 293.

2. Ziring, 'The Phases of Pakistan's Political History', 139.
3. Stanley Wolpert, *Jinnah of Pakistan* (Karachi: Oxford University Press, 1999).
4. Ibid.
5. Ibid.
6. Sikandar Hayat, *The Charismatic Leader: Quaid-i-Azam Mohammad Ali Jinnah and the Creation of Pakistan* (Karachi: Oxford University Press, 2008). All subsequent references to the book, including citations are from its second, revised edition, published in 2014. In 2018, the Oxford University Press published its Pakistan Paperbacks edition.
7. Ibid., 345.
8. Saleem M. M. Qureshi, 'Iqbal and Jinnah: Personalities, Perceptions and Politics', in *Iqbal, Jinnah and Pakistan*, 23.
9. K. H. Khurshid, *Memoirs of Jinnah*, ed. Khalid Hasan (Karachi: Oxford University Press, 1990), 53.
10. Fatima Jinnah, *My Brother*, ed. Sharif al Mujahid (Karachi: Quaid-i-Azam Academy, 1987), 50. Another date of birth is also mentioned, based upon some school record. But Jinnah himself always insisted that 25 December indeed was the correct date. Even today, in Pakistan, this day is celebrated as his birth day officially and publicly.
11. Ibid., 47.
12. Ibid.
13. Ibid.
14. Ibid., 69.
15. Sharif al Mujahid, ed., *In Quest of Jinnah: Diary, Notes and Correspondence of Hector Bolitho* (Karachi: Oxford University Press, 2007), xi.
16. Nanda, *Road to Pakistan*, 3.
17. Wolpert, *Jinnah of Pakistan*, 15.
18. Mujahid, *In Quest*, xii.
19. Ibid.
20. Ibid.
21. Nanda, *Road to Pakistan*, 3.

22. Ibid., 4.
23. Fatima Jinnah, *My Brother*, 76.
24. Nanda, *Road to Pakistan*, 8.
25. Ibid.
26. Ibid.
27. Cited in Ajeet Jawed, *Secular and Nationalist Jinnah* (Karachi: Oxford University Press, 2009), 3.
28. M. C. Chagla, quoted in Nanda, *Road to Pakistan*, 9.
29. William Metz, *The Political Career of Mohammad Ali Jinnah*, ed. Roger D. Long (Karachi: Oxford University Press, 2010), 5.
30. Ibid., 2.
31. Ian Bryant Wells, *Ambassador of Hindu-Muslim Unity: Jinnah's Early Politics* (Delhi: Permanent Black, 2005), 17.
32. Ibid.
33. Ibid.
34. Ibid.
35. Ibid., 17–18.
36. Ibid., 8.
37. Ibid., 18.
38. Ibid., 24.
39. Ibid., 18.
40. Ibid.
41. Ibid.
42. Ibid.
43. Ibid.
44. Syed Sharifuddin Pirzada, ed., *The Collected Works of Quaid-i-Azam Mohammad Ali Jinnah*, Vol. 1 (Karachi: East and West Publishing Co., 1984), 1.
45. Nanda, *Road to Pakistan*, 12.
46. Pirzada, *Collected Works*, Vol. 1, 4.
47. Ibid.
48. Ibid., 2.
49. Wells, *Ambassador of Hindu-Muslim Unity*, 26.
50. Nanda, *Road to Pakistan*, 13.
51. For a detailed systematic analysis of his charisma and charismatic leadership see, Sikandar Hayat, *The Charismatic Leader: Quaid-i-Azam Mohammad Ali Jinnah and the Creation of Pakistan*, 2nd ed. (Karachi Oxford University Press, 2014).
52. Riaz Ahmad, *Quaid-i-Azam Mohammad Ali Jinnah: The Formative Years, 1892–1920* (Islamabad: National Institute of Historical & Cultural Research, 1986), 89.
53. Wells, *Ambassador of Hindu-Muslim Unity*, 36–7.
54. Ibid., 37.
55. Ibid.

56. Sharif al Mujahid, *Quaid-i-Azam Jinnah: Studies in Interpretation* (Karachi: Quaid-i-Azam Academy, 1981), 2.

57. Ibid., 2–3.

58. Ibid., 8.

59. Pirzada, *Collected Works, 48.*

60. Ibid.

61. Ibid.

62. Ibid., 9.

63. Ibid. 9–10.

64. Earlier presidents were Gokhale, Mehta, and such eminent leaders.

65. Cited in Riaz Ahmad, ed., *The Works of Quaid-i-Azam Mohammad Ali Jinnah, Vol. III (1916–1917)* (Islamabad: Quaid-i-Azam University, 1998), 380.

66. Ibid.

67. Wells, *Ambassador of Hindu-Muslim Unity*, 53.

68. Ibid., 58.

69. Ahmad, *The Formative Years*, 147–8.

70. Nanda, *Road to Pakistan*, 33.

71. Ibid., 34.

72. Muhammad Saleem Ahmad, *The All-India Muslim League: A History of the Growth and Consolidation of Political Organization* (Bahawalpur: Ilham Publishers, 1988), 229.

73. A. G. Noorani, *Jinnah and Tilak: Comrades in the Freedom Struggle* (Karachi: Oxford University Press, 2010), 19.

74. Wells, *Ambassador of Hindu-Muslim Unity*, 60.

75. Singh, *India—Partition—Independence*, 86.

76. Wells, *Ambassador of Hindu-Muslim Unity*, 60.

77. Stanley Wolpert, *Tilak and Gokhale: Revolution and Reform in the Making of Modern India* (Berkeley: University of California Press, 1977), 225. Cited in Ahmad, *The Formative Years*, 121–2.

78. Wells, *Ambassador of Hindu-Muslim Unity*, 65.

79. Ibid., 66.

80. Cited in Ibid., 68.

81. Ibid., 69

82. Ibid.

83. See, Hayat, *The Charismatic Leader*, 62.

84. Ibid.

85. Ibid.

86. Ibid.

87. Wells, *Ambassador of Hindu-Muslim Unity*, 74.

88. Ibid.

89. Nanda, *Road to Pakistan*, 46.

90. Rafique Afzal, ed., *Selected Speeches and Statements of the Quaid-i-Azam Mohammad Ali Jinnah*, 1911–1934 and 1947–48 (Lahore: Research Society of Pakistan, 1976), 112–13.

91. Sikandar Hayat, *Aspects of the Pakistan Movement*, 3rd rev. ed. (Islamabad: National Institute of Historical & Cultural Research, 2016), 92.
92. Marc Jason Gilbert, 'The Era of British Rule', in *A History of Pakistan*, ed. Roger D. Long (Karachi: Oxford University Press, 2015), 303.
93. Ibid.
94. Hayat, *Aspects of the Pakistan Movement*, 89–90.
95. Wells, *Ambassador of Hindu-Muslim Unity*, 85–6.
96. Afzal Iqbal, ed., *Select Writings and Speeches of Maulana Mohamed Ali*, Vol. II (Lahore: Sh. Muhammad Ashraf, 1969), 21–3.
97. Hayat, *Aspects of the Pakistan Movement*, 14.
98. Hayat, *The Charismatic Leader*, 63.
99. Ibid.
100. Pirzada, *Collected Works of Quaid-i-Azam*, 388.
101. Ibid., 375.
102. Hayat, *The Charismatic Leader*, 63.
103. Ibid., 63–4.
104. Cited in Ibid., 64.
105. Hayat, *Aspects of the Pakistan Movement*, 15.
106. Hayat, *The Charismatic Leader*, 66.
107. Hector Bolitho, *Jinnah: Creator of Pakistan* (Karachi: Oxford University Press, 1964), 78.
108. Hayat, *The Charismatic Leader*, 66–7.
109. Hayat, *Aspects of the Pakistan Movement*, 16.
110. Cited in Wells, *Ambassador of Hindu-Muslim Unity*, 126.
111. Ibid., 128. Gandhi's ascendancy in politics also demonstrated that there was 'no longer any hope of keeping Indian nationalism a predominantly non-religious movement of the educated classes.' Metz, *The Political Career of Mohammad Ali Jinnah*, 139.
112. Wells, *Ambassador of Hindu-Muslim Unity*, 128.
113. Cited in Nanda, *Road to Pakistan*, 96.
114. Wells, *Ambassador of Hindu-Muslim Unity*, 142.
115. Ibid., 128.
116. Metz, *The Political Career of Mohammad Ali Jinnah*, 41.
117. Ibid., 39.
118. Incidentally, Hindu Mahasabha, an anti-Muslim organization, was also revived in 1924. Ibid., 42.
119. M. Naeem Qureshi, 'Jinnah and the Khilafat Movement (1918–1924)', *Journal of South Asia and Middle Eastern Studies* 1, no. 2, Iqbal Centennial Issue (December 1977), 107.
120. Cited in Hayat, *The Charismatic Leader*, 68.
121. Wells, *Ambassador of Hindu-Muslim Unity*, 146.
122. Mujahid, *Studies in Interpretation*, 11.
123. For that list of all participants see, Ibid., App. 8 'Delhi Muslim Proposals, 1927', 467.
124. Ibid., 17.

125. Wolpert, *Jinnah of Pakistan*, 94.
126. Metz, *The Political Career of Mohammad Ali Jinnah*, 51.
127. Nanda, *Road to Pakistan*, 102–3.
128. Wells, *Ambassador of Hindu-Muslim Unity*, 164.
129. Ibid.
130. Ibid.
131. Ibid.
132. Ibid., 165.
133. Noorani, *Jinnah and Tilak*, 89.
134. Chand, *History of the Freedom Movement in India*, 107.
135. Hayat, *The Charismatic Leader*, 71.
136. Wells, *Ambassador of Hindu-Muslim Unity*, 166.
137. Ibid., 169.
138. Ibid., 172.
139. Metz, *The Political Career of Mohammad Ali Jinnah*, 51.
140. Nanda, *Road to Pakistan*, 105.
141. Ibid.
142. Ibid., 106.
143. Ibid., 107.
144. See, Latif Ahmad Sherwani, ed., *Speeches, Writings and Statements of Iqbal* (Lahore: Iqbal Academy, 1977), 13, 19.
145. Jinnah's letter to the British Prime Minister, Ramsay MacDonald. Cited in M. H. Saiyid, *Mohammad Ali Jinnah: A Political Study* (Karachi: Elite Publishers, 1970), 142.
146. Wells, *Ambassador of Hindu-Muslim Unity*, 174.
147. Nanda, *Road to Pakistan*, 115–16.
148. Ibid., 116.
149. Wells, *Ambassador of Hindu-Muslim Unity*, 179.
150. See 'Nehru Report' on Minority Representation, in Mujahid, *Studies in Interpretation*, App. 9, 468–72.
151. Wells, *Ambassador of Hindu-Muslim Unity*, 179.
152. Hayat, *Aspects of the Pakistan Movement*, 18.
153. Cited in Ibid.
154. Wells, *Ambassador of Hindu-Muslim Unity*, 180. Significantly, the Nehru report 'repudiated the Lucknow Pact and offered no compensatory advantages to the Muslim community.' Wolpert, *Jinnah of Pakistan*, 97.
155. Nanda, *Road to Pakistan*, 118.
156. Hayat, *The Charismatic Leader*, 72.
157. Cited in Ibid., 71–2.
158. Nanda, *Road to Pakistan*, 119.
159. Ibid.
160. Ibid.
161. Ibid.
162. Wells, *Ambassador of Hindu-Muslim Unity*, 181–2.
163. Ibid., 184.

164. Wolpert, *Jinnah of Pakistan*, 99.
165. Prakash Almeida, *Jinnah: Man of Destiny* (Delhi: Kalpaz Publications, 2001), 92.
166. Bolitho, *Jinnah*, 89.
167. Patrick French, *Liberty or Death: India's Journey to Independence and Division* (New Delhi: Harper Collins, 1997), 62.
168. Metz, *The Political Career of Mohammad Ali Jinnah*, 57–8.
169. Ibid., 59.
170. Ibid.
171. Ibid.
172. Hayat, *Aspects of the Pakistan Movement*, 19. For the text of 'Fourteen Points' see, Mujahid, *Studies in Interpretation*, App 10., 473–81.
173. Hayat, *Aspects of the Pakistan Movement*, 19.
174. Ibid., 71.
175. Mujahid, *Studies in Interpretation*, App. 10, 480.
176. Jinnah 'had suffered considerably on account of his compromising stance on separate electorates' in the Delhi Muslim Proposals. Mujahid, *Studies in Interpretation*, 20. This provision of separate electorates now helped him win his 'critics' back. Wells, *Ambassador of Hindu-Muslim Unity*, 193.
177. Mujahid, *Studies in Interpretation*, 19.
178. Nanda, *Road to Pakistan*, 124.
179. Wells, *Ambassador of Hindu-Muslim Unity*, 194.
180. Wolpert, *Jinnah of Pakistan*, 120.
181. Nanda, *Road to Pakistan*, 128.
182. Wells, *Ambassador of Hindu-Muslim Unity*, 194.
183. Hayat, *The Charismatic Leader*, 75.
184. Ibid., 76.
185. Hayat, *Aspects of the Pakistan Movement*, 21.
186. Cited in Ibid.
187. Wells, *Ambassador of Hindu-Muslim Unity*, 216.
188. Cited in Hayat, *The Charismatic Leader*, 77.
189. Cited in Ibid.
190. Jamil-ud-Din Ahmad, ed., *Speeches and Writings of Mr. Jinnah*, Vol. I (Lahore: Sh. Muhammad Ashraf, 1968), 2.
191. Ibid., 3.
192. Aga Khan, *The Memoirs of Aga Khan: World Enough and Time* (New York: Cassel & Co., 1954), 232.
193. Metz, *The Political Career of Mohammad Ali Jinnah*, 65.
194. Ahmad, *Speeches and Writings*, Vol. I, 41–2.
195. Ibid., 42.
196. Hayat, *The Charismatic Leader*, 82.
197. Syed Sharifuddin Pirzada, ed., *Quaid-i-Azam Jinnah's Correspondence* (Karachi: East and West Publishing Co., 1977), 21.
198. Ibid.
199. Ibid.

200. Syed Shamsul Hasan, *Plain Mr. Jinnah* (Karachi: Royal Book Co., 1976), 55.
201. Z. A. Suleri, *My Leader* (Lahore: Nawa-i-Waqt Press, 1973), 59.
202. Hayat, *The Charismatic Leader*, 81.
203. Cited in Ibid., 81–2.
204. Ibid., 82.
205. Ibid.
206. Ibid.
207. Ibid.
208. Ibid., 83.
209. Hayat, *Aspects of the Pakistan Movement*, 80.
210. Ibid.
211. Ibid.
212. Ahmad, *Speeches and Writings of Mr. Jinnah*, Vol. I, 9. For a complete critique of the Act see, Jinnah's Speech on the Report of the Joint Parliamentary Committee on Indian Constitutional Reforms in the Legislative Assembly on 7 February 1935, in Ibid., 2–20.
213. Hayat, *The Charismatic Leader*, 83.
214. Cited in Ibid., 84.
215. Mujahid, *Studies in Interpretation*, 24.
216. Ibid., 25.
217. Ibid., 27.
218. Ibid., 29.
219. Nanda, *Road to Pakistan*, 235. In fact he wrote to Jinnah that 'Muslim India cannot afford to lose you. Men of clear vision, independent judgement and strength of character are very few.' Cited in Ibid. Earlier, of course, he had sent his nominees to the Round Table Conference in London 'mainly to undercut Jinnah' and his stand. Mohammad Waseem, *Politics and the State in Pakistan* (Lahore: Progressive, 1989), 70.
220. Waheed Ahmad, ed., *Letters of Mian Fazl-i-Hussain* (Lahore: Research Society of Pakistan, 1976), 528.
221. M. Rafique Afzal, *A History of All-India Muslim League, 1906–1947* (Karachi: Oxford University Press, 2013), 212.
222. Cited in S. M. Burke, *Landmarks of the Pakistan Movement* (Lahore: Research Society of Pakistan, 2001), 273.
223. Cited in Hayat, *The Charismatic Leader*, 84.
224. Cited in Afzal, *A History of the All-India Muslim League*, 218.
225. Cited in Ibid.
226. Ibid.
227. Ibid.
228. Noorani, *Jinnah and Tilak*, 160. In fact, Noorani felt that it was 'an irrational dislike of Jinnah bordering on hate. It existed even in the early thirties when Jinnah was universally hailed as an Indian nationalist. It drove Nehru repeatedly to say of Jinnah things which he knew were not true.' Ibid., 109.

229. Afzal, *A History of the All-India Muslim League*, 219.
230. Ibid.
231. Ian Talbot, *Freedom's Cry: The Popular Dimension in the Pakistan Movement and Partition Experience in North-West India* (Karachi: Oxford University Press, 1996), 10.
232. Sailesh Kumar Bandopadhaya, *Quaid-i-Azam Mohammad Ali Jinnah and the Creation of Pakistan* (New Delhi: Sterling Publishers, 1991), 126.
233. Ahmad, *Speeches and Writings*, Vol. I, 27.
234. Hayat, *The Charismatic Leader*, 86–7.
235. Cited in Khalid bin Sayeed, *Pakistan: The Formative Phase 1858–1948*, 2nd ed. (Karachi: Oxford University Press, 1994), 82.
236. Ironically failure of the negotiations 'suited Jinnah more than their success. He could make it a grievance against the Congress. The induction of one or two League legislators into the cabinet of the government of one province out of 11 provinces ... made little sense to him.' Nanda, *Road to Pakistan*, 210.
237. Penderel Moon, *Divide and Quit* (London: Chatto & Windus, 1961), 15.
238. Younus Samad, *A Nation in Turmoil: Nationalism and Ethnicity in Pakistan, 1937–1958* (New Delhi: Sage Publications, 1995), 54.
239. S. Gopal, ed., *Selected Works of Nehru*, Vol. I (Delhi: Orient Longmans, 1978), 52.
240. Afzal, *A History of the All-India Muslim League*, 220.
241. Hayat, *The Charismatic Leader*, 87.
242. Abul Kalam Azad, *India Wins Freedom*, 2nd ed. (New Delhi: Orient Longmans, 1988), 171.
243. Ibid.
244. Singh, *India—Partition—Independence*, 234.
245. Benjamin Zacharia, *Nehru* (London: Routledge, 2004), 93.
246. Ahmad, *Speeches and Writings*, Vol. I, 25–6.
247. Nanda, *Road to Pakistan*, 212.
248. Mujahid, *Studies in Interpretation*, 401.
249. Sayeed, *The Formative Phase*, 87.
250. Mujahid, *Studies in Interpretation*, 35.
251. Ahmad, *Speeches and Writings*, Vol. I, 29. For a complete address of Jinnah see, Ibid, 25–39.
252. Ibid., 31.
253. Ibid.
254. Ibid.
255. Ibid., 32.
256. Ibid., 39.
257. Akbar S. Ahmad, *Jinnah, Pakistan and Islamic Identity: The Search for Saladin* (Karachi: Oxford University Press, 1997), 89.
258. Sayeed, *The Formative Phase*, 100.
259. Mujahid, *Studies in Interpretation*, 433.

260. Afzal, *A History of the All-India Muslim League*, 302. Jinnah had been addressed with at least a dozen titles before, including *Amirul Mulk, Mujahid-i-Millat, Ghazi, Mohibb-i-Millat, Quaid-i-Muslimin* etc. Ibid.

261. On 12 August 1947, the Constituent Assembly of Pakistan adopted an official resolution to that effect, making it part of the official correspondence, documents, records, henceforth.

262. For a detailed discussion of Jinnah's emergence as the charismatic leader see, Hayat, Chp. 2, 'Jinnah's Early Political Career: The Emergence of Quaid-i-Azam', in *The Charismatic Leader*, 54–128.

263. Samad, *A Nation in Turmoil*, 57.

264. Mujahid, *Studies in Interpretation*, 35.

265. Mushirul Hasan, ed., *India Partitioned: The Other Face of Freedom*, Vol. I (New Delhi: Roli Books, 1997), 15.

266. Hayat, *The Charismatic Leader*, 92.

267. Pirzada, *Quaid-i-Azam Jinnah's Correspondence*, 46.

268. Ibid., 93.

269. Nanda, *Road to Pakistan*, 222.

270. Noorani, *Jinnah and Tilak*, 169.

271. Ibid., 233.

272. Khurshid Ahmad Khan Yusufi, ed., *Speeches, Statements, and Messages of the Quaid-i-Azam*, Vol. I (Lahore: Bazm-e-Iqbal, 1996), 334.

273. Sherwani, *Speeches, Writings and Statements of Iqbal*, 23. This correspondence, in fact, reinforced 'the kind of ideological feedback that Iqbal had been constantly providing to Jinnah impelling him to strike an independent course of political action for the All-India Muslim League.' Mauzooruddin Ahmad, 'Iqbal and Jinnah on the "Two-Nations" Theory', in *Iqbal, Jinnah and Pakistan*, 60.

274. A. M. Zaidi, ed., *Evolution of Muslim Political Thought*, Vol. V (Delhi: S. Chand & Co., 1979), 121.

275. Cited in Allen H. Jones, 'Mr. Jinnah's Leadership and the Evolution of the Pakistan Idea: The Case of the Sind Provincial Muslim Conference, 1938', in *World Scholars on Quaid-i-Azam Mohammad Ali Jinnah*, ed. Ahmad Hassan Dani (Islamabad: Quaid-i-Azam University, 1979), 191–203. (Italics added).

276. Ibid.

277. Ahmad, *Speeches and Writings*, Vol. I, 79.

278. Ibid., 95.

279. Ibid., 96. There is a repeated reference to India as a 'continent' (not a country), in his speeches now.

280. Ibid., 97.

281. Ibid., 104–5. The Congress ministries were formed in July 1937, and thus the Congress rule lasted for about two and half years.

282. Even Nehru was of the view now that the 'Hindu-Muslim problem has not so far been settled in a satisfactory way ....' Cited in Nanda, *Road to Pakistan*, 268.

283. Ahmad, *Speeches and Writings*, Vol. I, 133.

284. Pirzada, *Quaid-i-Azam Jinnah's Correspondence*, 95–6.

285. Hayat, *The Charismatic Leader*, 251.

286. Ibid.

287. Ahmad, *Speeches and Writings*, Vol. I, 130–1. For the full article see, Ibid., 122–31.

288. See the full text in Ahmad, *Speeches and Writings*, Vol. I, 151–72.

289. Ibid., 167–8.

290. Ibid., 169.

291. Ibid.

292. Ibid., 168.

293. Ibid.

294. Ibid., 169.

295. Ibid., 171.

296. Ibid., 170.

297. Ibid., 171.

298. Liaquat Ali Khan, comp., *Resolutions of the All-India Muslim League, from December 1938 to March 1940* (Delhi: All-India Muslim League, n.d.), 47–8.

299. Ibid., 48.

300. Saleem M. M. Qureshi, 'Mohammad Ali Jinnah: A Personality Assessment by his Contemporaries', in *Quaid-i-Azam and Pakistan*, ed. Ahmad Hassan Dani (Islamabad: Quaid-i-Azam University, 1981), 115.

301. Zaidi, *Evolution of Muslim Political Thought*, Vol. VI, 170.

302. See, Hayat, Chp. 5, 'The Formula: A Separate State of Pakistan', in *The Charismatic Leader*, 238–301; and Hayat, Chp. 6, 'The Lahore Resolution and its Implications', in *Aspects of the Pakistan Movement*, 141–79.

303. Wolpert, *Jinnah of Pakistan*, 182.

304. Anwar H. Syed, 'Iqbal and Jinnah on the Issues of Nationhood and Nationalism', in *Iqbal, Jinnah and Pakistan*, 92.

305. Christopher Jafferlot, ed., *Pakistan: Nationalism without a Nation* (London: Zed books, 2000), 15.

306. Syed Jaffar Ahmad, 'The Lost Jinnah', in *M. A. Jinnah: Views & Reviews*, ed. M. R. Kazmi (Karachi: Oxford University Press, 2005), 171.

307. Ibid.

308. Nanda, *Road to Pakistan*, 319.

309. See, for instance, Hayat, Chp. 7, 'Mission Accomplished: The Creation of Pakistan', in *The Charismatic Leader*, 355–443.

310. Hayat, 'The Political Mobilization and Organization of the Muslims', in *The Charismatic Leader*, 302. See Chapter 6 (302–54), for all the details. Also see another detailed chapter on the subject, Chp. 7, 'Jinnah, Muslim League, and Political Strategy for the Achievement of Pakistan', in Hayat, *Aspects of the Pakistan Movement*, 180–221.

311. Ibid., 183–4.

312. Wilfred Cantwell Smith, *Modern Islam in India: A Social Analysis* (London: Victor Gollacz, 1946), 275.
313. Phillips Talbot, *An American Witness to India's Partition* (New Delhi: Sage Publications, 2007), 239.
314. Hayat, *The Charismatic Leader*, 306.
315. Ahmad, *Speeches and Writings*, Vol. I, 47.
316. *The Constitution and Rules of the All-India Muslim League,* published by Liaquat Ali Khan, Honorary Secretary, All-India Muslim League (Delhi: All-India Muslim League, 1944), 17. Interestingly, enhanced powers of the president in these successive constitutions closely followed the steady rise in Jinnah's charisma and charismatic leadership.
317. Moon, *Divide and Quit*, 38.
318. Hayat, *The Charismatic Leader*, 316–17.
319. Talbot, *An American Witness*, 240.
320. Hayat, *The Charismatic Leader*, 317.
321. Talbot, *Freedom's Cry*, 25.
322. Ibid.
323. Keith Callard, *Pakistan: A Political Study* (London: George Allen & Unwin, 1968), 20. Another writer, Stephen Cohen remarked that 'he was Pakistan's Tom Paine and George Washington.' Stephen Philip Cohen, *The Idea of Pakistan* (Lahore: Vanguard, 2005), 28.
324. V. P. Menon, *Transfer of Power in India* (Princeton: Princeton University Press, 1957), 438.
325. Nanda, *Road to Pakistan*, 303.
326. Hayat, *The Charismatic Leader*, 335–6.
327. Noor-ul-Haq, *Making of Pakistan: The Military Perspective* (Islamabad: National Institute of Historical & Cultural Research, 1993), 38.
328. Stanley Wolpert, *Nehru: A Tryst with Destiny* (London: Oxford University Press, 1997), 273. Linlithgow and Amery, in fact, saw Gandhi as 'an "intolerable nuisance" during the war years, only keen to maintain his nuisance and his bargaining value at as high level as possible, with a view to post-war designs ....' Nanda, *Road to Pakistan*, 295.
329. Jinnah's speech in the League's meeting in April 1943 in New Delhi. Cited in Stanley Wolpert, *Shameful Flight: The Last Years of the British Empire in India* (Karachi: Oxford University Press, 2006), 57.
330. Hayat, *The Charismatic Leader*, 357.
331. Metz, *The Political Career of Mohammad Ali Jinnah*, 109.
332. N. Mansergh and Penderel Moon, eds. *Constitutional Relations between Britain and India: The Transfer of Power*, Vol. IV (London: Her Majesty's Stationery Office, 1973), 962.
333. French, *Liberty or Death*, 167.
334. Singh, *India—Partition—Independence*, 264.
335. N. Mansergh and E. W. R. Lumby, eds., *Constitutional Relations between Britain and India: The Transfer of Power*, Vol. II (London: Her Majesty's Stationery Office, 1971), 872.

336. Hayat, *The Charismatic Leader*, 357.
337. Mansergh, *The Transfer of Power*, Vol. II, 811.
338. Singh, *India—Partition—Independence*, 264.
339. Menon, *Transfer of Power in India*, 90.
340. Ibid.
341. Menon, *Transfer of Power in India*, 78.
342. Cited in Hayat, *The Charismatic Leader*, 359.
343. Ibid.
344. Ibid., 360.
345. In fact, this was so well known that the Secretary of State, Lord Amery, had to tell the Viceroy Linlithgow, to keep Jinnah 'quiet till Cripps arrives'. N. Mansergh and Penderel Moon, eds., *Constitutional Relations between Britain and India: The Transfer of Power*, Vol. I (London: Her Majesty's Stationery Office, 1970), 396.
346. Hayat, *The Charismatic Leader*, 360.
347. Mansergh, *Transfer of Power*, Vol. I, 565.
348. Cited in R. J. Moore, *Churchill, Cripps, and India, 1939–1945* (Oxford: Clarendon Press, 1979), 82.
349. N. Mansergh and Penderel Moon, eds., *Constitutional Relations between Britain and India: The Transfer of Power*, Vol. VI (London: Her Majesty's Stationery Office, 1976), 938.
350. Ahmad, *Speeches and Writings*, Vol. I, 391.
351. Ibid., 392.
352. D. G. Tendulkar, *Mahatma: Life of Mohandas Karamchand Gandhi*, Vol. VI (Delhi: Ministry of Information and Broadcasting, 1959), 72.
353. H.V. Hodson, *The Great Divide* (London: Hutchinson, 1969), 105.
354. Tendulkar, *Mahatma*, Vol. VI, 268.
355. Nanda, *Road to Pakistan*, 311.
356. Ibid.
357. *Jinnah-Gandhi Talks*, with a Foreword by Nawabzada Liaquat Ali Khan (Lahore: Book Talk, 1991), 12.
358. Ibid.
359. Ibid., 23.
360. Ibid.
361. Ibid., 40.
362. Ibid., 65.
363. Ibid., 67.
364. Ibid., 69.
365. Ibid., 82.
366. Ibid., 91.
367. N. Mansergh and Penderel Moon, eds., *Constitutional Relations between Britain and India: The Transfer of Power*, Vol.V (London: Her Majesty's Stationery Office, 1974), 758.
368. Khurshid, *Memories of Jinnah*, 30.
369. Ibid.

370. Yasmin Khan, *The Great Partition: The Making of India and Pakistan* (New Delhi: Penguin, 2007), 129.

371. In the case of Gandhi–Jinnah talks, what complicated matters further was the fact that 'Gandhi's lack of technical precision and consistency, his bringing into discussion matters which, in Jinnah's opinion, had no relations to the points in dispute, and his acting as an individual rather than as official representative of the Congress all grated upon Jinnah and helped to prevent a meeting of minds.' Metz, *The Political Career of Mohammad Ali Jinnah*, 119.

372. Hodson, *Great Divide*, 115.

373. Jamil-ud-Din Ahmad, ed., *Speeches and Writings of Mr. Jinnah*, Vol. II (Lahore: Sh. Muhammad Ashraf, 1976), 186.

374. Ibid., 186–7.

375. See, for instance, Ayesha Jalal, *The Sole Spokesman: Jinnah, the Muslim League and the Demand for Pakistan* (Cambridge: Cambridge University Press, 1985), 130.

376. Khurshid, *Memories of Jinnah*, 47.

377. Mansergh, *The Transfer of Power*, Vol. VI, 208.

378. Ibid., 113. Ironically, the Simla conference 'confirmed the hostility between Congress and the Muslim League'. *Liberty or Death*, 200.

379. Mansergh, *The Transfer of Power*, Vol. VI, 174.

380. Wolpert, *Jinnah of Pakistan*, 245.

381. Jalal, *The Sole Spokesman*, 132.

382. N. Mansergh and Penderel Moon, eds., *Constitutional Relations between Britain and India: The Transfer of Power*, Vol. VII (London: Her Majesty's Stationery Office, 1977), 582.

383. Hayat, *The Charismatic Leader*, 374.

384. Ibid., 375.

385. Ibid.

386. Cited in Ibid.

387. Cited in Ibid.

388. Ahmad, *Speeches and Writings*, Vol. II, 293.

389. Ibid., 295–6. The Muslim League had sent its proposals, including 'a union', on 12 May 1946, but they were 'not appreciated'. They were 'further diluted'. See Kazimi, *A Concise History of Pakistan*, 150.

390. Ahmad, *Speeches and Writings*, Vol. II, 293.

391. For a detailed result, both of the Muslim-majority and Muslim-minority provinces, and its analysis, see, Afzal, *A History of the All-India Muslim League*, 598–9.

392. For a detailed discussion on Jinnah's acceptance and ultimate rejection of the Cabinet Mission Plan see, Hayat, Chp. 8, 'Jinnah's Acceptance of the Cabinet Mission Plan', in *Aspects of the Pakistan Movement*, 222–39.

393. M. A. H. Ispahani, *Quaid-e-Azam Jinnah As I Knew Him* (Karachi: Forward Publications Trust, 1966), 200.

394. Hayat, *The Charismatic Leader*, 376.

395. Ibid., 377.
396. Ibid., 379.
397. Ibid., 380–1.
398. Ibid.
399. Ibid., 382.
400. Mansergh, *The Transfer of Power*, Vol. VII, 689.
401. Ibid., 614.
402. Rajmohan Gandhi, *Eight Lives: A Study of the Hindu-Muslim Encounter* (Albany, New York: State University of New York Press, 1986), 176.
403. S. K. Majumdar, *Jinnah and Gandhi: Their Role in India's Quest for Freedom*, (Lahore: Peoples Publishing House, 1976), 238.
404. N. Mansergh and Penderel Moon, eds., *Constitutional Relations between Britain and India: The Transfer of Power*, Vol. III (London: Her Majesty's Stationery Office, 1979), 26. Noorani felt that: 'Things went wrong between 1937 and 1939 [Congress rule of the provinces]. But there was another opportunity for a rapprochement in 1946 [Cabinet Mission Plan]. The Congress wrecked it once again.' Noorani, *Jinnah and Tilak*, Preface, XVI. In the process, it did not occur to the Congress 'that its alternative was partition.' Ibid., 189.
405. Jalal, *The Sole Spokesman*, 193.
406. Archibald Wavell, *Wavell: The Viceroy's Journal*, ed. Penderel Moon (Karachi: Oxford University Press, 1974), 271.
407. French, *Liberty or Death*, 215.
408. N. Mansergh and Penderel Moon, eds., *Constitutional Relations between Britain and India: The Transfer of Power*, Vol. VIII (London: Her Majesty's Stationery Office, 1979), 333.
409. Ibid., 439.
410. Wavell, *The Viceroy's Journal*, 324, 287.
411. Wolpert, *Jinnah of Pakistan*, 260.
412. Ahmad, *Speeches and Writings*, Vol. II, 315.
413. This may have helped, as Wolpert claimed, 'Jinnah's 'pendulum strategy' of swinging the ballast of Muslim support from Congress to the British and then back again, which thus won the greatest concessions for the Muslims at every stage of the long, tough struggle towards a negotiated transfer of power ....' Wolpert, *Jinnah of Pakistan*, 136.
414. Metz, *The Political Career of Mohammad Ali Jinnah*, 122.
415. Ibid., 305, 308.
416. Ibid., 308–16.
417. Syed Sharifuddin Pirzada, ed., *Foundations of Pakistan: All-India Muslim League Documents, 1906–1947*, Vol. II (Karachi: National Publishing House, 1970), 558.
418. Ibid., 560–1.
419. Gandhi, a barrister though, was not interested in constitutions, constitutionalism in itself. In 1942, for instance, he confessed to a flabbergasted Viceroy, Lord Lingthow, that he had not read the 1935

Act, a major, defining Act of the British Parliament in the late 1930's till the partition of India. See C. H. Philips, *The Partition of India* (London: George Allan & Unwin, 1970), 1. He never entered any legislative assembly in India, and did not practice law (in India).

420. Mujahid, 'Preface', in *In Quest of Jinnah*, xix.
421. Noorani, *Jinnah and Tilak*, 211.
422. Ahmad, *Speeches and Writings*, Vol. II, 323.
423. Afzal, *A History of the All-India Muslim League*, 648.
424. Ibid., 640.
425. Mansergh, *The Transfer of Power*, Vol. VIII, 323.
426. Percival Spear, *India: A Modern History* (Ann Arbor: University of Michigan Press, 1961), 415–16.
427. Afzal, *A History of the All-India Muslim League*, 648.
428. Ibid.
429. Cited in Ibid., 649.
430. Spear, *India*, 416.
431. Wavell, *the Viceroy's Journal*, 299.
432. Menon, *Transfer of Power in India*, 305–6.
433. N. Mansergh and Penderel Moon, eds., *Constitutional Relations between Britain and India: The Transfer of Power*, Vol. IX (London: Her Majesty's Stationery Office, 1980), 141.
434. Mansergh, *The Transfer of Power*, Vol. VIII, 311.
435. Afzal, *A History of the All-India Muslim League*, 650.
436. Hayat, *The Charismatic Leader*, 390.
437. Menon, *Transfer of Power*, 307.
438. Mansergh, *The Transfer of Power*, Vol. VIII, 311.
439. Ahmad, *Speeches and Writings*, Vol. II, 353–4.
440. Ibid., 355.
441. Hayat, *The Charismatic Leader*, 393.
442. Mansergh, *The Transfer of Power*, Vol. VIII, 709.
443. Ahmad, *Speeches and Writings*, Vol. II, 363.
444. Ibid., 364.
445. Hayat, *The Charismatic Leader*, 396.
446. Hayat, *Aspects of the Pakistan Movement*, 222.
447. Menon, *Transfer of Power in India*, 337–8.
448. Mansergh, *The Transfer of Power*, Vol. IX, 128.
449. Ibid.
450. For a detailed discussion on the 'Breakdown Plan' see, Muhammad Iqbal Chawla, *Wavell and the Dying Days of the Raj: Britain's Penultimate Viceroy in India* (Karachi: Oxford University Press, 2011), 228–44.
451. Full text of Attlee's announcement is available in Menon, *Transfer of Power*, App. IX, 506–9.
452. Ibid.
453. See, Hayat, *The Charismatic Leader*, 409–10, for some details.

454. N. Mansergh and Penderel Moon, eds., *Constitutional Relations between Britain and India: The Transfer of Power,* Vol. X (London: Her Majesty's Stationery Office, 1981), 187.

455. Nirad C. Chaudhuri, *Thy Hand, Great Anarch! India: 1921–1952* (London: Chatto & Windus, 1987), 824.

456. Ibid.

457. On 28 April 1947, Rajendra Prasad, Congress President of the Constituent Assembly had warned that 'no constitution will be forced upon any unwilling part of it ... This means not only the division of India, but also a division of some provinces ... the Assembly may have to draw up a constitution based on such a division.' Stanley Wolpert, *Nehru: A Tryst with Destiny* (London: Oxford University Press, 1997), 355.

458. Mansergh, *The Transfer of Power,* Vol. X, 521.

459. Ibid.

460. Ibid., 280.

461. Hayat, *The Charismatic Leader,* 406.

462. Ibid., 405. For some detailed discussion on Jinnah's efforts to save unity of the Punjab and Bengal see, Ibid., 405–8.

463. Ian Talbot, *India and Pakistan: Inventing the Nation* (London: Arnold, 2000), 143. It needs to be stressed that this plan was confirmed to eleven provinces of British India. It had nothing to do with the princely states.

464. S. M. Burke and Salim al-Din Quraishi, *Quaid-i-Azam Mohammad Ali Jinnah: His Personality and His Politics* (Karachi: Oxford University Press, 1997), 375.

465. Alan Whaites, 'Political Cohesion in Pakistan: Jinnah and the Ideological State', in *M. A. Jinnah,* 114.

466. For details of this process see, Hayat, *The Charismatic Leader,* 412–13.

467. N. Mansergh and Penderel Moon, eds. *Constitutional Relations between Britain and India: The Transfer of Power,* Vol. XI (London: Her Majesty's Stationery Office, 1982), 139.

468. French, *Liberty or Death,* 316.

469. Ian Copland, 'Quaid-i-Azam and the Nawab Chancellor: Literary Paradigms in the Historical Construction of Indian Muslim Identity', in *Islam, Communities and the Nation,* ed. Mushirul Hasan (Delhi: Manohar, 1998) 118.

470. French, *Liberty or Death,* 365.

471. 'The claim', Patrick French, who examined the archives of Indian Political Intelligence (IPI) thoroughly among other official documents, 'that the British had secret plans all along to partition India (an allegation that is still believed by many Indians of certain age) cannot be supported from the internal memoranda and documentation of Whitehall officialdom.' French, *Liberty or Death,* 222.

Conclusion

The main finding of this study is that Muslim separatism in British India, in the given representative system of government, based on numbers, and thus inherently biased against the Muslims, was an 'instrumentalist' choice, a conscious and deliberate choice, made by the Muslim political leadership to articulate, promote, and secure the interests of their own community. The Hindu majority community, led by the Congress (and Hindu Mahasabha), ignored their interests, denied them a share in power and left them no choice but to seek separatism, nationhood, and, ultimately, a separate state of Pakistan. Their religio-cultural basis in Islam, as a community, as a common bond, as a rallying point, certainly helped the Muslims in the pursuit of this goal. But this pursuit was essentially political, not religious, nor religiously motivated or 'primordial' for that matter. Pakistan, like all nationalist goals of national movements, was a political goal and for political ends, to secure for the Muslims power and security in a separate, sovereign state of their own. This, of course, could not have been achieved but for the odyssey of six prominent Muslim leaders—Syed Ahmad Khan, Aga Khan, Syed Ameer Ali, Maulana Mohamed Ali, Allama Muhammad Iqbal, and Quaid-i-Azam Mohammad Ali Jinnah—who helped transform Muslim separatism into the concrete, crowning achievement of the separate state of Pakistan.

Muslim separatism was a salient phenomenon in Indian politics long before the arrival of the British. It was present during centuries of Muslim rule of India despite the best efforts of some rulers to develop, in alliance with the Hindus, an integrated socio-political system catering to the interests of both Muslims and Hindus, the bulk of the population. The separatism, however, was natural and mutual, in some ways a given, based on the religio-cultural differences between the two communities following different, and indeed diametrically opposed, religions of Islam and Hinduism.

Separatism was a norm, a value system and tradition, and was generally acceptable by both Muslims and Hindus.

The British rule and its system of representative government introduced in India in the early twentieth century, promoting the elective principle, not only formalised and institutionalised this separatism but made it contentious too, dividing Hindus and Muslims into majority and minority communities, respectively, into a kind of opposing communities, and for good. The Muslims, given their small numbers (about a quarter of the population before Partition), became a 'minority community'. There was no way they could turn the system around in their favour. The system had a built-in bias towards the majority community. There was little the Muslims could do about it. Even the so-called constitutional safeguards, such as separate electorates which the Muslims fought for and retained throughout the colonial rule, were not of much help in the face of an overwhelming majority of a religious kind, especially as the fulcrum of power began to shift towards the centre. Hindu rule stared at them. To complicate the matters further, there were certain provinces of British India, such as the North-West Frontier Province (now Khyber Pakhtunkhwa), Punjab, Sind (Sindh), Baluchistan (Balochistan), and Bengal, where the Muslims were in majority. On top of it, all these Muslim-majority provinces, except Bengal, were contiguous, sharing borders. They were like a separate territory, a Muslim territory, already.

The earliest proponent of Muslim separatism, Syed Ahmad Khan, saw the Muslim position as a minority with considerable concern for their well-being and progress under the new British dispensation. He saw little prospects for their future unless the Muslims got together to promote their own interests and demands themselves, independent of the newly formed Indian National Congress (1885), primarily pursuing interests of the Hindu-majority community which, to the detriment of the Muslims, also included demand for further extension of the representative system of government in India. Syed Ahmad Khan, therefore, opposed the Congress and, in the process, went on to found a Muslim separatist political movement, pressing upon the Muslims the need to pursue their own interests separately and for their own sake. That was the only way they could deal with the new threats and challenges brought about by the new order which made them a permanent minority community in the country.

The Aga Khan, following the lead, helped in establishing a separate political organisation for the Muslims to advance and secure their separate interests in the emerging polity, the All-India Muslim League, in 1906. Realising the precarious situation of the Muslims in the representative system of government as a minority, he also went ahead and demanded the right for the Muslims to choose their own representatives through 'separate electorates', that is, Muslims voting for the Muslims. While the British, given the peculiar circumstances of India, saw the merit of this demand, they were reluctant to concede lest it upset the Hindus, the majority community, till another separatist leader, Syed Ameer Ali (in concert with the Aga Khan, of course) and his London Muslim League (a branch of the Muslim League), forced them to do so. The 1909 Act granted separate electorates to the Muslims. In the process, both the Aga Khan and Ameer Ali went on to strengthen and consolidate the Muslim separatist political movement in Indian politics.

The movement, however, suffered a setback, ironically at the hands of one of Syed Ahmad Khan's followers, Maulana Mohamed Ali who, in his desperate effort to save the Khilafat in Turkey from the onslaught of the British and Western allies during World War I, joined hands with Mohandas Karamchand Gandhi and the Congress (and the Hindu Mahasabha) leadership. Thus, a formidable Hindu–Muslim alliance took shape. But, not surprisingly, it did not last long. The inherent conflicts of interest ruptured the alliance soon, and with a vengeance. Communal riots and bloodshed followed for years. Mohamed Ali not only parted ways with Gandhi and the Congress but indeed came back to lead the Muslim separatist political movement with a clear commitment and clarity, highlighting the significance of Muslim-majority provinces in a federal set-up as a way out of difficulties the Muslims were facing in India. Indeed, the separatist movement was revived and made ready for a separate goal to be formulated by Allama Muhammad Iqbal.

Allama Iqbal formulated the idea of a separate state (in 'North-West India and Bengal') for the Muslims, based on 'Muslim nationalism', necessitated by their peculiar situation in India where they were bound to lose their identity, culture, and tradition. The 'life of Islam as a cultural force' required its 'centralization' in a certain 'specified territory'. Iqbal did not only make this clear to Jinnah in a series of personal, confidential letters but also, more importantly, urged him to come forward and lead the Muslims out of their 'present difficulties'.

Jinnah, of course, given his own long experience of Indian politics, having worked with the Congress closely to secure Hindu–Muslim unity for the common cause of self-government and freedom for India, and having been thwarted in all such efforts by the late 1930s, could not agree more. He had reached the dead-end already. He readily embraced the concept of Muslim nationalism, propounded his 'two-nation theory', and demanded a separate state of Pakistan in the Lahore Resolution of March 1940, thus elevating the Muslim separatist movement to its highest level and purpose, the Pakistan Movement and Pakistan. He took full advantage of the opportunities granted by World War II, largely due to various acts of omission and commission of both the Congress and the British, and, indeed, failures of these two parties in the triangular fight, and thus mobilised the Muslims for Pakistan (the result was the overwhelming victory of the Muslim League in 1945–6 elections). He went on to demonstrate his superb negotiating skills throughout this period and when that did not help, as in the case of the Cabinet Mission Plan, he resorted to 'Direct Action' to achieve his Pakistan. The ensuing Hindu–Muslim riots and a general breakdown of authority in the country created a situation where partition and the separate state of Pakistan emerged as the only solution to impending civil war and chaos in India. The British ultimately conceded in February 1947. The Congress accepted it through the Partition Plan in June 1947. In August 1947, the Muslims had their separate state, not the way they desired or demanded it (Punjab and Bengal were divided), but still their separate, sovereign state. Muslim separatism in India, present since ages but more as a value, norm, and tradition, had finally been actualised in a tangible, objective form in the separate state of Pakistan.

This is not to suggest that alternate paths of development did not exist or were not conceivable. Pakistan was not in the 'womb of history', so to speak. It was neither inevitable nor a given. But the Congress or the British did not think or do much about it. The Congress did not realise that the Hindu–Muslim problem was not simply a 'communal' issue between the two communities. It was more of a 'national' problem and had to be dealt with accordingly. Indeed, the Congress refused to acknowledge Muslim-particular interests after the 1919 Act, with a semblance of power transferred to provinces through a system of 'dyarchy'. The Nehru Report of 1928 not only failed to make room for Muslim interests in the future constitution of independent India, it even denied them their present privilege with regard to some specific constitutional safeguards, such as separate electorates. In provincial governments that the Congress formed in 1937, it refused to share power with the Muslims through the Muslim League which, in spite of its poor showing in terms of seats in the recently held elections, was their most representative political party. Worse, its provincial rule of 1937–9 clearly demonstrated Hinduising tendencies, as if the 'Hindu Raj' had arrived. The Muslims were duly alarmed and distressed, wondering if this could happen to them when the British were still around and in charge of the centre, what would be their fate once India was free and the centre was placed in the hands of the Hindu majority for all time. The imminent departure of the British after the war thus impelled the Muslims to hasten their demand for a separate state in 1940.

The British, on their part, could not truly gauge the extent of constitutional difficulties—eventually crisis—that the Muslims faced since the introduction of the representative system of government in India based on numbers on the British parliamentary model. In addition, given their own experiences and practices, they kept on pressing a unitary form of government on a racially, ethnically, and religiously diverse and divided population of India. They did not try a genuine, responsive federation, with a weak centre and strong provinces. With powers vested in Muslim-majority provinces, this may have satisfied Muslim grievances at the early stages—in the 1920s—before they really developed into core, conflictual issues between the Muslims and Hindus and then even federalism was no help. It had little value or appeal left for the Muslims. In the early 1940s, the British, of course, thought of the Swiss model but, by then, it was proverbially too little and too late. In 1946, they could not even be honest and fair with the Muslims about their own federal/confederal Cabinet Mission Plan, which, ironically, Jinnah had accepted first for his own reasons, and which happened to be the last and the most critical scheme to save the unity of India, if at all.

There was no denying that the conduct of the Congress leadership and the behaviour of the Hindu majority community since the first signs of transfer of power into Indian hands, and the devolution of powers under the 1919 and 1935 Acts, particularly after the 1937–9 rule of the provinces, had shown the Muslims, clearly and convincingly that federalism, provincial autonomy, even if granted, would still not ensure them a fair share of power in the government. They will always be vulnerable and at the mercy of the Hindu leaders. Gandhi and, particularly, Jawaharlal Nehru's haughty and harsh attitude, left them in no doubt about it. Besides, with the passage of the Lahore Resolution, which ensured them power and security in their own separate, sovereign state, the federal objectives had totally lost appeal for them. Federalism in India, however strong, could not be a substitute for freedom in Pakistan, absolute freedom, where they would be able to live their lives their own way. They would be free and independent. Thus, they committed themselves to a new destiny and goal. It was only left to Jinnah to lead them into the 'promised land' which he ably did in a short span of seven years, 1940–7, helped by a host of factors brought about by World War II.

But Jinnah primarily succeeded in this remarkably short span of time only because of the long, arduous, and dedicated journey, odyssey indeed, of Muslim leaders, Syed Ahmad Khan, Aga Khan, Ameer Ali, Mohamed Ali, and Allama Iqbal, in the pursuit of Muslim separatism. They developed it into a Muslim separatist political movement for him to take over, transform it into a nationalist Pakistan Movement, and lead it all the way to the realisation of its ultimate goal of Pakistan. Jinnah, of course, realised this goal through his able, extraordinary, charismatic leadership, a leadership marked by his determination, devotion, discipline, focus, clarity, organisational skills, and, above all, a strategic sense and direction. Pakistan could not have been achieved without his leadership of the Pakistan Movement. He achieved it through his brilliant strategy and against all odds.

But still, all said and done, the fact remained that this achievement was the end result of a long collective, cumulative effort on the part of all the aforementioned leaders, from Syed Ahmad Khan to Jinnah. This leadership odyssey made it possible for Muslim separatism to grow and develop into a separatist political movement, eventually the Pakistan Movement, which, led by Jinnah, culminated in the achievement of the separate state of Pakistan. Muslim separatism and its persistent pursuit had finally come to fruition.

Bibliography

Primary Sources

Afzal, M. Rafique, ed. *Selected Speeches and Statements of the Quaid-i-Azam Mohammad Ali Jinnah, 1911–1934 and 1947–1948*. Lahore: Research Society of Pakistan, 1976.

Aga Khan. *The Memoirs of Aga Khan: World Enough and Time*. London: Cassell and Company Ltd, 1954.

Aga Khan. *India in Transition: A Study in Political Evolution*. Bennett, Coleman and Co., Ltd, 1918; Osmania University digital publication, 2005.

Ahmad, Jamil-ud-Din, ed. *Speeches and Writings of Mr Jinnah*, Vols. I and II. Lahore: Sh. Muhammad Ashraf, 1968 and 1976.

Ahmad, Riaz, ed. *The Works of Quaid-i-Azam Mohammad Ali Jinnah, Vol. III (1916–1917)*. Islamabad: Quaid-i-Azam University, 1998.

Ahmad, Waheed, ed. *Letters of Mian Fazl-i-Husain*. Lahore: Research Society of Pakistan, 1976.

Akhtar, Rafique, ed. *Historic Trial: Maulana Mohamed Ali and Others*. Karachi: East and West Publishing Co., 1971.

Allami, Abu'l-Fazl. *The Ain-i-Akbari*. Translated by H. Blochmann. Lahore: Sang-e-Meel Publications, 2003.

————. *The Akbar Nama of Abu-l-Fazl*. Translated by H. Beveridge. Lahore: Sang-e-Meel Publications, 1975.

Allana, Gulam, ed. *Pakistan Movement: Historical Documents*. 3rd ed. Lahore: Islamic Book Service, 1977.

Ambedkar, B. R. *Pakistan, or the Partition of India*. Bombay: Thacker & Co., 1945.

Azad, Abul Kalam. *India Wins Freedom*, 2nd ed. New Delhi: Orient Longmans, 1988.

Aziz, K. K. *Ameer Ali: His Life and Work*. Lahore: Research Society of Pakistan, 2006.

————, ed. *The Indian Khilafat Movement, 1915–1933: A Documentary Record*. Karachi: National Publishing House, 1972.

Aziz, Shah Abdul. *Malfuzaat-e-Shah*. Karachi: Pakistan Educational Publishers, 1960.

Badaoni, Abdul Qadir, *Muntakhab-ut-Tawarikh*, Vol II. Translated by W. H. Lowe. Calcutta, India: J. W. Thomas, Baptist Mission Press, 1884. Reprinted Karachi: Karimsons, 1976.

Banerjee, Anil Chandra, ed. *Indian Constitutional Documents: 1757–1945*. Calcutta: A. Mukherjee & Co., 1946.

de Bary, William Theodore, ed. *Sources of Indian Tradition*. New York: Columbia University Press, 1958.

Batalvi, Ashiq Hussain. *Iqbal Kay Akhri Do Saal*. Karachi: Iqbal Academy, 1961.

Besant, Annie. *The Future of Indian Politics*. London: Theosophical Publishing House, 1922.

Chand, Duni. *The Ulster of India*. Lahore: Navajivan Press, 1936.

Char, Desika, ed. *Readings in the Constitutional History of India, 1757–1947*. Delhi: Oxford University Press, 1983.

Chaudhuri, Nirad C. *Thy Hand, Great Anarch! India: 1921–1952*. London: Chatto & Windus, 1987.

———. *The Autobiography of an Unknown Indian*. London: Macmillan, 1951.

Chirol, Valentine. *India: Old and New*. London: Macmillan, 1921.

Chughtai, Mohammad Abdullah. *Iqbal ki Suhbat Mein*. Lahore: Majlis-i-Taraqi-i-Adab, 1971.

Coatman, J. *Years of Destiny: India, 1926–1932*. London: Jonathan Cape, 1932.

The Constitution and Rules of the All-India Muslim League, published by Liaquat Ali Khan, Honorary Secretary, All-India Muslim League. Delhi: All-India Muslim League, 1944.

Coupland, Reginald. *The Indian Problem, 1833–1935*. London: Oxford University Press, 1968.

———. *India: A Re-Statement*. London: Oxford University Press, 1945.

Cumming, Sir John, ed. *Political India, 1832–1932*. London: Oxford University Press, 1932.

Dar, Bashir Ahmad, ed. *Letters and Writings of Iqbal*. Karachi: Iqbal Academy, 1967.

Dembo, Morris. 'Introduction'. In *Political Profile of Sir Sayyid Ahmad Khan: A Documentary Record*, edited by Hafeez Malik. Islamabad: Institute of Islamic History, Culture and Civilization, Islamic University, 1982.

Dunbar, George. *A History of India: From Earliest Times to 1939*, Vol. I. London: Nicholson & Watson, 1949.

Dutt, R. P. *India Today*. London: Victor Gollancz, 1940.

Elliot, Henry Miers and John Dowson, eds. *The History of India, as Told by its Own Historians*, Vols. V and VII. Lahore: Islamic Book Service, 1976.

Fatehpuri, Farman. *Sir Syed Ahmad Khan, The Present State of Indian Politics: Speeches and Letters*. Lahore: Sang-e-Meel Publications, 1982.

Ferishta, Mahomed Kasim. *History of the Rise of the Mahomedan Power in India till the year A.D. 1612*. Translated by John Briggs. Calcutta: Editions Indian, 1966.

Gandhi, Mohandas Karamchand. *The Collected Works of Mahatama Gandhi*. Delhi: Publications Division, Ministry of Information, 1979.

Gopal, S., ed. *Selected Works of Jawaharlal Nehru*, Vol. I. Delhi: Orient Longmans, 1978.

Government of India. Statutory Commission. *Report of the Indian Statutory Commission*, Vol. I. London: HMSO, 1930.

Graham, G. F. I. *The Life and Work of Sir Syed Ahmad Khan*, With a New Introduction by Zatuna Y. Umer. Karachi: Oxford University Press, 1974.

Gwyer, Maurice and A. Appadorai, eds. *Speeches and Documents on the Indian Constitution, 1921–1947*, Vol. II. Bombay: Oxford University Press, 1957.

Hali, Maulana Altaf Hussain. *Hayat-i-Javed*. Lahore: National Book House, 1986.

Hasan, Mushirul, ed. *Mohamed Ali in Indian Politics: Select Writings*. Delhi: Atlantic Publishers, 1982.

Hasan, Syed Shamsul, *Plain Mr Jinnah: Selections from Quaid-e-Azam's Correspondence Relating Mainly to Personal Matters*. Karachi: Royal Book Co., 1976.

Hodson, H. V. *The Great Divide*. London: Huchinson, 1969.

Hunter, W. W. *The Indian Musalmans*. Calcutta: Comrade Publishers, 1945.

Hussain, Altaf. 'Memories of the Quaid-i-Azam'. In *Quaid-i-Azam As Seen by His Contemporaries*, edited by Jamil-ud-Din Ahmad. Lahore: Publishers United, 1966.

Iqbal, Afzal, ed. *My Life, A Fragment: An Autobiographical Sketch of Maulana Mohammad Ali Jauhar*. Islamabad: National Press Trust, 1987.

————, ed. *Selected Writings and Speeches of Maulana Mohamed Ali*, 2 Vols. Lahore: Sh. Muhammad Ashraf, 1969.

Iqbal's address to the All-Parties Muslim Conference, 29 December 1928 – 1 January 1929. In *Guftar-i-Iqbal*, edited by Rafique Afzal. Lahore: Research Society of Pakistan, 1969.

Iqbal, Allama Muhammad. *The Development of Metaphysics in Persia: A Contribution to the History of Muslim Philosophy*. Lahore: Sang-e-Meel Publications, 2004.

_____. 'Islam as a Moral and Political Ideal'. In *Thoughts and Reflections of Iqbal*, edited by Syed Abdul Vahid. Lahore: Sh. Muhammad Ashraf, 1973.

_____. *The Reconstruction of Religious Thought in Islam*. Lahore: Sh. Muhammad Ashraf, 1965.

_____. 'Presidential Address, Allahabad Session, December 1930'.

Ispahani, M. A. H. *Qaid-e-Azam Jinnah As I Knew Him*. Karachi: Forward Publications Trust, 1966.

Jafri (Nadvi), Syed Rais Ahmad, comp. *Selections from Maulana Mohammad Ali's Comrade*. Lahore: Mohamed Ali Academy, 1965.

Jinnah, Fatima. *My Brother*, edited by Sharif al Mujahid. Karachi: Quaid-i-Azam Academy, 1987.

Jinnah-Gandhi Talks. With a Foreword by Nawabzada Liaquat Ali Khan. Lahore: Book Talk, 1991.

Khan, Liaquat Ali, comp. *Resolutions of the All-India Muslim League, from December 1938 to March 1940*. Delhi: All-India Muslim League, n.d.

Khan, Sir Syed Ahmad. *The Causes of the Indian Revolt*. With an Introduction by Francis Robinson. Karachi: Oxford University Press, 2000.

_____. *The Present State of Indian Politics: Speeches and Letters*, edited by Farman Fathepuri. Lahore: Sang-e-Meel Publications, 1982.

_____. *Akhri Mazameen* (Urdu). Lahore: Matba Rafai Aam Press, 1898.

Khurshid, K. H. *Memories of Jinnah*, edited by Khalid Hasan. Karachi: Oxford University Press, 1990.

Letters of Iqbal to Jinnah. Preface by M. A. Jinnah (Lahore: Sh. Muhammad Ashraf, 1968).

Lyall, Alfred. *Asiatic Studies: Religious and Social*. London: John Murray, 1884.

Macdonald, Ramsay. *The Awakening of India*. London: Hodder & Stoughton, 1910.

Manglori, Syed Tufail Ahmad. *Musalmanon Ka Roshan Mustaqbil*. Delhi: Ilmi Delhi, 1945.

Mansergh, N., E. W. R. Lumby, and Penderel Moon, eds. *Constitutional Relations between Britain and India: The Transfer of Power*, 11 Vols. London: Her Majesty's Stationery Office, 1970–82.

Vol. I: Cripps Mission, January–April 1942 (1970).

Vol. II: 'Quit India', 30 April–21 September 1942 (1971).

Vol. III: Reassertion of Authority, Gandhi's Fast and the Succession to the Viceroyalty, 21 September 1942–12 June 1943 (1971).

Vol. IV: The Bengal Famine and the New Viceroyalty, 15 June–31 August 1944 (1973).

Vol. V: The Simla Conference, Background and Proceedings, 1 September 1944–28 July 1945 (1974).

Vol. VI: The Post-War Phase: New Moves by the Labour Government, 1 August 1945–22 March 1946 (1976).

Vol. VII: The Cabinet Mission, 23 March–29 June 1946 (1977).

Vol. VIII: The Interim Government, 3 July–1 November 1946 (1979).

Vol. IX: The Fixing of a Time Limit, 3 November–22 March 1947 (1980).

Vol. X: The Mountbatten Viceroyalty, Formulation of a Plan, 22 March–30 May 1947 (1981).

Vol. XI: The Mountbatten Viceroyalty, Announcement and Reception of the 3 June Plan, 31 May–7 July 1947 (1982).

Menon, V. P. *Transfer of Power in India*. Princeton, N.J.: Princeton University Press, 1957.

Mitra, N. N., ed. *The Indian Annual Register, 1939*, Vol. II. Calcutta: Annual Register Office, 1939.

————. *The Indian Annual Register, 1936*, Vol. II. Calcutta: Annual Register Office, 1936.

————. *The Indian Annual Register, 1921–22*, Vol. I. Calcutta: Annual Register Office, 1921.

Muhammad, Shan, ed. *The Right Hon'able Syed Ameer Ali: Political Writings*. New Delhi: Ashish Publishing House, 1989.

Mujahid, Sharif al, ed. *In Quest of Jinnah: Diary, Notes, and Correspondence of Hector Bolitho*. Karachi: Oxford University Press, 2007.

Nehru, Jawaharlal. *An Autobiography*. London: Bodley Head, 1958.

'Nehru Report' on Minority Representation. In *Quaid-i-Azam Jinnah: Studies in Interpretation*, App. 9. edited by Sharif al Mujahid. Karachi: Quaid-i-Azam Academy, 1981.

Niazi, Syed Nazir. *Iqbal Kay Hazoor*. Karachi: Iqbal Academy, 1971.

Nizami, Khaliq Ahmad. *Shah Waliullah Kay Siyasi Maktubat*. Aligarh: Aligarh Muslim University Press, 1950.

Noman, Muhammad. *Muslim India: Rise and Growth of the All India Muslim League*. Allahabad: Kitabistan, 1942.

O'Dwyer, Michael. *India As I Knew it, 1885–1925*. London: Constable, 1925.

Panipati, Muhammad Ismail, ed. *Maqalat-i-Sir Syed*, Vol. II. Lahore: Majlis-e-Tarraqi-e-Adab, 1962.

Phatak, N. R., ed. *Source Material For a History of the Freedom Movement in India (1885–1920)*, Vol. II. Bombay: Government Central Press, 1957. Cited in Matiur Rahman. *From Consultation to Confrontation: A Study of the Muslim League in British Indian Politics, 1906–1912*. London: Luzac & Co., 1970.

Pirzada, Syed Sharifuddin, ed. *The Collected Works of Quaid-i-Azam Mohammad Ali Jinnah*, Vol. 1. Karachi: East and West Publishing Co., 1984.

———. *Quaid-i-Azam Jinnah's Correspondence*. Karachi: East & West Publishing Co., 1977.

———. *Foundations of Pakistan: All-India Muslim League Documents, 1906–1947*, Vol. II. Karachi: National Publishing House, 1970.

Prasad, Beni. *India's Hindu-Muslim Questions*. London: George Allen & Unwin, 1946.

Prasad, Rajendra. *India Divided*. Bombay: Hind Kitab, 1947.

Ravoof, A. A. *Meet Mr Jinnah*. Lahore: Sh. Muhammad Ashraf, 1955.

Sachau, Edward C., ed. *Alberuni's India*, Vol. I. Lahore: Sh. Mubarak Ali, 1962.

Saiyid, M. H. *Mohammad Ali Jinnah: A Political Study*. Karachi: Elite Publishers, 1970.

Salik, Abdul Majid. *Zikr-i-Iqbal*. Lahore: Bazm-i-Iqbal, 1955.

Sherwani, Latif Ahmad, ed. *Speeches, Writings and Statements of Iqbal*, 3rd ed. Lahore: Iqbal Academy, 1977.

Sitaramayya, B. Pattabhi. *The History of the Indian National Congress, 1885–1935*. Madras: Working Committee of the Congress, 1935.

Smith, Wilfred Cantwell. *Modern Islam in India: A Social Analysis*. London: Victor Gollacz, 1946.

Suleri, Ziauddin Ahmad. *My Leader*. Lahore: Lion Press, 1945.

Tagore, Rabindranath. *A Tagore Reader*, edited by Amiya Chakravarty. Boston: Macmillan Co., 1966.

Talbot, Phillips. *An American Witness to India's Partition*. New Delhi: Sage Publications, 2007.

Tariq, A. R., ed. *Speeches and Statements of Iqbal*. Lahore: Sh. Ghulam Ali, 1973.

Tendulkar, D. G. *Mahatma: Life of Mohandas Karamchand Gandhi*, Vol. VI. Delhi: Ministry of Information and Broadcasting, 1959.

Thomas, F. W. *The History and Prospects of British Education in India*. Cambridge: Cambridge University Press, 1891.

Topa, Ishwa Nath. *Sidelights on the Problems of Indian Nationality.* Allahabad: Kitabistan, 1933.

Wasti, S. Razi, ed. *Memoirs and Other Writings of Syed Ameer Ali.* Lahore: Peoples Publishing House, 1968.

Wavell, Archibald. *Wavell: The Viceroy's Journal,* edited by Penderel Moon. Karachi: Oxford University Press, 1974.

Wilder, John W., trans. and ed. *Selected Essays by Sir Sayyid Ahmad Khan.* Lahore: Sang-e-Meel Publications, 2006.

Yusufi, Khurshid Ahmad Khan, ed. *Speeches, Statements, and Messages of the Quaid-i-Azam,* Vol. I. Lahore: Bazm-e-Iqbal, 1996.

Zaidi, A. M. ed. *Evolution of Muslim Political Thought in India,* Vol. V. Delhi: S. Chand & Co., 1979.

Secondary Sources

Abbasi, M. Yusuf. 'Syed Ameer Ali (Pioneer of Muslim Politics)'. In *Founding Fathers of Pakistan,* edited by Ahmad Hasan Dani. Lahore: Sang-e-Meel Publications, 1998.

————. *The Political Biography of Syed Ameer Ali.* Lahore: Wajidalis, 1989.

————. 'Sir Syed Ahmad Khan and the Re-awakening of the Muslims'. *Journal of Pakistan Studies,* Vol. II (1980).

Abbott, Freeland. 'View of Democracy and the West'. In *Iqbal: Poet-Philosopher of Pakistan,* edited by Hafeez Malik. Lahore: Iqbal Academy, 2005.

Afzal, Muhammad Mujeeb. *Bharatiya Janata Party and the Indian Muslims.* Karachi: Oxford University Press, 2014.

Afzal, M. Rafique. *A History of the All-India Muslim League, 1906–1947.* Karachi: Oxford University Press, 2013.

Ahmad, Akbar S. *Jinnah, Pakistan and Islamic Identity: The Search for Saladin.* Karachi: Oxford University Press, 1997.

Ahmad, Aziz. 'Iqbal's Political Theory'. In *Iqbal As a Thinker: Essays by Eminent Scholars.* Lahore: Sh. Muhammad Ashraf, 1973.

————. *Islamic Modernism in India and Pakistan.* London: Oxford University Press, 1967.

————. *Studies in Islamic Culture in the Indian Environment.* Oxford: Clarendon Press, 1964.

Ahmad, Muhammad Saleem. *The All-India Muslim League: A History of the Growth and Consolidation of Political Organization.* Bahawalpur: Ilham Publishers, 1988.

_____. 'Iqbal and Politics – Part I'. *Journal of Pakistan Studies* II, no. 3 (1983–4).

_____. 'Iqbal and Politics – Part II'. *Journal of Pakistan Studies* II, no. 4 (1984).

Ahmad, Qeyamuddin. *The Wahabi Movement in India.* Calcutta: Firma K. L. Mukhopadhyay, 1966.

Ahmad, Riaz. *Quaid-i-Azam Mohammad Ali Jinnah: The Formative Years, 1892–1920.* Islamabad: National Institute of Historical & Cultural Research, 1986.

Ahmad, Syed Jaffar. 'The Lost Jinnah'. In *M. A. Jinnah: Views & Reviews,* edited by M. R. Kazimi. Karachi: Oxford University Press, 2005.

Ahmad, Waheed. *Road to Indian Freedom: The Formation of the Government of India Act 1935.* Lahore: Caravan Book House, 1979.

Ahmed, Manzooruddin. 'Iqbal and Jinnah on the "Two-Nations" Theory'. In *Iqbal, Jinnah and Pakistan: The Vision and the Reality,* edited by C. M. Naim. Lahore: Vanguard, 1984.

Alavi, Hamza. 'Pan-Islam in British Indian Politics'. *Pakistan Perspectives* 7, no. 2 (July–December 2002).

Ali, Maulana Muhammad. 'Editorial'. *Hamdard.* 15 January 1929. In *Quaid-i-Azam Jinnah: Studies in Interpretation,* edited by Sharif al Mujahid. Karachi: Quaid-i-Azam Academy, 1981.

Ali, Parveen Shaukat. *The Political Philosophy of Iqbal.* Lahore: Publishers United, 1978.

Almeida, Prakash. *Jinnah: Man of Destiny.* Delhi: Kalpaz Publications, 2001.

Ashraf, K. M. 'Muslim Revivalists and the Revolt of 1857'. In *Rebellion 1857,* edited by P. C. Joshi, pp. 78–111. Delhi: People's Publishing House 1957.

Aziz, K. K. *The Making of Pakistan: A Study in Nationalism.* London: Chatto & Windus, 1967.

Bandopadhaya, Sailesh Kumar. *Quaid-i-Azam Mohammad Ali Jinnah and the Creation of Pakistan.* New Delhi: Sterling Publishers, 1991.

Baxter, Craig. *Jana Sangh: A Biography of an Indian Political Party.* Philadelphia: University of Pennsylvania Press, 1959.

Becker, Mary Louise. 'Some Formative Influences on the Career of Quaid-i-Azam M. A. Jinnah'. In *World Scholars on Quaid-i-Azam Mohammad Ali Jinnah,* edited by Ahmad Hassan Dani. Islamabad: Quaid-i-Azam University, 1979.

Bhatnagar, S. K. *History of the M.A.O. College Aligarh.* Lahore: n.p. n.d.

Bolitho, Hector. *Jinnah: Creator of Pakistan*. Karachi: Oxford University Press, 1964.

Brass, Paul. 'Elite Groups, Symbol Manipulation and Ethnic Identity among the Muslims of South Asia'. In *Political Identity in South Asia*, edited by David Taylor and Malcolm Yapp. London: Curzon Press, 1979.

————. *Language, Religion, and Politics in North India*. Cambridge: Cambridge University Press, 1974.

Breeher, Michael. *Nehru: A Political Biography*. Boston: Beacon Press, 1962.

Brown, D. Mackenzie. *The White Umbrella: Indian Political Thought from Manu to Gandhi*. Berkeley: University of California Press, 1964.

Brown, Judith. *Gandhi's Rise to Power: Indian Politics, 1915–1922*. Cambridge: Cambridge University Press, 1977.

Brown, W. Norman. *The United States and India, Pakistan, Bangladesh*. Cambridge, Massachusetts: Harvard University Press 1972.

Burke, S. M. *Landmarks of the Pakistan Movement*. Lahore: Research Society of Pakistan, 2001.

————. *Mainsprings of Indian and Pakistani Foreign Policies*. Minneapolis: University of Minnesota Press, 1974.

————, and Salim al-Din Quraishi. *Quaid-i-Azam Mohammad Ali Jinnah: His Personality and His Politics*. Karachi: Oxford University Press, 1997.

Callard, Keith. *Pakistan: A Political Study*. London: George Allen & Unwin, 1968.

Chand, Tara. *Influence of Islam on Indian Culture*. Lahore: Book Traders, 1979.

————. *Society and State in the Mughal Period*. Lahore: Book Traders, 1979.

————. *History of the Freedom Movement in India*, Vol. 4. Lahore: Book Traders, 1972.

Chandra, Satish. 'Religious Policy of Aurangzeb during the Later Part of his Reign—Some Considerations'. *Indian Historical Review* Vol. XIII, nos. 1–2 (1987).

Chaudhry, Mohammed Ahsen. 'The Impact of the Revolt of 1857 on British Colonial Policy'. *Journal of the Pakistan Historical Society* (July 1963).

Chavan, Sheshrao. *Mohammad Ali Jinnah: The Great Enigma*. New Delhi: Author Press, 2006.

Chawla, Muhammad Iqbal. *Wavell and the Dying Days of the Raj: Britain's Penultimate Viceroy in India*. Karachi: Oxford University Press, 2011.

Cohen, Stephen Philip. *The Idea of Pakistan*. Lahore: Vanguard, 2005.

Cohn, Bernard S. *India: The Social Anthropology of a Civilization*. Englewood Cliffs: New Jersey: Prentice-Hall, 1971.

Copland, Ian. 'Quaid-i-Azam and the Nawab Chancellor: Literary Paradigms in the Historical Construction of Indian Muslim Identity'. In *Islam, Communities and the Nation*, edited by Mushirul Hasan. Delhi: Manohar, 1998.

Dani, A. H., ed. *World Scholars on Quaid-i-Azam Mohammad Ali Jinnah*. Islamabad: Quaid-i-Azam University, 1979.

Dar, Bashir Ahmad. *Articles on Iqbal*. Lahore: Iqbal Academy Pakistan, 1997.

————. *Religious Thought of Sayyid Ahmad Khan*. Lahore: Institute of Islamic Culture, 1957.

Dhulipala, Venkat. *Creating a New Medina: State Power, Islam, and the Quest for Pakistan in Late Colonial North India*. Cambridge: Cambridge University Press, 2015.

Dodge, Norris Steven. 'Political Behavior and Social change: Causes of the Growth of the Indian Electorate in the last half Century'. Unpublished PhD Dissertation, Cornell University, 1971.

Edwards, Michael. *The Last Years of British India*. London: Cassell, 1963.

Elphinstone, Mountstuart. *Aurangzeb*. Edited by Sri Ram Sharma, with introduction by Robert Nichols. Karachi: Oxford University Press, 2008.

————. *The History of India: The Hindu and Mohometan Periods*. London: John Murray, 1889.

Embree, Ainslie T. *India's Search for National Identity*. New York: Alfred A. Knopf, 1972.

Evans, Walter Bennett. *The Genesis of the Pakistan Idea: A Study of Hindu-Muslim Relations*. Karachi: Oxford University Press, 2013.

Farooqi, Hafiz Abdullah. 'Iqbal's Concept of State'. In *Studies in Iqbal's Thought and Art*, edited by Saeed Sheikh. Lahore: Bazm-i-Iqbal, 1972.

Faruki, Zahiruddin. *Aurangzeb: His Life and Times*. Lahore: Al-Biruni, 1977.

Farooqi, Ziya ul-Hasan. *The Deoband School and the Demand for Pakistan*. Bombay: Asia Publishing House, 1963.

French, Patrick. *Liberty or Death: India's Journey to Independence and Division*. New Delhi: Harper Collins, 1997.

Frischauer, Willi. *The Aga Khans*. London: Bodley Head, 1970.

Gallagher, John. 'Nationalism and the Crisis of Empire, 1919–1922'. In *Power, Profit and Politics*, edited by Christopher Baker, Gordon Johnson, and Anil Seal. Cambridge: Cambridge University Press, 1981.

Gandhi, Rajmohan. *Eight Lives: A Study of the Hindu-Muslim Encounter.* Albany, NY: State University of New York Press, 1986.

Gilbert, Marc Jason. 'The Era of British Rule'. In *A History of Pakistan*, edited by Roger D. Long. Karachi: Oxford University Press, 2015.

Gopal, Ram. *Indian Muslims: A Political History (1858–1947).* Lahore: Book Traders, 1976.

Gordon-Polonskaya, L. R. 'Ideology of Muslim Nationalism'. In *Iqbal: Poet-Philosopher of Pakistan*, edited by Hafeez Malik. Lahore: Iqbal Academy, 2005.

van Grondelle, Marc. *The Ismailis in the Colonial Era: Modernity, Empire and Islam.* New Delhi: Foundation Books, n.d.; London: C. Hurst & Co., 2009.

Hamid, Abdul. *On Understanding the Quaid-i-Azam.* Islamabad: National Committee for Birth Centenary Celebrations of Quaid-i-Azam Mohammad Ali Jinnah, 1977.

————. *Muslim Separatism in India: A Brief Survey, 1858–1947.* Lahore: Oxford University Press, 1967.

Hardy, Peter. *The Muslims of British India.* Cambridge: Cambridge University Press, 1972.

————. *Partners in Freedom and True Muslims: The Political Thought of Some Muslim Scholars in British India, 1912–1947.* Lund: Student Literature Scandanavian Institute of Asiatic Studies, 1971.

Haq, Mushirul. *Muslim Politics in Modern India, 1857–1947.* Meerut: Meenakshi Parakashan, 1970.

Hasan, Mushirul, ed. *India Partitioned: The Other Face of Freedom*, Vol. I. New Delhi: Roli Books, 1997.

————. *Nationalism and Communal Politics in India, 1916–1928.* Delhi: Manohar, 1979.

Hassan, Riffat. 'The Development of Political Philosophy'. In *Iqbal: Poet-Philosopher of Pakistan*, edited by Hafeez Malik. Lahore: Iqbal Academy, 2005.

Hayat, Sikandar. *Aspects of the Pakistan Movement*, 3rd rev. ed. Islamabad: National Institute of Historical & Cultural Research, 2016.

————. *The Charismatic Leader: Quaid-i-Azam Mohammad Ali Jinnah and the Creation of Pakistan.* 2nd ed. Karachi: Oxford University Press, 2014.

————. 'Syed Ahmad Khan and the Foundation of Muslim Separatist Political Movement in India'. *Pakistan Journal of Social Sciences* VIII, nos. 1–2 (Jan–July–Dec 1982).

Hussain, M. Hadi. *Syed Ahmad Khan: Pioneer of Muslim Resurgence.* Lahore: Institute of Islamic Culture, 1970.

Ikram, Shaikh Muhammad. *History of Muslim Civilization in India and Pakistan: A Political and Cultural History.* Lahore: Institute of Islamic Culture, 2013.

————. *Modern Muslim India and the Birth of Pakistan.* Lahore: Sh. Muhammad Ashraf, 1970.

————. *Raud-i-Kausar.* Lahore: Institute of Islamic Culture, 1958.

Iqbal, Afzal. *Life and Times of Mohamed Ali.* Lahore: Institute of Islamic Culture, 1974.

Iqbal, Javid. *Zinda Rood.* Lahore: Sang-e-Meel Publications, 2014.

————. *Intellectual Legacy: Articles of Dr. Javid Iqbal on Academic, Literary, Educational Issues, Political Thought and Pakistan.* Lahore: Iqbal Academy Pakistan, 2012.

————. *Ideology of Pakistan.* Lahore: Ferozsons, 1971.

Jafferlot, Christopher, ed. *Pakistan: Nationalism without a Nation.* London: Zed Books, 2000.

Jain, M. S. *The Aligarh Movement: Its Origins and Development, 1858–1906.* Agra: Sri Ram Mehra, 1965.

Jalal, Ayesha. *Self and Sovereignty: Individual and Community in South Asian Islam since 1850.* Lahore: Sang-e-Meel Publications, 2007.

————. *The Sole Spokesman: Jinnah, the Muslim League and the Demand for Pakistan.* Cambridge: Cambridge University Press, 1985.

Jawed, Ajeet. *Secular and Nationalist Jinnah.* Karachi: Oxford University Press, 2009.

Jones, Allen H. 'Mr. Jinnah's Leadership and the Evolution of the Pakistan Idea: The Case of the Sind Provincial Muslim Conference, 1938'. In *World Scholars on Quaid-i-Azam Mohammad Ali Jinnah*, edited by Ahmad Hassan Dani. Islamabad: Quaid-i-Azam University, 1979.

Kazimi, M. R. *A Concise History of Pakistan.* Karachi: Oxford University Press, 2009.

————, ed. *M. A. Jinnah: Views and Reviews.* Karachi: Oxford University Press, 2005.

Khan, Mohammed Ahmad. *Iqbal Ka Siyasi Karnama.* Lahore: Iqbal Academy, 1977.

Khan, Yasmin. *The Great Partition: The Making of India and Pakistan.* New Delhi: Penguin, 2007.

Khurshid, Abdus Salam. *Sarguzashat-i-Iqbal*. Lahore: Iqbal Academy, 1977.

Lane-Poole, Stanley. *Mediaeval India under Mohammedan Rule, 712–1764*. Lahore: Sang-e-Meel Publications, 1979.

Lewis, Bernard. *The Emergence of Modern Turkey*. Lahore: Oxford University Press, 1967.

Majumdar, Ramesh Chandra. *History of the Freedom Movement*, Vol. III. Calcutta: Firma K. L. Mukhopadhyay, 1962.

Majumdar, S. K. *Jinnah and Gandhi: Their Role in India's Quest for Freedom*. Lahore: Peoples Publishing House, 1976.

Malik, Hafeez. *Iqbal in Politics*. Lahore: Iqbal Academy Pakistan, 2009.

———. *Sir Sayyid Ahmad Khan and Muslim Modernization in India and Pakistan*. New York: Columbia University Press, 1980.

———. 'The Man of Thought and the Man of Action'. In *Iqbal: Poet-Philosopher of Pakistan*, edited by Hafeez Malik. Lahore: Iqbal Academy, 2005.

———. *Iqbal: The Poet Philosopher of Pakistan*. New York: Columbia University, 1971.

———. *Moslem Nationalism in India and Pakistan*. Washington DC: Public Affairs Press, 1963.

———, and Lynda P. Malik, 'The Life of the Poet-Philosopher'. In *Iqbal: Poet-Philosopher of Pakistan*, edited by Hafeez Malik. Lahore: Iqbal Academy Pakistan, 2005.

Malleson, George Bruce. *Rulers of India: Akbar and the Rise of the Mughal Empire*. Lahore: Islamic Book Service, 1979.

Marck, Jan. 'Perceptions of International Politics'. In *Iqbal: Poet-Philosopher of Pakistan*, edited by Hafeez Malik. Lahore: Iqbal Academy, 2005.

Maruf, Mohammed, ed. *Contributions to Iqbal's thought*. Lahore: Islamic Book Service, 1977.

Masud, Muhammad Khalid. *Iqbal's Reconstruction of Ijtihad*. Lahore: Iqbal Academy Pakistan, 2009.

Mathur, Y. B. *Growth of Muslim Politics in India*. Lahore: Book Traders, 1980.

Mehrotra, S. R. *Towards India's Freedom and Partition*. New Delhi: Rupa & Co., 2007.

Metcalf, Thomas R. *The Aftermath of Revolt*. Princeton: Princeton University Press, 1964.

Metz, William. *The Political Career of Mohammad Ali Jinnah*, edited by Roger D. Long. Karachi: Oxford University Press, 2010.

Mian, Mohammed, ed. *Jamiyat-ul-Ulama Kiya Hai*. Delhi: Jamiat-ul-Ulama, 1946.

Minault, Gail. *The Khilafat Movement: Religious Symbolism and Political Mobilization in India*. New York: Columbia University Press, 1982.

Moon, Penderel. 'Jinnah's Changing Attitude to the Idea of Pakistan'. In *World Scholars on Quaid-i-Azam Mohammad Ali Jinnah*, edited by A. H. Dani. Islamabad: Quaid-i-Azam University, 1979.

_____. *Divide and Quit*. London: Chatto & Windus, 1961.

Moore, R. J. *Churchill, Cripps, and India, 1939–1945*. Oxford: Clarendon Press, 1979.

Morris-Jones, W. H. *The Government and Politics of India*. London: Hutchinson & Co., 1971.

Muhammad, Shan. *Sir Syed Ahmad Khan: A Political Biography*. Lahore: Universal Books, 1976.

Mujahid, Sharif al. *Quaid-i-Azam Jinnah: Studies in Interpretation*. Karachi: Quaid-i-Azam Academy, 1981.

_____, comp. 'The Khilafat Movement'. In *Mohammad Ali: Life and Work*. Karachi: Pakistan Historical Society, 1978.

_____. 'Communal Riots'. *A History of the Freedom Movement*, Vol. IV, Part II. Karachi: Pakistan Historical Society, 1970.

Mujeeb, M. *The Indian Muslims*. London: George Allen & Unwin, 1967.

Mujtabai, Fathullah. *Aspects of Hindu Muslim Cultural Relations*. New Delhi: National Book Bureau, 1978.

Mukherjee, Ramkrishna. *The Rise and Fall of the East India Company: A Sociological Appraisal*. Bombay: Poplar Prakashan, 1958.

Munawwar, Muhammad. *Dimensions of Iqbal*. Lahore: Iqbal Academy Pakistan, 2003.

Naim, C. M. 'Afterword'. In *Iqbal, Jinnah and Pakistan: The Vision and the Reality*, edited by C. M. Naim. Lahore: Vanguard, 1984.

Nanda, B. R. *Road to Pakistan: The Life and Times of Mohammad Ali Jinnah*. New Delhi: Routledge, 2010.

Nizami, Khaliq Ahmad. *Some Aspects of Religion and Politics in India during the Thirteenth Century*. Bombay: Asia Publishing House, 1961.

Noor-ul-Haq, *Making of Pakistan: The Military Perspective*. Islamabad: National Institute of Historical & Cultural Research, 1993.

Noorani, A. G. *Jinnah and Tilak: Comrades in the Freedom Struggle*. Karachi: Oxford University Press, 2010.

Panikkar, K. M. *Asia and Western Dominance*. New York: Collier, 1969.

Pakistan History Board. *A Short History of Hind-Pakistan*. Karachi: Pakistan Historical Society, 1955.

Philips, C. H. *The Partition of India*. London: George Allan & Unwin, 1970.

Pirzada, Syed Sharifuddin. *Evolution of Pakistan*. Lahore: All-Pakistan Legal Decisions, 1963.

Prasad, Ishwari. *A Short History of Muslim Rule in India: From the Advent of Islam to the Death of Aurangzeb*. Allahabad: The Indian Press, 1956.

Prawdin, Michael. *The Builders of the Mogul Empire*. London: Allen & Unwin, 1963.

Purohit, Teena. *The Aga Khan Case: Religion and Identity in Colonial India*. Cumberland, US: Harvard University Press, 2012.

Qureshi, Ishtiaq Husain. *Akbar: The Architect of the Mughul Empire*. Karachi: Ma'aref, 1978.

———. *Ulema in Politics: A Study Relating to the Political Activities of the Ulema in the South-Asian Subcontinent from 1556 to 1947*. Karachi: Ma'aref, 1977.

———. *The Struggle for Pakistan*. Karachi: University of Karachi, 1974.

———. *The Administration of the Mughul Empire*. Karachi: Karachi University, 1966.

———. *The Muslim Community of the Indo-Pakistan Subcontinent (610–1947): A Brief Historical Analysis*. The Hague: Mouton & Co., 1962.

———, 'Hindu Communal Movements'. In *A History of the Freedom Movement, Vol. III, Part I*. Karachi: Pakistan Historical Society, 1961.

———. *The Administration of the Sultanate of Delhi*. Karachi: Pakistan Historical Society, 1958.

Qureshi, M. Naeem. *Ottoman Turkey, Ataturk, and Muslim South Asia: Perspectives, Perceptions, and Responses*. Karachi: Oxford University Press, 2014.

———. *Pan-Islam in British India: The Politics of the Khilafat Movement, 1918–1924*. Karachi: Oxford University Press, 2009.

———, 'The Indian Khilafat Movement (1918–1924)'. *Journal of Asian History* 12, No. 2 (1978).

———. 'Jinnah and the Khilafat Movement (1918–1924)'. *Journal of South Asia and Middle Eastern Studies* 1, no.2. Iqbal Centennial Issue (December 1977).

Qureshi, Saleem M. M. 'Iqbal and Jinnah: Personalities, Perceptions and Politics'. In *Iqbal, Jinnah and Pakistan: The Vision and the Reality*, edited by C. M. Naim. Lahore: Vanguard, 1984.

Qureshi, Waheed. *Iqbal aur Pakistani Qaumiyat*. Lahore: Maktaba-e-Aliya, 1977.

Rahim, Muhammad Abdur. *History of the Afghans in India,* A.D. *1545–1631, with especial reference to their relations with the Mughals.* Karachi: Pakistan Publishing House, 1961.

Rahman, F. 'Muslim Modernism in the Indo-Pakistan Sub-Continent'. *Bulletin of the School of Oriental and African Studies* 21, no. 1 (1958): 82–99.

Raja, Masood Ashraf. *Constructing Pakistan: Foundational Texts and the Rise of Muslim National Identity, 1857–1947.* Karachi: Oxford University Press, 2010.

Rajput, A. B. *Muslim League Yesterday and Today.* Lahore: Sh. Muhammad Ashraf, 1948.

Ranade, Mahadeo Govin. *Rise of the Maratha Power, and Other Essays.* Bombay: University of Bombay, 1961. Cited in Thomas R. Metcalf, ed. *Modern India: An Interpretative Anthology.* London: Collier Macmillan, 1971.

Rizwan-ul-Islam. 'Iqbal's Concept of Muslim Nationalism (Millat)'. In *Contributions to Iqbal's Thought,* edited by Mohammad Maruf. Lahore: Islamic Book Service, 1977.

Robinson, Francis. *Separatism Among Indian Muslims: The Politics of the United Provinces' Muslims, 1860–1923.* Cambridge: Cambridge University Press, 1974.

———, 'Islam and Muslim Separatism'. In *Political Identity in South Asia,* edited by David Taylor and Malcolm Yapp. London: Curzon Press, 1979.

Rosen, George. *Democracy and Economic Change in India.* Berkeley: University of California Press, 1966.

Ross, Nancy Wilson. *Three Ways of Asian Wisdom: Hinduism, Buddhism, Zen, and their Significance for the West.* New York: Simon & Schuster, 1966.

Saeed, Ahmad. *Iqbal Aur Quaid-i-Azam.* Lahore: Iqbal Academy, 1977.

———, and Kh. Mansur Sarwar. *Trek to Pakistan.* Lahore: Al-Fouzi Publishers, 2012.

Samad, Yunas. *A Nation in Turmoil: Nationalism and Ethnicity in Pakistan, 1937–1958.* New Delhi: Sage Publications, 1995.

Sarila, Narendra Singh. *The Shadow of the Great Game: The Untold Story of India's Partition.* New Delhi: Harper Collins, 2005.

Sayeed, Khalid bin. *Pakistan: The Formative Phase, 1857–1948.* 2nd ed. Karachi: Oxford University Press, 1994.

Seal, Anil. *The Emergence of Indian Nationalism: Competition and Collaboration in the Later Nineteenth Century.* Cambridge: Cambridge University Press, 1968.

Seervai, H. M. *Partition of India: Legend and Reality.* Rawalpindi: Services Book Club, 1991.

Sen, Sachin. *The Birth of Pakistan.* Calcutta: General Printers & Publishers, 1955; Lahore, 1978.

Shaikh, Farzana. *Community and Consensus in Islam: Muslim Representation in Colonial India, 1860–1947.* 2nd ed. Delhi: Imprint One, 2012.

Sharma, Sri Ram. *The Religious Policy of the Mughal Emperors.* Bombay: Asia Publishing House, 1962.

Sherwani, H. K. *Cultural Trends in Medieval India.* Bombay: Asia Publishing House, 1968.

Siddiqui, Iqtidar Husain. *Some Aspects of Afghan Despotism in India.* Aligarh: Three Men Publication, 1969.

Singh, Jaswant. *Jinnah: India—Partition—Independence.* New Delhi: Rupa & Co., 2009.

Smith, Anthony D. *Nationalism in the Twentieth Century.* Oxford: Oxford University Press, 1979.

Smith, Wilfred Cantwell. *Islam in Modern History.* Princeton: Princeton University Press, 1957.

Spear, Percival. *India, Pakistan and the West.* 3rd ed. London: Oxford University Press, 1958.

Srinivas, Mysore Narasimhachar. *Social Change in Modern India.* Berkeley: University of California Press, 1973.

Stepaniants, Marietta, 'Development of the Concept of Nationalism: The Case of Muslims in the Indian Sub-continent'. *The Muslim World*, Vol. LXIX, No. 1 (January 1979).

Stokes, Eric. *The English Utilitarians and India.* London: Oxford University Press, 1959.

Syed, Anwar H. 'Iqbal and Jinnah on Issues of Nationhood and Nationalism'. In *Iqbal, Jinnah and Pakistan: The Vision and the Reality*, edited by C. M. Naim. Lahore: Vanguard, 1984.

Syed, Muhammad Aslam. *Muslim Response to the West: Muslim Historiography in India, 1857–1914.* Islamabad: National Institute of Historical & Cultural Research, 1988.

Talbot, Ian. *India and Pakistan: Inventing the Nation.* London: Arnold, 2000.

_____. *Freedom's Cry: The Popular Dimension in the Pakistan Movement and Partition Experience in North-West India*. Karachi: Oxford University Press, 1996.

Tinker, Hugh. *India and Pakistan: A Political Analysis*. New York: Frederick A. Praeger, 1967.

_____. *South Asia: A Short History*. New York: Frederick A. Praeger, 1966.

Truschke, Audrey. *Aurangzeb: The Man and the Myth*. Karachi: Oxford University Press, 2017.

_____. *Culture of Encounters: Sanskrit at the Mughal Court*. New Delhi: Penguin Random House India, 2017.

Vahid, Syed Abdul. *Studies in Iqbal*. Lahore: Sh. Muhammad Ashraf, 1976.

Waheed-uz-Zaman. *Towards Pakistan*. Lahore: United Publishers, 1969.

Waseem, Mohammad. *Politics and the State in Pakistan*. Lahore: Progressive, 1989.

Wasti, S. Razi. 'The Role of the Aga Khan in the Muslim Freedom Struggle'. In *Founding Fathers of Pakistan,* edited by Ahmad Hasan Dani. Lahore: Sang-e-Meel Publications, 1998.

_____. *Lord Minto and the Indian Nationalist Movement, 1905 to 1910*. Oxford: Clarendon Press, 1964.

Wells, Ian Bryant. *Ambassador of Hindu-Muslim Unity: Jinnah's Early Politics* (Delhi: Permanent Black, 2005), 17.

Whaites, Alan. 'Political Cohesion in Pakistan: Jinnah and the Ideological State'. In *M. A. Jinnah: Views & Reviews*, edited by M. R. Kazimi. Karachi: Oxford University Press, 2005.

Wolpert, Stanley. *Shameful Flight: The Last Years of the British Empire in India*. Karachi: Oxford University Press, 2006.

_____. *Jinnah of Pakistan*. Karachi: Oxford University Press, 1999.

_____. *Nehru: A Tryst with Destiny*. London: Oxford University Press, 1997.

_____. *A New History of India*. New York: Oxford University Press, 1977.

_____. *Tilak and Gokhale: Revolution and Reform in the Making of Modern India*. Berkeley: University of California Press, 1977.

_____. *India*. Englewood Cliffs, New Jersey: Prentice Hall, 1965.

Woodruff, P. *The Men Who Ruled India: The Founders*, Vols. I and II. London: Jonathan Cape, 1953 and 1954.

Zachariah, Benjamin. *Nehru*. London: Routledge, 2004.

Zaman, Mukhtar. *Students Role in the Pakistan Movement.* Karachi: Quaid-i-Azam Academy, 1979.

Ziring, Lawrence. 'The Phases of Pakistan's Political History'. In *Iqbal, Jinnah and Pakistan: The Vision and the Reality,* edited by C. M. Naim. Lahore: Vanguard, 1984.

Zobairi, R. H. 'Sir Syed Ahmad Khan's Interpretation of Muslim Society and his Reform Movement in the Indian Context'. *Islamic Culture* VII, No. 3 (July 1983).

Index

B

Balfour, Arthur 146
Balkan Wars 88, 93, 144, 161
Baluchistan 92, 158, 164, 185, 225, 231, 254, 261, 273, 291
Banerjee, Surendranath 115
Barailvi, Sayyid Ahmad 38, 40
Bari, Maulana Abdul 148, 150–1, 170–1
Bengal 9, 17, 32, 40, 42, 44, 47, 53, 69, 74–6, 88, 92–3, 100, 110–11, 113–16, 125, 129, 138, 142, 158, 161, 164, 193, 201, 203, 218, 226–7, 229, 231, 237, 241, 245, 248, 251, 254, 256, 261–3, 267, 271–3, 289, 291, 293
Bengalis 63–5, 67
Bengal Legislative Council 113
Besant, Annie 73, 171, 218–19
Bhakti movement 29, 34
Bharatiya Janata Party (BJP) 19
Bihar 92, 217, 241, 261, 267
Bilgrami, Syed Hasan 124
Bombay 82–3, 92, 94, 117, 146, 195, 207, 209, 211–17, 219–20, 222, 236, 244, 257, 261, 267–8, 270
Bombay Home Rule League 222
Bombay News Chronicle (newspaper) 220
Bombay Provincial Conference (1916) 216
Bose, Sarat Chandra 272
Bose, Subhas Chandra 243, 272
Brahmos 52
Brahmo Samaj 40, 73
Brass, Paul 1–6, 20, 78
Breakdown Plan 270, 288
British: government 4, 52–3, 55–8, 82, 99, 102–4, 122, 124, 128, 136, 140, 143, 146–7, 163, 189–90, 195, 207, 217–8, 221, 226–7, 232, 234, 247, 255–6, 259–60, 270–1; imperial rule 5; India 1, 16–17, 19, 47–8, 50, 56, 75–7, 82, 110, 135–6, 166, 170–3, 175, 186, 200, 210, 231, 266, 273, 289–91; parliament 69, 85,

288; parliamentary model 294; rule 10, 13, 17, 50–1, 71, 75, 82, 85, 89, 110, 114, 118, 130, 136–7, 140, 277, 291; system of representative government 41, 51
Brown, Mackenzie 36

C

Cabinet Mission Plan (1946) 208, 261–2, 264, 266–7, 269–71, 286–7, 293, 295
Calcutta 69, 80, 93, 111, 117, 129, 137–8, 149, 212–13, 227, 229–30, 245, 267
Cambridge University 57, 59, 82, 176
centralisation in a certain territory 185, 293
Central Legislative Assembly 209, 224, 231, 236, 262
Central National Muhammadan Association 69, 113, 130
central parliamentary board 238
Central Provinces (CP) 69, 261
Chagla, M. C. 211, 275
Chand, Duni 39, 48
Chand, Tara 13, 24, 34, 41–2, 46, 274
Chandra, Satish 31–2
Chaudhri, Nirad C. 13
Chauri Chaura incident 97, 152, 222
Chhatari, Sir Muhammad Ahmad Said Khan (Nawab of Chhatari) 238
Christians 19, 56, 87, 182
Civil Disobedience Movement 99, 101, 233, 253
civil war 68, 164, 184, 190, 195, 267–8, 293
Communal: Award 102–3, 190, 236–7; basis 5; card 9; riots 43, 167, 172, 195, 207, 292
Communalism 1, 37, 160–1, 184, 244, 270
composite culture 2
Congress: 6–8, 10, 14–15, 19, 23, 33, 41, 50–1, 60, 65–70, 78–80, 82–5, 94, 98–9, 101–4, 108, 110, 112, 120, 127,